The East Came West

Muslim, Hindu, and Buddhist Volunteers in the German Armed Forces 1941-1945

A study of East European & Middle Eastern Collaboration with the German Armed Forces In World War II

For Oilda Lopez

The East Came West
Muslim, Hindu, and Buddhist Volunteers in the German Armed Forces 1941-1945

Edited by
Antonio J. Munoz

AXIS EUROPA BOOKS
53-20 207th Street, Bayside,
New York 11364-1716 USA
Phone: (718) 423-9893 Fax: (718) 229-1352
URL- http://www.axiseuropa.com

ISBN: 1-891227-39-4

Printed in Korea
For information on quality printing at low prices visit-
asianprinting.com

Acknowledgement

I would like to thank several persons who, without their help and aid, this book would not have been possible. First let me thank my fellow writers- Oleg Romanko, Martin Bamber, Moustafa Assad, and H.L. DeZeng. Although not a regular contributor, Mr. DeZeng's chapter appeared originally in Axis Europa Magazine. I also want to thank Patrick Cloutier, who translated the first part of this work from the Russian. Patrick, thank you for your help!

Acknowledgement should be given to the following archives and institutions: U. S. National Archives, Croatian Museum – Zagreb, Bundesarchiv, Berlin Document Center (now called the Bundesarchiv – Berlin), and the Museum of Modern History, Ljubljana.

I am also indebted to Justin Horgan, Rudolf Hartog, P. Krappe, Schintone-Sigro, Jean Luis Roba, Keith Williams, Al Barrows, Kevin Henderson, Michael Boothe, and Douglas D. Hammond for their photographic contributions to this book. Thank you one and all! Without these rare photographs, my colleagues and I would not have been able to present as clear a picture on the history of these volunteers. For purposes of confidentiality, the American photographic collections have been generalized and referred to as "Private American Collector."

Special thanks go out to Miss Miriam Ordoñez, who'se small contribution, according to her account, was actually very helpful and extremely important in my being able to complete this work. Thank you, Miriam! Finally, thanks should also go to my supportive wife. Without her beside me, my writing would not have any meaning.

"Allah above us,
And Hitler beside us"

-

The motto of the newspaper "Gazavat" ("Jihad")
Political organ of the North-Caucasian
National-Liberation Movement

"Do not rejoice you men,
For though the world stood up
And stopped the bastard,
The bitch that bore him is in heat again."

-

Berthold Brecht

CONTENTS

LEFT: General Ernst Köstring, who commanded eastern troops, composed of volunteers from the Soviet Union during the Second World War. He is considered by many to have been the best German commander of eastern troops during the war. *Bundesarchiv.*

Part - I

The East Came West: Muslim and Hindu Volunteers In German Service, 1941-1945

By Oleg Valentinovich Romanko
Post-graduate sub-faculty student
Of Modern History at
Tavricheskiy National University

TRANSLATOR'S NOTES

Translation of this book presented a few challenges: the first was the terminology for soldiers from the Caucasus region. In addition to designations for those legionnaires from Georgia, Armenia, and Azerbadjian, they were sometimes collectively referred to for the Caucasus Mountians. In the Russian and German languages, the adjective description of Caucasus is *kavkazskiy* and *kaukasiche*, respectively. In English, the adjective is rendered *Caucasian.* The term 'Caucasian' also refers to Europeans and white Americans. In the case of the Legions recruited from the inhabitants of the region, the words *kavkazskiy* and *kaukasiche* better refer to their geography of origin, rather than their distinctive nationalities. In place of the term 'Caucasian,' I employ the word 'Caucasus' as an adjective, in order to emphasize the geography of origin and avoid confusion with common racial terminology.

In at least two other instances, I translate reference to the inhabitants of the northern Caucasus as 'tribes.' The Russian author referred to a *severo-Kavkazkiy Legion* or a Northern-Caucasian Legion. Again, as there are a multitude of languages and ethnic groups from that location, I decided that 'Northern Caucasian' would confuse geographical origin with racial identity. Since many of these language-users and ethnic groups vary in number from 1,000 to 800,000, they seem to better constitute 'tribes,' which are organized around family groupings, rather than 'nations' or 'nation-states' as people in the west might understand them. Hence, I rendered them as *Northern Caucasus tribes*, or *North Caucasus tribes.* A map published in the February 1996 *National Geographic,* article titled: *The Fractured Caucasus,* influenced my decision to go with the term 'tribes' when refering to those recruits. I strongly recommend this issue to the reader, as it will enhance his understanding of the ever-present linguistic and racial factors in the recruitment and deployment of the Eastern Legions.

Another challenge in translating this work was the author's reference to light units. In one case, the author used the word *melkiy* for 'light.' The Defense Language Institute Russian Basic Course, Glossaries and Indexes, RU 0383 S, defines *melkiy* as "small; shallow." Modern armies have light infantry divisions, as did those of World War Two. These are formations of considerable force, so I decided that the term'light'did not apply on this occasion, at least. Battalion-size units and smaller often did not have their own artillery support, or the logistical organizations that make brigades and divisions independent. For this reason, I decided to use the term *unsupported* to describe some of the units in Tunisia, meaning that they did not have their own combat support.

Last, I used the Library of Congress style to transliterate Russian characters to English-alphabet equivalents. This was a really great project and I hope you enjoy this history of Foreign Volunteer Legions in the German Army. I thank D.L.I., UCONN, and the University of Illinois Study Abroad Program for the training they gave me, and I thank you for your readership.

Sincerely,
Patrick Cloutier, Translator.

EDITOR'S NOTE

It has been 56 years, or about five and a half decades since the Second World War ended. Yet, more books continue to be written and published concerning the history of that tragic conflict in which millions of lives were lost and the entire political and economic sphere of the world was transformed forever. The reason for this is quite simple. The war was so all encompassing, so large scale in its scope and depth that centuries will pass and historians will still be writing about it. The amount of data yet to be uncovered in dusty archives and other out of the way places is just that substantial.

It is with great pleasure that I was able to contribute and to put together this collection of historical data on one of the least known, little understood, and much forgotten aspect of World War II. The history of Arab, Indian, and Russian volunteers in German uniform may surprise the general reader, but more fascinating is the fact that these collaborator units were made up of people who called Islam, Hinduism, or even Buddhism as their religion! While most authors and academics have chosen to cover the war in general or specific campaigns or battles, my colleagues and I have chosen to seek the esoteric. The subject of the German Army as well as Allied forces has also been very much written about. There are literally dozens of books on the D-Day landings alone! Less so however, is the story of the Axis allied armies and of the millions of foreign volunteers who chose for one reason or another, to serve the Third Reich.

I am proud of the research that Oleg Romanko, Martin Bamber, and the other contributors to this book have made. I believe that our efforts will make it much easier for researchers and common laymen alike to better understand this little known aspect of the Second World War. The story of the units that are covered here may not have been the elite panzer formations which have been written about so often but they had a specific and important story to convey to mankind and future generations.

Take for instance, the subject of this work, which is the participation of Muslim, Hindu, and Buddhist volunteers in the German Armed Forces during the Second World War. There are many lessons to be learned from this history, even though not a single one of these Arab, Indian, Bosnian, Albanian, Tartar, or Kalmyk volunteers ever rode on a German tank. The repercussions of their participation on the German side can still be heard in the streets of Ramahlla, Israel, or war torn Bosnia, Kosovo, or in the resurgence of independent Muslim republics within the former USSR. The list of lessons and warnings from history abound. My hope is that this work will help to better understand that conflict which occurred so long ago and yet still echoes loudly in this present world. It is a history that needs to be told. My belief is that we have given justice to the subject and the result is a fascinating story.

Antonio J. Munoz, Editor.

INTRODUCTION

The process of forming Muslim Legions, just as with other foreign volunteer formations in the German Armed Forces, was not a one-time phenomenon. The defining characteristic, in our [Russian] opinion, was the German national interest, if one could call it that, which in turn depended on the evolution of German occupation policy.

An important milestone in this process, as it is divided into two stages, were events that occurred in the period from autumn 1942 to autumn 1943. Among these of course, is what was subsequently called the battle of Stalingrad (September 1942-February 1943), the rout of the Germans in North Africa, the fall of the Mussolini regime in Italy, and that country's subsequent capitulation in September 1943. All of these events without a doubt played a paramount role in the defeat of Hitler's Germany. But we should not forget that they also led to many changes in the political sphere.

In the first place, the process of creating and using Muslim volunteer formations under German command clearly shows the predominance of military objectives over political ones. When Germany held victory, she had no need of such allies. Therefore political goals in the war played a subordinate role and served, for the most part, as propaganda. Their main task was to bring about the undermining of the loyalty of national groups to the central, Stalinist government, but nothing more.

Therefore generally speaking, at any given stage all efforts for creating and employing Muslim and foreign volunteer formations were in part decided primarily by military authorities, i.e. Armed Forces High Command (OKW), the Army High Command (OKH), and Military Intelligence (Abwehr), with insignificant interaction with political agencies, such as the newly established Eastern Ministry.[1]

Apart from this, on Himmler's initiative, the formation of auxiliary security police units was undertaken in the occupied territories, principally in the Balkans and USSR. These units serve primarily in keeping order and to combat Partisans behind the front lines. They were originally not intended to take part in battles with regular Russian Army units but were often thrown into the front lines. This proved more so as the war progressed and the German military situation became worse.

Secondly, with the goal of bringing the local population into closer cooperation with the occupation authorities, a balance between military and political objectives was struck: Germany needed soldiers for service on the front and against Partisans in the rear, as well as workers for German industry and agriculture. This task would be difficult to fulfill without creating the illusion of self-determination among the population. It is necessary to point out, that the second stage was realized only in the Balkans and the still-occupied territories of the USSR. The defeat in the Caucasus and North Africa compelled the Germans to abandon plans for penetrating the Near East and India.

---

[1] This was the Eastern Ministry for Occupied Territories, which was headed by Alfred Rosenberg.

Therefore, Alfred Rosenberg's Eastern Ministry for Occupied Territories began to play a key role in the process of creating and using foreign volunteer formations. The role of the military came to nothing. Toward the end of the war, particularly after the attempted assassination of Hitler on July 20th, 1944, Himmler became the supreme commander of all foreign volunteer formations, including the Muslim units, which at that time had only been subordinate to the SS command.

One can say with confidence therefore, that in the period 1941-1945, the following numbers of Muslim volunteers came to serve in the German Armed Forces:

1. Arabs and Indians of the Muslim faith: around 5,000 and 2,000 men, respectively.[2]
2. Balkan Muslims: around 30,000 men in three SS Divisions; in the Bosnian Militia in Herzegovina and Sanjak—around 10,000; in the militia created by the Albanian "Balli Kombetar" organization in Kosovo, Metokii, and Western Macedonia, from 12,000 to 15,000 men; in various auxiliary police units in Kosovo and Metokii, and from 14,500 to 16,500.
3. In all, a rough estimate of from 70,000 to 72,000 men.[3]

Besides this, it is necessary to take into consideration that until autumn 1943, around 80,000 Muslims from Albania, Bosnia, and Kosovo served in various units created by the Italian Command (Volunteer Anti-Communist Militia, the Muslim Legion, and so on.) After the capitulation of Italy, many of these were disbanded and a number of them, an average number of up to 30,000 men, replenished various auxiliary units in the German occupation forces.[4]

The general strength of the different foreign volunteer formations in the Wehrmacht in the Balkans fluctuated from 270,000 (September 1944) to 190,000 (January 1945.) Therefore, one may say with full certainty that the Muslim portion of volunteer formations fluctuated from one third to ½ that number. Naturally, this number was tied to their losses in ongoing military operations in the Balkans during that period.[5]

The greatest difficulty arises from the characteristic question as to how many ordinary Soviet citizens turned up in the ranks of the German military during the war, and what percentage of that number were Muslim volunteers. For understandable reasons, that question is not generally raised in Soviet historiography. Even now, that subject is often side stepped.

According to the calculations of contemporary Russian researcher S.I. Drobyazko, out of a general figure of 1,300,000-1,500,000 Soviet citizens that volunteered for the Germans, 500,000-675,000 served as volunteer auxiliaries or "Hiwis" as they were called. Seventy thousand served in auxiliary police detachments, and 285,000-295,000 men were found in "Eastern" combat units. Out of these figures, Muslim units in the above-mentioned categories of volunteer

---

[2] [141: vol. 4, p. 127]

[3] [120, pages 61-62, 110, 198-199, 292.]

[4] [55, pp.7-25.]

[5] [77, p. 98.]

formations comprised around 200,000 men, 40-45,000 and 150,000 men. Altogether this number totaled 400,000 men, or more than 25%.[6]

It should be pointed out that more than 60,000 of these were Georgians, Armenians, and Kalmyks, who the Germans also included in their roster of "Eastern Legions" units.[7] These are strengths taken only from the Armed Forces. The strengths of the remaining national "Eastern Legions" units were, according to the data of a historian from the Federal Republic of Germany, Hans Werner Nuelen, as follows:

1. Northern Caucasus, about 70,000 to 75,000 men.
2. Volga Tartars, 40,000 men.
3. Kazakhstan and Central Asia, 180,000 men.
4. Crimean Tartars, 15,000 to 20,000 men.[8]

Thus the general strength of the Muslim volunteer formations stood at around 510,000 men, which equaled about 1/3rd of the general strength of foreign volunteers in the German military for the period 1935-1945. The total figure of volunteers was in the neighborhood of 1.6 million to 1.8 million men.[9] What then, were the main reasons that motivated the Nazi military-political leadership to play the "Muslim card" in the war years? In spite of the general significance of this process—the effort to sow religious and ethnic dissension between peoples, using the old principle of every invader, "divide and conquer,"—nevertheless differed greatly, depending on various military-political conditions in various regions of the USSR and the Balkans.

In the question of Arab and Indian volunteers, political considerations dominated over military objectives. One of Hitler's comrades-in-arms, H. Rausching, thought of them as a tactic for sowing discord between the peoples of Europe, most of all England and France, and the Muslim countries. Everything else that remained was a slogan of Hitlerian propaganda.[10]
Operationally, the military value of units formed of Arabs and Indian Muslims, if only in comparison with units formed from Balkan Muslims and Muslim citizens of the USSR, practically equaled zero. This can be explained by the fact that the German Army never made it to the Near East and India, and that the leaders of the pro-German Arabs, the Grand Mufti of Jerusalem, Al-Hussein, and the Prime Minister of Iraq, Al-Gailani, constantly fought each other for supremacy in the Arab World. The leader of the pro-German Indians, Subhas Chandra Bos in the end turned to Japan, having seen no real creation of a large pro-Axis Indian army formed in Germany, other than a token infantry regiment. Therefore, only about 5,000 Arabs and 2,000 Indian Muslims and Hindus turned up in the ranks of the German military. For all that, the volunteer's desire was not enough to turn them into a "liberation army" for the Near East and India.

---

[6] [92, pp. 127-134.]
[7] [93, p. 4.]
[8] [147, p. 342.]
[9] See Appendix 1.
[10] [51, p. 271-272.]

On the other hand, the same course of events said something different. Hitler and his military-political entourage understood quite well that there would not be a general Arab uprising, or an Indian one for that matter, if the German Army was not advancing to the borders of those regions. In the current military-political situation, this possibility was practically non-existent. Therefore, all political and military negotiations with the Arab and Indian leaders were plain fiction-mere attempts to use their authority to win over public opinion in the Muslim World. "German-Arab" and "German-Indian" unions sprang up in propaganda circles.

As already mentioned above, toward spring 1943 the Arab-Indian aspect in the process of creating Muslim volunteer formations disappeared on its own after the defeats on the Eastern and North African fronts, simply no one enlisted for the Arab and Indian Legions. But despite this, there was another side to the issue, not related to German plans to penetrate the Near East and India; how much depended on those Arabs and Indians wearing the German uniform? Then again, what ever depended on it? *"Nationalism,"*-concluded Spanish researcher Carlos Cavallero-Jurado and English author C. Lyles, *"was this cause...National motives were clearly paramount in the efforts of Indian and Arab volunteers."*

The creation of Muslim volunteer formations in the Balkans touches on the classic example, of how one can preserve control in that region by playing on religious differences. Here, the German occupation policy emphasis was on using the ancient enmity between Orthodox Serbs, Muslims in Bosnia, Kosovo, and Metokii, and the Catholic Croats. Even in 1914, immediately after the start of the First World War, the Austro-Hungarian government, under whose authority Bosnia fell, *"strove to ignite the national and religious antagonisms in that region: it sponsored volunteer units, named 'Legions,' which were raised in Bosnia and Herzegovina from Muslim fanatics,"* and set them upon the Serbs.[11]

During the Second World War, history repeated itself. *"In Bosnia-Herzegovina,"* writes English researcher R. West, *"since time immemorial, the Orthodox Serbs have considered the Muslims their chief enemies...To fan the old hatreds, the occupiers enlisted the help of the Ustashe—Muslim cutthroats to take part in the mass-killing of Serbs, who, in their turn, in May 1941 slaughtered a thousand Muslims near Banja Luka."*[12]

But the Germans exploited the Muslim factor not only for their occupation policy in the Balkans against the Serbs, who now formed the basis of Josef Tito's Partisan Army, but covertly against the ally in the Tripartite Pact—The Independent State of Croatia. By including the territory of Bosnia and Herzegovina in its boundaries, the German authorities found a very effective counterweight in the Ustashe. As already pointed out, Ante Pavelich uselessly protested against the formation of a Waffen-SS Muslim Division.

The division of the Balkans into spheres of influence between Germany and Italy until September 1943 added one more political detail to the creation of Muslim volunteer formations. Almost the entire region of the compact Muslim community fell under the authority of Italy. Here, the Italians no doubt left their

---

[11] [97; T.1, p. 669.]

[12] [124, p. 125.]

mark on the process of creating Muslim Legions. For a long time, there existed the opinion in patriotic historiography [*of the USSR - translator's note*] as expressed by M.I. Kalinin, on 4 August 1943, in a conference with front-line political canvassers working among fighters of non-Russian nationality. Speaking of the traitors of the People, who had gone over to the enemy's side, he said *"For a nation as great as the USSR, encountering such worthless exceptions has no significance."*[13]

But judging by the previous figures this was not quite so, if one views the events of the Great Patriotic War through the eyes of a second-class citizen. Upon starting the war with the USSR, one of the main tasks before the military-political leadership of Germany was the destruction of the multi-national state, and the recruitment to its side of the leadership of the non-Russian peoples and national minorities of our country *"in the struggle against Bolshevism and Muscovite imperialism."* A special staff was created for the peoples of the Volga, the republics of the Caucasus, and Central Asia. One of the methods for attracting the leadership of these peoples to Germany's side became the creation of national "Eastern Legions," in the capacity of a nucleus for future armies of "independent" states.

Moreover, Hitler reacted very negatively to the possibility of using Slavs in the war on the German side. He did not however object, although with several reservations, to suggestions for using the people from the above-listed regions. In meeting the national aspirations of the peoples of the Volga, the Caucasus, Central Asia, and most of all, the Muslims, he seriously reckoned on support from Turkey and the Islamic World. *"New weapons of the Reich"*, in the form of Muslim units, writes contemporary Russian researcher V.P Yampolskiy, actively proved themselves not only in the vanguard, but in the rear as well, where these units hunted Partisans, carried out punitive actions against the peaceful citizens, and so on. Hearth and blood were all that remained after Muslim formations swept through, as with those similar to them. [14]

This was a large-scale and long-term action of the German political-military leadership, which knew how to play the "Muslim card" for its ends: that is, to tear the USSR apart from within with the help of national conflicts and tremors and by the same token pave the way for the cherished blitzkrieg. It was the same idea for the Near East and the Balkans. A variety of people served in the Muslim volunteer formations: among them were low-count traitors of the people, who cannot be pardoned; those forced to join, driven by suffering and hunger and torment in the prison camps; those who had lofty ideals and were sincerely misled; and those possessed by the idea of settling a grudge, no matter what regime was in power. But one thing must be understood: there is nothing more terrible or criminal than fratricide--especially when it is done in league with the Nazis. No ideas or theories can justify it.

All this is important not just of itself, but also in the very thought that the rulers of Nazi Germany inserted into the use of the Muslim volunteers. In order to gain world hegemony, they tried to portray themselves as friends of the Muslims,

---

[13] [43, p 89.]
[14] [47, p 24.]

to gain their favor and use it their own ends. Similar occurrences did not sink into the past--in our own difficult times we may observe something like it. Therefore, it is worth remembering, that these events are not merely some kind of tale, but that they are very real and occurred. BELOW: Some of the many emblems used by these volunteers.

CHAPTER 1
Arabs and Representatives of the Muslim Peoples of India in the German Armed Forces 1941-1945

On 12 February 1941, General Rommel's German Afrika Korps landed on the coast of North Africa. From a military viewpoint, this was of no particular significance, but nevertheless, its political meaning represented the apogee of German aspirations in the Near East. The Near and Middle East, and even India, with their rich oil reserves and other natural resources, were already a bone of contention between the leading European powers at the end of the 19th Century: Great Britain and France on one side, and Germany on the other. Coming to power in 1933, the National Socialist government held to the same line on the Near East Question as Imperial Germany.[15]

Already on 7 August 1939, in a session with representatives of England, *Reichsminister* Goering announced that *"The Near and Middle East is a natural economic sphere of influence for Germany and represents an issue of vital importance for her."* From England he demanded recognition of that region *"as a sphere of German influence."* Thus, even before the Second World War, the calculations of the Hitler government were directed toward isolating England, by any means, from Arab oil.[16] After the start of preparations in June 1940 for Operation Barbarossa (the plan for war against the USSR,) the Near East region acquired military significance as a strategic staging area for an advance into the Soviet Caucasus from the rear, and a subsequent junction with forces attacking through the European portion of the USSR.[17]

Attempting to penetrate North Africa, the Near East, and India, Germany used the old method of supporting the local populations in their struggle against the Anglo-French colonizers. Toward 1941, ideological preparation of the populations of the near and Middle Eastern coutries, and India also, increased sharply. German propagandists (usually information center staff,) stigmatized the colonists in the name of the military-political government of the Third Reich. They promised the populations of these countries that a German victory over England and France would bring them liberation from the colonial yoke.[18]

German agents in Near and Middle Eastern countries increased their search for contacts with widely varying groups that had hostile intentions toward England and France, hoping to turn them into political weapons.[19] In April-May 1941, Rommel's *Afrika Korps* drove to the borders of Egypt, creating a favorable

[15] [76, pp. 39-41; 95 pp.66-69.]
[16] [12, pp. 2-3.]
[17] [6, pp. 41-42.]
[18] [74, p. 301; 105, pp. 42-44.]
[19] [105, pp. 43-44; 117, pp. 27-28.]

situation then for increased covert and propaganda activity in the Near and Middle East countries.[20] With the goal of systematically developing this activity (including military means,) the Supreme Command of the Wehrmacht (OKW) issued Special Directive No. 30 on 23 May 1941, under the heading "Middle East." This directive was worked out by generals of the General Staff under OKW orders signed by Hitler. The scope and vision of the directive was aimed at preparing the political soil in the Arab East for strategic positioning for conducting a giant encircling maneuver with forces of the *Afrika Korps* coming from Egypt, and other Army Groups from the Caucasus or Turkey. Thus was the plan to defeat the USSR. These plans assumed more concrete form in OKW Directive No.32 "Preparation for the period after the implementation of Operation Barbarossa," from 11 June 1941.[21]

To coordinate all the measures for the near and Middle East, a special agency was created: *Sonderstab "F"* (Special Staff F.) It was under the control of Major-General of Aviation, Helmuth Felmy.[22] Along with his responsibilities went management of diversionary acts, intelligence agents, and so on. But the chief aspect of his duties was the formation, training, and employment of special units created from the native peoples of the near and Middle East, and the Caucasus. Directive 32A - Responsibilities of Special Staff F ["F" for Felmy] issued on 21 June 1941, was dedicated to this last question, and was supplemental to Directive 32. It emphasized, among other things, an invasion of the near and Middle East at the proper time with the presupposed support of civil unrest and revolts.[23]

General Felmy and the staff under him were thus the factual commanders of all future Arab units. But this required finding a nominal figurehead and representative of all pro-German Arab factions, desirably from anti-British factions of the local elite. Here the Nazis, true to the politics of "divide and conquer," immediately placed their bets on two leaders. One of them was the Grand Mufti of Jerusalem, Hadji Muhammed Amin Al-Hussein. As the contemporary researcher H. Kontselman writes, the Mufti was the kind of person who *"could find the words necessary for mobilizing Muslim self-awareness. He and his supporters succeeded in creating significant difficulties for the British Protectorate authorities in Palestine".*[24]

After bloody clashes between Arabs and Jews in Jerusalem in 1929, a British military court sentenced the Grand Mufti to ten years in prison. The spiritual leader fled, was later pardoned, and returned.[25] Al-Hussein attempted to create the foundations of a future Palestinian state after a British departure. To this end, he founded the Pan-Arab Committee in 1936. This agency demanded that the English immediately forbid further Jewish entry into Palestine. The English replied with a refusal and began to persecute the Committee. The Grand

---

[20] [35; T.1 p.730; 59, pp.45-46.]

[21] [64, pp.129-130.]

[22] [34, T.2, pp.509-510.]

[23] [64, p.151.]

[24] [99, p.27.]

[25] [83, p.167.]

Mufti, disguised as a beggar, fled to Egypt, and afterwards to Syria, Iraq, and Iran. In mid-1941 he reached Berlin.[26]

While still in Baghdad, on 20 January 1941, the Grand Mufti wrote Hitler a letter in which he spoke of the decision of Arabs to fight against England, if they were guaranteed material and moral support. On the instructions of Hitler, State Secretary of the Foreign Affairs Ministry, Ernst von Weizacker, answered the Grand Mufti. In the letter an agreement of financial and military assistance was given, and even projected the supply of weapons, if a way could be found to deliver them.[27]

On the night of 29/30 April 1941, events occurred which showed that such a path of delivery could be found. In answer to the entry of British troops into Iraq, its Prime Minister, Rashid Ali Al-Gailani, took military action against them. Thus started the so-called '30-day war.' While simultaneously breaking relations with England, the Iraqi government turned to Hitler with a request to furnish military assistance, first in the form of air support. In the afore-mentioned Directive No. 30 *"The Middle East,"* Hitler emphasized his resolution *"to enable the development of operations in the Near East by way of military support for Iraq."*[28]

How much significance the Nazi military-political leadership attached to events in Iraq is shown by the fact that, Rudolf Hess who had already been in England, stated in a conversation with English representatives: *"Hitler would not leave Iraq in a fix, so long as it fights on the German side."*[29] The call for volunteers from the Arab population was among the first tasks of this undertaking, aimed at supporting Iraq. The responsibility for this lay with R. Ran, an advisor of diplomatic rank and Special Plenipotentiary for the German Foreign Affairs office in Syria. In line with this task, he created groups to carry out diversionary acts on the trail of the British Army in Iraq. Major F. Kaukji, organizer of an anti-British revolt not long ago in 1936, commanded one of these groups. This column successfully campaigned against the British throughout the course of the Anglo-Iraq War.[30]

After the occupation of Aleppo (where the headquarters of the Arab Legion being formed by Ran was located) by English and "Free French" forces under General de Gaulle at the beginning of July 1941, Kaukji fled to northern Syria, and then to Germany. The Legion was disbanded, but a number of its volunteers went on to bring the covert branch of the *Abwehr* apparatus up to strength. *"If only the transportation situation were improved, I could send you the appropriate people,"* wrote Ran in a letter to an *Abwehr* member residing in Athens, under whose aegis the recently created Special Staff F was located.[31]

But none of these measures could help Iraq. Already on 29 May 1941, the war was over. The government led by Al-Gailani, and the Grand Mufti, who was

---

[26] [99,pp.27-28.]
[27] [95, p.42.]
[28] [Tsit. Po. 117, p.37.]
[29] [111, p.371.]
[30] [109, pp.214-216.]
[31] [Tsit. po. 117, p.43.]

also in Iraq, hid in Iran, and then made it to Berlin. There, the former Prime Minister of Iraq also started to proclaim his pretensions to being leader of the Arab World.[32] Nevertheless, from the beginning, the German government attached importance to the cooperation of the Grand Mufti and Al-Gailani. First of all, in the event of an invasion of the Arab region, they could render help in influencing the tribal chiefs, and create a propaganda counter-weight to the English.

With their help, OKW established close contacts with major Muslim leaders and clerics in the countries of the Arab East, using their anti-British sentiments to its advantage. In part, Al Gailani and the Grand Mufti readied the creation of an "Iraqi-Arab Army" under the aegis and leadership of the *Wehrmacht* Command. In return, Germany would have use of the national raw materials and mineral wealth of the Arab countries. It was reported to them in Hitler's name, that in accordance with OKW Directive 30, they could consider the Arab Legion, which Staff F proposed to create, as the core of a future "Iraq-Arabic Army." It was planned to include 1 Syrian, 1 Palestinian/Trans-Jordanian, and 3 Iraqi Divisions.[33]

To work out and generalize materials on the Near East, an "Arab Committee" was created in the Foreign Affairs Ministry in Germany. F. Grobba, a diplomat with a great length of service in the Near East, became its chairman. Simultaneously, he was Special Plenipotentiary to Arab countries for Special Staff "F," since the day of its foundation.[34] On 28 November 1941, there was a meeting between Hitler and the Grand Mufti in Berlin. Striving to reach an accord on a declaration by Germany, which would guarantee independence to the Arab countries, the Mufti suggested the formation of an Arab Legion and its inclusion in the Wehrmacht for joint operations against England. Hitler declined the declaration, motivated by the fact that *"The gentlemen (the diplomats) obviously forgot completely that such kinds of promises—when up to this point, we have not driven to Mosul—are complete rubbish and absurd. The English will simply slaughter all those Arabs who appear in support of our operations."*[35]

But he turned with interest to the creation of a legion, as it agreed with the goals outlined in Directive 32. In a subsequent session with Grobba, the Grand Mufti suggested bringing the Legion up to strength with:

1. Palestinian Arabs, who had fallen prisoner to German forces;
2. Arab officers from Syria, Palestine, and Iraq who were in need after the removal from Turkey to Germany;
3. Arab POWs from French North Africa, located in German-occupied territories of France;
4. Arab emigrants from North Africa, living in France;

---

[32] [95, pp.42-44.]
[33] [152, p.317.]
[34] [152, p.317.]
[35] [50, p.298.]

5. Trustworthy Arabs from Morocco connected with the Grand Mufti.[36]

On the recommendation of Grobba, the military leadership was limited to Iraqis, Syrians, and Palestinian students studying in education establishments in countries occupied by Germany. Grobba also recommended making the future Arab Legion subordinate to General Felmy's staff. At the start of December 1941, Al-Gailani met with the Chief of the Foreign Ministry, Joachim von Ribbentrop. He, like the Mufti, solicited a declaration, and personal recognition of himself as the Prime Minister of Iraq, as well. He was rebuffed. But on 22 December Ribbentrop wrote and signed a letter to him, in which he assured him about the readiness *"to discuss terms of cooperation between Iraq and Germany"*, as soon as possible.[37] Nevertheless, the question of creating an Arab Legion did not come onto the day's agenda.

LEFT: The emblem of the Arab volunteers. This arm patch read "FREE ARABIA" and was written in both Arabic and German.

On 4 January 1942, General Felmy visited Al-Gailani and the Grand Mufti. Grobba took part in the meeting. Al-Gailani expressed the desire to conclude with an agreement about "German-Iraqi military cooperation." Grobba and Felmy constructed a project about the agreement after the talks. Al Gailani and the Grand Mufti calculated that in the event the *Wehrmacht* approached Arab territory, almost the entire Iraqi Army (3 divisions) would join it. A further 1 or 2 divisions could be formed from Arab volunteers in Syria. They also counted on the tribes in the Persian Gulf zone, among whom, in their opinion, as many as "10,000 recruits were ready to co-operate with the German military." Reliable divisional cadres and corresponding junior officer cadres should already be created single-mindedly for them, by means of forming an Arab Legion.[38]

Al Gailani and the Grand Mufti announced that they would supply the personnel resources for the legion. Special Staff F would take on the remaining tasks. From the start, the legion was conceived of as a "school for junior commanders" which would prepare one hundred NCOs and Junior Lieutenants from the Arabs. Next, they in their turn would take upon themselves the training for the next groups of 500-1,000 men. In the long-term, the greater part of the commanders, in accordance with the plans of the German command, would become instructors for the forming Iraqi and Syrian divisions.

But in these projects nothing was said about a leadership role for the Arabs. Therefore, unacknowledged in Berlin, the Grand Mufti headed to Rome, where on 7 May 1942, he met with Mussolini. In the course of the discussion, he

[36] [152, p.354.]
[37] [95, p. 131.]
[38] [152, p.357.]

suggested forming an Arab Legion to him, but with significant changes *"an independent Arab military formation,"* under the command of Arab officers, and with Arab banners.[39] The anti-British Arab nationalists leaned more closely to Hitler than to Mussolini: they hoped that a German victory would deliver them from English domination. And not without foundation, they feared that Italy planned to take the place of the latter in the Arab East.[40]

But in the same period (April-June 1942) the mutual tension between Al-Gailani and the Grand Mufti, waxing at the time of their joint stay in Baghdad, increased so much that it grew into mutual open hostility. This hostility between two leaders of the Arab World reflected on the situation of the "German-Arab Training Sub-unit" at Special Staff "F." Al-Gailani would not agree to cooperate with that detachment without a military agreement with Germany. More significant obstacles were created by the position taken by the Grand Mufti in summer 1942. Having his uncompromising attitude in mind, Hitler said: *"Our ally in that region—the Grand Mufti—besides being a fervent defender of his nation, always proceeds from the real interests of the Arabs, and is never ruled by some ridiculous fantasy."*[41] Not receiving real support from either Germany or Italy in his efforts to assume leadership of the Arab World, he ceased recruiting Arabs for the Axis Powers.

This is how the political situation took shape around the plans for creating Arab units in the German Army. The plans were realized by altogether different means with completely different goals. First of all, they were connected with the previously mentioned Special Staff "F," whose political role in these developments was already discussed. This organization was conceived, first of all, as the Headquarters for all future units which were to be formed from the natives of the Near East and North Africa. Therefore, let us switch our view for a look at the military side of its activities, which were preeminent.

As stated already, Special Staff "F" was created in May 1941. The place selected for its center of operations was Cape Sunion in Southern Greece. In so far as the subject of its operations was work with emigres from the near and Middle East, its personnel were selected accordingly. Special Staff "F" was named for Major General Felmy, who long worked as a flight instructor in Turkey, and had spent time in the tropical countries of Africa. The Chief of Staff was Major R. Mayer, who in his time, served in Turkey, Palestine, Iraq, and Algeria. Attached to Staff "F" from the *Abwehr* was Oskar Ritter von Niedermayer, who was an officer of importance and a famous Near East specialist. In 1915-1916 he was part of a special German mission in Kabul, which had the goal of bringing Afghanistan into the war on the side of the Central Powers.[42]

By personal recommendation of Ribbentrop and the Foreign Ministry, the afore-mentioned General Grobba was named Special Plenipotentiary to the Arab countries. He was the former German envoy in Baghdad in 1932. But from 1-3

[39] [152, pp.360-361.]
[40] [64, p.140.]
[41] [50, pp.397-398.]
[42] [75, pp.18-26; 104, pp.352-355.]

September, he was the envoy to Saudi Arabia. Thus, Special Staff "F" was immediately subordinate to OKW, but in questions of politics it answered to the Foreign Ministry.[43] The standing orders for it were the "Special Instructions to Staff F," worked out and signed 21 September 1941 by the Deputy Chief of Staff of the *Wehrmacht* Operations Center, General Walther Warlimont. In accordance with this, Staff "F" was given the powers of *"a central command, concerning all questions of the Arab World, which touched on the Wehrmacht."*[44]

RIGHT: Emblem of Special Staff "F". This insignia sported a white Nazi swastika at its base, surrounded by two white wreaths and a white palm tree with yellow sunrise. The background was an olive green *Author's Collection..*

In agreement with Directive 32, the recruitment of Arab-nationalists was placed in its sphere of operations, in order to strengthen Staff "F." Their recruitment was delegated to R. Ran.[45] After going through special military training, they were to form the kernel of future military formations, for a specially designated "F" Corps. The formation of the latter would happen by the following method: First, a contingent of 27 Arabs from different Near East peoples was assigned to Special Staff F (it was planned to increase that number to 200,) as well as 20 officers and 200 NCO's and enlisted men, most of whom were serving in the specially designated *"Brandenburg Division."* From the end of May to the beginning of June 1941, two small specially designated units were formed from them in Potsdam: *Sonderverbande No.287 and No.288.*[46] They were to have a structure, such as would enable them to carry out particularly difficult tasks, including operations in the desert (and independent of whether they were operating as one, or separately.)

Sonderverbande No. 288 had a strength that was equivalent to a battalion and was composed mostly of Germans. Therefore, by July-August 1942, it was deployed to North Africa to reinforce Rommel's *Afrika Korps*.[47] *Sonderverbande No. 287* had a somewhat different fate. It was to be the spearhead for the capture of the Near East. Therefore, in the main, its personnel were mainly emigres from there. In accordance with "Mission Instructions," preparation of unit 287 considered such questions *as "clothing issue, weapons, organization, and unit cohesion."*[48] By July 1941, an instructional group was formed from Arabs *"for use in the Great Syrian Desert."* In it were Arab students who had studied in Germany, as well as anti-British military factions who had left Syria.

[43] [95, pp.124-125.]
[44] [64, pp.134-135.]
[45] [152, p. 256.]
[46] [128 p.32.]
[47] [107, pp. 112-113.]
[48] [152, p.315.]

These Arab volunteers were to be in propaganda and sabotage and espionage units, which were called "Death's Commandos."[49] They were instructed by German officers fluent in Arabic, in eight instructional groups of various military types, and clothed in *Wehrmacht* uniforms. *Sonderverbande No. 287* was completely motorized. From the beginning 2,200 men enlisted to serve in it. The unit was referred to as a regular battalion in documents, but in reality it was far stronger than that. According to the established organization of the German Army, a normal battalion would consist of 3-4 companies, but unit No. 287 had seven. The first company was manned by volunteers from the near and Middle East who all together spoke more than 20 languages. The 2nd Company was Mountain Jaeger; the 3rd Company--Infantry; 4th Company--Reconnaissance; 5th Co.--Artillery, whose pieces were light and heavy mortars; 6th Co. was Anti-aircraft Artillery; and 7th Co. was an anti-tank outfit.[50] The unit was furnished with the most modern weapons and ammunition *"It speaks of their mission importance,"* that aside from military units, the 287th also had hydro-graphical and topographical companies.

Sonderverbande No. 287 was earmarked *"first for later use in"* battle operations *"in the Syrian Desert, between Syria and Iraq, where it would be deployed in dispersed battle groups, for joint operations with Arab cadres and volunteer forces."*[51] At the end of October 1942, *Sonderverbande 287* was transferred to North Africa, where in the course of several months it received *"special combat training."* In 1942, Special Staff F was to receive two to three more similar units.

Toward July 1942, *"an Arab instructional group"* of 24 Iraqis, 112 Syrians and Palestinians, and 107 Arabs from the Magreb countries completed special military reconnaissance training. Thus, by 20 August 1942 OKW took the decision to upgrade Special Staff “F” to a Corps-size unit, based on *Sonderverband 287*. The Corps would receive the special designation "F," and be deployed as a reserve of Army Group “A” HQ in Stalino. At this time, Army Group “A” was advancing toward the Caucasus. In accordance with OKW plans, after Army Group “A” arrived in Tbilisi, “F” Corps would entrain and transfer by rail through Rostov on the Don River and on to the Caucasus. It would then detrain and attack in the direction of Western Iran/Iraq, and its exit to the Persian Gulf—Basra. [52]

On 29 August 1942, the major portion of the Corps, located before that time in Rumania, arrived Mayorskoye village, near Stalino. By 3 October 1942 it was training as an Army Corps—an independent manuever unit.[53] “F” Corps had military units of all types that allowed it to operate with complete independence, without the help or support of other units. The Corps contained three reinforced motorized battalions, each rated at 1,000 officers and men; 1st and 2nd Battalions were composed exclusively of officers and soldiers of the *Wehrmacht*; 3rd

---

[49] [152, p.316.]
[50] [62, p. 1.]
[51] [152, p.315.]
[52] [95, p.149.]
[53] [33, p.137.]

Battalion was composed fully of Arabs training in Special Staff F's "instructional group."
By roster, every battalion was the equivalent of a regiment in weapons and tactics, and firepower potential. Besides that, assigned to “F” Corps were: a separate tank battalion (25 heavy and medium tanks,) an aviation detachment (25 aircraft,) a communications company, an engineer company, a mortar company, a recon detachment with armored cars and motorcycles, a cavalry squadron, a meteorlogical service platoon, and a truck column (Opel-Blitz.) Artillery consisted of four 105mm gun divisional fire-support batteries, four heavy divisional anti-aircraft cannon, and 20mm light anit-aircraft guns. “F” Corps also had a HQ and rear echelon units, which included medical, bakery, butcher, plus various skilled workshops, etc.[54]

The Corps was completely mechanized and possessed the capability to arm an additional complete division of "volunteers" and defectors, in the event that the Wehrmacht invaded Iraq. In its organization table were special sub-units, composed of Germans who were former French Foreign Legionnaires.[55] The distinguishing personal insignia was the image of an oval wreath, in which was a leaning palm, with a rising sun over a gold sand desert, and beneath--a black swastika. From the beginning, the Corps numbered 6,000 soldiers and officers. After deployment in the Caucasus it was expanded into a still larger unit: additional tank battalions, a cavalry regiment, and other sub-units were attached to it. In addition to military and political training, “F” Corps personnel studied the geography and history of the near and Middle East countries (particularly Iran, the Arab countries, and India.) For a short term, soldiers studied the relief and natural conditions of the region, from the northern Iranian border down to India. Soldiers and officers were taught Turkish, Persian, Arabic, and other eastern languages. Besides this, they knew French and English. Émigré soldiers from the Near East countries, except students, studied German.[56]

According to OKW plans, “F” Corps should have deployed as a strike/assault force unit and political center for the German march on the Caucasus and the countries of the near and Middle East. The duties of carrying out intelligence-gathering, diversionary acts, propaganda/agitation tasks, and readying preparations for anti-Soviet revolts in the Caucasus were delegated to its personnel. Because of the responsibilities of its mission, “F” Corps *"moved only at night,"* but Soviet intelligence agents noticed *"many dark-brown people among its soldiers, dissimilar to Germans, speaking in an unknown language."*[57]

But upon its arrival in the Caucasus, it was necessary to become a combat unit. On 3 October, the HQ of Army Group “A” reported to the HQ of 1st Panzer Army, along with a summary of unit distributions from the OKW reserve, that as of 5 October 1942, “F” Corps was transferred to its command. On 5 October it dispatched an order to “F” Corps about its imminent operational subordination to 1st Panzer Army. On 15 October, “F” Corps first went into battle under the

---

54 [36, pp.231-232.]
55 [36, pp.231-232.]
56 [95, p.151.]
57 [36, p.12.]

command of General Felmy. On the north flank of 1st Panzer Army, and north of Achikulak, they *"came into contact with a strong cavalry force"* of the 4th Guards Kuban Cossack Cavalry Corps.[58]

It should be noted that the OKW decision to transfer "F" Corps and its maneuver units to the Caucasus, where it was drawn into a positional battle, rather than the Near East--its primary responsibility, roused the dissatisfaction of the Grand Mufti Al-Hussein. As early as 29 August 1942, knowing of Special Staff F's transfer, he appealed in a letter to the OKW Chief of Staff, General Field Marshal Keitel. He sharply spoke against such a decision. Not receiving an answer, he again tried to turn to the Italians at the end of August 1942. Here too, he found disappointment. Al-Gailani, on the other hand, decided to stay with the Germans to the end. Expressing the desire for further cooperation, he presented only one condition. This was presentation of written assurances that after the conquest of the Caucasus and the entry of the *Wehrmacht* into Iraq, command of the Iraqi Army would be placed in the hands of Iraqi officers. He also asked that Iraqi officers in "F" Corps would be released to the disposal of the Iraqi Army.[59]

Al-Gailani's position further embroiled him in conflict with the Grand Mufti, who decided to leave Germany in September/October 1942. He went to Bosnia where he offered his help to the authorities "of the Independent State of Croatia" in the matter of recruiting local Muslims into sub-units for combat against Josip Broz Tito's partisans. The Yugoslav government declared him a war criminal for this in 1945, and sentenced him to death by hanging in absentia. By mid-autumn 1942 there was a turning point in the battle for the Caucasus, and by December 1942 "F" Corps was so worn in battle, that the German Command expressed serious reservations in regard to its military readiness.

In December 1942 / January 1943 "F" Corps was replenished along with sub-units of the 1st Panzer Army, with a combined force of: the "von Jungschultz" Cavalry Regiment, a cavalry detachment,[60] the 506th Motorized Battalion, and a Field Police Battalion. So the Steppe Battle Group was returned to its base under the command of General Felmy.[61] By January 1943, Soviet forces destroyed this group. At the end of January, the Corps was again formed as Special Staff "F," and placed at the disposal of Army Group Don's commander, General Field Marshal Eric von Manstein. In February, the remnants of the Corps, together with its commander, were deployed to Tunis.[62] Its deployment there was necessary to reinforce the Italo-German Army in Africa. Subsequently, "F" Corps was strengthened on account of Arab volunteers, and a number of separate Arab formations from Iraq, Syria, Transjordan, and Libya.

In contemporary historical literature dedicated to World War Two, there is a strong misconception that "F" Corps and the "Free Arab Legion" was one and the same. But "F" Corps never officially had that designation--which term was an

---

58 [95, p.153.]

59 [95, pp.153-154.]

60 This cavalry unit may have possibly been part of the Kalmuck Cavalry Formation [for more on this unit, see chapter 8].

61 [36, p.245.]

62 [95, pp.161, 246.]

easy way to distinguish those Arabs who fought under German command, from other volunteer groups who fought in the German Armed Forces. Although the Free Arab Legion found it operationally subbordinate to the "F" Corps headquarters, they were nevertheless a separate unit, formed independently of "F" Corps during 1941-42. France and the North African colonies belonging to her can be named as the next place for forming similar units.

As early as the end of 1940, the German propaganda service in the Arab countries began to widely advertise the special regard of the Nazis for the Muslims. The Germans released 10,000 Arabic soldiers from the Magreb, who had been on duty in the French Army and fallen prisoner, to their homes. With the help of Algerian emigrés, the Germans began to publish the newspaper *"Al-Rashid,"* in occupied Paris. This helped the *Abwehr* and propaganda services create the illusion of a friendly attitude on the Reich's part toward the Arab peoples.[63]

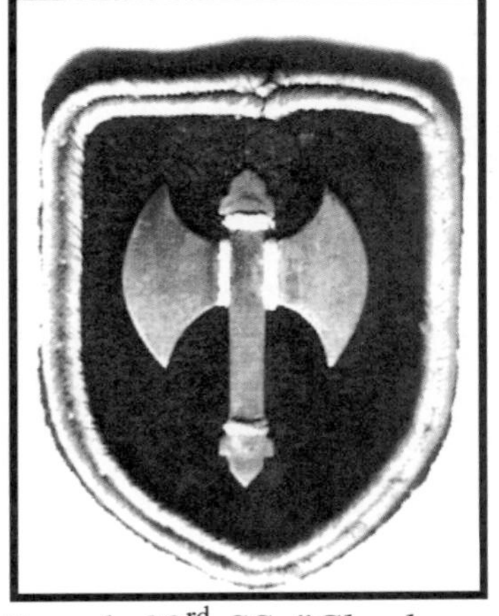

LEFT: Arm Patch of the "Phalange Africaine." It sported a gold surround shield, and gold double headed battle axe on a black background. *Author's Collection.*

With this objective, the Germans formed a North African unit from Muslims living in France. They were used in anti-Partisan operations. A significant number of French Muslims were also enrolled in a French Volunteer Legion that was sent to the Eastern Front in October 1941. There it took part in the German attack on Moscow. In 1941-42, it battled Soviet Partisans in Army Group Center's rear area. Subsequently, the legion was assigned to the French 33rd SS *"Charlemagne"* Division.[64] The German 715th Infantry Division, stationed in garrison in southern France, also accepted Muslims into its ranks. The command created a sub-unit for experimental purposes, under the designation "German-Arab Infantry Battalion No. 845."[65]

On 8 November 1942, the Anglo-American landings in North Africa began. Before long, they had captured the entire Southern Mediterranean coast, and only Tunisia remained under the control of the Axis Powers. For its defense, the German Command decided to use local nationals as volunteers. Thus was created the important unit known as German-Arab Training Division (Deutsch-Arabische Lehr Abteilung,) or simply, the German-Arab Troop (Deutsch-Arabische Truppen.) It numbered five battalions, including the previously discussed unit, *Sonderverband No.288*, which it absorbed. The German-Arab Training Division was subordinate to 5th Panzer Army Headquarters. In it were Muslim personnel who from the beginning, were assigned to the "African Phalange" *("Phalange Africaine")* volunteer unit. The Vichy Government created

---

63 [95, p.277.]

64 [128, pp. 6, 32.]

65 [128, p.32.]

this in 1942 for the defense of Tunisia from the Anglo-Americans.[66] There were also other lighter, unsupported units, under the command of German officers, used for rear-area security. In February-March 1943, the previously mentioned "F" Corps, newly reformed, was added to these units. Finally, on 15 May 1943, all these units capitulated with the 250,000 personnel of the Italo-German Army on Cape Bon.

With the same objectives in mind as with Arab units, the Nazi military-political government created an Indian volunteer formation. In December 1941-January 1942, the formation of the Indian National Legion (or as it is better known, the Legion *"Azad Hind,"* or "Free Indian Legion" was started in training camps in Frankenburg and Koenigsbruck in Saxony. In time, this would become the core of an "Indian National Army" *("Jai Hind")*.[67]

The Indian Legion was formed of volunteers from Hindu POWs who had served in the English Army and had been taken prisoner in the course of battle in North Africa. It was also formed from supporters of a leader in the Indian National Congress: Subhas Chandra Bose, who was located in Germany. Until then, Bose was working at the "Free India" radio station in Nauen, occupied with anti-English propaganda.[68] On 26 August 1942, the Legion took an oath of loyalty to Hitler and was brought in as the 950th Indian Infantry Regiment *(Indisches Infanterie Regiment No.950)* and had a strength of 2,000 men.[69] *Wehrmacht* Colonel Kurt Krappe was designated commander of the Legion, and served in that capacity until 25 June 1943.

LEFT: The emblem of the Indian 950th Infantry Regiment – the "Springing Tiger". The words "FREE INDIA" were written in German. The arm patch sported the Indian national colors of yellow, white and green. The Tiger was painted in a white-reddish orange. *Author's Collection.*

The Legion was organized as a standard German Army infantry regiment, with three battalions of four companies each (1st-12th) and a machine gun company (13th), an anti-tank company (14th), and a sapper company (the 15th). Besides that, an Honor Guard and Convalescent Hospital were assigned to the Legion.[70] The Legion was partly motorized: it was furnished with 80 motor vehicles and 700 horses, which later served as the basis to change its designation to the 950th Motorized Regiment (Indian).[71] In contrast to the British practice of creating units of the Indian Army, units of mixed nationality and religion were assigned to the Legion. Thus, Muslims, Hindus, and Sikhs served in it side by

---

[66] [128, pp.7, 32-33.]
[67] [141; v.4, p.127.]
[68] [74, p.303; 85, pp. 413-415.]
[69] [128, p.31.]
[70] [128, p.31; 141; v.4 p.126.]
[71] [128, p.31.]

side. Out of respect for their religious traditions, the Sikhs were allowed to wear the turban as regular field head gear. Approximately 2/3rd of the Legions soldiers were Muslim, and 1/3rd Hindus.[72]

At the end of 1943 all Indians of the Muslim faith were conclusively transferred into the SS; to the 13th SS Mountain Infantry Division *"Handschar,"* which was in the forming stage in Bosnia.[73] *Reichsfuhrer-SS* Heinrich Himmler was filled with enthusiasm about the prospect of forming a Muslim SS Division in general, and recruiting Muslim Indians in particular. But *SS-Obergruppenfuhrer* Gottlob Berger, the Chief of Operations for the SS, warned him in November 1943 that Indian Muslims felt that they were Indians first, and that likewise, the Bosnian Muslims considered themselves Europeans first. The idea was forgotten.[74]

In January 1942 a unit of Indian fighters from the Legion took part in an operation worked out by the *Abwehr* called "Bayadera." In the eastern part of Iran 100 agent provocateurs were dropped by parachute. *Abwehr* officer Captain Khabikht headed the group. The task of the group was to penetrate India by foot through Belujistan and unite with pro-Nazi detachments of Indian nationalist organizations, counted at 5,500 men acting under the control of the *Wehrmacht.* The group was to occupy itself with diversions and sabotage of English communications. Its chief goal, however, was to make fertile ground for a general national Indian uprising.[75] It is necessary to point out that the German military-political authorities tied the start of Operation Bayadera with the capture of the Caucasus and the fall of Tbilisi; from there, German diplomats intended to proclaim the creation of pro-German cabinets of the "New" Iran, Iraq, India, and Syria.

In spring 1943 an unsuccessful attempt was made to direct the Legion to Burma, where at that time the Japanese Army was at the very borders of India and had created their own "Indian National Army."[76] After that, the Legion was brought to the Netherlands to guard the Atlantic Wall, but by September 1943, it was transferred to southern France to guard the coast.[77] In August 1944 the Western Allies landed in southern France, and the Legion, in order not to be cut off, was brought to

ABOVE: An Indian NCO of the 950th Infantry Regiment. *Bundesarchiv.*

[72] [136, p.63.]
[73] For more details about this, see Chapter 2.
[74] [140, p.117.]
[75] [95, p.67.]
[76] [112, pp.51-62.]
[77] [136, p.63.]

Germany. All along the way, it was subject to attacks by French Maquis Partisans. As early as 8 August 1944 the Legion, now numbering about 2,300 men, was placed under the control of SS High Command, like other foreign volunteer units. It now called itself "The Indian Army Volunteer Legion, SS" *("Indische Freiwillige Legion Waffen-SS.").* *SS-Oberfuehrer* Heinz Bertling became the new commander of the Legion.[78] In May 1945, during an attempt to escape to neutral Switzerland, the Americans and Free French, who turned them all over to the English Army, captured all the personnel of the Legion.

RIGHT: Hitler greets the Iraqi leader, al Gailani. *Historical Museum, Evpatoria, Crimea, Ukraine.*

BELOW: Field Marshal Erwin Rommel inspects the 950th (Indian) Infantry Regiment while stationed in Holland in 1943. The regiment had been stationed on the Dutch coast for a brief time before it was transferred to the Bay of Biscay area of southwestern France. *Bundesarchiv.*

[78] [125, p.402; 141; v.4, p.127.]

CHAPTER 2
Balkan Muslim Volunteer Formations In the Armed Forces of the Axis Powers 1939-1945

For the entire length of its history, the Balkans has been considered the powder keg of Europe. In our century, it is namely from the Balkans that the First World War started. The Second World War received an impulse from the Balkans, which for its relative significance compares with the start of the Russian campaign. Now, at the end of the 20th Century, we are witnesses to a new Balkan crisis, with the potential to lead to serious consequences. History shows that the Balkans became the border between the Christian and Muslim worlds, after their conquest by the Ottoman Empire in the 15th Century. Therefore, any conflict here at once carries religious and ethnic ramifications—conflict in which those striving to establish their hegemony over that peninsula always play roles. Nazi Germany was particularly successful at this; the creation and use of Balkan Muslim volunteer formations were one of the instruments of its occupation policy in the region. *"German thinking was simple"* - wrote Yugoslav historian Y. Maryanovich: *"Dismember Yugoslavia, kindle colliding national and religious tinder, bring servile puppet governments to power, composed of local collaborationists...apply the very most severe methods of pressure on the population, all of which should furnish...Germany with dominance for a minimal use of military force."*[79]

The Balkans has three major compact Muslim-populated regions. These are: Albania (65%) and former Yugoslavia (11% of the population). Those in Yugoslavia lived in two areas: Bosnia and Herzegovina (around 30% of the population), and Kosovo and Metokhii (around 60% of the population).[80]

Before the start of World War Two, and during its course, the region was occupied by Italy and Germany; that naturally left its mark on occupation politics and the process of forming "volunteer formations," as well as their activities. On 7 April 1939, the Italian Expeditionary Corps landed in Albania, and in the course of a week, occupied the country. King Zog fled, and the Albanian Army was dispersed. By 10 April 1939, the Italian military completed occupation of the country. On 12 April a puppet Albanian government was formed with the important landowner, Sh. Verlyatsi at its head. This government was designated the "Provisional Administrative Council." The Council began to fulfill the functions of an auxiliary agency for Italian General Iacomoni—the factual head of government. King Victor Emmanuel III was proclaimed the Supreme Head of State, or its King. Henceforth, Albania became a part of the Italian Empire.[81]

On the night of 6 April 1941, German forces, supported by the Italians and Hungarians, invaded Yugoslavia. Twelve days after the start of the war, Belgrade

---

[79] [103, p.45.]

[80] [53.]

[81] [55, p.11; 148, p.25.]

fell, and young Peter II Karageorgevich flew away to British-controlled Egypt. According to Hitler's plans, Yugoslavia was to be partitioned like Czechoslovakia and Poland. The greater part of its territory would go to Germany and Italy. Portions of it would go to Hungary and Bulgaria.[82] On 10 April 1941 the "Independent State of Croatia" (ISC) was proclaimed in Zagreb. Included within its borders were strictly Croatian lands and Bosnia-Herzegovina. On 11 April, on the basis of a law concerning the Army and Navy, the Armed Forces for the ISC began to be built. But they were so weak that Hitler and Mussolini did not decide to move these forces from Croatia, where they remained until the end of the war, guaranteeing her "independence." On that basis, on 23 April 1941, the border between the German and Italian occupation zones was demarcated. It ran almost down the middle of Bosnia-Herzegovina.

RIGHT: A Bosnian SS volunteer in the "Handschar" Division's engineer battalion. *Bundesarchiv.*
BELOW: Members of the Reconnaissance Battalion of the 13th SS "Handschar" Division stop by a creek to water their horses. *Author's Collection.*

Italy occupied the greater part of Kosovo and Metokhii, which were formally annexed to Albania on 12 August 1941. A High Citizens Committee, and later a "Ministry of the Liberated Regions" ran these areas. The Germans themselves took only one small, but mineral-rich (zinc and tin) portion of Kosovo called Trepcha.[83] Thus, a large portion of territories populated by Balkan Muslims wound up under the control of Italy. From the first, Italy started to recruit them for service in its army: not with the rights of volunteers, but forming them on the basis compulsory national military units.

From 1939 through early 1941, an Albanian Royal Guard was formed in Rome, and four Albanian Fascist Militia Legions, battalions in size, were formed and designated 1-4. After Italy's attack on Greece in October 1940, the Verlyatsi

[82] [120, pp.15-20.]
[83] [120, pp.21-22.]

ABOVE: Officers of the SS "Handschar" Division during 1944. Some of these officers and men were eventually transferred over to the forming 23rd SS Mountain Division "Kama", which was supposed to become the "sister" division of the "Handschar". The "Kama" Division was also to have been made up mainly of Moslem volunteers from Bosnia and Herzegivina. *US National Archives.*

government declared a state of war with the latter. The 1st and 2nd Legions were sent to the Greek Front. Simultaneously, mobilization was declared in Albania. But once sent to the front, Albanian soldiers refused to fight and units experienced mass desertions.[84] Besides this, six Royal Albanian Infantry Battalions were created, three artillery batteries, two light anti-aircraft batteries, and five irregular volunteer battalions.[85]

In 1940-1941 Albanians began to be called up for service in the Regia Nave, the Regia Aeronautica, border police and customs guards, and the Carabinieri. In Albania itself local police forces were created to maintain order.[86] With the increase in Partisan activity at the end of 1941, Albanian infantry regiments *(Cacciatori d'Albania)* were created (designated Nos. 1-3) Each regiment numbered from 2,000-3,000 soldiers in two infantry battalions, a machine gun company, and an artillery battery. On 10 January 1943 a decision was taken at a meeting of the Italian General Staff to raise a fourth Albanian regiment, and a brigade from volunteers. In the opinion of Chief of Staff, Ugo Cavallero, this was done with the goal of inculcating a feeling of duty in the Albanians, in the presence of their new people, the Italian Empire. *"It is undesirable"*-he emphasized in his diary, *"that in Albania they should turn to Italian soldiery as to occupiers."*[87]

Therefore, by spring 1943, a fourth regiment was created in Kosovo as the 4th Regiment, and included in the 1st Albanian Infantry Brigade. But because of low readiness and massive desertions from the 2nd and 3rd Regiments, it was disbanded before the capitulation of Italy.[88] In Western and Central Bosnia, the Italians formed the 20,000-strong paramilitary Anti-Communist Volunteer Militia to combat partisans. In the Sanjak Region (western Serbia and northern

---

[84] [55, p.12.]
[85] [148, p. 26.]
[86] [148, pp.26-27.]
[87] [39, p.272.]
[88] [148, p.27.]

Montenegro) a Muslim Legion was formed with the same goals. It was disbanded towards 1943.[89] But the Albanians did not want to fight for Italian interests. Thus, the attempt by the M. Kruya Administration, who had replaced Verlyatsi in December 1941, to mobilize Albanians for war against England in Libya, and later to form a unit for dispatch to the Russian Front, ended in total failure.[90]

Business went somewhat differently in the German occupation zone. In as much as significantly fewer Muslims lived here, the Germans recruited Slovenians, Croats, and Serbs for the volunteer formations. Thus, for the period 1941-1942, they formed a Serbian government guard, a Serbian Volunteer Corps, and a Slovenian Home Guard, with the help of local collaborationists.[91] Nevertheless, in the second half of 1941, an Albanian gendarme (about 1,000 men) was created to maintain order under the direction of the German authorities. Its headquarters was in Kosovska-Mitrovitse. It had about 1,000 Albanian volunteers in detachments, which were commanded by village elders.[92]

BELOW: Parade of Bosnian Moslem troopers of the 13th SS Mountain Division "Handschar." Notice the distinctive right collar tab, which contained a swastika and a hand holding a Turkish Scimitar (curved sword). Notice also the specialized fez cover. The history of this division now follows in Chapter 2, as well as in Chapter 13. *US National Archives.*

In 1942-43 a fundamental turning point occurred in the course of the Second World War. The German Army and its allies suffered a defeat at Stalingrad. A result of that was the weakening of the pro-German coalition, and efforts by Italy to exit the war. The latter increased further after the Western

[89] [148, pp.21,23.]
[90] [55, p. 15.]
[91] [148, pp.22, 23.]
[92] [120. Pp.33-34.]

Allies landed in Sicily in July 1943. Thus, not counting on the stamina of its Italian ally, the German Supreme Command distributed a plan to lower-level military commands on 30th August 1943, code-named "Axis." With their own forces, (15 divisions) they were to subdue Italy, and as soon as possible, re-arm those Italian units entering on the German side and agreeing to fight under their command as "volunteer formations." On the eve of 8 September, a few hours before the Italian capitulation, the Supreme Command of the *Wehrmacht* (OKW) gave the order to immediately carry out *"Unternehmen Achse"* (Operation Axis).[93] Now came the second phase in the process of forming and using Muslim Volunteer Formations. It was characterized by the following traits. In the first instance, the reformation and creation of new units for police duties and partisan combat was already ongoing.

As a result, at the start of 1944 Muslim Volunteer Formations included the following: four Albanian Rifle Regiments (1-4,) four Fascist Militia Battalions, and gendarmes, created in spring 1943 under the command of General Prenka Prevesi.

RIGHT: A recruiting poster specifically designed by the Germans to attrack Bosnian Moslems for the German SS "Handschar" Mountain Divi-sion. The theme of the poster was anti-communist, and the Croatian shield on the top right hand of the poster reminded all that the Croatian defense was involved. The poster sported a German SS mountain trooper fighting alongside a Bosnian SS soldier and was meant to show solidarity between the German and Muslim peoples of Bosnia and Herzegovina. See page 18 for a full color view. *Author's Collection.*

93 [59, pp.21-22.]

ABOVE: SS General Karl Sauberaweig decorates a Bosnian SS volunteer in the 13th SS "Handschar" Division. *Museum of Modern History, Ljubljana, Slovenia.*

In addition, a number of Italian collaborationists came to be included in the armed formations of the *"Balli Kombetar"* organization. Anti-Communist forces created this at the end of 1942 in southern Albania, with the support of the Italian occupation authorities. *"Important landowners, wealthy peasants, and groups representing various bourgeois interests"* joined the ranks of the organization. In order to attract the local population to its side, the *Ballisti* made declarations about the democratic character of their organization. But by 15 March 1943, they openly turned to collaborating with the occupiers, signing the Dalmatsto-Keltsyura Protocol.[94] By the terms of the Protocol the *Ballisti* not only refused to fight the occupiers, but were required to take part in suppressing resistance movements and render aid to the gendarmes of the Albanian authorities.[95]

The *Ballisti* formations numbered several weak battalions, which were kept inactive, however, out of fear of repressions from the Italian side. After the October 1943 occupation of Albania by the German Army, the *Ballisti* adhered to the Germans, believing their promises that after a German victory Kosovo would go to the Albanians. At the beginning of 1944, twenty of their battalions that were located in Macedonia, Kosovo, and Metokhii (in all about 15,000 men) fought

[94] Dalmatsto was the head commander of Italian Forces in Albania, and Keltsyura was one of the Ballisti leaders.

[95] [55, p.18.]

against the Partisans, together with German units under the command of the German 21st Corps.[96] A number of Albanian formations also operated against Partisans in Kosovo and Metokhii: the previously-mentioned gendarmes, "the Kosovo Regiment," formed in 1943 in Kosovska-Mitrovitse as an operational unit; two territorial police regiments—formed in January 1944—one with an HQ in Pech, the other with its HQ in Pristina. The general strength of these units was around 8,000 men. Besides that, an Albanian militia with strength of around 5,000 was created by the Ballisti in western Macedonia, and was subordinate to German authorities.[97] In the words of American historian Gordon Williamson: *"The conduct of some of these auxiliary formations in relation to their fellow countrymen was such that in any given situation their brutality exceeded that of the German punitive expeditions."*[98]

That is how it went in Bosnia and Herzegovina. But, above all, events were tied to a different aspect of the second phase in creation and operations of Muslim volunteer formations—the creation of foreign *Waffen-SS* divisions. The defeat at Stalingrad and in Africa, and continued military operations, which entailed more and more losses in manpower, forced *Reichsfuehrer-SS* Heinrich Himmler to lower racial standards. He turned away from long-standing "blood" regu-lations, which until then were considered the decisive standard for acceptance to the SS. Therefore, in February 1943, the SS Chief of Operations was permitted to take "non-Aryans" into military service. Thus, by this year, divisions of the *Waffen-SS* were filled-out by Slav, Baltic, Asian, and Muslim volunteers. In February 1943, Himmler gave an order about the creation of new *Waffen-SS* divisions from Bosnian Muslim volunteers for the conduct of anti-Partisan operations in Yugoslavia. But the leader of Croatia, Ante Pavelich, regarded the order of the *Reichsfuehrer* suspiciously: *"Suspecting it was a Machiavellian plan, having the goal of turning the Muslims loose against the Catholic Croats, and destabilizing the situation in the Croat State."*[99]

Moreover, all Muslims living in the territory of Bosnia-Herzegovina were officially considered citizens of the Independent State of Croatia, and therefore should have been serving in its army. Incredibly, but true, the Bosnian Muslims and Croat Catholics co-existed very peacefully in one state—their common hatred of the Orthodox Serbs united them. Situated under the authority of Croatia, the *Ustashe* organization established close ties with the leaders of the Bosnian Muslims before the war.[100] After the formation of the ISC on 10 April 1941, the first independent Croatian government was created in Zagreb—the "Croatian Government Administration," to which two representatives of the Bosnian Muslims (Osman Kulenovich and Ismet Muftich) belonged.[101] By the middle of the war, Pavelich's deputy, Mile Budak, in his efforts to achieve a base of support from the mass of Bosnian Muslims, even apparently agreed that Croatia belonged to two faiths—Catholicism and Islam: "The ISC," he said *"is an Islamic state*

[96] [55, p.19; 77, p.78.]
[97] [118, p.113; 120, p.164.]
[98] [125, p.182.]
[99] [131, pp.122-123.]
[100] [119, p.74.]
[101] [119, p.79.]

everywhere that the people profess belief in Islam only. I particularly emphasize that it is important to know that we are a state of two religions—Catholicism and Islam."[102]

At the order of Pavelich, even a Mosque was founded in Zagreb. With the goal of attracting Muslims to the defense of their common homeland (the ISC) a number of units were raised by the *Ustashe* authorities, composed entirely of Muslims under the command of Muslim officers. Thus, just 10 days after the German attack on the USSR, Pavelich appeared on radio and called for volunteers to go to war on the German side. Towards the end of August 1941, a voluntary Croatian Legion was formed, better known as the 369th (Reinforced) Croatian Infantry Regiment *(Verstarken Kroatischen Infanterie Regiment No. 369).* It consisted of three four-company strength infantry battalions, a HQ Company, an anti-tank company, and heavy weapons company. Colonel Pavarich commanded the Legion. One battalion of the Legion was drawn exclusively from Muslims in Bosnia-Herzegovina.[103] After going through basic training in Dollersheim (Austria) and taking an oath of allegiance to Hitler and Pavelich, the unit was given to the German 100th *Jaeger* Division and sent to the southern sector of the Russian Front.[104] Subsequently, it took part in the battle for Stalingrad, where its personnel were either destroyed or captured.[105]

The "Hadzhieffendicha Legion" *("Hanziefendiceva Legija")* was yet another Muslim unit of no less grave reputation, used by the *Ustashe.* This was an autonomous combat command, up to brigade strength, which fulfilled the function of a Croat-Muslim militia in the northeast part of Bosnia (the Tuzla region.) Major Muhammed Hadzhieffendich, a government commissar, led the Legion. The unit was weakly armed and had few experienced officers and NCOs in all. In September 1943, Hadzhieffendich was included in a new formation—The Muslim-Croat *"Handschar"* SS Division (discussed in more detail below), but by October of that year he was killed together with 55 of his soldiers while battling Tito's Partisans. After his death the Legion was disbanded and its surviving fighters were either included in the Croatian Army, or the 13th SS *"Handschar"* Division, or they defected to the Partisans.

In the summer of 1943, the *"Guski"* Legion *(Huskina Legija)* was formed by the Croatian government in western Bosnia. It also fulfilled the functions of a Muslim militia. Its strength was around 3,000 men, consisting of eleven battalions, under the command of Husko Milyakovich. The battle-worthiness of the Legion was very low. In February 1944 Milyakovich and a group of his legionnaires defected to the Partisans. After this, the Legion was disbanded. Part of the fighters was assigned to the Handschar Division, and the remainder replenished the *Ustashe* combat units.[106]

The desire to use Muslims in the ISC military compelled Pavelich to consider Himmler's initiative with distrust. But this final protest of Pavelich was

---

102 [Tsit, po. 124, p.106.]
103 [128, pp.9-10.]
104 [120, pp.31-32.]
105 [128, p.10.]
106 [140, pp.89-91, 92-93.]

abandoned without heed, and new SS divisions continued to form. It should be noted that the pro-German Muslim, the aforementioned Grand Mufti of Jerusalem, Hadzhi Muhammed Amin al-Hussein, rendered very active help to Himmler in this matter. Not long before this, he traveled to Bosnia from Berlin, where he did not find Hitler's support for the creation of Arabic volunteer units.[107]

Thus, by July 1943 the 13th Mountain Rifle Khandshar Division SS (Waffen-Gebirgs-Division der SS *"Handschar"* No.13 (kroatische No.1)) was raised. From the start, it was better known as "Bosnia-Herzegovina." Two Mountain Jaeger Regiments were included in it, Nos. 1 and 2. In January 1944 the numbers were changed to 27 and 28. Initially *SS-Standarfuehrer der Reserve* Herbert von Obwurzer was named commander of the division. On 8 September 1943 *SS-Brigadefuehrer* Karl Gustav Zauberzweig replaced him, although the "official" date was August 1st. The last division commander was *SS-Brigadefuehrer* Desiderius Hampel.[108] The level of volunteer training in the division left something to be desired. Therefore, in September 1943 the division was sent for refresher training in France, where almost immediately, problems arose. The German officers frequently showed contempt for their Muslim subordinates. As a result, they mutinied and killed several German officers. The revolt was put down and the ringleaders sentenced. But the division, the only formed SS formation to ever mutiny, was not disbanded.[109]

In February 1944, the division was sent to Yugoslavia, where it participated in Partisan battles in the Brcko region (spring 1944.) Here it earned a sinister reputation for its atrocities.[110] At the end of 1944, the German retreat through the Balkans began. The Muslim volunteers proved useless in a war of movement, and in the end, the Muslim detachments were disbanded in September 1944. The Germans, who held all the command positions in the division, were formed into an assault group, "Regimental Group of the 13th Mountain Infantry Division *"Handschar"* or *"Kampfgruppe Hanke."* It took part in fighting during the retreat through Hungary and Austria, finally surrendering in May 1945 to Soviet forces. In January 1944, an enlistment of Bosnian Muslims into one more division was announced: the 23rd Mountain Infantry Division-SS *"Kama" (23.Waffen-Gebirgs-Division der SS "Kama.").* It was proposed that the division would consist of Muslims, Germans, and Croats. Muslim officers and NCOs would be transferred to it from the *"Handschar"* SS Division.

Two mountain-jaeger regiments were successfully assembled towards June 1944: the 55th and 56th. *SS-Standartenfuehrer* Helmut Reithel was named division commander. On 9 August 1944 *SS-Brigadeführer* Gustav Lombard replaced him.[111] The division participated in fighting with Partisans and committed countless atrocities, but on the eve of the arrival of the Red Army, the Muslims began to desert, literally by the dozen. In the end, in October 1944 the division was disbanded. The Muslims were sent home and the German officers

---

[107] [124, p. 178.]

108 [153, pp.16-17.]

109 [107, pp.277-279; 131, p.123.]

110 [107, p.191; 120, p. 218, 220, 232; 153, p.16.]

[111] [125, pp.231-232; 153 p.20.]

and NCOs were included in a new assault group, from the remnants of the Khandshar Division.[112]

In April 1941, Himmler gave the order to form still another division—this time from Kosovo Albanians: the 21st SS Mountain Infantry Division *"Skanderbeg" (21.Waffen-Gebirgs-Division der SS "Scanderbeg" [albanische No.1]).* Towards August 1944 the division was completely reformed to a strength of about 6,500 men, distributed in two mountain infantry regiments (the 50th and 51st.) *SS-Oberfuehrer* August Schmidthuber was designated its first commander, although he was soon replaced with *SS-Obersturmbannfuehrer* Graaf. The divisional cadre was drawn from soldiers and officers of the 14th Regiment *Skanderbeg,* the 7th Waffen-SS Mountain Infantry Division *"Prinz Eugen,"* composed of ethnic-German Serbs living in the Balkans before the war:[113] *"The Division was considered fit for police actions only,"* writes American author Gordon Williamson, *"although even in this area its operations were of little effect. The majority of the division, Muslims it turns out, were only interested in settling scores with old enemies—the Serbs. As a result, there were many atrocities."*[114]

In the course of only two months there were 3,500-recorded cases of desertion; as a result, by October 1944 its ranks were reduced to 1,500 men.[115] Resultantly, the division was disbanded: the German cadres were assigned to *Kampfgruppe "Skanderbeg,"* and later united back with the 14th Regiment, 7th Waffen-SS Division *"Prinz Eugen."* The Muslims continued to take part in anti-Partisan campaigns near Zvornik, Bijelinja, and Brcko between December 1944 and January 1945. In February 1945, the 5th SS Volunteer Mountain Corps, which controlled these two divisions, was sent to the Oder Front, where it served in the battle for Berlin.[116] Himmler thought that raising divisions from believers in Islam, with their lasting traditional hatred of the Orthodox Christian Serbs (who later comprised the basis of Tito's Partisan ranks) was brilliant. The divisions were given many privileges: for example, special rations, and permission to practice religious rites. These privileges went against the anti-religious ideology of the SS, but Himmler exclaimed to Goebbels that *"he had nothing against Islam, because it promised Paradise to Muslims if they died in battle, religion is very practical and appealing to the soldier!"*[117] But reality differed somewhat from what was desired. Himmler made a mistake deploying these units against the peaceful population of Yugoslavia. Barbaric reprisals committed by the Muslim SS meant that the same could be expected in return. As author Gordon Williamson writes: *"In military terms, the effectiveness of these divisions was almost zero, in so much as the Partisans began to fight with greater ferocity; the war took on the character of a grand vendetta, replete with punishments and*

---

[112] [131, p.129; 153, p.20.]

[113] 142, p.35.]

[114] [125, p.229.]

[115] [107, p. 191; 125, p. 229; 153, p.20.]

[116] [153, p. 20.]

[117] [Tsit, po: 125, p.232.]

tortures of the Middle Ages."[1] On the other hand, Himmler refused to consider these divisions, like the other "non-Aryan" divisions, as *"members-in-full of the SS Brotherhood."*

This scornful attitude produced a nomenclature used to distinguish these units. For example, the official designation of the *"Handschar"* Division was: 13th Mountain Infantry Division of the SS *(13.Waffen-Gebirgs-Division der SS)* and not 13th SS Mountain Infantry Division (SS Gebirgs Division.) Subsequently, the volunteers were in the service of the SS, but not part of the very SS. Such scorn led to mutinies and massive desertions.[2]

ABOVE: Reichsführer-SS Heinrich Himmler inspects an honor guard company of the 13th SS Mountain Division "Handschar." The divisional emblem can be seen on the left. The emblem was a Turkish Scimitar, or curved sword on a shield. SS-General Sauberzweig can bee seen here behind Himmler, wearing a fez and an eye patch. *US National Archives*.

RIGHT: The right collar tab of the Bosnian Moslem SS "Handschar" Division. *Antonio J. Munoz Collection.*

---

[1] [125, p.382.]

[2] [153, pp.16-17.]

ABOVE LEFT: German propaganda poster aimed at the Russian population. The gist of the story told here is that the German soldier was the defender of the Russian people against the tyranny of the Commisars. *Antonio J. Munoz Collection.*
BELOW LEFT: Another German propaganda poster. The story line here was basically the same. The German Army was defending the Russian peasant farmer from the tyranny of Communism. *Antonio J. Munoz Collection.*

CHAPTER 3
Muslim Formations Raised From Citizens of the USSR In the German Armed Forces 1941-1945

To this very day, one of the most difficult and intricate issues of World War Two is the use of Soviet citizens in the ranks of the German Armed Forces. Only in recent years has there been the opportunity among native historians [*read as Russian historians –the translator*] to delve deeply into this question, on which countless publications have been written.[120] It turns out that the issue is not one-sided and contains numberless facets. One such facet, which draws the attention of historians, along with the moral and ethical side of a phenomenon such as collaboration; whether it be political, national, and military, is the question of the membership of our fellow countrymen in a foreign army. These were men who served in the *Wehrmacht* and in the *Waffen-SS* in the national ranks of so-called 'volunteer formations.' In the opinion of contemporary Spanish & English researchers Carlos Caballero-Jurado and C. Lyles: *"Among the first volunteers counted in the regular units of the German Army, were members of the peoples who populated the Caucasus and Asian territories of the USSR."*[121]

This was not accidental: the use of national issues played and important role in German occupation policies and Nazi propaganda. It had a special significance prior to preparations and during the implementation of Operation Barbarossa. In preparing for war against the Soviet Union, *"the German government regarded it as an artificial and loose union of and enormous number of nations and peoples, like an ethnic conglomerate, void of inner unity."*[122] After the start of the war with the Soviet Union, one of the main tasks of the German military-political government was to break it up as a multi-national state, by drawing members of the national minorities to its side. As the Nazis thought: "*In the struggle with Bolshevism, it has become important to draw to our side the numerous Muslim peoples of the Soviet Union."*[123] A special staff was created for co-operation with these peoples. *"Among other things, one of the methods for attracting Turks and Caucasus peoples of the USSR to their side was creation of national Eastern Legions."*

This is what contemporary Russian researcher S.I. Drobyazko, wrote regarding this matter.[124] On 20 July 1941, a meeting of the upper military-political leaders of Germany took place. In it, newly made *Reichsminister* of the Occupied Eastern Territories, Alfred Rosenberg, presented a plan to Hitler of the structure

---

[120] [45, 47, 91, and 92 and others.]
[121] [128, p.17.]
[122] [96, pp.265-266.]
[123] [93, p.3.]
[124] [93, p.3.]

of the future political administration of what would remain (so the Nazis proposed) of the USSR. In accordance with this plan, it proposed to create five administrative entities - *Reichskomissariats*: *"Moskovia," "Ostland," "Ukraine," "Kavkaz"*. Kavkaz also included the northern Caucasus it would also include Zakavkaz, or the area beyond the Caucasus. The last, "Turkestan" would include the Povolzhe and Bashkiria. Bashkiria also included the republics of Central Asia and Kazakhstan. The last two would have the status of *Reichskomissariat* only temporarily; it was proposed to make them imperial protectorates, with relatively wide autonomy and their own armed forces.[125] This last point of the plan did not receive Hitler's approval, which reacted very negatively to any form of autonomy in the East, and even more so, spoke categorically against weapons for the local population: *"Even if found to be in specific circumstances that would make it easy to turn to any one of the conquered peoples for military assistance, it would be a mistake. Sooner or later they will turn those weapons against us,"* he thought.[126]

Thus, the question of creating and using Muslim volunteer formations on any given military level in which the Army was occupied was only very weakly supported by political agencies. From the very beginning of the Great Patriotic War [*the war on the Eastern Front-translator*] deserters from the Red Army and former detainees started to offer their services in the capacity of auxiliary service troops to German Army units. The number of these "Hiwis" (abbreviation for the German term *"Hilfswilligen"*-"volunteers") in time reached several hundred thousand men. They served as cooks, drivers, medics and in general, they were members of all categories of the army auxiliary services, which were joined to units and placed at the disposal of German formations. Standard infantry divisions of 1943 provided 2,005 positions for Hiwis,[127] but in practice, there were far more—up to 25%-30% of the strength of many divisions. Thus, in the ranks of Ferdinand Paulus' 6th Army itself surrounded in Stalingrad, there were 52,000 "Russian auxiliary personnel," out of a general strength of 290,000 men. In any case, the term "Russian" has to be understood more loosely as a general term for all peoples of the USSR.

An enormous number of people live in the Caucasus and Central Asia, but the Germans strove to place them all under two categories. One was "Kaukasier" ("Caucasians,") that is, those who lived on either side of that mountain range, (*hereafter referred to as Caucasus peoples—translator.*) The other was "Turkestaner" ("Turkestanis")—in the German understanding, all Asian peoples living beyond the Volga and the far-off regions of Asia.[128] In October-November 1941 the German military intelligence service *(Abwehr)* started work on the creation of two battalions from POWs. With a special designation, they were created to operate jointly in the German Army push to the Caucasus and Central Asia. Besides fulfilling special tasks, such as fighting Partisans and intelligence-diversion operations: *"The battalion's personnel were trained for propaganda work to recruit defectors from the leadership ranks of the Central Asian and*

---

125 [37, pp. 527-528.]
126 [Tsit. Po: 78, p.85.]
127 [107, p.177,]
128 [128, p.17.]

Caucasus peoples. They also trained to organize anti-Soviet revolts on the territories of the national republics."[129]

INSET: The commander of the 804th Azerbaijani Infantry Battalion addresses the volunteers, somewhere in the Caucasus Mountain in the summer of 1942. *Bundesarchiv.*

It was suggested to create the battalions, where the *Wehrmacht's* 444th Security Division, was operating in Army Group South's zone of operations. In the words of OKH Chief, Colonel-General Franz Halder, there were many POWs, who *"surrendered at the first moment...there was a great percentage of Mongol peoples in the ranks of the enemy."*[130] It was proposed to designate the battalions correspondingly, the 444th Turkestani Battalion *(Turkestaner Bataillon No. 444,)* and the 444th Caucasus Battalion *(Kaukasier Bataillon No. 444).*[131] But the so-called "Turkestan Regiment" *(Turkestaner Regiment)* became one of the first Muslim units in the Wehrmacht created on the Eastern Front. It was later renamed the 811th Infantry Battalion. Quarter Master-General of the Armed Forces High Command (OKW), Ernst Wagner of the 444th Security Division created the regiment in accordance with an order, on 15 November 1941. It consisted of four companies under the command of German officers and NCOs. By the winter of 1941/42 it carried out security duties on the territory of Northern Tavrii.[132] At the end of 1941 and beginning of 1942 the German Command turned to preparations for an attack on southern Russia and the Caucasus. To achieve maximum success, occupation policy methods were revised. According to remarks by German

---

129 [93, p.4.]
130 [34; T.3; book 1, p.60.]
131 [19, 35770/1; 134, pp.25-28.]
132 [134, p.26; 135, p.161-163.]

historian N. Muller, it: *"Intended to Germanize the Baltics, convert Belarus into an enormous transitional concentration camp, make the Ukraine a granary of the future Greater German Reich, while in the Caucasus the Germans proposed to conduct an 'experiment' in granting broad rights to the people"*[133]

RIGHT: Arm patch of the Azerbaijani volunteers. See page 18 for a full color view of this and other color arm patches shown in this book. *Author's Collection*

This special policy was defined by Germany's intention to use the Caucasus as a German oil supply source. Realizing that its "Caucasus experiment" led to far-reaching goals, the German military-political leadership also projected the creation of "national" Caucasus military formations. One of the documents, drawn up by Rosenberg on 27th March 1942, four months before the attack on the Caucasus, stated:

RIGHT: The Georgian Legion arm patch, which was worn by all volunteers in the Georgian infantry battalions. *Author's Collection.*

"On the basis of a decision of the Fuehrer, the creation of Caucasus military units from POWs is foreseen, which should be used in battle in the Caucasus. They should be brought up to strength with the chief nationalities of the Caucasus, mainly from the peoples of the Trans-Caucasia, although not any single nationality. They should consist of four groups: Georgians, Armenians, Azerbaijanis, and one group including the mountain tribes. We may now already say that use of Caucasus military units by the Greater German Empire will produce a deep impression on these peoples, in part, when they find out that the Fuhrer has conferred this honor upon them and the Turkestanis only."[134]

The strength of the national formations was predetermined in a "Memo" in order that they should not exceed 1,000 men. Thus, the Germans backed away from the danger *"that they should be able to pressure the German authorities on any account."*[135] On the basis of the above-indicated plans and an OKW directive on 30 December 1941, which authorized the formation of several volunteer legions from the various peoples of the Caucasus and Central Asia, legions were

133 [106, p.258.]
134 [48, T.2 pp.212-219.]
135 [Tsit, po: 90 p.139.]

created during the first half of 1942, just before the invasion of the Caucasus. A specially created "Organizational Staff K" *("K" for "Kaukaser")* renewed active recruiting operations for legion volunteers among POWs and natives of the Caucasus and Central Asia.[136] For propaganda/organizational work in the POW camps, a special agency, *"Dienststelle Ts,"* was created under the auspices of *Stab K* (Staff "K"). Its task was to create a commission for *"filtration of the POW camps"* and *"separation of persons of Caucasus origin from Russians for later...recruitment."*[137] It is very interesting, from the German viewpoint on nationality policy, how recruits for these legions were produced, writes émigré historian A.S. Kazantsev: *"When one of the Turkestani battalions was formed, there were Tartars, Uzbeks, and Kalmyks in it. There were several Russian and Trans-Baikal Cossacks, who the Sonderfuhrer gathered according to such standards as high cheek-bones, slanted eyes, and skin color...Speaking Russian was prohibited."*[138]

The émigré leadership circles rendered great help to the Germans in creating national legions. In late 1941/early 1942, a number of "national councils" and "committees" were created in Germany. In the opinion of their creators, they should have played a distinctive role as "governments in exile," of which the legions were to become the "Armed Forces." But, in the eyes of the Germans, they carried no political weight and were used for propaganda purposes.[139] Four legions were first created from December 1941 through June 1942; later, a further two Eastern Legions were added. *"Moreover"* write Spanish and English researchers Carlos Cavallero-Jurado and C. Lyles, *"they were created with complete success; by their military qualities, they were the equivalent of volunteer legions raised from West Europeans."*[140] And their status, writes German historian K. H. Pfeffer, *"in no way differed from the condition of the latter."*[141] Their first base was located in Poland, where these formed:

1. A Turkestani Legion (muster center at Legionovo).[142]
2. A Caucasus-Mohamedan Legion (muster center at Edlin station).[143]
3. A Georgian Legion (muster center in Krushne).[144]
4. An Armenian Legion (muster center in Pulavach).[145]

The rosters of the Turkestan Legion had members of various Central Asian peoples in its ranks—Uzbeks, Kazakhs, Kirgizians, Turkomen, Karakalpaks, Balkatsevians, Karachians, and Caucasus Muslims—Azeris, Dagestanis,

[136] [95, pp.199-200.]
[137] [96, p.269.]
[138] [42, p.233.]
[139] [47, pp.27-31; 90, pp.85-93.]
[140] [128, pp.17-18.]
[141] [110, p.512.]
[142] [16, N 62-0/4; 134 pp.30-32.]
[143] [16 N 62-0/8; 134, pp.30-32.]
[144] [16, N 62-0/5; 134 p.32.]
[145] [16, N 62-0/8; 134, p.32.]

Ingushetians, and Chechens. Only the Armenian Legion had ethnically pure ranks.[146] On 2 August 1942 the Caucasus-Mohamedan Legion was renamed the Azerbaijani Legion. As with the Georgian Legion, recruits from the mountain tribes were taken into its ranks, they were assigned to a Northern Caucasus training center in Vesoly (Wesola). In addition, on 15 August 1942, a Volga Tartar Legion was formed at Edlin. The Legion contained Volga Tartars, Bashkirs, Maris, Mordvians, Chuvashi, and Urmurti in its ranks.[147]

The General Headquarters of the Eastern Legions *(Kommandeur der Ostlegionen)* which brought about the common formation and training of the national legions was located at Rembertov in the beginning, but in summer 1942 was transferred to Radom.[148] At Legionovo Station a school was also situated, which trained junior grade field commanders *(Gruppenfuhren)* and officers/captains *(Kompanienfuhren)* and lieutenants *(Zugfuhren).* [Platoon leaders - the translator].[149] Arriving from POW camps, the future legionnaires were sorted by company, platoon, and squad in prepared camps. They reported for training, which included first phase physical training, and drill and ceremony—as well as mastery of German commands and regulations. German company commanders, with the help of interpreters and section commanders from the legion ranks who had completed a two-week course at an NCO school in Legionovo, conducted drill and ceremony exercises.[150] As émigré historian A.S. Kazantsev wrote: *"The entire command structure of these battalions, down to platoon level, was German, or those who were specially trained or long-suffering from the Nazi sickness."*[151]

BELOW: A Georgian emigré Prince serving in the ranks of the Georgian Legion battalions.

Upon completion of the basic course of instruction, the recruits were transferred to battalions, where they received standard issue, and went on to tactical training and study of unit weapons material.[152] The ideological training of legionnaires ended in working up their national spirit, although no political goals were before them. Thus, the creation of a 'Turkestani State' or 'Greater Turkestan' under a German protectorate was promised to the soldiers of the Turkestani Legion. At the same time, the Germans told the Volga Tartars that they were *"by far, the most educated, active, and politically valued element of all*

---

146 [134, p.33.]
147 [16, N 62-0/6; 29, pp.1-6.]
148 [15, RN 53-52/v.30.]
149 [134, pp.34-35.]
150 [93, p.6.]
151 [42; p.234.]
152 [93, p.6.]

the Turkish peoples of the USSR."[153] Emigres—members of the above-mentioned "national committees," played an important role in the ideological training of the legionnaires. They worked under the aegis of the Minister of the Occupied Eastern Territories. Of this training, the previously-noted A.S. Kazantsev wrote: *"To set the partition of Russia into place, battalions were formed from POWs of various nationalities, who were not only indoctrinated with a beastly hatred toward Bolshevism, but towards everything Russian as well. Journals and newspapers were published for them, and lectures were given, which artfully fanned an ugly, malicious, chauvinism."*[154]

LEFT: A Turkestani volunteer. He is wearing the 1st version of the Turkestani Legion arm patch (see center, below). The second design of the Turkestani arm patch was much more colorful and completely different from the first design. *Author's Collection.*

The newspaper *"Yani-Turkestan"* (New Turkestan) was published for the military service-members of the Turkestan Legion, as were the *journals "Milli-Turkestan"* (National Turkestan) and *"Milli-Edabiat"* (National Literature.) The basic political thrust of the material printed on the pages of these publications, ended with a call for the *"liberation of Central Asia from Bolshevism."*[155] Among the personnel of the Armenian Legion, the newspaper *"Ayyastan"* (Armenia) was circulated, with the active cooperation of the émigrés-Dashnaks.[156] Among the legionnaires of the Volga Tartar Legion, the newspapers *"Idel-Ural"* (Volga-Ural) and *"Tartar-Edabiat"* (Tartar Literature) were circulated; they were printed in Germany in the Tartar language. The newspapers called for: *"The unity of all*

---

153 [86, p.98.]
154 [42, p.233.]
155 [47, p.28; 126, p.51; 134, pp.128-129.]
156 [90, pp.85-91; 134, pp.128-129.]

Tartars and Muslims living between the Volga and the Urals, the expulsion of the Russian population, and the establishment of friendly relations with Germany."[157]

The pan-Turkish organizations and the Muslim émigré circles in Turkey connected with them were of great help to the Germans in propagandizing the Eastern Legions, foremost the Muslim Legions. In pursuit of the goal of uniting all Turkish peoples into one state under the aegis of Turkey, they hoped that Germany would render them help in this area by destroying the Soviet Union.[158] At the beginning of October 1941, a trip to the Eastern Front for two Turkish Army Generals was organized with the help of the German Ambassador in Turkey, Franz von Papen. The generals, Ali Faoud Erden and Khyusnyu Emir Erkilet, also toured the Crimea. Both expressed serious concern for the fate of Turkish POWs. Their visit, in the opinion of a Staff "K" analyst, Gerhard von Mende, became the final impetus toward creating the Eastern Legions.[159]

In the training of the legionnaires, particularly the Muslims, their religious convictions occupied a very important place. In the Muslim legions, the position of Mullah was included, which mixed religious functions with command roles; sometimes, they were simultaneously platoon leaders. All of them were 25 to 32 years of age and completed training in Germany. In the words of one fighter of the Turkestani Legion: *"Many of them did not display strong comprehension of the 'duties,' as they confused the sequence of prayers and ceremonies.*"[160]

Besides this, the Mullah collected 10 *Deutschmarks,* every ten days from the legionnaires in a mandatory formation. They told

BELOW LEFT: The 2nd design of the arm patch for the North Caucasian volunteers. Units of the North Caucasian Legion, as well as other North Caucasian volunteers serving with the 162nd (Turkic) Infantry Division and Sonderverband Bergmann were allowed to wear this special arm patch. *Author's Collection.*
BELOW RIGHT: An Azerbaijani volunteer of the Bergmann Formation. *Bundesarchiv.*

[157] [29, p.2; 47, p.30; 134, pp.128-129.]
[158] [86, pp.92-103.]
[159] [86, p.98.]
[160] [57, p.42]

the soldiers that this money was *"destined for the construction of a future Mosque."* From this, two DMs went to the Mullah for his own use. Daily prayer services were established in the Legion, which were conducted once a week. The services ended in prayer. The Mullahs gave sermons and speeches, as required.[161] The Grand Mufti of Jerusalem, Al-Hussein, repeatedly visited the camps of the Muslim Legionnaires, appearing with calls for Holy War against the "unbelievers," in alliance with Germany.[162] Military and political training of the soldiers concluded with a collective oath and reception of a national banner. After this, the battalion was sent to the front, while in the emptied camps, the formation of new units began. Each battalion contained three infantry companies, one machine-gun company, and an HQ company. Each company had from 130-200 men.

In the infantry companies there were three rifle platoons, a HQ platoon, and anti-tank, engineer, mortar, and communications platoons (one each). The general strength of the battalion consisted, as written above, of 800-1,000 men and officers. In that number were up to 60 German cadre personnel *(Rahmenpersonal:)* 4 officers, 1 bureaucrat, 32 NCOs, and 23 "other" ranks. Among the German battalion and company commanders there were reciprocal deputy representatives from the given nationalities listed. The command structure below company level was exclusively national.[163]

Toward spring 1942 the legions completed their training and were directed from Poland by battalion, to the Eastern Front. The first unit to take part in battlefield operations was the 450th Battalion of the Turkestan Legion, under the command of Major Andreas Mayer-Mader. He was a cadre intelligence officer and a well-known specialist of Central Asia. He earlier commanded the 444th Turkestani Battalion.[164] The deployment of the legions to the Eastern Front occurred in three stages:

1. Toward the end of 1942: six Turkestani battalions (450th, 452nd, the 781st thru 784th,) two Azerbaijani (the 804th and 805th,) three Northern Caucasus (800th, 801st, and 802nd,) two Georgian (795th and 796th,) and two Armenian battalions (808th and 809th).[165]
2. In the beginning of 1943 came five Turkestani battalions (the 785th thru 789th,) four Azerbaijani (806th, 807th, 817th, and 818th,) one Northern Caucasus (803rd,) four Georgian (the 797th thru 799th, the 822nd,) three Armenian (810th, 812th, and 913th,) and three Volga-Tartar battalions (825th, 826th, and 827th).[166]
3. In the second half of 1943: three Turkestani battalions (790th, 791st, and 792nd,) two Azerbaijani (819th and 820th,) three Northern Caucasus (835th, 836th, and 837th,) two Georgian (823rd and

---

161 [57, p.42.]

162 [93, p.6.]

163 [134, pp.35-37.]

164 [8, pp.1-35; 134, pp.31-32; 135, pp. 156-159.]

165 [8, pp.1-35; 134, p.38.]

166 [8, pp.1-35; 134 p.38.]

824th,) three Armenian (814th, 815th, and 816th,) and four Volga-Tartar battalions (828th thru 831st).[167]

Before the abolition of the HQ Command for Eastern Legions at the end of 1943, 52 battalions were formed: 14 Turkestani, 8 Azerbaijani, 7 Northern Caucausian, 8 Georgian, 8 Armenian, and 7 Volga-Tartar Legions. The general strength all told was about 52,000 men in.[168] Rosenberg suggested to Hitler in one of his report memos on The Question of Caucasus Military Units,

ABOVE: A member of the Volga-Tartar Legion. This volunteer is wearing the 3rd version of the Volga-Tartar insignia on his right sleeve. *Bundesarchiv.*
RIGHT: The 2nd version of the arm patch for members of the Volga Tartar Legion. There were a total of three arm patch designs that were manufactured for the Volga Tartar volunteers. The last one sported a bow and arrow. The first arm patch had shown a straight sword and arrow, while the 2nd version shown here depicted two curved swords and an arrow. *Author's Collection.*

---

[167] [134, pp.38-39.]
[168] [134, p.39.]

"The differentiation of the tribes and peoples amidst the Caucasus should ease German government control over them the strength of separate formations may be determined by military considerations, but deploying them among different peoples—only by political considerations the very idea of the use of a military unit, with the object of renewed conflict between different peoples, is already a political factor."[169]

The Eastern Legions were deployed on the front in accordance with these suggestions. Wide use of Legion units began in autumn 1942, when the first of the battalions in Poland were sent to the Caucasus and close to Stalingrad. In the zones of Army Groups "A" and "B," from September 1942 to January 1943, twenty-five battalions were engaged in security operations close to the German rear, and also carried out the most diverse combat duties on an equal footing with Werhmacht units. In the Tuapsinskiy sector, the 452nd and 781st Turkestani, 796th Georgian, 808th Armenian and 800th Northern Caucasus Battalions attacked as part of the German 17th Army.[170] The 804th Azerbaijani Battalion operated in the Sukhumi sector.[171] More easterly, in the region of Nalchik and Mozdok (1st Panzer Army) operated the 805th and 806th Azerbadjianian, 795th Georgian, and

BELOW RIGHT: The officer on the extreme left of this picture is wearing the 2nd version of the Volga-Tartar arm badge. *Museum of Modern History, Ljubljana, Slovenia.*
BELOW LEFT: Members of a Muslim infantry battalion from the Caucasus raise a German military sign near a Mosque (see tower in the background). *Antonio J. Munoz Collection.*

[169] [48; T.2, p.216.]
[170] [7, pp.1-9; 135, pp.163-170, 203-212, 327-334.]
[171] [22 pp.1-6; 135 pp.221-235.]

809th Armenian Battalions.[172] The Turkestani 450th, 782nd, and 811th Battalions were located in the Astrakhan sector, subordinate to the 16th Panzergrenadier Division. Here they were concentrated for future moves into Central Asia and Kazakhstan.[173]

In evaluating the use of the Legions in the Caucasus, Army Group "A" Chief of Staff, Lieutenant-General H. von Greifenberg, indicated that several of them. For example, the 804th and 805th Azerbaijani, and 809th Armenian Battalions, operated in densely forested regions, often independently, successfully engaging bandits [partisans—Russian Editor's note] and enemy units. They made a great contribution to pacification operations in these areas.[174] But many other battalions did not meet the expectations of the German Command: they did not display a state of battle-readiness. In connection with this, a portion of those legionnaires who were recruited against their will deserted or defected to the Red Army. Soviet propaganda played a substantial role in this, as well as the desire of

BELOW: Eastern Legion volunteers wearing legion insignia. The *Waffenfarbe* worn by these volunteers as shoulder patches varied in color depending on ethnic nationality: Light Blue for the Turkestani volunteers; Brown for the North Caucasian volunteers; Pink for the Georgian volunteers; Yellow for the Armenian volunteers; And Light Green for the Azerbaijani volunteers. *Antonio J. Munoz Collection.*

[172] [135, pp.235-250, 274-291, 334-346.]
173 [12, pp.1-12; 135, pp.156-183.]
[174] [Tsit. po: 93, p.10.]

many legionnaires not to battle with their countrymen.[175]

Thus, of the personnel of the 795th Georgian Battalion, 10 fled while traveling to the front, 50 deserted at the front, and 33 legionnaires went over to the Red Army. In the Georgian 796th Battalion, the number of defectors amounted to 82 individuals, and in the 781st Turkestani Battalion, 43 men deserted.[176] The German Command adopted corresponding measures toward the unreliable units. Thus, the 452nd Turkestani Battalion was disbanded, and the 796th Georgian and 808th Armenian Battalions were disarmd and reorganized as road-construction units.[177] However, the 795th Georgian Battalion was purged of its unreliable elements from the German Command's viewpoint, and reduced to two companies—an infantry and a machinegun company. From then on, it acquitted itself well.[178]

LEFT and BELOW: Two more examples of Eastern Legion insignia. These are Turkestani volunteers. The one below, on the far left can be seen wearing the 1st design of the Turkestani Legion arm patch. *Antonio J. Munoz Collection.*

[175] [56, p.250; 95, pp.205-206.]
[176] [95, pp.205-206.]
[177] [135, pp.163-166, 291-304, 327-334.]
[178] [135, pp.274-291.]

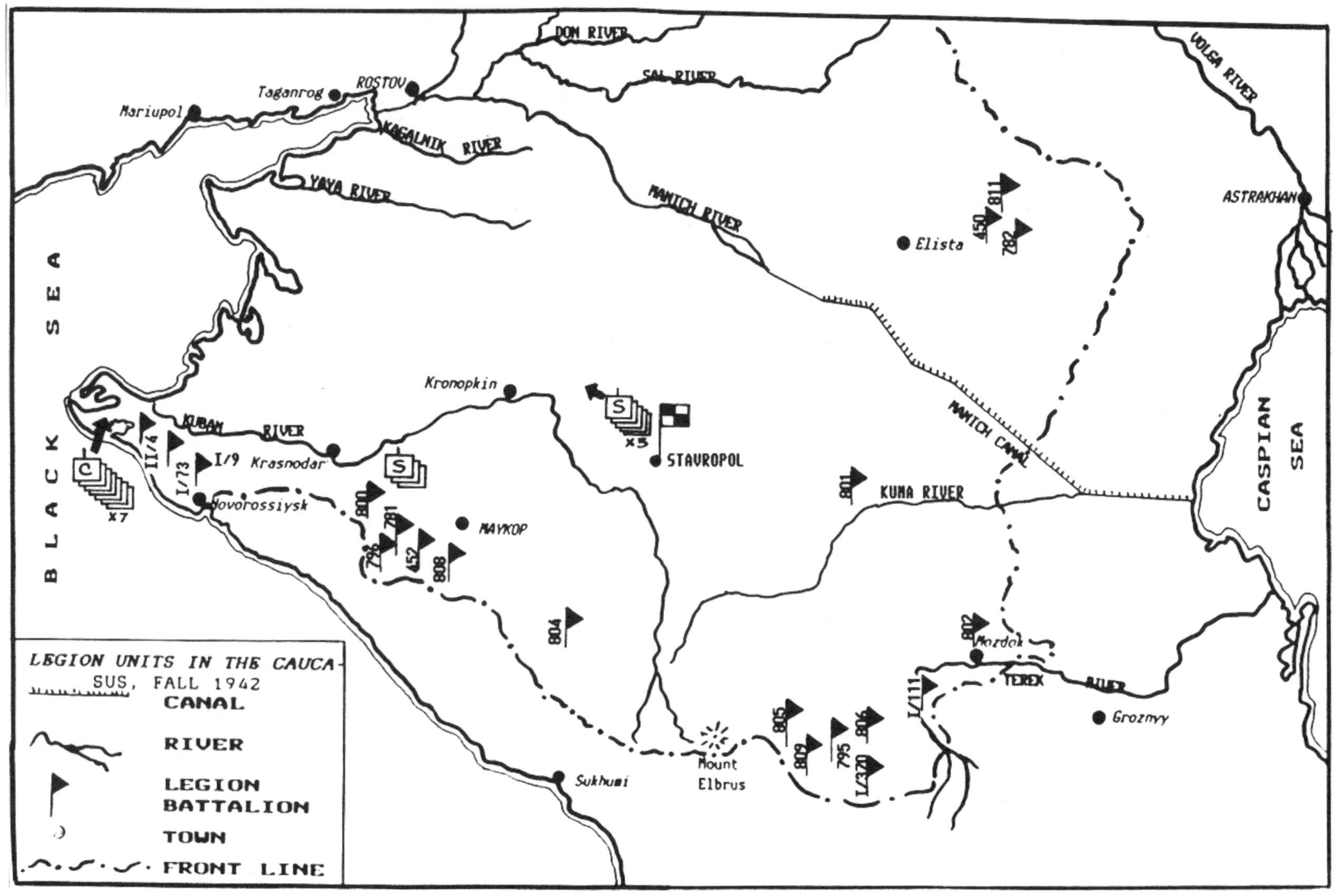
DON RIVER
SAL RIVER
VOLGA RIVER
ASTRAKHAN
Mariupol
Taganrog
ROSTOV
KAGALNIK RIVER
YAYA RIVER
MANYCH RIVER
Elista
811
450
782
BLACK SEA
CASPIAN SEA
Kronopkin
KUBAN RIVER
Krasnodar
STAVROPOL
x5
MANYCH CANAL
801
KUMA RIVER
II/4
I/73
I/9
x7
Novorossiysk
800
781
452
808
MAYKOP
804
802
Mozdok
TEREK RIVER
I/111
Grozny
805
809
795
806
I/370
Mount Elbrus
Sukhumi
LEGION UNITS IN THE CAUCASUS, FALL 1942
CANAL
RIVER
LEGION BATTALION
TOWN
FRONT LINE

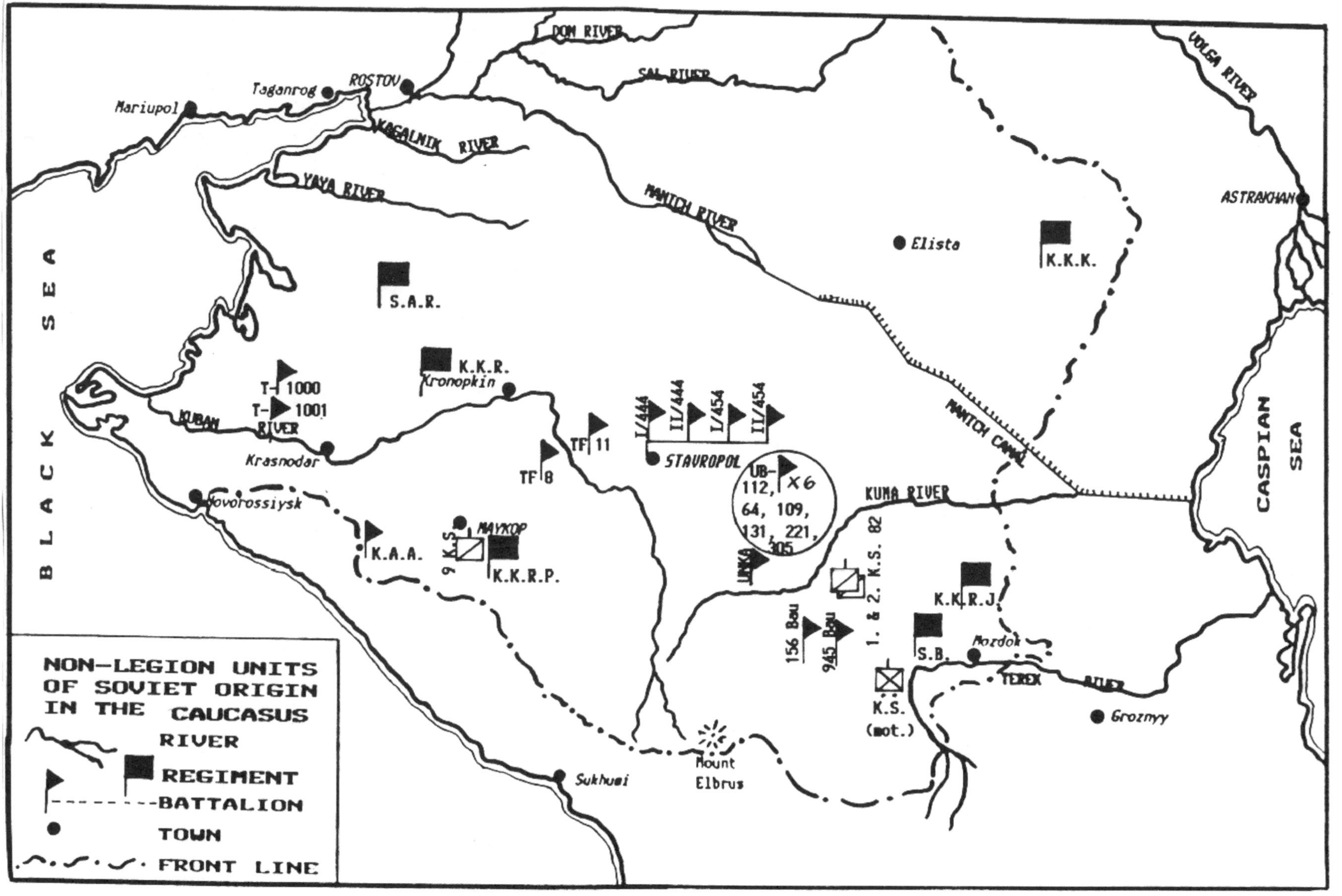
DON RIVER
SAL RIVER
VOLGA RIVER
Taganrog
ROSTOV
Mariupol
KAGALNIK RIVER
YAYA RIVER
MANYCH RIVER
ASTRAKHAN
Elista
K.K.K.
BLACK SEA
S.A.R.
K.K.R.
Kronopkin
T-1000
T-1001
KUBAN RIVER
Krasnodar
TF 11
TF 8
I/444
II/444
I/454
II/454
STAVROPOL
MANYCH CANAL
CASPIAN SEA
UB-
112,
X 6
64, 109,
131, 221,
305
KUMA RIVER
Novorossiysk
MAYKOP
K.A.A.
9 K.S.
K.K.R.P.
1. & 2. K.S. 82
K.K.R.J.
156 Bau
945 Bau
S.B.
Mozdok
K.S.
(mot.)
TEREK
RIVER
Groznyy
Sukhumi
Mount
Elbrus
NON-LEGION UNITS
OF SOVIET ORIGIN
IN THE CAUCASUS
RIVER
REGIMENT
BATTALION
TOWN
FRONT LINE

In several battalions, from the time of their formation and training, underground cells were formed. They were prepared to march their units over to the Red Army and Partisan lines. The first successful attempt was undertaken in February 1943, when the 825th Volga-Tartar Battalion arrived in the Vitebsk region. Another incident occurred on 13 September 1943, when one of the Turkestani battalions in Oboloni area slaughtered its German officers and personnel from three companies and with weapons in hand, crossed over to Red Army lines.[179] As seen, Hitler was correct when, in December 1942 he announced: *"I do not know how the Georgians will conduct themselves. They do not belong to the Turkish peoples. I only consider Muslims reliable…I consider the formation of these purely Caucasus battalions as a very grave risk, but I see no danger in forming purely Muslim units."*[180]

In connection with this, the Eastern Legions Command in Poland was disbanded towards the end of 1943. All battalions created by it were either reorganized or transferred from the Russian Front to Western Europe.[181] From reorganization, part of them became security detachments that provided auxiliary security police forces in the *Reichskomissariats,*[182] and others became detachments that had auxiliary designations. One of them, the *Bohler Brigade,* consisted of four reinforced Turkestani construction battalions *(Turkestanische-Arbeits-Bataillone),* and one reserve battalion *(Turkestanische-Arbeits-Ersatz-Bataillon).* The *Bohler Brigade* had a general strength of 20,000 men. Ten other auxiliary battalions were created: artillery, supplies, construction, and reserve battalions with a general strength of 10,000 men. There were 202 separate companies: supply, construction-engineers, railroad, and repair. Of those, 111 were formed from Turkestanis, 30 from Georgians, 22 from Armenians, 15 from Volga Tartars, and 3 from Northern Caucasus nationalities. The total number who did service in these units was 174,000 men.[183]

A portion of the battalions were reorganized as reserves, transferred to southern France and stationed in the cities of Castre: Georgian, Turkestani, and Northern Caucasus battalions; and

RIGHT: Turkestani Volunteers and their German NCO. Notice the easily recog-nizable Asiatic features of the volunteers. *Private American Collector.*

[179] [57, pp.44-46.]

[180] [82, pp.418-419; 130, p.251.]

[181] [17, RH 2/1435.]

[182] [90, pp.140-143; 94, p.140,]

[183] [128, pp.19-20; 134, p.39.]

Mande: Armenian, Azerbaijani, and Volga-Tartar battalions. These were respectively combined into the 1st and 2nd Volunteer Cadre Regiments. They were put together with Russian, Ukrainian, and Cossack units in the Cadre Volunteer Division *(Freiwilligen-Stamm-Division)* with its HQ in Lyon.[184] Other battalions, not assigned to the Cadre Division, gave service guarding the Atlantic Wall. These included the 795th, 797th, 798th, 822nd, and 823rd Georgian; the 800th, 803rd, and 835th Northern Caucasus Battalions, the 781st and 782nd Turkestani, and the 809th, 812th, and 813th Armenian Battalions, and others; or operated in the central regions of France against Partisans, like the 799th Georgian, and the 829th Volga-Tartar Battalions.[185]

In the struggle against the Anglo-American invasion, the majority of Eastern battalions turned out to be incapable of standing up to the superior enemy in any situation, due to poor weaponry and low morale: several were crushed by the allies, while several were disarmed by the Germans themselves. The remnants of the battalions defeated on the Western Front were assembled on the drill field in Neuhammer (Silesia.) Here, the 12th Caucasus Tank Destroyer Formation was formed on the foundation of the better Georgian, Armenian, Azerbaijani, and Northern Caucasus Legion cadres in the winter of 1944-45. In the spring of 1945 it operated on the Oder Front and took part in the defense of Berlin.[186] It should be said that Poland was not the only place where the Eastern Legions were

ABOVE: Members of the 787th Turkestani Infantry Battalion, which was attached to the 346th German Infantry Division while stationed in France. This photo was taken in 1944. *Private American Collector.*

[184] [93, pp.11-12.]
185 [90, pp.147-166; 136, pp.60-64.]
[186] [93, p.12.]

formed. Thus, after the winter battles of 1941-42, and because of the great losses in personnel by Army Group Center, the *Wehrmacht's* 162nd Infantry Division was sent to the Ukraine. OKW ordered the division transformed into a drill center for the training of Eastern Legions.

BELOW LEFT & RIGHT: Several more Turkestani volunteers in various types of German uniforms. *Private American Collector*.

New centers with training camps were created on the territory of Poltava Region, with the Turkestani Legion in Romnax, the Azerbadjiani in Prilukax, the Georgian in Gadyache, the Armenian in Loxvitse, and the Northern Caucasus Legion in Mirgorod, where the Legion Formation HQ and translator/interpreter courses were located.[187] Doctor Oskar Ritter von Niedermayer, an *Abwehr* Colonel and one of the best German specialists on Russia and the Muslim East was appointed Director of the Legion Formation HQ. From 6 September 1942 he was a Major General. As stated earlier, until summer 1941 he was an *Abwehr* special plenipotentiary officer with Special Staff "F" involved in training Arab volunteer units. Until May 1943 twenty-five Eastern Legion battalions were successfully formed:

1. Twelve Turkestani (I/29, I/44, I/76, I/94, I/100, I/295, I/297, I/305, I/370, I/371, I/384, I/389;)
2. Six Azerbaijani (I/4, I/73, I/97, I/101, I/111, II/73;) four Georgian (I/1, I/9, II/4, II/198;)

[187] [14, RH 26-162/15; 134, pp. 58-65.]

3. Three Armenian (I/125, I/198, II/9;) and
4. Two reinforced Northern Caucasus semi-battalions (842 and 843.)
5. There were also seven construction and two reserve battalions—in all, more than 30,000 men. In numbering the battalions, the Roman Numerals represent order of appearance and the Arabic Numerals signify the division number to which cadre personnel belonged.[188] The majority of the Turkestani battalions were attached to Paulus' 6th Army.[189]

In May 1943 the national legions' training center was transformed into the experimental 162nd Turkish Infantry Division *(162.Turkestaner-Infanterie-Division)* under the command of von Niedermayer. The base for creating the division served the battalions that were in a formative stage. The division's cadre personnel were transferred to the drill field at Neuhammer, where formation was continued. The division had a two-regiment organization 303rd Turkestani and the 314th Azerbaijani Infantry Regiments. Sultan Alim, a former Master Sergeant in the Red Army led the 303rd, while the 314th was commanded by Colonel M.N. Israfilov, or Israfil-Bey. The Division also contained the 162nd Artillery Regiment, a cavalry battalion, rear units, and sub-units. In principle, they were manned on a 1:1 ratio—50% German, chiefly ethnic-German *Volksdeutsch.*[190]

BELOW LEFT: Turkestani volunteers in France, circa 1944. *Bundesarchiv.*
BELOW RIGHT: Closeup view of a Turkestani Muslim volunteer. *Private American Collector.*

[188] [134, p.76.]
[189] [79, p.363.]
[190] [20; 30.]

Upon completion of forming and training, the 162nd Division, in accord with the policy of deploying Eastern troops away from the Eastern Front, was first sent to Slovenia, and then in August 1943 it was re-stationed in Italy. There it was used for security duty and combat with Partisans until the very end of the war. After the Allied amphibious landing in southern Italy, it twice (September-December 1944 and January-April 1945) took part in battles against them.[191]

Colonel Oskar von Niedermayer was relieved from his post as commander of the 162nd Division on 4 June 1944. The reason cited was lack of necessary combat experience. Major-General R. von Heigendorf, who in his own time worked at the Eastern Legions Command HQ in Radom, replaced him.[192] In April 1945, the division was withdrawn to Austria, where in 4 May 1945 it surrendered to the English Army. Practically all the personnel of the Division were handed over to the USSR, in accordance with an agreement at the Yalta Conference.[193] Until 12 April 1947, Major-General Heigendorf was in English captivity. In addition to OKW occupying itself with forming Muslim volunteer units, *Abwehr,* the *Wehrmacht's* military intelligence service, did so likewise. The Special Regiment Gorets *(Sonderverband "Bergmann,")* created by the *Abwehr* from the start, was to carry out tasks of punitive and diversionary nature in the Caucasus. The formation of that unit began in autumn 1941 on the drill field in Neuhammer, at the personal order of *Abwehr* chief, Admiral Wilhelm Canaris.

It was intended for punitive-diversionary operations in support of the "New Order" in the Caucasus, and for fulfilling police functions in the rear area

BELOW: Extremely rare photograph of Turkestani Muslim volunteers at Legionovo in the General Government (Poland). *Private American Collector.*

191 [14, 34427/8; 20.]
192 [20.]
193 [52, pp. 149-152; 122, pp.347, 348-349.]

of the German Army. The personnel of the division were collected in POW camps from member peoples of the Northern Caucasus, Georgians, and Armenians. The officers were selected from among Caucasian emigres into a unit that included around 130 Georgians. They composed the Abwehr Special Unit *"Tamara,"* created for the purpose of *"organizing a revolt in Georgia."*

Koenigsberg University Professor and *Abwehr* cadre officer, *Oberleutnant* Theodor Oberlander, was designated unit commander. He was a useful authority of great expertise on Russia and "Eastern Affairs." In addition to this, he already had experience in creating and using similar units. In summer 1941 he occupied the position of political administrator of the infamous *"Nachtigal"* (Nightingale) Battalion, raised from Ukrainian nationalists.[194] *Sonderfuhrer* Baron W. von Kuchenbach, who was brought up in Russia, was named Oberlander's deputy. The selection of POWs for the unit continued until the end of November 1941, when they were transferred to Mittelwald, Bavaria. There, its personnel were occupied with infantry and mountain warfare training until March 1942. To that time there were 1,200 men in the unit (300 Germans and 900 Caucasus folk) organized into five companies:

Legions Bataillon "Tamara"

1st Company, composed of Georgians and Armenians,
2nd Company, composed of Dagestani peoples,
3rd Co.—Azeris and Germans,
4th Co., with Georgians and Armenians, and
5th Co., a HQ unit composed of Georgian émigrés.

The command element of the unit consisted solely of Germans. It had primarily light weapons for armaments: hand-held automatic machine-guns, company mortars, anti-tank weapons, and German-manufactured carbines.[195] In June 1942, all the personnel of the unit took an oath and in August-September 1942 were sent to the Caucasus, where they took parts in a number of diversionary

RIGHT: Another extremely rare photograph of Turkestani volun-teers in late 1941. The volunteers are still wearing Russian Army style uniforms with German collar tab insignia. *Private American Collector.*

[194] [44, pp.7-8, 24-25; 54, p.672.]
[195] [6p.2; 10, pp.1-10; 109; 135, pp.104-106.]

operations: Operation *"Shamil"* (August 1942) and operations for capturing the oil refineries of Grozny in September 1942.[196] From September 1942 the unit operated against Soviet Partisans in the Mozdok-Nal'chik-Mineralnye Vody area, where it became 'famous,' thanks to its cruelty and mass-executions. On 29 October it was sent to forward areas: 1st and 4th companies went to Nalchinskoye, and the 2nd and 3rd companies went to the Ishcherskoye sector. In order to prove the worth of the unit, it went to the most difficult sectors of the front, where they sustained heavy casualties.[197]

During this time, they succeeded in raising additional four-infantry companies of Georgian, Northern Caucasus, Azerbaijani, and a mixed reserve unit from defectors, POWs, and local volunteers. An equal number of cavalry squadrons was raised as well: (a) Georgian, commanded by Prince Dadiani an émigré; (b) Kabardian, commanded by K. Beshkitov, a Red Army deserter; (c) Balkarian; and (d) Russian. The cavalry squadrons each had 200 men, who were earmarked mainly for security duty and punitive actions in the German rear. This went on until the end of 1942. The unit expanded into a three-battalion strong regiment, with a general strength of 2,300 men:

I. 1st Battalion - Georgian
II. 2nd Battalion - Azerbaijani
III. 3rd Battalion - Northern Caucasus[198]

As Paul Leverkuehn, an officer of the *Abwehr* testifies his book, *"The Regiment became unreliable when the German retreat from the Caucasus began."* Therefore, in February 1943 the regiment, covered by its cavalry squadrons, withdrew through the Taman Peninsula to the Crimea. There, its infantry units were obliged to carry

RIGHT: General Andrei Andreiivich Vlasov, head of the Russian Army of Liberation (ROA), sponsored by the Germans. Vlasov strove to gather all anti-Stalinist formations from the USSR under one Russian command in order to create an anti-communist Russian Liberation Army. His efforts were supported by one German faction, while opposed by another German faction of government and the minority peoples of the USSR. *US National Archives.*

196 [25, pp.1-10; 101, p.72; 102, pp.112-113.]
197 [93, p.13.]
198 [41, pp.248-253; 44, p.27; 135, pp.113-114.]

out patrol duties to secure the coast along the Koktebel—Dvuyakornaya Bay line. The cavalry squadrons were occupied with combating Partisans.[199] According to records of the Crimean HQ's of the Partisan Movement, during that period the regiment numbered 1,150 men: 60 Germans, with the remainder being Azerbaijanis and Georgians. For armament it had: 80 heavy machineguns, 42 light machineguns, 10 battalion mortars, 10 regimental mortars, and 16 anti-tank weapons.[200] According to some records, an attempt was made to form a Caucasus Division based on the regiment, but things never went further than planning and propaganda announcements.[201]

LEFT: Major-General Viktor Ivanovich Maltsev, the commander of the Russian ROA Air Force. Historical Museum, Evpatoria, Crimea, Ukraine.

Toward late autumn and winter 1943/44, all battalions in the regiment, together with German troops, participated in the terrific battles on the Perekopskiy Isthmus. Later, they were evacuated from the peninsula and sent to Greece (1st and 3rd Battalions) and to Poland (2nd Battalion) where their main task became combating Partisans.[202] Things turned out a little differently with the volunteer formations created in a different region that had a concentrated population of Muslim residents—the Crimea. There, as Russian historians M.Y. Heller and A.M. Nekrich write: *"The Germans, as in the Caucasus, carried on the policy of using non-Russian peoples in the war against the USSR."*[203]

On September 1st 1941 the *Reichskomissariat Ukraine* began to function. The territory was administratively divided into General Komissariats. The Crimea was to be assigned to *General-Komissariat "Tavrida"* or *"Krim,"* after its final conquest. *Reichstag* Deputy and NSDAP senior member A. Frauenfeld was named its General Komissar.[204] He suggested to Hitler that the entire population of Crimea be expelled, and replaced with inhabitants of the Southern Tyrol, transforming the peninsula into a "German Riviera." In as much as the Crimea was not completely transferred to the jurisdiction of a civilian administration (making it the whole time, either an area of operations or a rear area,) the chief task of the occupation authorities became winning the hearts and minds of the people. Thus, the main emphasis was on supporting the forces of law and order, and everything else that would enable its establishment. From the end of 1941, the Partisan resistance became the main factor to exert influence on German

199 [93, p.14.]

200 [2; d.28, sheet 29.]

201 [3; d. 173-a, sheets 35-36, 37-37 reverse side; 93, p.14]

202 [44, pp.29-30.]

203 [84, p.432.]

204 [37, pp.381-381.]

occupation policy. One German officer later recalled: *"The Partisan resistance was not, of course, a simple manifestation of disorder in the rear areas, as the Germans thought at first. Quite the opposite, it was a political resistance movement, which was impossible to bring under control with no more than German Police forces."*[205]

Therefore, the German Command came to the conclusion that it was necessary to create "local auxiliary police forces," which besides having military uses would have a not inconsiderable propaganda effect. The Crimea, with its mixed national composition, could not be a better place to adopt such a policy. The organization of the policy, intelligence, and punitive services in the Crimea was implemented immediately under the leadership of the notorious *Einsatzgruppe D*, headed by *SS-Oberfuehrer* Otto Olendorf. *Einsatzgruppe D* officials created city and regional security-police departments.[206] In November 1941, all "local auxiliary police forces" in the Reichskomissariats were organized into sub-unit "auxiliary security police*" (Schutzmannschaft der Ordnungs Polizei* or *"Schuma.")* These sub-units were divided into several categories:

1. *Schutzmannschaft-Einzeldienst*—police in the cities and rural areas;
2. *Selbstschutz*—self-defense units or "self security;"
3. *Schutzmannschaft-Bataillone*—battalions for anti-Partisan combat;
4. *Feuerschutzdienst*—auxiliary fire-fighters;
5. *Hilfsschutzdienst*—reserve police for concentration camp security.

BELOW: Volunteers from a Turkestani construction battalion. There were numerous companies and battalions made up of eastern volunteers who formed work units for the German Army. *Museum of Modern History, Ljubljana, Slovenia.*

205 [58, p.82.]
206 [59, pp.19-21.]

Those enlisting in such formations were promised very good material compensation. City and rural police were formed right after the occupation of cities and important population centers in the Crimea. One may say that their rosters included three main national groups: Russians, Tartars, and Armenians. Thus the Tartars predominated in the police of Alushti, Yalta, Sevastopol, Karasubazar, and Zui, but were significantly fewer in the police of Evpatoria and Feodosia.[207] But neither city nor rural police could fight the Partisans independently, or destroy them, for that matter. Therefore, the Germans did all that was possible to form stronger, more battle-worthy units, which could provide relative security, if only in their own region. In connection with this, by 18 August 1942, the Chief of the Central HQ of the Partisan Movement, P.K. Ponomarenko reported to I.V. Stalin: *"The Germans are using all means to bring Partisans to battle contingents from our population in the occupied areas, creating military units, punitive, and police detachments from them. They wish to raise these up, in order to draw the Partisans into battle, not with Germans, but with formations from the local population. Rabid, nationalistic propaganda goes around the formations... kindling national dissension, accompanied by anti-Semitism."*[208]

LEFT AND ABOVE: A sample of a Turkestani *soldbuch.* The man served in one of the Turkestani battalions that altogether made up the Turkestani Legion. *Private American Collector.*

Advantages and privileges were created for their families. Thus, in accordance with an OKW resolution, *"any person who actively fights or struggles with the Partisans and Bolsheviks, may submit an application for an allotment of land or payment to him in reward, for up to 1,000 rubles."*[209] By October 1941-writes English and German researchers Charles Dickson and Otto Heilbrun: *"The Germans started to attract Crimean Tartars, who always related to the Bolshevik regime with hostility, for the struggle with the Partisans. So-called 'Tartar self-*

[207] [2; d. 28, sheets 40-41; d. 505, sheet 3, 18 reverse side, 19.]
208 [38, pp.120-122.]
[209] [3; d. 24, sheet 31.]

defense detachments' were formed, which rendered great help to the Germans."[210]

In the words of General-Field Marshall Erich von Manstein, commanding the German 11th Army located in Crimea, the main task of these detachments: *"Lay in securing their villages from Partisan attack."*[211] In November 1941, Tartars from the village of Koush created one of the first self-defense detachments. At the start, it numbered 80 men, and towards April 1942, was already at 345 men. Someone named Raimov was designated the commander of the detachment. He served afterwards in the German Police up to the rank of Major. O Khasanov, a former member of the All-Union Communist Party (b) *["b" for Bolshevik—the translator]* and village elder, took an active part in the creation of the detachment. The main task of the detachments was that of: *"Frequent attacks and diversions to hold the Partisans in a constant state of tension, destroy their manpower, and raid their supply bases."*

Thanks to three strong lines of defense, Koush was invulnerable to the Partisans for a long time.[212] By December 1941, self-defense detachments were formed in such populated areas as: Uskut (130 men,) Tuak (100 men,) and Kuchuk-Uzen (80 men.) The villages of Eni-Sala, Sultan-Sarai, Bashi, Karasu-Bashi, and Molbay also had self-defense detachments.[213] But the presence of

BELOW: Every *Soldbuch* contained these distinctive insignia so that the eastern volunteer could distinguish rank and badges of ethnic origin. *Private American Collector.*

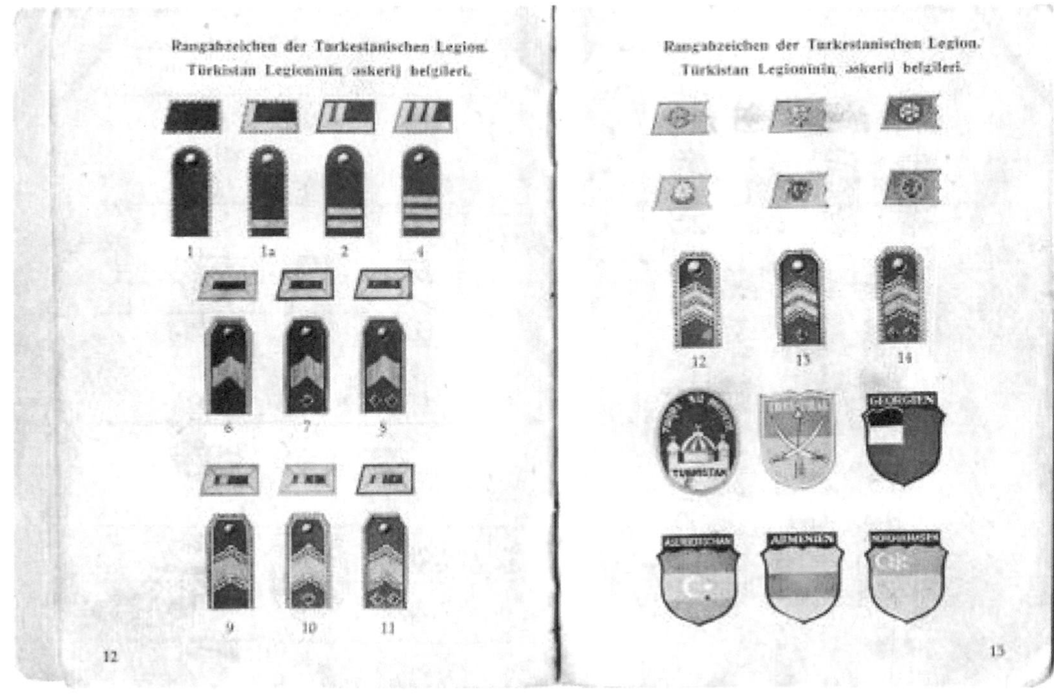

[210] [89, pp.172-174.]

[211] [46, p.262.]

[212] [2; d. 26, sheets 57, 64; d. 56, sheet 20.]

[213] [2; d. 26, sheet 57.]

these forces appeared inadequate to the occupation authorities. Therefore, they adopted a number of different measures for the organization and use of self-defense detachments. On 2 January 1942, a report took place in the Intelligence section of the 11th Army, in which it was declared that Hitler decided to raise volunteers from the Crimean Tartars. Army Headquarters gave all recruitment questions to the leadership of *Einsatzgruppe D*. Before it stood the following operational tasks: *"Involve all able-bodied Crimean Tartars, capable of service in the 11th Army on a volunteer basis; also create Tartar self-defense companies, which will be used jointly with Einsatzgruppe D for combat with Partisans."*[214]

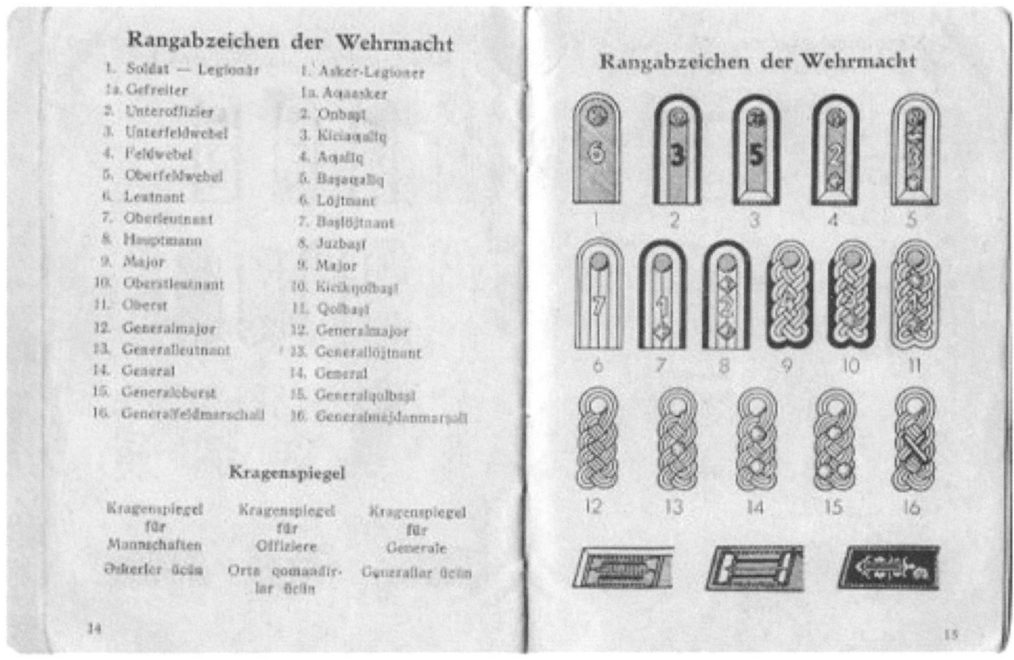

Rangabzeichen der Wehrmacht

1. Soldat — Legionär	1. Asker-Legioner
1a. Gefreiter	1a. Aqaasker
2. Unteroffizier	2. Onbaşı
3. Unterfeldwebel	3. Kiçiaqalıq
4. Feldwebel	4. Aqalıq
5. Oberfeldwebel	5. Başaqalıq
6. Leutnant	6. Löjtnant
7. Oberleutnant	7. Başlöjtnant
8. Hauptmann	8. Juzbaşı
9. Major	9. Major
10. Oberstleutnant	10. Kiçikqolbaşı
11. Oberst	11. Qolbaşı
12. Generalmajor	12. Generalmajor
13. Generalleutnant	13. Generallöjtnant
14. General	14. General
15. Generaloberst	15. Generalqolbaşı
16. Generalfeldmarschall	16. Generalmejdanmarşalı

Kragenspiegel

Kragenspiegel für Mannschaften	Kragenspiegel für Offiziere	Kragenspiegel für Generale
Askerler üçün	Orta qomandirlar üçün	Generallar üçün

14

ABOVE: Every *Soldbuch* contained these distinctive insignia so that the eastern volunteer could distinguish rank and badges of ethnic origin. *Private American Collector.*

On 3 January 1942, at 1000 hours, the first meeting of the "Tartar-Muslim Committee" in Simferopol began, under the chairmanship of J. Abdureshidova. This meeting was to initiate the start of Tartar recruitment for the *"common struggle against Bolshevism."* The conference took place under the leadership of Otto Ohlendorf.[215] On 5 January 1942, with the formal concurrence of the chairman of the Committee, a recruitment center was opened in Simferopol and began recruiting volunteers under the slogan: *"All Tartars who want the Partisans to stop robbing you—Volunteer to take arms against them!"*[216] The recruitment of volunteers continued through the course of January 1942 in two hundred and three populated areas and five POW camps. As a result, 9,255 men were recruited; the

---

[214] [45, p.91.]

[215] [45, p.91.]

[216] [21 d. 26, sheet 57.]

greatest number in Karasubazar - 1,000 men; the least number in Biyuk-Onlar, 13 men. Of these, 8,684 men were sent to units of the 11th Army. The rest, 571 men, were judged unfit for service in line units, and sent back to their villages. These had been deemed too elderly or too young, or too sick to serve. Simultaneously, *Einsatzgruppe D* enlisted 1,632 men, who were sent to 14 self-defense companies and billeted, respectively, in:

i. Simferopol (1st Company)
ii. Biyuk-Onlar (2nd Company)
iii. Beshu (2nd Company)
iv. Baksan (3rd Company)
v. Molbay (5th Company)
vi. Biy-Eli (6th Company)
vii. Alusht (7th Company)
viii. Bakhchisarai (8th Company)
ix. Koush (9th Company)
x. Yalta (10th Company
xi. Taraktarsh (12th and 13th Company) and in
xii. Dzhankoe (14th Company) [217]

ABOVE: Eastern legion troops during the winter of 1942-1943. The man holding the machine gun seems to be wearing a German World War I helmet. In addition, the machine gun itself is a "hand-me-down" from the First World War. *Bundesarchiv.*

[217] [45, pp.92-93.]

The German campaign to recruit volunteers from the Crimean Tartars worried the Partisans very much. Thus, the Chief of the II Partisan Region, I.V. Genov, reported on 31 January 1942, to great land: *"Local Tartar population successfully armed...by the Germans; the goal...combat with Partisans...Necessary to assume that in coming days they will begin to train in battle with us. We are prepared for this...although we understand that armed Tartars are far more dangerous than Germans or Rumanians."*[218] But by February 1942 separate Tartar-volunteer detachments, with a strength of up to 200-250 men, were sent to the front near Kerch, where they took part in battles with the Red Army. Subsequently, these units were used near Sevastopol.[219] Hitler, appearing in the Reichstag on 24 May 1942, announced in his speech that: *"In units of the German Army, Tartar auxiliary units, together with Lithuanian, Latvian, Estonian, and Ukrainian Legions, are participating in battles with the Bolsheviks...Crimean Tartars always display their military valor and readiness to fight. But under the Bolshevik government they were always forbidden to display these qualities...It is fully understood, that they stand shoulder to shoulder with the soldiers of the German Army in the struggle against Bolshevism."*[220]

In August 1942, the Chief of the OKH, Colonel-General F. Halder signed instruction No. 8000/42 concerning *"The use of local auxiliary forces in the East."* In it, all volunteer formations were categorized by their political loyalty and battle-worthiness. It read: *"Cossacks and peoples of the Turkish race, fighting against the Bolshevik enemy arm in arm with German soldiers, stand out as full-fledged brothers-in-arms. Here also are included: Turkish battalions, Cossack sub-units, Crimean Tartars..."* [221] In the first half of 1942, they began to create *Schuma* battalions from the local populations in the occupied territories. They were considered as operational sub-units for Partisan combat, and differed from self-defense companies in mobility. In connection with this, all Tartar self-defense companies were assigned to such battalions in July 1942. Thus, toward November 1942, eight Schuma battalions were formed in the Crimea and quartered in the following populated areas: Simferopol (147th and 154th,) Karasubazar (148th,) Bakhchisar (149th,) Yalta (150th,) Alusht (151st,) Dzhankoe (152nd,) and Feodosia (153rd).[222] On 11th November 1942, the *Wehrmacht* Command in the Crimea announced a renewed recruitment effort of a number of Crimean Tartars into the German *Army "for use in the Crimea."* The "Tartar Muslim Committee" in Simferopol fulfilled the tasks of the recruitment centers.[223 and 224] As a result, one more battalion was formed in spring 1943, and several battalions and harvest companies were in a formative stage.

In organizational and operational matters, all these units were subordinate to the SS and Police Command "Tavrida" (Simferopol). Simultaneously, they

---

[218] [2; d. 26, sheet 58.]
[219] [2; d. 26, sheet 64.]
[220] [68; 1942, No.42, p.2.]
[221] [18, H 1/524.]
[222] [2; d. 28, sheet 38; 134, p.47.]
[223] [ulitsa Pushkina, 14]
[224] [49, 53.]

made up a Crimean-Tartar Legion of the Wehrmacht.[225] Usually, local volunteers commanded a battalion, but in every one of them there were nine German cadre personnel (1 liaison officer and 8 NCOs). For weapons, the personnel had automatic, light, and heavy machine guns and mortars.[226] Every battalion had its own area of operations, in which it was to maintain order. For example, 148th Battalion operated in the Argin-Baksan-Barabanovka, Sartana-Kurtluk, and Kamyshli-Beshuy region; the 149th Battalion, in the Kokoshi-Koush-Mangush region; and the 151st Battalion—in the Korbek-Ulu-Uzen-Demerdzhi region.[227]

Here they performed guard duty of civilian and military objectives, and together with units of the *Wehrmacht* and German police, participated in combat against Partisans. Thus in a summary report of the German HQ, Battalions 148, 149, and 150 participated in six important actions against Partisans from 9 November to 27 December 1942. During these operations, eight Partisans were killed and five captured. Battalion losses are not mentioned in summaries, but were most likely not low.[228]

After the German retreat from the Caucasus, and the blockade of the Crimean groups, it became more frequent for soldiers of the Crimean Tartar units to go over to Partisan lines. The most significant of these became the defection of the 152nd Battalion under the command of the previously named Raimov, who was shot by the Partisans anyway. Underground organizations were created in a number of units, as was the case with the Eastern Legions. Thus, the commander of the 154th Battalion, A. Kerimov, was arrested by the Germans as "untrustworthy;" in the 147th Battalion, 76 men were arrested and shot "as pro-Soviet elements."[229] According to German data, about 1/3rd of the battalions turned out unreliable, and were disarmed. Their personnel were thrown into concentration camps.[230] In April-May 1944, the remaining battalions fought with the Red Army, and in June were sent to Rumania, where an SS unit was raised from them (more on this later.) Thus, according to the data of western researchers, the general strength of the Crimean Tartars serving in the German Armed Forces fluctuated from 15,000 to 20,000 out of a population of 220,000 in 1939.[231]

It follows to say that in the course of 1942, several batches of Eastern Legion battalions were sent to the Crimea, which, during the German invasion of the Caucasus, served as a rear area for the attacking forces. So, toward the end of summer 1943, their average strength in the Crimea reached 1,500-2,000 men. After the evacuation from the Caucasus, their strength grew to 10,000 men.[232] The most famous of these battalions was the I/73rd Azerbaijani Infantry Battalion, quartered in Koktebel. As early as August 1943, an underground organization was formed within it, which established communications with the Partisans. This

---

[225] [93, p.32.]
[226] [134, p.47.]
[227] [134, p.147.]
[228] [2; d. 391, sheet 113, reverse side-115 reverse side.]
[229] [4, d. 16, sheet 37.]
[230] [2; d. 390, sheet 26; d. 505, sheet 2, 148 reverse side, 151, 210-v.]
[231] [143, p.61.]
[232] [2; d.28, sheet 29, 72; d.34, sheet 2 reverse side; d. 40, sheet 3; d.312, sheet 8.]

organization operated for more than a month until October 8th 1943 when a loyal pro-German Azerbaijani volunteer betrayed it. The Germans shot eight men, disbanded the battalion, and sent its personnel to concentration camps. Nevertheless, sixty men managed to flee and form a Partisan detachment; it operated successfully until the liberation of Crimea.[233] On 18 December 1942, on the eve of the Stalingrad disaster, a conference took place in Berlin of leadership officials, ministers of the occupied Eastern territories, administrators of military operational rear-areas, and representatives of the central military government who were responsible for carrying out work in the occupied Soviet territories.

RIGHT: Another photo of General A. Vlasov and German Army & SS officers in November 1944. This meeting was held in the Czech capital. The so-called "Prague Manifesto" was signed and declared by all peoples of the USSR who were opposed to Stalin and communism. *US National Archives.*

The basic theme of the conference was the question of the possibility of more widely attracting the Soviet population to collaborate with the Germans. A number of measures were proposed that would provide the Wehrmacht with complete goal fulfillment, augment detachments in the battle against the Partisans, and solve the worker shortage question in Germany itself: *"The conclusion reached at the conference"* writes American historian Allan Bullock, was expressed by two sentences:

"The difficult situation makes creating a positive collaboration with the population urgent. Russia could be shattered by these very same Russians."[234] Rosenberg ferociously dismissed these ideas, and *Reichskomissar Ukraine*, Erich Koch, and a portion of the military opposed it.[235] Hitler also *"excluded any step (toward a political settlement with the anti-Bolshevik forces) until the moment that the German Army had secured the decisive victory..."*[236]

Hitler's position had influence in determining Turkey's decision not to enter the war on the side of the Axis Powers; conversely, the creation of the Eastern Legions from Muslim peoples of the USSR began to play a part in Germany's

---

233 [2; d.312, sheet 1.]
234 [81, p.368.]
235 [106, pp.260-261.]
236 [81, p.432.]

influence on the Turkish government. Nevertheless, party and government factions were forced to make a number of concessions to the nationalists, to bring their political activity in line with the propaganda war against the USSR. In the still-occupied territories the Nazis began to create all kinds of 'councils' and 'committees,' in order to plant the illusion among the populace that they had a hand in deciding their own fate.

In Germany, a whole number of "national committees," that had arisen at the start of the war, but had played no role, were rejuvenated and reorganized by the Nazis. The formation of all nationalist organizations in Germany was done with the approval and cooperation of Alfred Rosenberg, the Minister of the Occupied Eastern Territories. A bureau was created for communications with the Ministry and guidance of the committees. The tasks of the bureau and the 'committees' included conduct of the propaganda work in volunteer formations; and guidance of subversive activities of émigrés and POWs from the nationalist ranks located in Germany, against the USSR. Thus was created the "Turkestan Committee." It was led by émigré Veli Kayum-Khan. The "Azerbaijani Staff' was led by A.A. Dudanginskiy a former Soviet officer who was now a *Wehrmacht* Major and *SS-Standartenführer* M.N. Israfilov, another *émigré.* There was also a "Northern Caucasus Staff," led by A.I. Magomaev, an émigré, and "Idel-Ural" under "The War Union of Volga Tartars", led by A.G. Shafaev and S.A. Alkaev, both former Soviet Citizens.[237]

The creation of Tartar Committees took place on Crimean territory under any conditions and for any cause. At the end of December 1941 the first "Muslim Tartar Committee" was formed in the city of Bakhchisarai. Afterwards, a committee like it was formed in Simferopol. In the thoughts of its founder, Dzh. Abdupeshidava, and his two deputies, I. Kermenchikli and O. Memetova, this committee should have guided the lives of all Crimean Tartars. But the German Security Service *(SD* or *Sicherheitsdienst)* immediately forbade him to call it "Crimean," permitting only the word "Simferopol" in the title. In the opinion of the leader of the SS and Police Command "Tavrida," (a.k.a.- "Simferopol"), *SS-Brigadefuehrer* Ludolf von Alvensleben, it should have served only as an example of Regional Muslim Committees, which started to form in different cities and populated points in the course of 1942.[238]

Organizationally, the Simferopol Tartar Committee was divided into six departments. One was to combat the "bandits" (i.e.- Soviet Partisans); One for the assembly of volunteer formations; One for rendering help to families of volunteers; One for culture and religion; One for propaganda and agitation; and one for administrative and economic needs.[239] The program of the Tartar Committee Leadership included: organization of the Crimean Tartar population for combat against the Partisan Movement. It also sought the destruction of Communist and Soviet activists, re-establishment of ancient traditions and customs; open prayer; propaganda and agitation to serve the creation of a Crimean

---

237 [32, pp.131-159; 47, pp.27-28; 134, pp.128-129; 135, pp.131-136.]

238 [2; d. 26, sheet 55; d. 388, sheet 26, 9; 3; d.41, sheet 4.]

239 [3; d.41, sheet 4-5.]

ABOVE: General Vlasov inspects a unit of ROA troops stationed at Münsingen Training Camp while undergoing training. Two Russian armored infantry divisions, numbered 600th and 650th were formed as the cadre of a future Russian Liberation Army. *US National Archives.*

Tartar nation under a German protectorate; and assist the occupation regime and the German Army with labor resources and food production.[1]

The chief media organs of the Committee were *"Azad Krim"* (Free Crimea (chief editor M. Kurtiev)) and the journal *"Ana-Yurt"* (Motherland.) They largely propagandized calls to render help to the occupation authorities and other appeals, primarily of a nationalist character. They conducted agitation for enlistment to the volunteer detachments and self-defense detachments, and distributed material about the operations of volunteers in action against the Partisan Movement.[2] In May 1943 one of the senior Crimean Tartar nationalists, A. Ozenbashli, gave a memorandum addressed to Adolf Hitler, in which the following program for cooperation between Germany and the Crimean Tartars was laid-out:

1. Crimea should become a Tartar State under a German protectorate.
2. On the basis of existing volunteer formations it was necessary to create a Tartar Army.
3. **Return of all Tartars in Turkey, Bulgaria, and other states to the Crimea and "cleansing" the Crimea of other nationalities.**

---

[1] [2; d.388, sheets 7-32, reverse side.]
[2] [2; d.388, sheets 7-9.]

4. Until the decisive victory over all the Bolsheviks, the entire population, including the elderly, should be issued arms.
5. Until the Tartar government could stand on its own feet, Germany should take trusteeship over it.[242]

Nevertheless, leaders of the Committee who were seeking favor from the SD, the *Sicherheitsdienst* (SS Security Service) did not send the document on its way and did not even discuss it in print. The document was passed by hand among Committee members in manuscript form. Instead, a decision was taken to continue recruiting Crimean Tartars into the German Armed Forces. But as Russian historians M.Y. Heller and A. M. Nekrich wrote: *"The occupiers everywhere firmly held authority in their hands and fiercely suppressed attempts to seek national independence. National organizations were formed everywhere under the strict control of the occupation authorities."*[243]

Thus, already by the close of 1943 almost all Tartar regional committees were practically non-functional. Thus, the Simferopol Committee in fact, consisted of only one member—its chairman Abdureshidova, who was directly responsible to the SD. Although there were eleven other committee members besides him, not a single one of them took part in its work. Even one of the chief branches of the Committee, that *"for combat with bandits,"* which A. Abdulaev headed, never complied with its responsibilities *"because of spinelessness and inexperience."*[244] In April-May 1944 several members of the committee fled to Germany, where in November 1943 a "Crimean Center" was still forming. The center and its corresponding Bureau for the Ministry of the Occupied Eastern Territories-"Crimean Tartar Leadership Department," were located in Frankfurt-am-Oder. E. Kirimal and Solzal administered it. In the beginning, Dr. Konelsen of the Ministry of Occupied Eastern Territories was the head of the Crimean Tartar Bureau, and after that, Dr. Mueller, a Baltic German.[245] It should be mentioned that Kirimal *"was very close with the Grand Mufti of Jerusalem, Al-Hussein. He used the influence of the latter when deciding on any questions."*[246]

In connection with the worsening situation on the Eastern Front, when it became obvious that the war had taken on a protracted character, the influence of the SS sharply grew in all sections of government administration. Therefore, in Department VI (foreign intelligence), the Main Administration of Reich Security (RSHA, headed by *SS-Brigadefuehrer* Walter Schellenberg), a "Scientific Research Method Service, Department G" was created, with H. Scheel as its head. Among its tasks were: organization and guidance of so-called 'research institutes,' which conducted work for the preparation of cadres for sabotage, propaganda, and espionage work directed against the USSR.

In part, Schellenberg took the decision to organize the so-called 'Turkestan' work group, setting down for it all decisions and questions pertaining

---

[242] [4; d.16, sheet 34.]

[243] [84, p.432.]

[244] [2; d.505, sheet 69-69 reverse side.]

[245] [45, p.90; 47, p.20.]

[246] [47, p.30.]

to covert work in Central Asia. *SS-Hauptsturmfuehrer* Rainer Orscha was placed at the head of the group. One of the tasks that this and similar groups had was selection of POW recruits into "volunteer units." This led to the opening of the "Mullah School" *("Mullakurse"),* which had about 250 students in branch groups in Dresden by 26th November 1944. Schellenberg placed an immigrant from Kazakhstan at the head of the school.[247] The creation of similar establishments is explained by the fact that national committees in Berlin, and those managed by Rosenberg and his ministry, were not trusted and obviously did not comply with the obligations set down for them.

In the military sphere real changes occurred, which seriously influenced the process of creating Muslim volunteer organizations. An Inspector-General of Eastern Troops *(General der Osttruppen)* was created as early as 16 December 1942 at Army High Command *(Oberkommando des Heeres, OKH.).* The commander of the Wehrmacht's 23rd Infantry Division, Major-General (later Lieutenant-General) H. Helmich was designated commander. Its tasks included training new units: infantry, engineer, construction battalions, cavalry squadrons, and artillery divisions. But they did not have the right to intervene in the tactical leadership decisions of the volunteer formations. In every Army Group Headquarters an office of Inspector-General of Eastern Troops was created subordinate to the authorities only in an administrative sense.[248] But the very designation of the new establishment was extremely unsuccessful: in did not take into account the national specifications of the volunteer formations. Russians, Ukrainians, Baltics, Caucasus tribes, and Turkish peoples—all fell under the general designation of "Eastern," as one German officer later wrote.[249]

Therefore, on 29 April 1943, the Chief of OKH, Colonel-General K. Zeitzler issued order No. P/5000/43: "Local Auxiliary Forces in the East—Volunteers." The order stated that, all *"those voluntarily coming to the German side shall not be declared POWs, but volunteers."* Besides this, they were presented with a choice: remain to serve in the German Army, or select *"one of the National Liberation Legions."*[250] Now the military-political leadership proposed to see not only helpers ("Hiwis") in the "Eastern Peoples," but allies: *"Eastern workers and...soldiers demonstrated the ability and desire of the Eastern Peoples to break with Bolshevism. Therefore, it is necessary to not turn the peasant into a Partisan, but influence him so that he will be ready to volunteer to make the first step toward a new world."*

The above statement was written in The German Crimean Gazette on 26 May 1943.[251] Soon after this, the Inspector-General of Eastern Troops was renamed the "Inspector General of Volunteer Formations" *(General der Freiwilligen Verband).* In January 1944, General Helmich was replaced by General of Cavalry E. Keistring, for blatantly not meeting the requirements of his duties. Keistring was more versed in "Eastern Affairs:" in 1932-1933 and 1935-

---

247 [11, pp.1-4; 80, pp.171-172; 113, pp.32-33; 134, pp.139-144.]
248 [128, p.14.]
249 [58, p.185.]
250 [13, RHD 7/8a/2.]
251 [3; d. 26, sheets 10-11.]

1941 he was Germany's military attache in Moscow, and in 1942 he spent some time in the Caucasus, where in the capacity of military advisor to General-Field Marshall Erich von Kleist he managed the Germans' "national policy."[252] But in the words of émigré historian A.S. Kazanteva: *"In relation to the Russian people, as toward other peoples of Russia, he differed from other German policy leaders only in his good knowledge of the Russian language."*[253]

After a November 1944 proclamation of the Vlasov "Committee on the Liberation of the Peoples of Russia," (KLPR), an attempt was made to unite all the above-indicated 'national committees' under its aegis, and to include their legions in the structure of "The Armed Forces of the KLPR." The majority of the leaders, Russophile supporters of A. Rosenberg, refused to go along with General A. Vlasov on such an agreement and in place of that announced the creation on the basis of the their national legions, a "Caucasus Liberation Army" and a "National Army of Turkestan." But this announcement remained at the planning stage.[254] Nevertheless, it did not hinder German propaganda to emphasize that: *"In battles against Bolshevism, a great friendship of nations was born. so, he who strives to sow national dissension...plays the hand of the Bolsheviks and is our enemy."*[255]

Another not insignificant aspect of the changes in the military sphere was the creation of foreign *Waffen-SS* divisions, among which were Muslims: the 13th SS Mountain Infantry *"Handschar"* and 23rd SS Mountain Infantry *"Kama"* divisions, composed of Bosnian Muslims, and the 21st Mountain Infantry Division *"Skanderbeg,"* composed of Kosovar Albanians.[256] Moving away from "racial principles" in recruiting for these divisions, Himmler ordered the acceptance of them and members of other "lower races."

Thus, at the end of 1943, Andreas Mayer-Mader, the former commander of the 1st Battalion of the Turkestan Legion, offered his services to the Chief Director of the SS, who presented him the opportunity to form a *Waffen-SS* Turkish Regiment. By

RIGHT: An officer of the Bergmann Formation. He is recognized by the metallic pin on the side of his soft cover, which represented a large Muslim knife called a *Kindjal,* or Caucasian knife. *Photo: Signal Magazine.*

[252] [27, pp.1-3; 36, p.217; 128, p.14.]

[253] [42, p.234.]

[254] [98, pp.66-68; 128, p.20.]

[255] [3; d.27, sheet 70.]

[256] for more about this division, see previous material.

way of recruiting POWs and enticing Turkestani officers and NCOs from other units, who were promised higher pay and quicker promotions in service, Mayer-Mader succeeded in gathering the necessary cadre personnel. The regiment he formed should have served as a model for the creation of a *Waffen SS* Division under the name of "New Turkestan" *("Neu Turkestan").* For this unit, the *Wehrmacht* had already earmarked several battalions: the 782nd, 786th, 790th, and 791st Turkestani, the 818th Azerbaijani, and the 831st Volga-Tartar Battalions.[257]

In March 1944, the 1st Eastern-Muslim SS Regiment, *(Ostmuselmanische SS-Regiment 1)* headed by Mayer-Mader, was transferred to Western Belorussia in the Yuratishki Region, where its commander disappeared without a trace. According to official reports, he died in a Partisan ambush. In the course of the next three months the Regiment went through still more commanders: *SS-Hauptsturmfuehrer* Billig and *SS-Hauptsturmfuehrer* Hermann. After the death of the latter in battle with Partisans near Grodno, a commander of one of the Turkestani Group companies - *SS-Obersturmfuehrer* Gulam Alimov, a former Uzbeki Red Army sergeant, headed the Regiment.[258] Under his leadership, in August 1944, the Regiment helped put down the Warsaw Uprising. It was attached to an SS penal brigade under the command of *SS-Oberfuehrer* Oskar Dirlewanger. It is worth mentioning that many other volunteer formations fought here together with the Regiment. These included: "The Russian National Liberation Army," (RONA) better known as the Kaminsky Brigade, one of the regiments of the "Cossack Group" of Ataman T.I. Domanov, three Ukrainian companies, and two Azerbaijani battalions from the *"Gorets" (a.k.a. Bergammn) Regiment.*[259]

Operations of the Regiment in Warsaw were highly rated by the German Command, which recognized many of the officers and ranks with medals, including the Iron Cross. At the end of October 1944, the 1st Eastern-Muslim SS Regiment was transferred to Slovakia, where on the night of 24/25 December, on the commander's initiative, a mutiny took place. As a result, Alimov, the officers, and about 400 Uzbek soldiers deserted to the Slovakian Partisans.[260] Though expecting his action to serve as a pardon, Alimov was shot instead, and after this many of his soldiers returned to the Germans.[261] In July 1944, Section III *(Amt – III)* of the SS Main Headquarters *(SS Fuehrungshauptamt)* was created in Berlin, especially for work with the Eastern Volunteer Formations, under the direction of Dr. Franz Arlt. The expansion of two Caucasus Police Battalions (the 70th and 71st) into the Northern Caucasus and Caucasian SS Regiments also began at this time in Belorussia.[262]

After the defeat of the German Crimean Group in May 1944 Hitler, enraged by the loss of the Russian peninsula, ordered the disbandment of all units withdrawn from the Crimea, the dispersal of their personnel, and fusion into new

---

257 [28, pp.1-4; 93, p.14.]

258 [47, p.28.]

259 [63, p.52; 125, p.242.]

260 [80, p.173.]

261 [93, p.15.]

262 [28, p.45]

ABOVE: During the summer of 1942 the German Army reached the lower Volga bend and the Caucasus region of the Soviet Union. Here there were numerous diverse peoples with varying faiths and political aspirations. The one factor which made many of these peoples side with the advancing Germans was their hatred of the Communist system. The Germans used this hatred to their own ends and recruited these Caucasian volunteers by the tens of thousands. *Antonio J. Munoz Collection.*

units. Thus in June 1944 the Tartar self-defense units remaining in the *Schuma* battalions and police detachments withdrawing from the Crimea to Rumania were assigned to form a three-battalion strength Tartar Mountain-Jaeger Regiment of the SS *(Tataren-Gebirgsjaeger-Regiment der SS).* In the course of a month, after participation in a number of operations, the Regiment was transferred to Hungary, where on July 8th 1944, by order of the Chief Director of the SS, it was reformed as the 1st Tartar Mountain-Jaeger Brigade of the SS *[Waffen-Gebirgsjaeger-Brigade der SS (tatarische No.1,)].* It had strength of around 2,500 fighters under the command of *SS-Standartenfuehrer* Willy Fortenbacher.[263]

A unit of the Crimean Tartar volunteers was transferred to France and assigned to the Volga-Tartar Legion reserve battalion in the city of Le Pieaux.[264] Still, several hundred served as *"Hiwis"* at the end of the war in the ranks of the 35th SS Police Division.[265] Besides this, a portion of the Tartars evacuated from the Crimea (mainly youths) enlisted in the Auxiliary Heavy Flak (Anti-Aircraft)

263 [30; 63, p.373f.]

264 [98, pp.187-188.]

265 [31.]

Service.[266] In October 1944, the Chief Director of the SS gave an order to reform the remnants of the 1st Eastern Muslim SS Regiment into a division-sized unit: the Eastern Turkish Unit of the SS *(Ostturkischer-Waffenverband der SS).* Organizationally, it was divided into several regimental sized battlegroups.[267] As a result, toward the end of 1944, the unit had the following elements:

1) Headquarters Unit-
    a. Commander: *SS-Standartenführer* Wilhelm (Harun Raschid el Bey) Hintersatz, a former officer in the Austro-Hungarian Army and SS communications officer with the Grand Mufti of Jerusalem; accepted the Muslim name of Harun-el-Rashid-Bey.[268]
    b. Adjutant: *SS-Untersturmfuehrer* Willy Bruckner (a German)
    c. JAG Chief: *SS-Hauptsturmfuehrer* Meyer-Herting (a German)
    d. Battle Review Officer and Unit and Assistant Commander for Propaganda: *Waffen-Obersturmfuehrer der-SS* Nazarov (an Uzbek).
2) Regimental Group "Idel-Ural" (Volga Tartars,) assigned to staff and 3rd Battalion.
3) Regimental Group "Turkestan," assigned to HQ plus 1st, 2nd, 6th, and 10th Battalions. Group Commander: *SS-Untersturmfuehrer* Tursunov (an Uzbek).
4) Regimental Group "Crimea," assigned to the unit on 31 December 1944, consisted of the remnants of the previously discussed Mountain-Jaeger Brigade SS. Included an HQ, 7th, 8th, 9th Battalions and a cavalry squadron. Group Commander: *SS-Brigadeführer* Fortenbacher.
5) Lastly, in March 1945, the unit was assigned Regimental Group "Azerbaijan" with HQ and 4th and 5th Battalions. Group Commander: *SS-Obersturmführer* Alekberli (an Azerbaijani.).[269]

At the end of 1944 a Caucasian-SS unit was created on the basis of Georgian, Armenian, Azerbaijan, and Northern Caucasus battlegroups stationed in northern Italy. Its strength was 4,800 men. It was intended to expand the unit into a Caucasus Cavalry Division under Major-General L.F. Bicherakhov, an émigré. Additionally, Colonel of the Terskiy Cossacks was to have accepted service in this command, but because of illness, he could not get about his duties. Therefore temporary control of the unit went to a Baltic German, *SS-Standartenfuehrer* Arved Theurmann.[270] Command of the regiments in this SS cavalry unit went to first-wave emigrants: (1) Prince P. Tsulukidze, (2) M.N. Israfilov, and (3) S.K. Ulagay – with each one holding the rank of *Waffen-Standartenführer der-SS.* But in connection with the situation at the front, this battle expansion plan was not realized.[271]

---

[266] [93, p.33.]
[267] [28, pp.5-6.]
[268] [47, p.28; 93, p.15;]
269 [28, pp.6-17; 47, pp.28-29.]
[270] Arved Theurmann had seen service in the Caucasus under the SS & Police Command there.
271 [9, pp.1-18; 47, p.29.]

Besides a Cossack SS unit, there were also about 6,500 refugees in northern Italy - husbands, elderly people, wives, and children - all led by Prince Sultan Kelech-Girce. All able-bodied men from the ages of 18 to 70 years of age were enlisted in two volunteer regiments, each of which consisted of companies formed according to national characteristics. These regiments were called upon to play the role of self-defense units in places that accommodated refugees and simultaneously served as a reserve to replenish the Caucasus unit.[272] In the words of historian Nicholas Bethell, the officers of these Caucasus units: *"Represented in themselves the aristocratic atavism of Tsarist Russia. Ten of them were princes, dressed in gleaming uniforms; they treated their soldiers as if they were serfs."*[273] On 26 August 1944, Hitler, after the assassination attempt against his life, decided that "all foreign national units and formations" of the ground forces must be placed under the direction of the *Waffen-SS* Command. This measure enabled Himmler to subordinate the remaining volunteer formations under his authority, which had not already to that time been under his leadership.[274]

ABOVE: North Caucasian volunteers reading a prayer over the tomb of a fellow member, somewhere in northern Italy in 1945. *Historical Museum, Evpatoria, Crimea, Ukraine.*

[272] [93, p.32.]
[273] [78, p.95.]
[274] [107, p.216.]

CHAPTER 4
Crimean Tartar Volunteer Formations In The German Armed Forces 1941-1945

One of the most difficult and intricate issues of World War Two to this very day is the use of Soviet Citizens in the ranks of the German Armed Forces. Only in recent years has there been an opportunity among native historians to delve deeply into this question, on which countless publications have been written.[275] It turns out that the issue is not one-sided and contains numberless facets. Once such facet, which brings the attention of historians to itself, along with the moral and ethical side of a phenomenon such as national, military collaboration and its political essence etc., is the question of the membership of our fellow countrymen, who served in the *Wehrmacht* and in the *Waffen-SS* in the national ranks of so-called 'volunteer formations.'

Besides, in our difficult social-political conditions, conditions of a scornful attitude to the historical past of our People and the profiteering thereby, this issue takes on a sudden current significance. The other side of the issue is the insufficient study of a topic like the national policy, if one could call it that, of Nazi Germany in the occupied territories of the USSR during the period of the Great Patriotic War. German historian K.G. Pfeffer wrote: *"The attitude of the German government toward other peoples…has a very great significance….the widespread belief that the Germans treated other peoples badly as a rule is incorrect. In practice…the attitude varied greatly."*[276]

With this emphasis comes agreement that, namely, the use of the nationality question in German occupation politics and Nazi propaganda played a very important role. It took on a particular significance prior to the preparation for, and in the course of Operation Barbarossa. In preparing for war against the Soviet Union, the German government regarded it as *"an artificial and loose union of an enormous number of nations, like an 'ethnic conglomerate,' lacking inner cohesion."*[277] Therefore, one of the chief tasks of the German military-political leadership after the war with the Soviet Union began, was its destruction as a multi-national state by way of attracting to its side members of non-Russian peoples and national minorities inside the Soviet Union. In this, the Nazis calculated that: *"For the struggle against Bolshevism it became possible to attract to their side the numerous Muslim peoples of the Soviet Union.A special staff was created for cooperation with these peoples."*[278]

The creation of "national volunteer formations" from the respective Turkish and Caucasus peoples of the USSR became one method of realizing such

---

[275] [1.]
[276] [2.]
[277] [3.]
[278] [4.]

cooperation.[279] With its mixed national population, the Crimea was among the first occupied regions in the Soviet Union where the Germans put their policy of using non-Russian Muslim peoples as military auxiliaries. It was here that in October-November 1941 that the Germans formed the first "Muslim Legions" from Crimean Tartars. The process of forming Crimean-Tartar volunteer formations was generally similar and had in its foundation military and political causes.

These played a role in the creation of similar formations from among other Muslim peoples of the USSR. But it had its own special traits, which left their own "local" fingerprints. In November 1941 the Crimea became assigned to one of the new administrative entities created by the Germans in the occupied Soviet territory—the *Reichskomissariat Ukraine*. It went by the designation "General District Tavrida." A civilian administration was to have been built there, owing to the fact that the Crimea was either a rear area for army operations, or a battle zone, it practically belonged to the units of the Wehrmacht and their Commands that were stationed there, until its liberation in 1944.

This authority strengthened even more when the Crimea became a rear area for German units attacking into the Caucasus in 1942-1943. From the end of 1941, the Partisan Movement became an important factor which influenced German occupation policy, including the Crimea. One German officer later wrote: *"The Partisan Movement was of course, not a simple manifestation of disorder in the rear areas, as some Germans thought at first. Quite the opposite: it was a political resistance movement, which was impossible to bring under control with German Police forces alone."*[280]

In the Crimea, this problem took on special importance for the German Command. The areas of Partisan concentration and activity were located in the immediate vicinity of communications and population centers that were important from an operational point of view. Thus from a military viewpoint, as an army rear area of operations, the peninsula's pacification became the main task of the German occupation authorities in the Crimea. This could be realized only after obtaining the loyalty of the population and the destruction of the Partisan Movement. All measures taken there by the occupation authorities were subordinated to this task without exception, including attempts to recruit the local population to its side in the interests of cooperation.

Therefore, the process of using volunteer formations for such cooperation, took on the form of "local auxiliary police forces," for support of public order and recruitment of volunteers, and their inclusion by small groupings in the German Army operating in the Crimea, in the capacity of "volunteer helpers" or "Hiwis," a German acronym for *"Hilfswillige."* The leadership of the infamous *"Einsatzgruppe D,"* headed by *SS- Oberfuehrer* Otto Ohlendorf, immediately implemented organization of the police, intelligence, and punitive agencies in the Crimea.[281] Created on the initiative of Chief Director of the Reich Main Security

[279] Among others - Russian editor's note.

[280] [6.]

[281] Olendorf, Otto, born 4.02.1907, one of the leadership of the German penal system, SS Gruppenfuehrer (1944.) In 1925 he was in the NSPAD and SA, in 1926 he transferred to the SS.

Office (RSHA) it was *"an instrument for carrying out racial policy"* in the occupied territories and was occupied with the extermination *"of Jews, Communists, and other undesirable elements."* In the course of summer-autumn 1941, this group exterminated 40,000 people in the southern Ukraine and the Crimea.[282] Two-thirds of its personnel (around 400 men) consisted of "local volunteers:" Ukrainians, Tartars, and Russians.

Besides these "basic" functions, it was tasked with the creation of an independent security police *(Ordnungspolizei)* in its areas of operations in the occupied territories. These pro-German collaborators under the control of the *Ordnungspolizei* created city and rural security police departments in the Crimea. In November 1941, all "local auxiliary police forces" on the *Reichskomissariat* territory were organized as auxiliary security police "sub-units" *("Schutzmannschaft der Ordnungspolizei"* or *"Schuma").* The Schuma police consisted strictly of the following categories:

1. *Schutzmannschaft-Einseldienst*—Security Police in the cities and rural areas;
2. *Selbstschutz*—self-defense units;
3. *Schutzmannschaft-Bataillone*—Police Battalions for combat with Partisans;
4. *Feuerschutzdienst*—Auxiliary Firefighters;
5. *Hilfsdienst*—Reserve Auxiliary Police for POW guard duty and for carrying out heavy labor service.

The Germans created the city and rural police departments immediately upon the capture of the cities and population centers of the Crimea. Usually, a director of the auxiliary security police department ran it under the City Authority. The main responsibility of its officials was the maintenance of order and to ensure that the regime's rules were obeyed.[283] One can say that the personnel element consisted of three main national groups: Tartars, Ukrainians, and Russians. The national composition varied in relation to the region. So, Tartars dominated the police in Alushti (Police Chief—Chermen Seit Memet,) in Yalta and Sevastopol (Police Chief—Yaya Aliev). Karasubazar and Zui (Police Chief—Senior Police Officer Aliev).Tartars were significantly fewer in number in Evpatoria and the Feodosia police departments.[284]

But neither the city nor rural police could fight the Partisans independently, much less destroy them. Therefore, the occupation authorities did everything possible to create stronger and better-armed formations, which could provide relative security, at least within the limits of their regions. On 2

On 27.09.1936 when the RSHA began to form, he headed its 3rd Directorate, managing the German Interior Security Service (SD.) From June 1941 until July 1942 he was Chief of Einsatzgruppe D. In May 1945 he was arrested by the Allies and pronounced guilty in the extermination of 91,000 people. On 10.04.1948 he was sentenced to death by hanging. On 8.06.1951 the sentence was carried out.

282 [7.]

283 [9.]

284 [10.]

December 1941 *Oberkommando des Heeres (OKH)* issued a directive and read in part: *"Special Orders for Fighting with Partisans: The use of local units in combat with Partisans is fully authorized. Their knowledge of the local terrain, climate, and language of the country make it possible, after all, to apply theories of operation in combat with Partisans."*[285]

The hostility of non-Russian peoples and national minorities toward the Russian people was in part, one of the principles of German occupation policy on the territory of the USSR in general, and in the creation of volunteer formations. In the Crimea this principle found its expression in cavorting of the German authorities with the Crimean-Tartar population and the raising of volunteer units from them, in the form of self-defense detachments and *Schuma* battalions, for use on the peninsula. In the words of Colonel-General Erich von Manstein, commander of the 11th Army which captured the Crimea in October-November 1941: *"The Tartars immediately went over to our side. They saw us as their liberators from the Bolshevik yoke, and what is more, that we respected their religious traditions."*[286]

Besides, as early as October 1941, there were the first indications that the Crimean Tartars began to desert from Soviet forces operating in the Crimea, usually hiding in its villages. In the words of an eyewitness: *"The Tartars did not simply desert, but under the guise of friendship, they corrupted the Russian fighters, persuading them to abandon their positions, and promising to hide them in their villages."*[287]

After the German military penetrated the Crimean peninsula, the Tartars came forward to serve in the capacity of guides for German units and led them to outflank and cut off retreating Soviet forces.[288] In Bakhchisarai the Tartars met the Germans with bread and salt in gratitude for liberation from the Russian authorities.[289] In a number of instances there were local open attacks on retreating Soviet units by Tartars, and also raids on Partisan supply bases created before the war.[290] Thus, for example, on 18th December 1941, a scout of the Feodosian Partisan detachment observed about forty carts in a forest with armed Tartars, who as it turned out, were going after the supplies of the detachment. A deserter led this group from the Sudakskiy Partisan detachment, a former Red Army lieutenant and All Union Communist Party (Bolshevik) member, Memetov.[291] The residents of the Tartar villages of Baksan, Tau-Kipchak, Mechet-Edi, Veirat, Konrat, Eurtuk, Eni-Sala, Molbay, Kamyshlyk, Argin, Eni-Sarai, Ulu-Uzen, Kazanly, Korbek, Koush, Biyuk-Uzenbash, Kuchuk-Uzenbash, and Uskut, all busied themselves with raiding Partisan supply bases.

After occupying the greater part of the Crimea, the Germans began to conduct open political dialogue with the Tartar population, playing on nationalist

---

285 [11.]
286 [12.]
287 [13.]
288 [14.]
289 [15.]
290 [16.]
291 [17.]

sentiments and giving Tartars material preeminence before the remaining Crimean peoples. A special line of stores was set up the best homes were given to Tartars, the best personal farming plots, and the best of collective farm inventories. For example, in Simferopol trade preference was given first to Tartars, then to Greeks and Armenians, and last of all, to the Karais and Russians. In many cases, the German occupation authorities did not support repression of Tartar Communists from the Komsomolets *[Communist Youth League—translator]* but absolved them, saying that: *"Tthey were mistaken earlier, but now with weapons in hand they shall make good of their mistakes."* [292]

Researchers Charles Dickson and Otto Heilbrunn wrote*: "By October 1941 for the struggle with the Partisans, the Germans began to recruit Crimean Tartars, who had always related with hostility toward the Bolshevik regime. So-called 'Tartar self-defense units' were formed, which rendered great help to the Germans."*[293] These detachments, numbering 70-100 men each, were given captured infantry weapons and assigned German NCO instructors. In the words of Eric von Manstein, the chief task of these detachments: *"Consisted in guarding their settlements from...Partisan attacks."*[294] The creation of similar units was facilitated by the presence of a significant number of military-age Tartar deserters in the villages. In November 1941, one of the first self-defense detachments was created in the village of Koush. In the beginning, it numbered about 80 men, but toward April 1942 its roster grew to 345 men. Someone named "Raimov," who was a local resident, was designated commander of the detachment and served with the German Police, attaining the rank of Major. Village elder O. Hasanov took an active role in the creation of the detachment. He was a recent member of the All Union Communist Party (Bolshevik) ["VKP(b)"]. The main task of the detachment was: *"Frequent attacks and diversions to hold the Partisans in a constant state of alert, destroy their manpower, and rob their supply bases."*[295]

Besides this, Koush was the Tartar-volunteer recruitment center for the region.[296] Thanks to three lines of defense and strongpoints, Koush was unapproachable to Partisans for a long time.[297] Thus, as a result of German association in organizing self-defense detachments, by December 1941, they were already formed in the following population centers: Uskut - 130 men, at Tuak - 100men, at Kuchuk-Uzen - 80 men, and at Eni-Sala, Sultan Sarai, Bashi, Karasu-Bashi, Molbay, and a number of others.[298] Until January 1942, the creation of detachments had an unorganized character and depended on the initiative of German military commanders. After the German defeat in front of Moscow, Rostov, and the Kerchensko-Feodosia airborne operation, the situation changed fundamentally. On 2 January 1942, a report was given in the intelligence section of the German 11th Army. During the course of it, it was announced that Hitler decided to summon volunteers from among the Crimean Tartars. Army

---

[292] [18.]
[293] [19]
[294] [20.]
[295] [21.]
[296] [22.]
[297] [23.]
[298] [24.]

Headquarters gave resolution of the issue to the leadership of *Einsatzgruppe D*. It was assigned the following tasks: *"Involve those Crimean Tartars who are able-bodied for military service, in operations at the front line with units of the 11th Army on a volunteer basis; also create Tartar self-defense companies, which jointly with Einsatzgruppe D, will be used in combat with Partisans."*[299]

On 3 January 1942, under the leadership of Otto Ohlendorf, a meeting of the Simferopol Muslim Committee, created 23 November 1941, began. It opened with the question of beginning Tartar recruitment into the German Armed Forces for the common "struggle against Bolshevism."[300] The Committee and its chairman, Dzh. Abdureshidova,[301] were given responsibility for preparing propaganda for the recruitment campaign in the respective population centers. The leadership of *Einsatzgruppe D* was given responsibility for the technical side of the recruitment campaign. Besides this, it was to work jointly with that section of the Committee which answered directly for work with volunteer recruitment: the Section for Combating Bandits (i.e.- Partisans), led by A. Abdulaev[302] and the Section for Recruitment and Organization of Volunteer Detachments, whose leader was T. Dzhemilev.[303] + [304] On January 5th 1942, with the formal agreement of the Chairman of the Muslim Committee, a recruitment office was opened in Simferopol and began to attract enlistees with the slogan: *"Tartars! If you want to stop the Partisans from robbing you, volunteer to take up arms against the Partisans!"*[305]

The Committee sent special representatives B. Adzhiev[306], Sh. Karabash[307], and A. Karabash[308] to facilitate the recruitment of local volunteers.

---

[299] [25.]

[300] [26.]

[301] Abdureshidova Dzhemil, the son of a merchant from the Evpatoriisk area, a Turkish national. In the first ranks of the Simferopol Muslim Committee as chairman, from May 1943 occupied the post of Second Deputy. In the beginning of 1944 he became Chairman once again. In March 1944 "for services to the Tartar People" the German Command awarded him The Order of Merit for the Eastern Peoples, Second Class.

[302] Abdulaev, Amet, Representative of the Sicherheitsdienst (SD) to the Simferopol Muslim Committee.

[303] Dzhemilev, Takhsin, son of a Mullah from the village of Urkusta Balaklavskiy region, by education an economist, until the war he worked in a union cooperative. In March 1944 the German Command awarded him The Order of Merit for the Eastern Peoples, Second Class.

[304] [27.]

[305] [28.]

[306] Adzhiev, Bekir, the ward of an important businessman from Alushti Cholbasa, until the war he worked in the Fruit and Vegetable Market Trust, managing the grocer's section.

[307] Karabash, Shamurat, in 1921 he was the leader of the Posse Commitatus in the village of Korbek; later, for this he was expelled from the VKP(b) in 1928. Until the war he worked in the Simferopol Nutrition Trust as a vegetable specialist. In January 1942, he was designated Tartar-volunteer recruiter, but as he never met the requirements of his duties, he was demoted in 1943 and designated manager of the Peasants' Home; he was a secret SD agent.

[308] Karabash, Abdulla, the nephew of the above; before the war he completed the Simferopol Pedagogical Institute and post-graduate work, after which he occupied the post of Assessor for the Crimean Council of People's Commissars (SNKK.) After the start of German recruitment efforts he became Chief Assistant and right hand of his uncle.

G. Appuz.[309] + [310] The recruitment of volunteers continued throughout January 1942 in 203 population centers and five POW camps. As a result, 9,255 Tartar volunteers were taken into service, the greatest number of volunteers in Crimea was taken in Karasubazar—1,000 men; the least number in Biyuk-Onlar—13 men. Of these 9,255 men, 8,684 were sent to units of the 11th Army. The remaining volunteers were pronounced unfit for duty in line units, and were returned to their villages. Simultaneously, *Einsatzgruppe D* recruited 1,632 men, who were divided into 14 self-defense companies, and stationed in the following populated areas: Simferopol, Biuk-Onlar, Beshu, Baksan, Molbay, Biy-Eli, Alushte, Bakhchisarai, Koush, Yalta, Taraktash (the 12th and 13th companies) and Dzhankoe.[311]

Every Tartar self-defense company consisted of three platoons and numbered from 50 (Dzhankoe) to 175 (Yalta) men. German officers commanded the companies. The fighters were clothed in standard German issue, but without distinguishing insignia. The personnel element was armed with standard infantry weapons, generally light types. Later they were also issued heavy machine guns and mortars.[312] In the creation of similar units, the German Command counted on a certain propaganda effect, in addition to having military objectives. By its thinking, the Partisans were to be made exhausted *"in battle, not with Germans, but with formations from the local population."*[313] In the words of the Chief of the Central Headquarters of the Partisan Movement, (Ts.Sh.P.D.) P.K. Ponomarenko, *"rabid nationalistic propaganda"* accompanied by *"smoldering national dissension, and anti-semitism"* was the norm around these units.[314]

The Simferopol Muslim Committee Department of Culture and Religion played a substantial role in the ideological development of the Tartar volunteer formations, whose leader was E. Gafarov.[315] A particular aspect of this dealt with the tutoring of the volunteer youths, who had received a Bolshevik education in Turko-Tartar history.[316] The newspaper Azad Krim ("Free Crimea"), which began publication from 11 January 1942, played a major guiding role in Crimean Tartar nationalist ideology. This newspaper was an agency of the Simferopol Muslim Committee and was published twice a week in the Tartar language (address of the editor: Pushkinskaya Street 14; printed in the presses of the Simferopol City Directorate at ulitsa Salgirnoy 23). [317] In the beginning the paper was published in small editions, in connection with the Propaganda Section, Crimea (the main German propaganda agency in the Crimea) in order to enlarge propaganda operations with the local population. Its circulation grew to 15,000 copies in the

---

309 In 1920-21 he was leader of an anti-Soviet Crimean-Tartar formation, for which he was later convicted.

310 [29.]

311 [30.]

312 [31.]

313 [32.]

314 [33.]

315 Gafarov, Ennan, until the war he was a criminal and occupied himself with speculation, for which he was repeatedly sentenced.

316 [34.]

317 [35.]

summer of 1943.[318] M. Kurtiev was its long-time chief editor and author of leading stories[319]. Colleagues of the newspaper editor were: F. Ablyaeva[320] (author of articles related to "Women's Issues"), A. Kurkchi[321] (author of nationalistic propaganda features, satire, and editorials), N. Seydametova[322] (author of correspondences related to economic issues), and M. Nizami, author of material related to cultural issues and propaganda; *"Questions of Conscience and Bolshevism"* was one of his best-known articles on the theme.[323]

Azad Krim printed materials about the organization of Muslim Committees in Crimean areas, their work in providing for the population, the re-distribution of landed property, cultural-religious influences on the Crimean Tartars, recruitment and service of Tartar volunteers in the German Armed Forces, reports from the military theater of operations, material about the opening of Mosques, toasts in honor of the German "liberation Army" and the *"liberation of oppressed peoples, and the faithful son of the German People, Adolf Hitler."*[324] Besides this, in 1943 the editor of the newspaper reported to his subscribers, that *"in foreign news much attention will be given to events taking place in the Near East and India."*[325] But alongside "spiritual food" appeared promises of material well being and the creation of all kinds of advantages and privileges for their families. Accordingly, a decision of OKW promised "any person who actively fought or fights with the Partisans and Bolsheviks" may submit an application for "his portion of land, or a payment to him of up to 1,000 rubles."[326] After publication of the "Law on the New Agrarian Order" on February 15th 1942, that had been drafted in the Ministry of the Occupied Eastern Territories by Alfred Rosenberg: *"They began to give full possession of two hectares of land to all Tartars and their families, who enlisted for the volunteer formations. They were presented with the best acreage, not considering that they had belonged to those peasants who did not enlist in the self-defense detachments."*[327]

The main role of the self-defense companies was to battle the Partisans jointly with German occupation troops. For this, the most educated and trained companies were used, for example, the 8th Bakhchisarai, and the 9th Koush. Those companies that had not achieved significant readiness were adapted for guard duty at military and civilian objectives: warehouses, railroad stations,

---

318 [36.]

319 Kurtiev, Mustafa, member of the Simferopol Muslim Committee, until 1941 was repeatedly subject to repression.

320 Ablyaev, Fevzi, until the war worked as a professor of the Tartar language and literature in Middle School No. 12 in Simferopol.

321 Kurkchi, Abdullah, until the war he worked as a translator in the Crimean Government Publishing House; two of his brothers were exiled from Crimea by the decision of NKVD bureaus. From the end of June 1941 he was a member of the Simferopol Muslim Committee and Chief Deputy Editor of Azad Krim.

322 Seydametov, Nedzhati, Karasubazar native, until 1928 he worked as a manager of an Evpatoriiskiy area land bureau, from 1929 to 1941 he worked in the Grocer-Trust system.

323 [37.]

324 [38.]

325 [39.]

326 [40.]

327 [41.]

administrative establishments, etc. The German recruitment campaign for Tartar volunteers worried the leadership of the Crimean Partisans very much. Thus, the leadership of the II Partisan Area, I.V. Genov, reported on January 31st 1942: *"Great Land: The local Tartar population is successfully armed...by the Germans; the goal—combat with Partisans...It is necessary to suppose that in the coming days they will begin to practice in battle with us. We are prepared for this...although we understand that armed Tartars are far more dangerous than Germans and Rumanians."*[328]

As a result, by autumn 1942, the Partisans in the Crimea were factually fighting on two fronts. According to an eyewitness, Deputy Chief of the Special Branch of the Crimean Headquarters of the Partisan Movement, (K.Sh.P.D.) Lieutenant Popov of Government Security, it was a front *"against the German fascist aggressor...and against traitors of the people—the Crimean Tartars."*[329] But by February 1942 separate detachments of Tartar volunteers, with a strength of 200 to 250 men, were sent to the front at Kerch, where they took part in battles against the Red Army. Subsequently, the German Command used these detachments at Sevastopol.[330] The recruitment campaign for self-defense companies continued during February-March 1942. As a result, by April 1942 their strength reached 4,000 men, with a ready reserve of 5,000 men.[331] Appearing in the *Reichstag* on May 24th 1942, Hitler announced in his speech

> *"That in units of the German Army there are also Tartar auxiliary units taking part in battle against the Bolsheviks, along with Lithuanians, Latvians, Estonians, and Ukrainian legions...Crimean Tartars always distinguish themselves with valor and a readiness to fight. But under the Bolshevik government they were prohibited from displaying these qualities...It it is fully understood, that they stand shoulder to shoulder with the soldiers of the German Army in the struggle against Bolshevism."*[332]

In August 1942 the Chief of Staff of the Army High Command (OKH) Colonel-General Franz Halder signed Order No. 8000/42 for *"The Disposition of Local Auxiliary Formations in the East,"* in which all volunteer formations were classified by category, according to their political reliability and military value. In this document, the respective Turkish peoples and Cossacks were divided into a separate category of *"equally vested allies, fighting shoulder to shoulder with German units against Bolshevism in the ranks of Special Combat Units,"* such as the Turkestani Battalions, the Cossack units, and the Crimean-Tartar formations.[333] The Tartars were very proud that such faith was bestowed upon them. In the words of an intelligence officer of the German 11th Army, *"they are*

---

[328] [43.]
[329] [44.]
[330] [45.]
[331] [46.]
[332] [47.]
[333] [48.]

proud to wear the German uniform."[334] In the first half of 1942, the German occupation authorities in the *Reichskomissariats* set about creating Schuma Battalions from local volunteers, which were recommended for use in anti-Partisan operations. In contrast to a self-defense company, whose area of operation was usually limited to the native region of the formation, *Schuma* battalions were designed to use on a wider front.

In July 1942, all Tartar self-defense companies in Crimea were formed into such battalions. As a result, toward November 1942 eight *Schuma* battalions were formed and quartered in the following population centers: In Simferopol were the 147th and 154th Battalions; In Karasubazar, the 148th Battalion; In Bakhchisarai the 149th Battalion; At Yalta the 150th Battalion; At Alushte the 151st Battalion; At Dzhankoe the 152nd Battalion; And at Feodosia the 153rd Battalion.[335] In an organizational and operational sense, all these units were subordinate to the Chief Director of the SS and Police of General Area "Tavrida," *SS-Brigadeführer* L. von Alvensleben.[336] Simultaneously, they were mostly on paper of the Wehrmacht's Crimean-Tartar Legion.[337] According to regulations, every battalion should have consisted of a headquarters company and four rifle companies of 124 men each. Each company was to consist of one machine gun and three infantry platoons. The nominal strength of a battalion was 501 men in theory, but in practice often fluctuated from 240 to 700 men.[338] As a rule, a local volunteer with former Red Army experience commanded the battalion, but in each of them there were 9 German cadre personnel - 1 communications officer, and 8 NCO's. The personnel element was armed with sub-machine guns, light and heavy machine guns, and mortars.[339]

On November 11th 1942 the Main Wehrmacht Command in Crimea announced an additional recruitment of Crimean Tartars into the ranks of the German Army "for use in Crimea." The Simferopol Muslim Committee fulfilled the functions of a recruiting office *(ulitsa Salgirnaya 14)*[340]. As a result, toward spring 1943 still another Schuma battalion was formed and several battalions and agricultural companies were in the formative stage.[341] Each battalion received standard infantry training, in accord with German regulations, but actually with a "policing orientation." Measures taken by the "Propaganda Section of Crimea," the main ideological agency on the Tavrida General Area territory, played a

---

334 [49.]
335 [50.]
336 Luedolf von Alvensleben was born on 17.03.1901. He was one of the leaders of the German penal agencies on USSR territory. Was an *SS-Gruppenführer* in 1944. In the 1920's he sided with the Nazi movement. From 4.05.1934 he was commander of the 46th SS Regiment (Dresden). Afterwards he commanded the 26th SS Regiment in Halle, then the 33rd SS Regiment in Schwerin-Mecklenburg. From November 1936 he was Chief Adjutant to *Reichsfuehrer-SS* Heinrich Himmler. From 1939 he was Chief of the SD and Security Police in Western Prussia. At the end of 1942—start of 1943, he was designated Senior Director of the SS and Police of Tavrida General Area, and stayed on in this capacity until April 1944.
337 [51.]
338 [52.]
339 [53.]
340 [54.]
341 [55.]

special role in the education of battalion personnel.[342] After taking an oath of allegiance to Hitler, and receiving a unit banner with the Tartar national coat-of-arms, each battalion was sent to an operational area designated to it.[343]

The main operating areas of the *Schuma* battalions in Crimea were: 148th Battalion in the Argin-Baksan-Barabanovka region; The 149th Battalion in the Kokoshi-Koush-Mangush region; The 151st Battalion in the Korbek-Ulu Uzen-Demerdzhi region. Here they carried out guard duty for military and civilian objectives, and together with units of the *Wehrmacht* and the German Police, took an active part in hunting for Partisans. Thus, according to reports of the German "Staff for Combat with Partisans," from 9 November to 27 December 1942, Battalions 148, 149, and 150 operated in the areas of Dzhankoe and Karasubazar, taking part in six important anti-Partisan actions. In these, eight Partisans were killed and five captured. The number of battalion losses is not mentioned in the reports, but probably were no fewer that those of the Partisans.[344]

In a number of instances, the German Command used these battalions for carrying out punitive expeditions and for guarding concentration camps. For example, on 4 February 1942, a group of Tartar volunteers from the village of Koush, headed by Yagai Smailom, jointly with a German punitive detachment, took part in the execution of citizens of the hamlet of Chair. In this incident, 15 people were brutally killed.[345] Starting in the spring of 1942, a concentration camp was erected on the territory of the Red Collective Farm, where the Germans tortured and shot no less than 8,000 Crimean inhabitants during the 2½-year occupation. According to eyewitnesses, the camp was securely enclosed by two rows of barbed wire and guarded by Tartar volunteers from the 152nd Schuma Battalion, whom the camp commander, *SS-Oberscharfuehrer* Schpeckman enlisted for completing *"the dirtiest work."*[346] Former Senior Red Army Lieutenant, V. Fayner, recalled: *"The taunting of the POWs...had no limits. The Tartar volunteers compelled an unknown POW to inform on him that he was a Jew. Afterward...they turned the unfortunate soul in, for which they received 100 German Marks."*[347]

Not surprisingly, similar behavior of the Tartar volunteers was observed. The leaders of the Crimean Partisans reported to the Ts.Sh.P.D. that: *"Members of the Partisan Movement in Crimea were living witnesses of the violence by the Tartar volunteers and their bosses, upon the captive sick and wounded Partisans (murder, cremation of the sick and wounded, etc.) In a number of cases, the Tartars were more merciless and professional than the fascist butchers."*[348] In creating the Tartar volunteer formations, the German political-military leadership was pursuing exclusively military goals, but also strove to use them and similar formations for propaganda purposes. But the leadership of the Tartar Muslim

[342] [56.]
[343] [57.]
[344] [59.]
[345] [60.]
[346] [61.]
[347] [62.]
[348] [63.]

Committees planned to use them differently: in order to receive greater political rights from the Germans, they hoped to make an original tool of these detachments for pressuring the people. Thus, in April 1942, a group of leaders from the Simferopol Muslim Committee worked out regulations and a Muslim Committee program, used for the following requests:

1. Establishment in Crimea of "Milli Firka" Party operations;
2. The creation of a Crimean-Tartar parliament;
3. Creation of a Tartar National Army;
4. The creation of an Independent Tartar State as a German protect-torate.[349]

This program was given to Hitler to review, but he did not approve of it. It was permitted only to increase the number of volunteers for the Wehrmacht and auxiliary police units, as a result of which the *Schuma* battalions were created. In May 1943, one of the senior Crimean-Tartar nationalists, A. Ozenbashly[350] wrote a memorandum to Hitler, in which he outlined the following program for cooperation between Germany and the Crimean Tartars:

1. Creation of a Tartar State under a German protectorate;
2. The creation of additional police units in a Tartar National Army,on the pattern of the *Schuma* battalions.
3. The return of all Tartars in Turkey, Bulgaria, and other states to Crimea; and the "cleansing" of Crimea of different nationalities.[351]
4. Arming the entire Tartar population, including the elderly, until the decisive victory over the Bolsheviks;
5. German Trusteeship over the Tartar State, until such time it could "stand on its own feet." [352]

The main similarity of this program with the previous one was the request for the creation of a "Tartar National Army." In the thoughts of Ozenbashly: *"just in case Germany turns out weakened by the war, with the help of a well-armed and trained army, it will be possible to demand independence from her."*[353] But the fulfillment of such demands was not in the plans of the Nazi regime; therefore, the Crimean Gestapo showed "greater prudence" and did not let the memorandum get out. Hitler learned nothing of it. Understanding the full strategic

[349] [64.]

[350] Ozenbashly, Amet, until 1928 he occupied a number of leadership posts in the Crimean Council of People's Commissars—Commissar of the People's Finance and Deputy People's Financial Commissar. Repressed by Veli Ibraimova. After serving his sentence, he worked as a doctor in Pavlodar. In the first half of 1943, he returned to Crimea, where he began a factional struggle with the Chairman of the Simferopol Muslim Committee, Abdureshidov. Ozenbashly's supporters on the Committee, (S. Ametov, A. Kurkchi, E. Kursi\eitov) invited the Germans to designate him Mufti of the Crimean Muslims.

[351] One may only suspect by which methods.—from the Russian editor.

[352] [65.]

[353] [66.]

importance of Crimea's position as a favorable launch-point for an attack on the Caucasus, the German Supreme Command had no desire to see some kind of 'national army' there alongside the *Wehrmacht* and the allied Rumanian Army. Therefore, all attempts by the leaders of the Crimean Tartar Nationalists Russian historians M.Y. Heller and A.M. Nekrich wrote:[354] "To use a situation of joint operations for their own ends" and create a *"Tartar National Army" were doomed to collapse in the course of the German occupation policy. "Everywhere the German occupiers firmly held authority in their hands and fiercely suppressed the minor attempts to find...national independence."*

After the German retreat from the Caucasus, and the blockade of its Crimean Group, demoralization set in and incidents of desertion to the Partisans began in the Crimean Tartar units. One of the most notable of these was the desertion of the 152nd *Schuma* Battalion, under the command of the previously named Major Raimova, who was nevertheless shot by the Partisans. An especially strong influx of Tartars to the Partisan detachments began in the autumn of 1943. By December, 406 men joined the Partisans, of whom 219 had previously served in the *Schuma* battalions or self-defense detachments.[355] Influenced by the mass agitation work of Partisans among the Tartar population and in the volunteer formations, pro-Soviet under ground organizations were created in many battalions in autumn/winter 1943. Thus, the CO of the 154th Battalion, A. Kerimov, was arrested by the Germans as "unreliable," and in the 147th Battalion seventy-six men were arrested and shot "as pro-Soviet elements."[356] By January 1944, the battalion's Chief of Staff, Kemalov, prepared to cross the unit over to the Red Army. The only obstacle which caused him to waiver was the thought expressed by him in a meeting with Partisan contacts: *"Even if...the whole detachment did this, it would make no difference after the occupation of Simferopol [by the Red Army—Russian translator] they would all be punished one by one."*[357]

As a result, according to German data, about 1/3rd of the *Schuma* battalions turned out to be unreliable and was disarmed by the Germans themselves, and their personnel thrown into concentration camps.[358] The real volunteers (in the opinion of the K.Sh.P.D.) who served in the remaining battalions were hitherto considered undesirable elements by the Soviet authorities." In April-May 1944 they fought against the Red Army that was liberating the Crimea. Thus, according to the recollections of I.I. Kupreev, Commissar of 5th Detachment of the 6th Eastern Brigade, volunteers from the Bakhchisarai Schuma battalion very earnestly fought for the city; after the liberation of Bakhchsarai many Tartars hid the surviving Germans in their homes.[359]

---

354 [67.]
355 [68.]
356 [69.]
357 [70.]
358 [71.]
359 [73.]

After the defeat of the German forces in May 1944, Hitler, raging over the loss of Crimea, ordered all units that had been evacuated from the peninsula disbanded, and that their personnel be mixed into new units. Therefore, by June 1944, the surviving Tartar Schuma battalions that were withdrawn from Crimea to Germany, were made into a three-battalion Mountain-Jaeger Regiment of the SS *(Tartaren-Gebirgsjaeger-Regiment der SS).* The Regiment underwent training on the drill field at Murlager, where on 8 July 1944, it was reformed as the Tartar-Mountain-Jaeger Brigade of the SS No.1 *[Waffen-Gebirgsjaeger-Brigade der SS (tartarische No.1)]* by an order of the Chief Operational Director of the SS. It was under the command of *SS-Standartenfuehrer* Willy Fortenbacher. Soon after this, the Brigade was deployed to Hungary, where it should have undergone further training, but also carried out garrison duties.[360]

In October 1944, the Chief Operational Director of the SS gave an order about the formation of "divisional type unit" from the remnants of the 1st Eastern Muslim Regiment of the SS, which participated in the August 1944 suppression of the Warsaw Uprising. This unit was to bear the name: "Eastern Turkish Unit of the Waffen-SS" *("Ostturkischer-Waffenverband der-SS")* and an organization consisting of battlegroups, or *Waffengruppe:* the *"Waffengruppe Turkestan"* (including volunteers from Central Asia and Kazakhstan,) *"Waffengruppe Idel-Ural,"* (including Volga-Tartar volunteers,) *"Waffengruppe Azerbaijan"* and lastly, *"Waffengruppe Krim."* The SS Mountain Brigade *"Krim"* whose unit was activated in August 1944 was disbanded on December 31st 1944. It consisted of the above-mentioned units in an SS mountain regiment/brigade headquarters. It also included an HQ, two infantry battalions, and two independent companies.[361] This disbanded SS Tartar Brigade was used as the basis for *SS Waffengruppe Krim.*

Besides this, the unit's HQ's had several officers who acted as points of contact with the SS Chief of Operations. One of them, with the rank of *SS-Untersturmfuehrer,* was a Crimean Tartar named Dairskiy.[362] A unit of Crimean-Tartar volunteers was deployed to France and included a reserve battalion of the Volga-Tartar Legion in its organization. The unit was stationed at Le Peaux. Here the battalion took part in battles against the French Partisans, the *"Marquis,"* and oppressed the peaceful population.[363] At the end of 1944, another 831 men from the rosters of the Crimean-Tartar units were directed to the ranks of the 35th SS Police Division in the capacity of *"Hiwi"* auxiliaries. They were distributed in this division in the following sub-units:

---

[360] [74.]
[361] [75.]
[362] Dairskiy was a Waffen-Untersturmfuehrer der-SS and a former Soviet POW. Until 1944 he had served in the 1st Eastern Muslim SS Regiment; he arrived in Berlin as a result of wounds, acted as Communications Officer with the Eastern Turkish unit of the SS and the Crimean Center, for the SS Chief Director. The Crimean Center was an agency of the Crimean Tartar émigrés created by the Minister of the Occupied Eastern Territories, Alfred Rosenberg.
[363] [77.]

1. 2nd Heavy Divisional Transportation Column: 125 men, two bureaucrats, and 3 officers under the command of Aslan Kugushova served in this unit.
2. The 7th Grenadier Company of *SS Polizei-Grenadier-Regiment 91:* 252 volunteers, a Muslim Chaplain, and seven officers under the command of *Waffen-Obersturmfuhrer der-SS* A.P. Shirinskiy[364] served in this unit.
3. 3rd Grenadier Company of *SS Polizei-Grenadier-Regiment 89*: 382 volunteers, one bearcat, four officers, under the command of *Sonderfuhrer* Mustafa Taiganskiy (he was the equivalent of a company commander).
4. Police Battle Group 147: Fifty-two volunteers, two officers, a translator and communications officer, under the command of *SS-Untersturmfuehrer* Mitte.
5. A unit of Tartar youths evacuated from the Crimea was also assigned to the Auxiliary Anti-Aircraft Artillery Service.[365]

After the conclusion of the Second World War, all of these volunteers were handed over to the USSR, by agreement with the Western Allies. One may say with confidence that in the years 1941-1945, 15,000 to 20,000 Crimean Tartars voluntarily joined to serve in the German *Wehrmacht,* out of a general population of 218,000 people, according to 1939 figures. This amounted to approximately 1/20th of the general total of Muslim volunteers from the USSR (about 400,000.) These figures support the veracity of German historians like M. Luther, I. Hoffmann, and Hans Werner Neulen.[366] For comparison, in 1941 there were 10,000 Tartars in the ranks of the Red Army; many of them deserted almost immediately when the war began. From 1941-44, 1,130 Tartars fought in Partisan detachments in the Crimea. The general strength of the Partisans in this period was around 11,000. Out of these, 96 died, 103 went missing in action, and 177 deserted; in underground Crimean organizations during the same period there were less than one hundred Tartars. In all, members of the Crimean underground numbered 2,500 people.[367] OKH Chief Colonel-General Franz Halder wrote in his daily journal for 8 August 1941, that *"from present experience...for every million people it is possible to form two divisions."*[368] If it is taken into account that on June 22nd 1941 the strength of a German infantry division was 15,859 men.[369] Then it follows that the German occupation authorities "trained" practically the entire able-bodied male population of the Crimean Tartars. For a long time, there was an opinion in patriotic historiography, expressed by M.I. Kalinin on August 4th 1943 at a meeting with agitators who were working among fighters of non-

---

[364] Shirinsky, Aleksandr Petrovich, born in 1922 in Feodosia.
[365] [79.]
[366] [80.]
[367] [81.]
[368] [82.]
[369] [83.]

Russian nationality. Speaking of the traitors of the People, he said: *"For a nation as great as the USSR, encountering such worthless exceptions is of no significance."*[370]

But the figures submitted above speak the opposite. When starting the war against the USSR, the military-political leadership of the Third Reich considered the destruction of the multi-national state as one of its first priorities, by attracting the respective non-Russian peoples and national minorities of our country to its side in the struggle against *"Bolshevism and Muscovite imperialism."* A special HQ was made for the numerous Muslim peoples of the USSR. *"One of the means used to attract these peoples to the German side was the creation of national Eastern Legions, in the capacity of cadres for the armies of future independent states"* as contemporary Russian historian S. I. Drobyazko considers.[371]

Moreover, Hitler was very skeptical to the creation of similar volunteer formations from the Slavic peoples, but nevertheless did not object to the suggestion of creating Muslim Legions: *"I consider the Muslims reliable...and see no danger in the creation of purely Muslim units"*—he stated at a conference in December 1942.[372] In the ranks of these Muslim volunteer units no certain type of lost soul was found; there were victims of circumstance, who had no chance to avoid serving the occupiers, or who dreamed of defecting to the Red Army at the first possible moment. But foremost, there were fierce nationalists. Émigré historian A.S. Kazantsev wrote in his time: *"In order to fulfill the plan of partition of Russia, battalions were raised from the various nationalities from among the POWs and volunteers. They were educated in a beastly hatred not only toward Bolshevism, but toward all Russians as well...artfully fanning ugly, malicious chauvanism."*[373]

In the background of such ideological training were the extremely absurd German propaganda and its yes-men from among the nationalists: *"In the battles against Bolshevism a great friendship of nations was born. And so, whoever strives to sow national discord...plays into the hands of the Bolsheviks and is our enemy."*[374] This "new weapon" of the Third Reich, in the form of Muslim volunteer formations actively announced itself not only at the front, but in the rear too, where these units, which hunted Partisans, carried out punitive missions against the peaceful population, and exterminated their countrymen and the citizens of different countries. Ashes and blood—are all that remained after the Muslim formations, just as in the Baltic States, the Ukraine, and the Caucasus. Nothing like Crimea has a similar place in the occupation period. Not surprisingly, a policy similar to the German one was carried out here with such expressions, and all the consequences emanating from them as: *"The Soviet Government granted greater privileges and gave greater indulgences, to the Tartar National Minority than to the Russians: the Tartars were less de-kulakized, less deported, less restricted in rights, and lo, the Tartars betray."*

---

370 [84.]
371 [85.]
372 [86.]
373 [87.]
374 [88.]

Footnotes:

1. Drobyazko S. I. "Vostochnye voyska" b vermakhte 1941-45// Nashi vesti.-1944.-No. 436. –S.15-17; No.437.-S. 8-10; Evo zhe. Sovetskie grazhdane v ryadakh vermakhta. K voprocu o chiclennosti// Velikaya Otechectvennaya voina v otsenke molodykh.-M., 1997.-C.127-134; Evo zhe. Vostochnye legiony i kazach'I chasti v vermakhte.-M., 1999; Kolesnik A.N. Grexopadenie? General Vlasov i ego okruzhenie.-Kharkov, 1991 i dr.
2. Pfeffer K.G. Nemtsi I drugie narodi vo vtoroy mirovoy voyne // Itogi vtoroy mirovoy voyny. Vyvody pobezhdennykh.-SPb.-M., 1999.-S.492.
3. Kozybaev M.K., Kumanev G.A. Bratskoye edinstvo narodov SSSR v gody Velikoy Otechestvennoy voyny// Narodniy podvig v bitve za Kavkaz. Sb. Statey.-M., 1981.-S.40
4. Gilyazov I. Pantyurkizm, panturanizm i Germaniya // Etnograficheskoye obozrenie.-1996.-No.2.-S.94.
5. Zaleskiy K.A. Vozhdi i voenachal'niki tret'ego reykha. Biograficheskiy entsiklopedicheskiy slovar'.-M., 2000.-S.381-382.
6. Shtrik-Shtrikfel'dt V.K. Protiv Stalina i Gitlera.-M., 1993.-S.82.
7. Entsiklopediya tret'ego reykha/Pod. red.A. Egazarova.-M., 1996.-S.19-21.
8. Niger T., Abbot P. Partisan Warfare 1941-1945.-London, 1983.-P. 14-15.
9. Golos Kryma (Simferopol').-1941.-No.1 (12.12.).-S.1.
10. Gosudarstvenniy arkhiv Avtonomnoy Respubliki Krym (dalee GAARK) (Simferopol'), f. P-151, op. 1, d.28, l. 40-41; d.505, l.3, 18ob., 19; f.P-156, op. 1, d.37, l.39.
11. GAARK, f. P-156, op. 1, d.391, l.88-89.
12. Manstein E. von. Uteryannie pobedi.-M.-SPb., 1999.-S.248.
13. GAARK, f. P-156, op.1, d.1, l.31; d.35, l.62.
14. GAARK, f. P-156, op. 1, d.35, l.62.
15. Tam zhe, l.60.
16. GAARK, f. P-151, op. 1, d.26, l.41; f.P-156, op. 1, d. 58, l. 41-42.
17. GAARK, f. P-151, op. 1, d.26, l.57.
18. GAARK, f. P-151, op. 1, d.26, l.40-41; f.P-156, op. 1, d. 37, l.112.
19. Dikson Ch. O., Geylbrunn O. Kommunisticheskie partizanskie deystviya.-M., 1957.-S. 172-174.
20. Manstein E. von. Ukaz. Soch.-S.262.
21. GAARK, f. P-156, op. 1, d.56, l.19-20.
22. GAARK, f. P-156, op.1, d. 41, l. 77.
23. GAARK, f. P-151, op. 1, d. 26, l. 57, 64.
24. Tam zhe, l. 57.
25. Krimsko-tatarskie formirovaniya: dokumenti tret'ego reykha svidetel'stuyut// Voenno-istoricheskiy zhurnal (dalee VIZh).-1991.-No.5-S.91.
26. Tam zhe.-S.91.
27. GAARK, f. P-156, op. 1, d.41, l. 4; Krimsko-tatarskie formirovaniya...-S.91.
28. GAARK, f. P-151, op. 1, d. 26, l. 57.
29. GAARK, f. P-156, op. 1, d.41, l. 4, 5, 5ob.
30. Krimsko-tatarskie formirovaniya...-S. 92, 93.
31. GAARK, f. F.P-156, op. 1, d. 41, l. 18; Krimsko-tatarskie formirovaniya...S. 91, 93.
32. "Idet beshenaya natsionalisticheskaya propaganda" // Istochnik.-1995. No.2.-S. 120-122.
33. Tam zhe.-S.122.
34. GAARK, f. P-151, op. 1, d.388, l. 17.
35. Tam zhe, l. 7.
36. GAARK, f. P-156, op. l, d. 26, l. 25.
37. GAARK, f. P-151, op. 1, d. 388, l. 7-8.
38. GAARK, f. P-151, op. 1, d. 388, l. 13-29; f. P-156, op. 1, d. 41, l. 43.
39. GAARK, f. P-151, op. 1, d. 388, l. 30.
40. GAARK, f. P-156, op. 1, d. 24, l. 31.

41. GAARK, f. P-156, op. 1, d. 38, l. 84ob.-85.
42. Krimsko-tatarskie formirovaniya...-S. 94.
43. GAARK, f. P-151, op. 1, d. 26, l. 58.
44. GAARK, f. P-151, op. 1, d. 35, l. 4.
45. GAARK, f. P-151, op. 1, d. 26, l. 64.
46. Hoffmann J. Die Ostlegionen 1941-43. Turkotataren, Kaukasier und Wolgafinnen im deutschen Heer.-Freiburg, 1976.-S.44.
47. Golos Krima (Simferopol').-1942.-No.42 (24.05.).-S.2.
48. Bundesarchiv-Militararchiv (Freiburg), Oberkommando des Heeres / Generalstab des Heeres, H 1/524.
49. Krimsko-tatarskie formirovaniya...-S.95.
50. Hoffmann J. Op. cit.-S. 47; GAARK, f. P-151, op. 1, d. 28. L. 38; d. 505, l. 49ob.
51. Drobyazko S. I. Vostochnie legioni...-S. 32.
52. Niger T., Abbot P. Op. cit.-S. 47.
53. Hoffmann J. Op. cit.-S. 47.
54. Okupatsiyniy rezhim v Krimu 1941-1944 pp. Za materialimi presi okupatsiynikh vlastey / Uporyadn. V.M. Gurkovich.-Simferopol'. 1996.-S. 53.
55. Drobyazko S.I. Vostochnie legioni...-S.32.
56. GAARK, f. P-156, op. 1, d. 26, l. 28.
57. GAARK, f. P-151, op. 1, d. 388, l. 22-23, 23-24.
58. Hoffmann J. Op. cit.-S. 47.
59. GAARK, f. P-151, op. 1, d. 391, l. 113ob.-115ob.
60. GAARK, f. P-151, op. 1, d. 26, l. 50; d. 392, l. 4.
61. GAARK, f. P-156, op. 1, d. 39, l. 104-104ob.; Krim v Velikoy Otechestvennoy voyne 1941-45 / Sost. V.K. Garagulya i dr.-Simferopol', 1994.-S.59.
62. GAARK, f. P-156, op. 1, d. 40, l. 135.
63. GAARK, f. P-151, op. 1, d. 41, l. 22.
64. Tam zhe, l. 15.
65. GAARK, f. P-652, op. 24, d. 16, l. 34.
66. GAARK, f. P-151, op. 1, d. 388, l. 31.
67. Geller M.Ya., Nekrich A.M. Istoriya Rossii 1917-1995.-M., 1996.-T.1.-S. 432.
68. Krim v Velikoy Otechestvennoy voyne...-S. 160.
69. GAARK, f. P-652, op. 24, d. 16, l. 37.
70. GAARK, f. P-151, op. 1, d. 505, l. 210-v.
71. GAARK, f. P-151, op. 1, d. 390, l. 26; d. 505, l. 2, 148ob., 151.
72. GAARK, f. P-156, op. 1, d. 388, l. 32ob.
73. GAARK, f. P-156, op. 1, d. 57, l. 31ob.-32.
74. Persoenliches Archiv des Werner Oschassek, Praesident der Union der Veteranen der 4. und 35. SS-Polizei-Grenadier-Division (Duesseldorf), mappe No.14 (35WSS) G (Heer Volunteers).-S. 14, 16; Klietmann K.G. Die Waffen-SS. Eine Dokumentation.-Osnabrueck, 1965.-S. 373f.
75. Persoenliches Archiv des Joachim Hoffmann, Wissenschatlicher Direktor a. D. am Militaergeschichtlichen Forschungsamt der Bundeswehr (Ebringen), The "Osttuerkische Waffenverband" of the SS // The Use by the Germans of Soviet Nationals against the Soviet Union in the Late War.-Intelligence Division, DRS.-(51) 29.-S. 1-17.
76. "Musul'manskaya plakha" dlya Rossii // VIZh. –1996.-No.5.-S. 29.
77. Kolesnik A.N. Ukaz. soch.-S. 187-188.
78. Persoenliches Archiv des Werner Oschassek..., mappe No.14. (35WSS) Q (35. SS-Polizei-Grenadier-Division).-S. 43-46.
79. Drobyazko S.I. Vostochnie legioni...-S. 33.
80. Luther M. Die Krim unter deutscher Besatzung im Zweiten Weltkrieg // Forschungen zur Osteuropaeschen Geschichte.-Berlin, 1956.-Bd.3.-S. 61; Hoffmann J. Op. cit.-S. 44; Neulen H. W. An deutschen Seite. Internationale Freiwillige von Wehrmacht und Waffen-SS.-Muenchen, 1985.-S. 342.
81. Krim v godi Belikoy Otechestvennoy voyni...-S. 161-162.
82. Gal'der F. Voenniy dnevnik. 1939-1942.-M., 1968-1971.-T.3. –Kn.1.-S.256.

83. Manstein E. von. Ukaz. soch.-S. 722.
84. Kalinin M.I. O sovetskoy armii. Sb. statey I rechey.-M., 1958.-S.89.
85. Drobyazko S.I. Vostochnie legioni…-S. 3.
86. Dallin A. German rule in Russia 1941-45: A Study of occupation policies.-London-New York, 1957.-P. 251.
87. Kazantsev A.S. Tret'ya sila. Rossiya mezhdu natsizmom i kommunizmom.-M., 1994.-S. 233.
88. GAARK, f. P-156, op. 1, d. 27, l. 70.
89. GAARK, f. P-156, op. 1, d. 31, l. 62.

LIST OF SOURCES AND LITERATURE

ARCHIVAL MATERIALS

I. Gosudarstvenniy arkhiv Avtonomnoy Respubliki Krim (Simferopol'):

1. F. P-1 (Dokumental'nie materiali Krimskogo obkoma KP Ukraini, 1936-1945.), op. 1, d. 2135, 2160, 2185, 2276, 2317
2. F. P-151 (Dokumenti Krimskogo shtaba partizanskogo dvizheniya), op. 1, d. 24, 26, 28, 30, 34-36, 312, 388-392, 505
3. F. P-156 (Dela Krimskoy komissii po istorii Belikoy Otechestvennoy voyni), op. 1, d. 1, 24-29, 31, 33, 35-41, 51, 56-58, 173-a
4. F. P-652 (Sovet Narodnikh Komissarov Krimskoy ASSR. 1921-1945.), op. 24, d. 9, 16, 17, 48
5. F. P-1289 (Krimskaya respublikanskaya komissiya po ustanovleniyu i rassledovaniyu zlodeyaniy nemetsko-fashistskikh zakhvatchikov i ikh soobshchnikov i prichinnego imi ushcherba grazhdanam, kolkhozam, obshchestbennim organizatsiyam, gosudarstvennim predpriyatiyam I uchrezhdeniyam), op. 1, d. 19, 24; op. 2, d. 70

II. Besitz des Militaergeschichtlichen Forschungsamtes (Potsdam):

6. Bericht ueber den Einsatz des Sonderverbandes "Bergmann" vom 1. Dezember 1942-15. Februar 1943.-16.02.1943
7. Besprechung ueber Unterbringung der neu aufzustellen den Tuerkvoelker-Legionen.-01.05.1942
8. Heygendorff R. v., Generalleutnant a. D. Tuerkvoelkische und Kaukasische Verbaende im Kampf an Deutschlands Seite im 2. Weltkrieg.-1949.-35s.
9. Nordkaukasische Freiwillige im 2. Weltkriege im Kampfe gegen die Sowjetunion auf Deutschlands Seite.-18s.
10. Oberlaender Th., Professor Dr. Dr. Geschichte der Einheit "Bergmann".-10s.
11. Spuler B., Professor Dr. Mullakurse.-4s.
12. Die Turkestaner.-12s.

III. Bundesarchiv-Militaerarchiv (Freiburg):

13. Kommandeur der Osttruppen z. b. V. 710, RH 58/73, RHD 7/8a/2
14. Kommandeur der 162. Infanteriedivision, RH 26-162/15, 34427/1-34427/8
15. Militaerbefehlshaber im Generalgouvernement / Wehrkreisbefehlshaber im Generalgouvernement, RH 53-23/v. 29, RH 53-23/v. 30, RH 53-23/44, RH 53-23/52, RH 53-23/58
16. Oberkommando des Heeres / Chef der Heeresruestung un Befehlshaber des Ersatzheeres, H 62-0/4-H 62-0/9

17. Oberkommando des Heeres / General der Freiwilligenverbaende, RH 2/1435, RH 2/2728
18. Oberkommando des Heeres / Generalstab des Heeres, H 1/136, H 1/143, H 1/524, H 1/1794, H 33/1
19. 444. Sicherungsdivision, 35770/1-35770/5

IV. Deutsche Dienststelle (WASt). Die Auskunftsstelle fuer Wehrmachtsnachweise (Berlin):

20. von Heygendorff, Ralph, geb. am 15.08.1897 in Dresden
21. von Pannwitz, Helmuth, geb. am 14.10.1898 in Botzanowitz

V. Persoenliches Archiv des Joachim Hoffmann (Ebringen):

22. Aserbeidschaner.-6s.
23. Behandlung der eintereffenden Turk-Bataillone, ihre Unterstellung, Ausbildung und Betreung.-Rz. AOK 1, Ic.-No. 8072/42 geh.-30.10.1942
24. Bericht ueber die Kaukasischen Freiwilligen-Verbaende in der Deutschen Wehrmacht.-26.03.1945 (Der Vorsitzende des Kaukasischen Kommitees Dr. Gabliani).-9s.
25. German Special Operations in the Caucasus. Operation "Schamil" // The Use by the Germans of Soviet Nationals against the Soviet Union in the Late War.-Intelligence Division, DRS.-(52)127.-10s.
26. Heygendorff, Ralph, v., Generalleutnant a. D. Erinnerungen an meine turkestanischen Waffenkameraden waehrend des 2. Weltkrieges
27. Koestring, Ernst, General der Kavallerie a. D. Stellungnahme zum Bericht Dr. Seraphim ueber Turkenheiten. 21.10.1948.-3s.
28. The "Osttuerkische Waffenverband" of the SS // The Use by the Germans of Soviet Nationals against the Soviet Union in the Late War.-Intelligence Division, DRS.-(51)29.-17s.
29. Wolgatatarische Legion.-6s.

VI. Persoenliches Archiv des Werner Oschassek (Duesseldorf):

30. Mappe No.14 (35WSS) G (Heer Volunteers)
31. Mappe No.14 (35WSS) Q (35. SS-Polizei-Grenadier-Division)

BIBLIOGRAPHY

32. Avtorkhanov A. Memuari. Glavni iz knigi // Oktyabr'-1992.-No.9-S.131-159.
33. Voenno-nauchnoe upravlenie Genshtaba. Voenno-istoricheskiy otdel. Sbornik materialov po sostavu, gruppirovke I peregruppirovke sukhoputnikh voysk fashistskoy Germanii i voysk bivshikh ee soyuznikov na sovetso-germanskom fronte za period 1941-1945.-Vip. II.-M., 1965.
34. Gal'der F. Voenniy dnevnik. 1939-1942.-M., 1968-1971.-T.1-3.
35. Dashichev V.I. Bankrotstvo strategii germanskogo fashizma. Dokumenti i materiali. Istoricheskie ocherki.-M., 1973.-T. 1-2.
36. Zakrutkin V.A. Kavkazskie zapiski // Zakrutkin V.A. Povesti i rasskazi.-M., 1989.-S 3-311.
37. Zaleskiy K.A. Vozhdi i voenachal'niki Tret'ego reykha. Biograficheskiy entsiklopedicheskiy slovar'.-M., 2000.
38. "Idet beshenaya natsionalisticheskaya propaganda" // Istochnik.-1995.-No.2.-S. 120-122.
39. Kaval'ero U. Zapiski o voyne.-M.,1968.

40. Kavkaz. 1942-43 godi: geroizm i predatel'stvo // VIZh.-1991.-No.8.-S. 35-43.
41. Kabardino-Balkariya v godi Velikoy Otechestvennoy voyni. Sb. dokumentov i materialov / Pod. red. M.K. Shekikhacheva.-Nal'chik, 1975.
42. Kazantsev A.S. Tret'ya sila. Rossiya mezhdu natsizmom i kommunizmom.-M., 1994.
43. Kalinin M.I. O sovetskoy armii. Sb. statey i rechey. M., 1958.
44. Krovavie zlodeyniya Oberlendera: otchet o press-konferentsii dlya sovetskikh i inostrannikh zhurnalistov, sostoyavsheysya v Moskve 5 aprelya 1960.-M., 1960.
45. Krimsko-tatarskie formirovaniya: dokumenti Tret'ego reykha svidetel'stvuyut // Voenno-istoricheskiy zhurnal (dalee-VIZh). 1991.-No.3.-S. 89-95.
46. Manstein E. von. Uteryannie pobedi.-M.-SPb., 1999.
47. "Musul'manskaya plakha" dlya Rossii // VIZh.-1996.-No.5.-S.24-31.
48. Nyurnbergskiy protsess nad glavnimi nemetskimi voennimi prestupnikami. Sb. materialov / Pod red. R.A. Rudenko.-M., 1965-1966.-T. 1-3.
49. Okupatsiyniy rezhim v Krimu 1941-1944 pp. Za materialami presi okupatsiynikh vlastey / Uporyadn. V.M. Gurkovich.-Simferopol', 1996.
50. Piker G. Zastol'nie razgovori Gitlera.-Smolensk, 1993.
51. Raushning G. Govorit Gitler. Zver iz bezdni.-M., 1993.
52. Sbornik deystvuyushchikh dogovorov, soglasheniy i konventsiy, zaklyuchennikh SSSR s inostrannimi gocudarstvami.-M., 1955.-Vip. IX (Deystvuyushchie dogovori, soglasheniya i konventsii).
53. Sovetskaya Istoricheskaya Entsiklopediya.-M., 1961-1965.-T.1.-S. 385-359; T.2.-S.637-641; T.7.-S. 994-995.
54. SS v deystvii. Dokumenti o prestupleniyakh SS / Pod. red. M.Yu. Raginskogo.-M., 1960.
55. Strani Tsentral'noy i Yugo-Vostochnoy Evropi vo vtoroy mirovoy voyne. Voenno-istoricheskiy spravochnik / Pod. red. M.I. Semiryagi.-M., 1972.
56. Sudaplatov P.A. Spetsoperatsii. Lubyanka i Kreml'. 1930-1950-e. gg.-M., 1997.
57. Turkestanskie legioneri // VIZh.-1995.-No.2. S. 39-46.
58. Shtrik-Shtrikfel'dt V.K. Protiv Stalina i Gitlera.-M., 1993.
59. Entsiklopediya tret'ego reykha / Pod. red. A. Egazarova.-M., 1996.
60. Beher H. Erinnerungen an den Sonderverband, drei Bataillone und an die Kameradenschaft Bergmann.-Krailling, 1985.
61. Braeutigam O. So hat sich zugetragen...Ein Leben als Soldat und Diplomat.-Wuerzburg, 1968.
62. Interview with an Afrikakorps Infantry Veteran.-London, January 23rd, 1999.
63. Klietmann K.G. Die Waffen-SS. Eine Dokumentation.-Osnabrueck, 1965.
64. Hitlers Weisungen fuer die Kriegsfuerung 1939-1945 / Hrsg. v. W. Hubatsch.-Frankfurt-am-Main, 1962.

PERIODICALS

65. "Azat K'rim" ("Svobodniy Krim").-1942-1944 (Simferopol').
66. "Byulleten' dobrovol'tsev Russkoy osvoboditel'noy armii".-1944 (Dabendorf).
67. "Gazavat. Ezhenedel'naya gazeta Severo-Kavkazskogo National-Osvoboditel'nogo Dvizheniya". 1944 (Berlin).
68. "Golos Krima".-1941-1944 (Simferopol').
69. "Krasniy Krim".-1941-1944 (Simferopol'-Krasnodar).
70. "Materiali dlya russkikh gazet. V pomoshch' redaktsiyam".-1943-1944 (Berlin).

71. Ofitserskiy byulletin' Russkoy osvoboditel'noy armii. Organ ofitserskogo korpusa Russkogo Osvoboditel'nogo Dvizheniya".-1943 (Dabendorf).
72. "Radiovestnik. Sbornik materialov peredach dlya radiouzlov".-1943-1944 (Berlin).
73. "Severniy Kavkaz. Organ Severo-Kavkazkogo Natsional'nogo Komiteta".-1944 (Berlin).

RESEARCH

74. Avetyan A.S. Krushenie kolonial'nikh planov germanskogo imperializma v godi vtoroy mirovoy voyni // Ezhegodnik Germanskoy istorii. 1976.-M., 1977.-S. 299-305.
75. Babakhodzhaev M.A. Missiya Nidermayera-Gentiga v Afganistan // Kratkie soobshcheniya Instituta vostokovedeniya AN SSSR.-1960.-Vip. XXXVII.-S. 18-26.
76. Bezimenskiy L.A. Razgadannie zagadki tret'ego reykha.-M., 1984.-T.2.
77. Belgradskaya operatsiya / Pod. red. D.A. Bolkogonova.-M., 1990.
78. Betell N. Poslednyaya tayna.-M., 1992.
79. Bivor E. Stalingrad.-Smolensk, 1999.
80. Brent'es B. Ispol'zobanie vostokobedov fashistskimi shpionskimi sluzhbami // Voprosi istorii.-1986.-No.2.-S. 171-173.
81. Bullok A. Gitler i Stalin. Zhizn' i vlast'.-Smolensk, 1998.-T.2.
82. Vert A. Rossiya v voyne 1941-1945.-M., 1967.
83. Voyni vtoroy polovini XX veka / Avt.-sost. F.N. Gordienko.-Minsk, 1998.
84. Geller M.Ya., Nekrich A.M. Istoriya Rossii 1917-1995.-M., 1996.-T.1.
85. Gertsshteyn R. Voyna, kotoruyu viigral Gitler.-Smolensk, 1996.
86. Gilyazov I. Pantyurkizm, panturanizm i Germaniya // Etnograficheskoe obozrenie.-1996.-No.2.-S.92-103.
87. Grechko A.A. Bitva za Kavkaz.-M., 1973.
88. Gunchak T. U mundirakh voroga // Viys'ko Ukraini.-1993.-No.9, -S.6-156.
89. Dikson Ch.O., Geyl'brun O. Kommunisticheskie partizanskie deystviya.-M., 1957.
90. Drambyan T.C. Oni srazhalic' za Frantsiyu.-Erevan, 1981.
91. Drobyazko S.I. "Vostochnie voyska" v vermakhte 1941-1945 // Nashi vesti.-1994.-No.436.-S.15-17; No.437.-S.8-10.
92. Drobyazko S.I. Sovetskie grazhdane b ryadakh vermakhta. K voprocu o chislennosti // Velikaya Otechestvennaya voyna v otsenke molodikh. Sb. statey studentov, aspirantov, molodikh uchenikh.-M., 1997.-S. 127-134.
93. Drobyasko S.I. Vtoraya mirovaya voyna 1939-1945. Vostochnie legioni i kazach'i chasti v vermakhte.-M., 1999.
94. Duda A., Starik V. Bukobins'kiy kurin'.-Chernivtsi, 1995.
95. Ibragimbeyli Kh.M. Krakh "Edel'veysa" i Blizhniy Vostok.-M., 1977.
96. Ibragimbeyli Kh.M. Krakh gitleroskogo okkupatsionnogo rezhima na Kavkaze // Narodniy podvig v bitve za Kavkaz. Sb. statey / Pod. red. G.A. Kumaneva i dr.-M., 1981.-S.265-285.
97. Istoriya Yugoslavii v 2-kh tomakh / Pod. red. L.B. Valeva i dr.-M., 1963.-T.1, 2.
98. Kolesnik A.N. Grekhopadenie? General Vlasov I ego okruzhenie.-Khar'kov, 1991.
99. Kontsel'man G. Yasir Arafat. Rostov-na-Donu, 1997.
100. Korkhmazyan R.S. Turetsko-germanskie otnosheniya v godi vtoroy mirovoy voyni.-Erevan, 1977.
101. Kukridzh E.Kh. Sekreti Stalina (glavi iz knigi)// VIZh.-1992.-No.1.-S.67-73.
102. Mader Yu. Imperializm: shpionazh v Evrope vchera i sevodnya.-M., 1985.

103. Maryanovich Y. Osvoboditel'naya voyna i narodnaya revolyutsiya v Yugoslavii.-M., 1956.
104. Masson V.M. Ramodin V.A. Istoriya Afganistana v 2-kh tomakh.-m., 1965.-T.2.
105. Miniaev V. Podrivnaya deyatel'nost' fashizma na Blizhnem Vostoke.-M., 1942.
106. Myuller N. Vermakht i okkupatsiya (1941-1944).-M., 1974.
107. Myuller-Gillebrand B. Sukhoputnaya Armiya Germanii. 1933-1945.-M., 1976.-T.3.
108. Neotvratimoe vozmezdie: po materialam sudebnikh protsessov nad izmennikam Rodini, fashistskimi palachami i agentami imperialisticheskikh razbedkov.-M., 1979.
109. Noveyshaya istoriya arabskikh stran Azii / Pod red. V.V. Naumkina.-M., 1988.
110. Pfeffer K.G. Nemtsi i drugie narodi vo vtoroy mirovoy voyne // Itogi vtoroy mirovoy voyne. Vivodi pobezhdennikh.-SPb.-M., 1999.-S. 492-515.
111. Pedfild P. Rudol'f Gess-spodvizhnik Gitlera.-Smolensk, 1998.
112. Raykov A.V. Indiyskoe "gosudarstvo" v Yugo-Vostochnoy Azii v godi vtoroy mirovoy voyne // Vostok.-1997.-No.2.-S. 51-62.
113. Romanov A. Allakh "chernorubashechnikov" // Nauka i religiya.-1964.-No5.-S.31-34.
114. Roman'ko O.V. Dobrovol'cheskie formirovaniya iz grazhdan SSSR v germanskoy armii na territorii Krima (1941-1944). Etapi sozdaniya i deyatel'nosti // Kul'tura naroda Prichernomor'ya.-1998.-No.5.-S.286-290.
115. Roman'ko O.V. "Musul'manskie formirovaniya"iz grazhdan SSSR v germanskoy armii (1941-1945) // Kul'tura narodov Prichernomor'ya.-1999.-No.6.-S. 203-210.
116.Roman'ko O.V. "Dobrovol'cheskie formirovaniya" iz balkanskikh musul'man v armiyakh gosudarstv "osi" (1939-1945) // Uchenie zapiski Tavricheskogo natsional'nogo universiteta.-1999.-No.51.-T.2.-S. 106-112.
117. Rumyantsev F.Ya. Taynaya voyna na Blizhnem i Srednem Vostoke.-M., 1972.
118. Slavin G.M. Osvoboditel'naya voyna na Yugoslavii (1941-1945).-M., 1965.
119. Stanoevich B. Ustashskiy ministr smerti. Anatomiya predatel'stva Andriya Artukovicha.-M., 1989.
120. Strugar V. Yugoslaviya v ogne voyni. 1941-1945.-M., 1985.
121. Tikhonov Yu. N. Kabul-42, ili kak bil sorvan pokhod Gitlera v Indiyu // VIZh.-2000.-No.1.-S. 24-30.
122. Tolstoy N.D. Zhertvi Yalti.-M., 1996.
123. Tupolev B.M. Germanskiy imperialism v bor'be za "mesto pod solntsem". Germanskaya ekspansiya na Blizhnem Vostoke, v Vostochnoy Afrike i v rayone Indiyskogo okeana v kontse XIX-nachale XX veka.-M., 1991.
124. Uest R. Iosip Broz Tito. Vlast' sili.-Smolensk, 1997.
125. Uil'yamson G. SS-instrument terrora.-Smolensk, 1999.
126. Shakibaev S. Padenie "Bol'shovo Turkestana".-Alma-Ata, 1970.
127. Shchevelev S.S. Palestina pod mandatom Velikobritanii (1920-1948 gg.).-Simferopol', 1999.
128. Caballero Jurado C., Lyles K. Foreign volunteers of the Wehrmacht. 1941-1945.-London, 1995.
129. Cooper M. The German Army, 1933-1945.-New York, 1978.
130. Dallin A. German rule in Russia 1941-1945: A Study of occupation policies.-London-New York, 1957.
131. Die SS: Hitlers instrument der Macht.-Hamburg, 1979.
132. Fricke G. Kroatien 1941-1945. Der "Unabhaengige Staat" in der Sicht des Deutschen Bevollmaechigen Generals in Agram, Glaise v. Horstenau.-Freiburg, 1972.
133. Hoffmann J. Deutsche und Kalmyken 1942 bis 1945.-Freiburg, 1974.
134. Hoffmann J. Die Ostlegionen 1941-1943. Turkotataren, Kaukasier und Wolgafinnen im deutschen Heer.-Freiburg, 1976.
135. Hoffmann J. Kaukasien 1942/43. Das deutsche Heer und die Orientvoelker der Sowjetunion.-Freiburg, 1991.
136. Houterman H. Eastern Troops in Zealand. The Netherlands, 1943-1945. Hitlers Osttruppen in the West.-Berlin, 1997.
137. Keiling W. Die Generale des Heeres.-Friedberg, 1983.

138. Kiszling R. Die Kroaten. Der Schicksalsweg eines Suedslawenvolkes.-Graz-Koeln, 1956.
139. Kumm O. Prinz Eugen, The History of the 7 SS Mountain Division "Prinz Eugen".-London, 1995.
140. Lepre G. Himmler's Bosnian Division. The Waffen-SS Handschar Division 1943-1945.-London, 1997.
141. Littlejohn D. Foreign Legions of the Third Reich (in four volumes).-San Jose, CA, 1979-1981.-Vol. 3-4.
142. Littlejohn D. The German struggle against Tito's Partisan // Military illustrated. 1993.-No.67.-P. 34-38, 40.
143. Luther M. Die Krim unter deutscher Besatzung im Zweiten Weltkrieg // Forschungen zur Osteuropaeischen Geschichte.-Berlin, 1956.-Band.3.-S.50-62.
144. Munoz A. For Croatia and Christ: The Croation Army in World War II, 1941-1945.-New York, 1996.
145. Munoz A. Lions of the Desert: Arab Volunteers in the German Army 1941-1945.-New York, 1997.
146. Muehlen P., von zur. Zwischen Hakenkreuz und Sowjetstern. Der Nationalismus der sowjetischen Orientvoelker im Zweiten Weltkrieg.-Duesseldorf, 1971.
147. Neulen H.W. An deutschen Seite. Internationale Freiwillige von Wehrmacht und Waffen-SS.-Muenchen, 1985.
148. Niger T., Abbot P. Partisan Warfare 1941-1945.-London, 1983.
149. Schnabel R. Tiger und Schakal. Deutsche Indienpolitik. 1941-1943.-Wien, 1968.
150. Seidler F.W. Oskar Ritter von Niedermayer im Zweiten Weltkrieg. Ein Bietrag zur Geschichte der Ostlegionen // Wehrwissenschaftliche Rundschau.-1970.-H.3.-S. 168-174.
151. Seidler F.W. Zur Fuehrung der Osttruppen in der deutschen Wehrmacht im Zweiten Weltkrieg // Wehrwissenschaftliche Rundschau.-1970.-H.12.-S. 683-702.
152. Tillman H. Deutschlands Araberpolitik im Zweiten Weltkrieg.-Berlin, 1965.
153. Windrow M. The Waffen-SS.-London, 1983.

Part - II

The East Came West: Hindu & Muslim IndianVolunteers In the Italian & German Army, and Waffen-SS, 1942-1945

By Dr. Martin J. Bamber
And
Antonio J. Munoz

CHAPTER 5
The *Battaglione Azad Hindostan* of the Royal Italian Army and the *Legion Freies Indien* of the German Army and Waffen SS, 1942-1945

Martin J. Bamber

Agitation for the end of British rule in India had existed for decades prior to the outbreak of the Second World War. Therefore it was logical for the Axis powers to attempt to capitalise on anti-British sentiments by attempting to recruit a military force from disaffected Indian prisoners-of war captured while serving with the British Empire forces in the North African campaign. The Italians were not the first in this field, but their efforts were comparatively shortlived and therefore will be considered first. In March 1942 a small group of Indian ex-POWs was gathered together by the Italian Army then in July 1942 the *"Raggruppamento Centri Militari"* was established. This was a special unit composed of foreign military personnel, ex-prisoners-of-war, foreign nationals living in Italy and Italians who had been resident abroad, with the intention of using them for intelligence gathering and sabotage operations behind enemy lines.[375]

Order of Battle: *Raggruppamento Centri Militari* - May 1942 [2]

Comando (Headquarters)
CO: *Tenente-Colonello di Stato* (Staff Lieutenant-Colonel) Massimo Invrea

1. Centro T: Italians from Tunisia
2. Centro A: Italians from Egypt, Palastine, Syria and Arabia; plus Arabs and Sudanese ex-prisoners-of-war
3. Centro I: Italians from India and Persia (Iran) and Indian ex-prisoners-of-war

In all the *Ragruppamento Centri Militari* collected together approximately 1,200 Italians, 400 Indians and 200 Arabs. In August 1942 the *Raggruppamento* was renamed as the *Raggruppamento Frecce Rosse* (Red Arrows Group) a name chosen by the commanding officer in memory of his service with the Italian Divisione *Frecce Nere* (Black Arrows Division) of the Italian *Corpo Truppo*

---

375 [1]

ABOVE: A German instructor inspects Indian soldiers. *Jean Luis Roba Collection.*

Volontari in the Spanish Civil War. The three *Centri Militari* received new desigations at the same time.[376]

Order of Battle: Raggruppamento Frecce Rosse - Late October 1942

Comando (Headquarters)

1. *Battaglione d'Assalto Tunisia* (Tunisia Assault Battalion) Ex-Centro T
2. *Gruppo Italo-Arabo* (Italo-Arab Group) Ex-Centro A
3. *Battaglione Azad Hindostan* (Free Indian Battalion) Ex-Centro I

The *Battaglione Azad Hindostan* was created out of *Centro I* using both the ex-Indian Army personnel (The Indian Army was under British operational command) and Italians previously resident in India and Persia (Iran). The units of the *Raggruppamento Frecce Rosse* were intended for operations behind enemy lines and were to be infiltrated by various means including insertion on the ground, via submarine and by parachute. This last means of transport leading to the establishment of a *Plotone Paracadutisti* (Parachute Platoon) within the *Battaglione Azad Hindostan,* its members receiving their parachute training at the Italian Army Parachute School at Tarquinia.[377] The soldiers of the *Battaglione Azad Hindostan* were attired in standard Italian military uniform with the addition of a turban. Their Italian *sahariana* tunics were worn with collar patches with three vertical stripes in the saffron (orange), white and green colors of the Indian National Congress (the main focus of Indian opposition to British rule) the saffron

[376] [3]
[377] [4]

stripe being closest to the wearer's neck. Stars on their collar patches distinguished Italians serving in the *Battaglione Azad Hindostan* while Indian troops had none. Those members of the battalion sent to Tarquinia for parachute training wore their own collar patces above paratroop pattern patches (again with and without stars for Italians and Indians respectively), as well as the paratroop badge depicting an open yellow parachute embroidered in rayon thread on the left upper arm.[378]

Nominal Order of Battle:
Battaglione Azad Hindostan - Late October 1942

1. *Compagnie Fucilieri* [Rifle Company] (Indians) - Motorised
2. *Compagnie Mitraglieri* [Machine-Gun Company] (Indians)- Motorised
3. *Plotone Paracadutisti* [Parachute Platoon] (Indians)
    a. CO: Tenente (1st Lieutenant) Danilo Pastorboni
4. *Overseas Italian Platoon*

However, despite their investment in the Indian's training the Italians considered the Indian troops of Battaglione Azad Hindostan to be of doubtful loyalty and this view was confirmed when the Indians mutinied on learning of the Axis defeat at El Alamein in November 1942. Following this the battalion was disbanded and the Indians returned to their prisoner-of-war camps.[379] Thus ended the disappointing Italian efforts to recruit Indians for service in the Axis armed forces. But their German partners, who began to recruit Indians earlier, do not appear to have been discouraged by the negative Italian experience as they perceived that they possessed a "trump card" not available to their Mediterranean allies.

"Netaji" ("Leader") Subhas Chandra Bose was a lawyer from Calcutta and an ex-president of the Indian National Congress who was a major rival to Mahatma Gandhi for the popular leadership of the movement to end British rule in India. Unlike Gandhi however, Bose was a not averse to the use of violence in the achievement of Indian independence. Using the old adage that "my enemy's enemy is my friend", Bose saw war between Britain and Germany as an opportunity to advance the cause of India's independence from the British Empire.

Thus on 17th January 1941, despite British surveillance, Bose escaped from his house in Calcutta and rapidly made his way across the breadth of India to Peshawar on India's North-West Frontier There, supporters of the Aga Khan helped him across the border into Afghanistan where he travelled on to Kabul. Here he was able to make contact with the Italian Embassy and the Italian government subsequently arranged for Bose's onward passage to Afghanistan's northern border with the Soviet Union. Using an assumed name, Bose crossed into the Soviet Union with the aide of a diplomatic passport provided by the Italians. Once in Russia the NKVD transported Bose to Moscow where he hoped

378 [5]
379 [6]

BELOW: Ceremony at the Hotel Kaiserhof, in Berlin to celebrate 'Indian Independence Day' – 26 January 1943. In the extreme right hand side of the photo is Colonel Kurt Krappe. *Jean Luis Roba Collection.*

that Russia's traditional enmity to British rule in India would result in support for his plans for a popular rising in India. However, Bose found the Soviets' response disappointing and was rapidly passed over to the German Ambassador in Moscow, Count von der Schulenberg. He had Bose flown on to Berlin in a special courier aircraft at the beginning of April where he hoped to receive a more favourable hearing from von Rippentrop and the German Foreign Ministry officials at the Wilhelmstrasse.[380]

Almost immediately Bose commenced broadcasting for the Germans for *"Azad Hind Radio"* ("Free India Radio"), transmitted from Nauen and later attempted to use the good favour he had established with Hitler to have himself named as leader of an Indian "Government-in-exile."[381] But Bose remained intent

380 [7]

381 [8]

on more direct opposition to the British than merely radio propaganda. He was handed an opportunity almost immediately when in April 1941 most of the members of the British 3rd (Indian) Motorised Brigade were taken prisoner by *Generalleutnant* Rommel's Deutsche Afrika Korps at El Mekili in Cyreniaca (Libya). On 15th May a *Luftwaffe* Major was sent to interview English-speaking members of the prisoners with a view to recruiting men for a proposed German Army (Heer) unit of Indian troops.[382]

This initial approach led to a 27 officers being flown to Berlin four days later, together with the establishment of a special camp for about 10,000 Indian POWs at Annaburg.[383] There, the Indian prisoners were visited by Bose and exposed to intensive propaganda with a view to their enlistment into the proposed unit, variously referred to as the *Legion Freies Indien* (Free Indian Legion), *Azad Hind* (Free India) Legion or the more exotically sounding: "Tiger Legion."[384] The first group of volunteers recruited both from ex-prisoners-of-war and also from Indian civilians resident in Germany, left Berlin's Anhalter railway station on Christmas Day 1941 for a camp at Frankenburg near Chemnitz in order to receive future groups of released Indian POWs.[385] Despite the recruitment of only eight resolute volunteers at this stage, in January 1942 the German Propaganda Ministry felt able to announce the establishment of the, in the circumstances, rather grandly titled "Indian National Army" or *"Azad Hind Fauj."*[386]

Subsequently 6,000 of the Indian prisoners who were considered most receptive to Bose's ideas were transferred to the camp at Frankenburg[387] where German officers and NCO's initiated military training.[388] Officially a cover story was maintained that the Indians were merely to be used as a labour unit and to lend credence to this, the unit was designated Arbeitskommando (Work detachment) Frankenburg. Of the 6,000 men at Frankenburg, 300 volunteers were transferred yet again to Königsbrück near Dresden in Saxony.[389] It was there that German Army uniforms were issued with the addition of a specially designed national arm badge in the shape of the shield. It was worn in German Army style on the right upper arm, with three horizontal stripes in the saffron, white and green Indian national colors. The Italians for the collar patches of the Battaglione Azad Hindoustan used this previously. It featured a leaping tiger superimposed over the white band of the tricolour and with the *legend "FREIES INDIEN"* ("FREE INDIA") in black characters on an integral white background above the tricolour. A saffron, white and green transfer may also have been used on the left side of their German steel helmets. Uniforms were of the usual army feldgrau (field grey) in winter and German or Italian tropical khaki in the summer.[390] Those Sikhs in the Legion were permitted to wear a turban (of a colour

---

382 [9]
383 [10]
384 [11]
385 [12]
386 [13]
387 [14]
388 [15]
389 [16]
390 [17]

appropriate to their uniform) as dictated by their religion instead of the usual peaked field cap *(einheitsfeldmütze).*[391]

These men now constituted the "Legion Freies Indien" of the German Army and took their oath of allegiance in a ceremony on 26th August 1942. The ranks of the new Legion were swelled by hundreds of new members some of whose participation was far from voluntary until by mid-1943 it boasted approximately 2,000 members and was also referred to as *Indisches Infanterie Regiment 950.*[392]

ABOVE: An Indian volunteer undergoing "kit" inspection in France during the summer of 1944. *Schintone-Sigro Collection.*

391 [18]

392 [19]

The *Legion Freies Indien / Indisches Infanterie Regiment 950* underwent a number of internal reorganisations as it grew in strength and developed. Ultimately it was organised as a standard German army infantry regiment of three battalions each of four companies.[393] Initially all the commisioned officers of I.R. 950 (ind) were German, but after a brief course some senior NCO's were commissioned in October 1943.[394] The unit was only partially motorised, being equipped with 81 motor vehicles and 700 horses[395] and was later sometimes even referred to as *Panzergrenadier Regiment 950 (indische)* presumably to reflect its semi-motorised status.[396] Unlike British practice in the Indian Army, the constituent units of the Legion were all of mixed religion and regional nationality so that Moslems, Hindus, Sikhs, Jats, Rajputs, Marathas and Garhwalis all served side-by-side.[397] Approximately two-thirds of the Legion's members were Moslem and one-third Hindu.[398]

Final Order of Battle:
(ind) Infanterie-Regiment 950 / Freies Indien Legion 1944-45 [399]

Legionskommandeur: Oberstleutnant (later *Oberst*) Kurt Krappe

1. Ausbildungs und Betreutungsstab (Training & Maintenance Staff) formed 27/4/43 then renamed on 7/7/43 as:- Regiments-Stab (ind.) Infanterie Regiment 950
2. Bataillon: 4 x Infanterie Kompanien (Nr. 1 - 4)
3. Bataillon: 4 x Infanterie Kompanien (Nr. 5 - 8)
4. Bataillon: 4 x Infanterie Kompanien (Nr. 9 - 12)
5. Infanteriegeschütz Kompanie (Nr.13) (Infantry-Gun Company) (6 x 7.5cm leichtes Infanteriegeschütz 18)
6. Panzerjäger Kompanie (Nr.14) (Anti-tank Company) (6 x Panzerabwehrkanone)
7. Pionier Kompanie (Nr.15) (Engineer Company)
8. Sonderkompanie (lit. "Special" but actually a Penal Company)
9. Hospital / Convalescent Home

In late 1943 Indians of the Moslem faith were also considered for recuitment into the *13. SS-Freiwilligen-Gebirgs-Division [Kroatiien],* or 13th SS Volunteer Bosnian-Herzegovinian Mountain Division (Croatia). This SS unit would later be known as the "Handschar" Division, which was then in the process of organizing mostly from Bosnians of the Moslem faith. Himmler was very enthusiastic about the formation of a Moslem SS division. However *SS-Obergruppenführer* Gottlob Berger, *Chef der SS Hauptamt* (Head of the SS Head

[393] [20]
[394] [21]
[395] [22]
[396] [23]
[397] [24]
[398] [25]
[399] [26]

Office) pointed out to Himmler in November 1943 that the Indian Moslems *"perceive themselves primarily as Indians, the Bosnians as Europeans"* and the idea was dropped.[400]

Officially the language of command was Hindustani, but since many of the members of the Legion came from regions of India were Hindustani was not widely spoken this was not always practical. In addition the German's almost total

ABOVE: Two friends, volunteers of the 950th Infantry Regiment, pose for a photograph somewhere in France in 1944. *Schintone-Sigro Collection.*

inability to provide personnel who could speak any of the languages of the Indian subcontinent bedeviled their relationship with the Indian troops throughout its existence and resulted in the Germans frequently using English for their communications with the Indians. English (together with some broken German learnt over the years) was also often used between Indians of different linguistic backgrounds within the Legion.[401] In this connection it is interesting to note that

---

[400] [27]
[401] [28]

one of the interpreters employed by the Germans was *Sonderführer* Frank Chetwynd Becker, an Englishman born in England to an English mother and a British-naturalised but German-born father who was posted to the Indian Legion in July 1942.[402] Difficulty with communication and German insensitivity in dealing with people of whose culture and customs they were largely ignorant led to the Legion suffering from poor discipline. Throughout its existence this low morale led to the shooting by his own men of one of the Indian Legion's most enthusiastic members, *Unteroffizier* Mohammed Ibrahim.[403]

The Indian Legion was presented with a regimental colour, most probably in the autumn of 1942 at the completion of the Legion's military training at Königsbrück during the oath taking ceremony. The flag was roughly rectangular in shape being slightly taller than it was long and with the same design on obverse and reverse. In a similar manner to the arm badges worn on the Legion's uniforms it featured a tricolor in the Indian national colors. These were saffron, white and green arranged in horizontal bands with the colors in the stated order from top to bottom but on the flag the white middle band was approximately three times the width of the two colored bands. The words *"AZAD"* and *"HIND"* were superimposed in white over the saffron and green bands respectively and a full color-leaping tiger was superimposed diagonally over the white band. The ultimate fate of the legionary colour is not known.[404] Bose also instituted an *"Azad Hind"* (Free India) decoration in 1942 in four grades, each of which could be awarded with or without swords in the German fashion. Both Indian and German members of the Legion were eligible to receive the decoration. Almost half of the Indian Legion's members received one or more of these awards.[405]

A. Order of *"Azad Hind"*[406]
B. Grand Star: *"Sher-e-Hind"* (Tiger of India)
C. 1st Class Star: *"Sardar-e-Jang"* (Leader of Battle)
D. 2nd Class Star: *"Vir-e-Hind"* (Hero of India)
E. Medal: *"Shahid-e-Bharat"* (Martyr of the Fatherland)

The *Abwehr* (*Wehrmacht* Military Intelligence) had envisaged this new Indian Nationalist military force as accompanying a future Axis campaign via the Caucasus through Iran into India to link-up with the Japanese Army advancing from the East through Burma thus bringing an end to British rule in India. As early as the end of August 1941 they had formulated an ambitious scheme to fly the Indian Legion to India and using parachute landings by them to start an anti-British revolt and this plan was shown to Bose. To this end some Indian POWs were recruited by *Rittmeister* Harbich of the Abwehr and incorporated as a part of *4.Regiment/800.Bau-Lehrdivision zur besonderen Verwendung Brandenburg* (Special Purpose Construction Training Division Brandenburg), which despite its

402 [29]
403 [30]
404 [31]
405 [32]
406 [33]

BELOW: Indian soldiers prior to an exercise, somewhere in France, 1944. They are seen here with weapons and full marching pack. *Schintone-Sigro Collection.*

innocuous sounding title constituted the "commando" (special forces) of the *Wehrmacht*. They were quartered at a training camp near Meseritz.

Axis defeats at Stalingrad and El Alamein at the end of 1942 made an attack into India appear an increasingly unlikely scenario. However, in the Far East the Japanese Army in Burma stood at the gates of India. Through their ambassador in Berlin, General Oshima, Bose was proposed as leader of a Japanese sponsored Indian Government-in-exile. On 9th February 1943 Bose, his adjutant Dr. Abid Hassan and two officers of the Indian Legion left Kiel on the long-range (Type IX D1) submarine, U-180. This submarine was under the command of *Fregattenkapitän* Musenberg.[407] The sub also also carried blueprints of jet engines and various other German secret projects to help the Japanese war effort. They transferred in rough seas to the Japanese submarine I-29 at a rendezvous near Madagascar[408] and arrived at Sabang harbor on We Island off the northernmost tip of Japanese occupied Sumatra on 6th May 1943.[409]

Subsequently Bose traveled via Singapore to Tokyo for talks with the Japanese Government. In the wake of these successful negotiations he moved into to his Japanese-provided residence in Singapore where his aides had assembled other like-minded Indians to form the "Provisional Government of Free India."[410] Ultimately Bose came to lead a much larger Japanese sponsored "Indian National Army" (eventually of almost three divisions) which fought alongside the Japanese

[407] [34]
[408] [35]
[409] [36]
[410] [37]

against the British (including British-Indian troops) 14th Army in Burma and in the extreme northeast of India.

Following Bose's departure for Singapore, discussions between the German Foreign Ministry and the Abwehr resulted in a plan to transfer the leadership of the Legion Fries Indien to the Far East. Department II of the Abwehr organised the operation in conjunction with the operations staff of the *Division Brandenburg* and the *Oberkommando der Marine* (German Naval High Command). The plan called for the use of four blockade-runners to take the officer corps and best men of the Indian Legion to Singapore.[411]

Given the war situation and allied domination of the Atlantic and Indian oceans the proposed operation was extremely audacious and called for careful planning. One blockade-runner was converted to resemble a iron ore carrier from neutral Sweden. Named the Brand III, it was manned by Brandenburgers with knowledge of Swedish and some Indians with experience as seamen. The majority of the Indians were however, concealed in specially consructed space at the bottom of the hold which was covered over with Iron ore so that inspection from above would give the impression of a normal hold full of ore. Brand III then proceded from Germany to Malmö in Sweden where it refueled, in the knowledge that British agents there would report its departure to London. The "neutral" vessel was allowed to make passage through the English Channel but was stopped in Gibraltar where its cargo manifest was examined but its cover story held well. A German agent in Capetown, South Africa had sent the order for the iron ore, which was ostensibly for a real iron foundry in South Africa to Sweden so that verification checks by the British authorities showed everything to be in order. Brand III carried on through the Suez Canal into the Indian Ocean and survived another inspection, this time by U.S. warships in the Bay of Bengal. Finally just west of the sunda strait the Brand III rendezvoused with a Japanese cruiser, which escorted it to Singapore.[412]

A second blockade-runner was less lucky; It elected to take the long sea route around the Cape of Good Hope but was intercepted at dusk by British warships just west of the Cape. In the fading light the captain decided to make a run for it and while making smoke headed off at top speed into the gathering darkness. In order to avoid the inevitable search the blockade-runner was forced to aim into the far southern latitudes and was not heard of again.[413] Back in Europe, the Legion Freies Indien was transferred to The Netherlands in April/May 1943, remaining there as part of the German *"Atlantikwall"* garrison until September of the same year.[414]

Legionskommandeur Oberstleutnant Kurt Krappe arrived in the Netherlands on 13th April 1943 in order to prepare for the transfer of the Indian Legion from Königsbrück. I./I.R. 950 (ind.) arrived at Truppenübungsplatz (Military Training Ground) Beverloo in Belgium on 30th April and was followed by II./I.R. 950 (ind.) on 1st-3rd May, III./I.R. 950 (ind.) left Germany somewhat

---

411 [38]
412 [39]
413 [40]
414 [41]

later and arrived at Truppenübungsplatz Oldebroek on the night of 13th-14th July but without its 12th Infantry Co. which was left behind in Germany as a replacement unit. On 5th May the 1st and 2nd Battalions were inspected at Beverloo by *General der Infanterie* Hans Reinhardt, *Kommandierender General der LXXXVIII. Armeekorps und Befehlshaber der Truppen des Heeres in den Niederlanden* (General Officer Commanding 88th Army Corps and Commander of the Army Troops in the Netherlands).

He later observed to the Wehrmachtsbefehlshaber in den Niederlanden (Higher Military Commander in the Netherlands) that the Indian troops should not be stationed in the Netherlands beyond the end of October as he thought that the cold climate on the North Sea coast would be detrimental to their health. Indeed on 17th September 1943 *Regiments-Stab (ind.) I.R. 950* left Haarlem and re-deployed to St. André de Cubzac in southwest France.[415] I./I.R. 950 (ind.) was assigned to the coastal sector near Zandvoort with an advance party arriving on 6th May and the main body on 17th, 19th & 21st May. Two companies were

ABOVE: Königsbrück, September 1942. This photograph was taken during the presentation of the new Standard to the Indian Legion. From left to right Adjutant (then Lieutenant) Adalbert Seifriz; unkbown German officer; "Netaji" Subhas Chandra Bose; the Commander of the 950th Infantry Regiment, Major (later, Colonel) Kurt Krappe; Back to camera- unknown. *P. Krappe Collection..*

stationed on the seaward front, two companies on the landward front, and one in Zandvoort as *Unterabschnittreserve* (subsector reserve).

[415] [42]

General der Infanterie Reinhard, *Reichsminister* Dr. Artur Seyss-Inquart (*Reichskommissar* in the Netherlands), envoy Otto Bene and *Oberst* Otto von Lachemair (CO *16. Luftwaffen Feld-Division*) inspected I./I.R. 950 (ind.) on 15th June. On 24th August I./I.R. 950 (ind.) was ordered relieved by *Georgien Infanterie Bataillon 822* and their last troop transport left on 31st August for their new base on the Atlantic coast of France west of Bordeaux on the Bay of Biscay.[416] Advance parties from II./I.R. 950 (ind.) arrived in Den Helder from Beverloo on 21st May and where ordered to the northern part of the Frisian Island of Texel (*6. Kompanie* at De koog, *7. Kompanie* at De Cocksdorp and *8. Kompanie* at Slufter). Following movement orders on 9th September, II./I.R. 950 (ind.) was relieved by Nordkaukasien Infanterie Bataillon 803 on 16th September. On 17th September 1943 II./I.R. 950 (ind.) passed through Den Helder en route to Les Sables d'Ollonne in France.[417]

III./I.R. 950 (ind.) remained at *Truppen-Übungs-Platz* Oldebroek as Corps Reserve. Its officers were visited by *General der Infanterie* Reinhard and *Generalfeld-marschall* von Rundstedt on 14th July, with *General der Infanterie* Reinhard and his Chief-of-Staff, *Generalleutnant* Erich Höcker (CO 719. I.D.). *Oberstleutnant* Kurt Krappe returned on 19th July to inspect the troops. III./I.R. 950 (ind.) left *Truppen-Übungs-Platz* (Troop Training Grounds) Oldebroek for France on 9th September 1943.[418]

The *Legion Freies Indien* was deployed in France on coastal defense duties in the area of Lacanau near Bordeaux. It was here that they were inspected by *Generalfeldmarschall* Rommel (who was, of course, responsible for their original capture!) in April 1944.[419] On 8th August 1944 the Free Indian Legion, now comprising about 2,300 men, like all the national legions of the German Army, was transferred to the control of the Waffen-SS. It was now being referred to as the *Indische Freiwillige Legion der Waffen-SS* and nominally received a new commanding officer: *SS-Oberführer* Heinz Bertling.[420] After a short period the Indian Legion continued under the command of *Oberst* Krappe. Despite the change in authority from Army to Waffen-SS, the Indian Legion continued to use Army ranks and uniforms until shortly before tha end of the war in Europe. The notorious SS map of February 1945 does show an SS collar patch featuring a tiger's head for the Free Indian Legion and their is some (albeit indistinct) photographic evidence of it having been worn in April 1945.

The Legion remained at Lacanau until over two months after the Allied Invasion of Normandy. However, following the allied breakout from the Normandy bridgehead and with the growing threat of allied landings on the Mediterranean coast of France, the Indian Legion was at risk of being cut off. On 15th August 1944 the same day that the feared Allied landings actually took place on the French Riviera the Legion left Lacanau to move back to Germany. The first part of their journey was by rail to Poitiers where they were attacked by

---

416 [43]
417 [44]
418 [45]
419 [46]
420 [47]

French FFI *(Forces Françaises de l'Interieur) "Maquis"* forces and a number of men were wounded. The French Resistance continued to harass the Legion when at the end of August it moved again to Allier via Chatrou, this time moving by road. The town of Dun on the Berry Canal was reached by the beginning of September and here French regular forces opposed the Indian Legion. In the resulting street fighting the *Indische Freiwillige Legion der Waffen-SS* suffered its first death in combat: *Leutnant* Ali Khan, later to be interred with full military honors at Sancoins cemetery. The Legion continued its withdrawal through Luzy marching at night but took more casualties in ambushes including *Unteroffizier* Kalu Ram and *Gefreiter* Mela Ram. The Loire was crossed and the Indians headed for Dijon. A short engagement was fought against allied armour at Nuits St. Georges.[421]

After several days halt for rest the Indians continued on to Remiremont, then, marching via Colmar in Alsace, they arrived at Oberhofen near the garrison town of Hagenau in Germany. During Christmas 1944 the Legion was billeted in the private houses of German civilians then moved in bitterly cold weather to the vacant *Truppenübungsplatz* at Heuberg.[422] In the summer of 1944 one company had been transferred to Italy but returned to the main body of the Legion at *Truppenübungsplatz* Heuberg in the spring of 1945.[423] The Germans always had a very low opinion of the fighting qualities of the Indian Legion (not that they had been given much opportunity to prove themselves in combat). Hitler is reputed to have commented: *"The Indian Legion is a joke."* and is said to have given a personal order that its arms be handed over to the *18. SS-Freiwilligen-Panzer-grenadier-Division "Horst Wessel."*[424]

The *Indische Freiwillige Legion der Waffen SS* remained at *Truppenü-bungsplatz* Heuberg until the end of March 1945. Then with the defeat of the Third Reich imminent, the Indians sought sanctuary in neutral Switzerland and undertook a desperate march along the shores of the Bodensee (Lake Constance) in an attempt to enter Switzerland via one of the alpine passes. However, this was unsuccessful and eventually the Legion was captured by United States and French Army forces. Before their delivery into the custody of British and Indian forces it is alleged that a number of Indian soldiers were shot by French troops.[425]

BELOW: Photograph of an original Indian National Army arm patch for the 950th Infantry Regiment. *Antonio J. Munoz Collectrion.*

421 [48]
422 [49]
423 [50]
424 [51]
425 [52]

Ultimately the members of the Free Indian Legion were transported back to India by sea. There, a number of senior personnel were imprisoned in the Red Fort in Delhi.[426] In view of the pressures used to recruit Indian prisoners-of-war during their captivity (and political expediency in an India in turmoil as independence approached) the members of the Free Indian Legion were dealt with leniently. But by then, the political leader of the Legion was already dead. Subhas Chandra Bose died from severe burns sustained when the Japanese Mitsubishi Ki-21 Army Type 97 "Sally" bomber he was flying in crashed on take-off from Taipei in Formosa (Taiwan) on 18th August 1945 while attempting to make his way to Manchuria in the wake of the Japanese surrender.[427] His remains were cremated and taken to Japan but rumours that he was still alive and working for the Chinese communists persisted for several years.[428] The German Brandenburgers and agents of Abwehr II who had remained with the "Indian National Army" in the Far East were rumoured to have joined the French Foreign Legion in Saigon, French Indo-China.[429]

Bibliography of Published Sources

Boyd, Carl & Yoshida Akihiko. The Japanese Submarine Force and World War II, Naval Institute Press, Annapolis, USA, 1995

Caballero Jurado, Carlos. Foreign Volunteers of the Wehrmacht 1941-45 (Men-at-Arms Series 147), Osprey, London, UK, 1993

Davis, Brian L.. Flags of the Third Reich 2: Waffen SS (Men-at-Arms Series 274), Osprey, London, UK, 1994

Fay, Peter Ward. The Forgotten Army: India's Armed Struggle for Independence 1942-1945, The University of Michigan Press, Ann Arbor, USA, 1993

Houterman, J. N.. Eastern Troops in Zeeland, The Netherlands, 1943-1945, Axis Europa, Bayside, USA, 1997

Kurowski, Franz. The Brandenburgers - Global Mission, J.J. Fedorowicz Publishing, Winnepeg, Canada, 1997

Lepre, George. Himmler's Bosnian Division: The Waffen-SS Handschar Division 1943-1945, Schiffer Publishing, Atglen, USA, 1997

Littlejohn, David. Foreign Legions of the Third Reich, Vol.4, R. James Bender Publishing, San Jose, USA, 1987

Lundari, Giuseppe. I Paracadutisti Italiani 1937/45 (Italian Parachutist Units 1937/45), Editrice Militare Italiana, Milano (Milan), Italy, 1989

Weale, Adrian. Renegades: Hitler's Englishmen, Weidenfeld and Nicholson, London, UK, 1994

[426] [53]
[427] [54]
[428] [55]
[429] [56]

References and Notes:-

1 Lundari, I Paracadutisti Italiani 1937/45, p. 90.
2 ibid. p. 90.
3 ibid. p. 90.
4 ibid. p. 90.
5 ibid. p. 99.
6 ibid. p. 91.
7 Kurowski, The Brandenburgers - Global Mission, p. 136.
8 ibid. p. 137.
9 Weale, Renegades, p. 213.
10 ibid., p. 213.
11 Littlejohn, Foreign Legions of the Third Reich, Vol.4, p. 127.
12 Davis, Flags of the Third Reich 2: Waffen SS, pp. 21-22.
13 Weale, op. cit. p. 213.
14 ibid. p.213.
15 Davis, op. cit., p. 22.
16 Weale, op. cit. p. 213 and Davis, op. cit., p. 22.
17 Littlejohn, op. cit., p. 128.
18 ibid., p. 128.
19 Weale, op. cit. p. 213 (other sources quote figures of up to 3,000).
20 Caballero Jurado, Foreign Volunteers of the Wehrmacht 1941-45, p. 31.
21 Littlejohn, op. cit., p. 126.
22 ibid., p. 127.
23 Caballero Jurado, op. cit., p. 31.
24 Davis, op. cit., p. 22.
25 Littlejohn, op. cit., p. 126.
26 Caballero Jurado, op. cit., p. 31 and Houterman, Eastern Troops in Zeeland, The Netherlands, 1943-1945, p. 63.
27 Lepre, Himmler's Bosnian Division, p. 117.
28 Littlejohn, op. cit., p. 126.
29 Weale, Renegades, p. 213 (Becker was travelling in Germany when war broke out in September 1939 and eventually found himself in the German Army. He was transferred to the Free Indian Legion at Königsbrück in June 1942 were he served as an unteroffizer and clerk in the company office of the 5.Kompanie. He later joined a company of III./I.R.950 (ind) and ended the war as a feldwebel. - Franz Fritsche via Rudolf Hartog, Letter 28/2/99)
30 ibid. p. 214.
31 Davis, op. cit., pp. 42-43.
32 Littlejohn, op. cit., pp. 130-132.
33 ibid pp. 130-131.
34 Kurowski, op. cit., p. 137.
35 Boyd, The Japanese Submarine Force and World War II, p. 117.
36 Fay, The Forgotten Army, p. 200.

37 Kurowski, op. cit., p. 137.
38 ibid., p. 138.
39 ibid., p. 138.
40 ibid., p. 138.
41 Houterman, op. cit., p. 63.
42 ibid., p. 63.
43 ibid., p. 63.
44 ibid., p. 63.
45 ibid., p. 63.
46 Davis, op. cit., p. 22.
47 Littlejohn, op. cit., p. 127.
48 Davis, op. cit., p. 22.
49 ibid., p. 22.
50 Houterman, op. cit., p. 63.
51 Littlejohn, op. cit., p. 127.
52 Davis, op. cit., p. 22.
53 ibid. p. 22.
54 Fay, op. cit. pp. 384-385.
55 Kurowski, op. cit., p. 139.
56 ibid., p. 139.

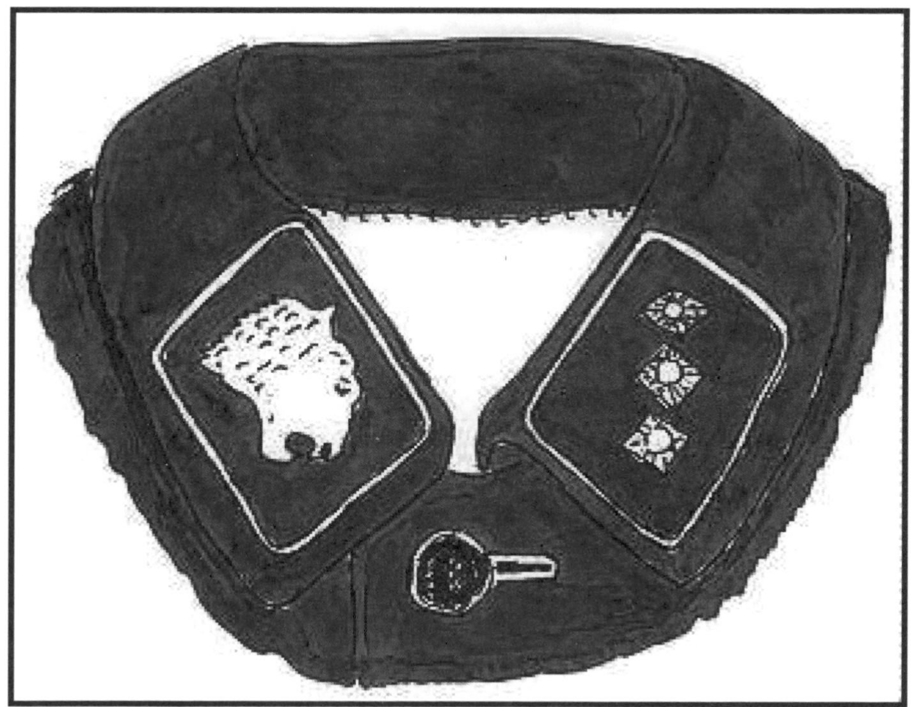

ABOVE: line drawing of the right and left collar tabs of an SS officer with the 950th Infantry Regiment after it was inducted into the Waffen-SS. Recently, one example of a right collar tab showing the tiger's head has shown up, which definitely proves that it existed and was used within the unit. *Antonio J. Munoz Collectrion.*

CHAPTER 6
Paper Tigers: The 950th (Indian) Infantry Regiment in the German Army and Waffen SS 1942-1945

Antonio J. Munoz

INTRODUCTION

During the Second World War the Allies and Axis made every effort to raise troops from North Africa, the Middle East and Asia. The Allies were the most successful since they basically controlled these regions for all or most of the war. Axis attempts to raise troops from these regions proved to have mixed results due to numerous reasons. First they never reached Iraq, Persia (Iran), Palestine, India, and other Middle Eastern countries and territories. Attempts to raise Arab units in Libya, Tunisia, and Morroco proved too little, too late. Secondly, political insensibilities at the outset (i.e.- German arrogance) also played a role in delaying the mass recruitment of Arab and other peoples of Africa and the Middle and Far East. Finally, Allied military gains in North Africa ended German efforts to correct their earlier mistake, almost as soon as recruitment and arming of these peoples had begun. By May 1943 North Africa was in complete allied hands. The Germans only partly managed to train and form a few Arab battalions, most of whose men were captured when the Axis surrendered in Tunisia.

Just as the North African campaign was drawing to a close, a new formation, made up mostly of Indian Hindus and some Muslims was being organized inside Nazi Germany. The unit, officially titled the *Infanterie-Regiment 950 (indische)* [950th Indian Infantry Regiment] in the German Army rolls, would eventually become known as the "Indian Legion" or "Springing Tiger Legion". This last reference was to its distinctive arm patch showing a leaping tiger with the Indian national colors in the background and the words "Free India" inscribed on the top part of the patch.

The regiment was formed and organized along regular German Army lines, although its actual aim was actually for propaganda purposes. Its appearance on the scene had taken about a year, since construction of the Indian regiment had begun in earnest in 1942. By the time the unit was dayviewed there was absolutely no chance that the German forces would ever reach India, and thus employ the regiment as a spearhead for their countrymen to rally around. But 1943 had brought some great reversals in German fortunes and Germany needed to show the World that many peoples were rallying to her cause. The Indian legion fit this need nicely. In 1943 the majority of the Muslim and Hindu world was still dominated and controlled by the British, a fact which many of these indegenous peoples resented greatly. The Germans realized this all too well.

Nationalism was just beginning to show itself fully in these third-world regions, and the peoples of these countries were trying to assert themselves. It was common therefore, that anti-colonialism (and therefore, anti-British) feelings ran high, especially among the intelligentsia and the less well to do, as is often the case. Only those directly benefited by English colonial occupation desired for a continuance of the status quo. These feelings were most extreme in Iraq, Iran, Palestine, and finally but not least, India where the independence movement had already begun even before the Second World War. Indian or Arab expectations of being "liberated" from the British had been pretty much dashed with the defeat of Paulus' *6. Armee* at Stalingrad, and Rommel's *Afrika Korps* at El Alamein.

LEFT: A very well posed photograph of a Sikh volunteer NCO staring intently into the distance. The only Allied force which the 950th (Indian) Infantry Regiment ever fought were the French partisans. *Bundesarchiv.*

Pretences had to be kept however, and the German propaganda department had orders to continue to try and undermine allied relations with the Arab and Indian world. Within this purpose, it's no small wonder that the only shots fired in anger by the Indian Legion turned out to be in self-defense and against French FFI *Maquisards*. Ironically enough, the French were trying to rid themselves of the German occupiers- much like the majority of Indians were trying to get rid of their British occupiers. This incident occurred in 1944, as the Indian Legion made a withdrawal from southern France.

ORIGINS OF THE LEGION, 1941-1942

The man most responsible for raising of the Indian Legion was Subhas Chandra Bose, an Indian lawyer and former leader of the Indian National Congress. Bose wanted India to be free as much as Mahatma Ghandi wanted India to be free. This was where both men agreed. However, in all other respects he was the complete antethesis of Ghandi, who supported Indian independence through non-violent methods. Bose was willing to take up arms for his ideals and principals. He had been an ardent supporter of Indian independence for a long time and was well known like Ghandi. Bose, a Hindu and the Mufti of Jerusalem

(Al Gailany), who was a respected Muslin leader, had been equally instrumental in formenting anti-British sentiment in their respective regions. Both men not only cited nationalistic reasons for siding with Nazi Germany, but also offered religious reasons for hoping for an Axis victory. It wasn't so much what the Nazis had to offer them, as much as what the Arabs and Indians would get rid of due to that Nazi victory. An old Arab proverb states that the enemy of my enemy is my friend. It seems that India's Subhas Chandra Bose, as well as other leaders with the same aspirations and background, took this proverb to heart.

RIGHT & BELOW RIGHT: Sikh Indian volunteer machine gunners. The regiment was magnificently armed and equipped. In 1945, as Adolf Hitler was scraping for weapons for his last levies, he complained that each man in the unit must be carrying two weapons. *Bundesarchiv.*

After traveling through Afghanistan, Bose crossed the frontiers of what was still neutral USSR and headed towards the German Reich. He arrived in Germany in the beginning of 1941. Bose soon established an office in the heart of Berlin and began to campaign for German recognition of an "Indian Provisional Government" in exile. Soon the German State offered Bose and his newly created "Center for a Free India" the status of a provisional government. Bose himself was made "preseident of the provisional government of Free India." This worked hand in glove with Germany's (and Bose's) attempts to undermine the British Empire.

Bose's staff grew quickly and soon he was putting out an Indian language newspaper for the Indian community in Europe. He soon expanded this to a radio show that was directed not only at Indians and Arabs in Europe, but in North Africa and the Middle East as well. His themes were always the same: magnifying the negative aspects of British colonial rule while explaining the benefits of an Axis victory. To long opressed Muslims and Hindus, his arguments seemed to make sense.

It wasn't long before Bose and his adherents were calling for the establishment of an Indian liberation army. The first Indian recruits were actually taken into the ranks of the German Army before Bose ever touched foot on German soil. As early as 1940 the German *Abwehr* (Secret Service) had begun recruiting Indian volunteers into their commando regiment (later a division)- the Brandenburg Formation. Most of these early volunteers had been rich or well to do privileged Indian College students who had been studying in Germany. Actual recruiting for the "Indian Liberation Army" began in earnest in September 1941. The initial recruit personnel came from Indian College students, businessmen and exiled Indians hiding from the British authorities.

The number of Indians recruited from German universities proved to be a trifle: just ten had volunteered. To this number were added five former Indian POW's who had served in the British Army in North Africa and had been captured. It was with this small group of men that Bose began his newspaper and radio show. In December 1941, Bose made a trip to a German prisoner of war camp, which was located near the town of Annaberg. The camp was home to a large percentage of Indian prisoners of war. These men were rather surprised to see Bose, whom many of them had heard about back home, walking without hindrance. It impressed them that an Indian was allowed to travel freely within Germany. Bose saw this and took the opportunity to explain in great detail his

BELOW: Summer of 1944, Bay of Biscay. Field Marshal Erwin Rommel inspects the 950th Indian Infantry Regiment, which at this time was attached to the 159th Infantry Division and located on the peninsula near Bordeaux. *Museum of Modern History, Ljubljana, Slovenia.*

reasons for being in Germany and his desire for an Axis victory over the British. He played heavily on any nationalistic tendencies, which he perceived in any recruit. Before he left on the following day, he had won over one hundred new volunteers to his cause. He told them that Britain's chokehold over India would

ABOVE: The Dutch coast, 1943. Units of the 950th Indian Infantry Regiment form up for morning inspection by their German NCO's. At this time the unit was still organizing and this lack of cohesion can be seen by the lax attitude of the men in this photo. *Bundesarchiv.*

end with an Axis victory. It was therefore their duty as Indians and as nationalists, to aid the Germans

Even though the Nazis expoused their theories of the superiority of the Germanic race, to Chandra Bose and Al Gailany, and all the other non-Germans who rallied to the Hakenkreuz (Swastika), it was enough for them that the Germans were fighting Communism, the Jews, French rule, or British hegemony. *"The enemy of my enemy is my friend."* That was an adage that became a dictum in the minds of these men. Many would pay with their lives for this, during and after the war. Britain, Bose argued, had used India and her people for the enrichment of the British Empire. Her army had abandoned them to their fate in German POW camps. In all of this, Indian blood was still being spilled in order to keep the English status quo. These were arguments that eventually won Bose an additional 600 volunteers from another POW camp, this one near Frankenberg. By August 1942 these 700 initial recruits had been sent to a new training camp. This camp was specifically erected for the Indian volunteers near Konigsbrueck near Dresden, Germany.

EMPLOYMENT OF THE REGIMENT

During September 1942 the Indian Legion was accepted into the ranks of the German *Wehrmacht* as *Infanterie-Regiment 950 (ind.),* or the 950th (Indian)

Infantry Regiment. Initially the unit had two battalions. Each battalion was composed of five infantry companies apiece. Even for 1943 German standards, the Regiment was magnificently armed and manned. Two years later, as the Third Reich lay in ruins and Hitler was reduced to scratching for arms with which to arm his last German levies, he would complain bitterly about the fact that foreign units were armed with more than one weapon, while German formations were left searching for World War I or foreign hand-me-downs. In November 1942 its order of battle was as follows:

UNIT:	Infanterie-Regiment 950. (ind.)
I. Bataillon	1.-5. Kompanie
II. Bataillon	6.-8. Kompanie
NOTES:	The 4.Kompanie (4th Company) was the submachine-gun company in the battalion. The 5.Kompanie was the heavy weapons unit. It contained one 75mm infantry gun, one 50mm anti-tank gun, and an engineer platoon. Each rifle company had two heavy 120mm mortars apiece, and four bazookas each.

By February 1943 the Regiment had the following strength returns:

Hindu Volunteers	1,503
Sikh Volunteers	516
Moslem Volunteers	497
"Other" Nationals	77
Grand Total:	2,593

An additional recruiting drive from the POW camps netted an additional 907 men so that by April 1943 the total strength rose to 3,500 men. This number was equivalent to the size of a small brigade. It was in April that the regiment and its two reinforced infantry battalions were sent to Beverloo, Holland where they were attached to the 16th Air Force Field Division. It too had only recently arrived on the Dutch coast a month before. The Indians were now relegated to guarding a part of Hitler's Atlantic Wall. It was during this time that the regiment experienced its first serious problem. A rebellion broke out within its ranks.

Most of the 170 men of the 3rd Company/ 1st Battalion had refused to comply with the order to transfer to Holland. The Germans took great care to settle the situation without causing much harm on the morale of the Indians, but in the end, 47 out of the 170 had to be court-martialed and sent back to POW camps. On August 31st 1943 the regiment was ordered moved further south and became attached to the German 344th Infantry Division, which was on garrison duty around the southwestern French city of Bordeaux, by the Bay of Biscay region. By September 17th the transfer was completed, although the 2nd Battalion did not quite fit itself in until October 7th, when its Headquarters' Company reached the town of Montalivet. The 950th Infantry Regiment now received the newly created 3rd Battalion, and would remain in this region until the beginning of its

ABOVE: German and Indian soldiers of the 950th Infantry Regiment prepare barbed wire defenses in France during the spring of 1944. *Museum of Modern History, Ljubljana.*
BELOW: When "Netaji" Subhas Chandra Bose went to Burna to help raise volunteers for the Japanese-sponsored Indian National Army, his political followers carried on in France. This meeting was held in Paris in 1944. *Museum of Modern History, Ljubljana.*

withdrawal from France in late June-early July 1944. By late 1943 the order of battle looked like this:

UNIT:	*Infanterie-Regiment 950. (ind.)*
I. Bataillon	1.-5. Kompanie
II. Bataillon	6.-8. Kompanie
III. Bataillon	9.-12. Kompanie
Infantry Gun	13. Kompanie
Anti-Tank	14. Kompanie
Engineer	15. Kompanie
Honor Guard	Ehren-Kompanie[430]

When the 344th Infantry Division withdrew from Bordeaux and was sent to Berck in Pas de Calais, in the region of 15th German Army, the Indian Legion remained behind. The 159th Infantry Division replaced the 344th Division in and around Bordeaux and the Bay of Biscay. The 950th Infantry Regiment was now attached to this new formation. This occurred on January 8th, 1944. Thirteen days later, on January 21st the Regiment was officially enrolled in the "Indian National Army." The Indian National Army was not the phantasy or machinations of some Axis propaganda machine, but a reality that the Japanese Army had brought to fruition. The story dates back to December 1942, when the British Army in Burma and Mayala was in retreat. It was in the northern Malayan town of Alor Star that Major Iwaichi Fujiwara of the Imperial Japanese General Staff interviewed a Sikh POW officer. The officer's name was Major Mohan Singh. Singh agreed to set up a special unit for Indians, Burmese, and Thai volunteers who opposed British and French control of their lands.

Bose who was then in Germany, had realized by then that the prospect the Germans would ever reach India was almost nil. He therefore decided to make a special trip to Japanese held territory. To Bose, it now seemed that the Japanese had produced a sizeable force that could truly become the core of n Indian Liberation Army. He now hoped to become the titular head of that fledgling army. The battle cry of this new Indian and East Asian force was *"Asia for the Asiatics,"*[431] which conveniently left the Japanese in the equation. This phrase had been uttered by other pro-Japanese collaborationist forces throughout the Empire of Japan and was obviously part of a calculated propaganda campaign by the Japanese. To the credit of the Japanese, this new force would eventually number some 33,000 men split into three divisions. These three divisions would fight alongside Japanese troops although their fighting morale was always low and their ranks thinned by desertions.

---

430 Bamber, Dr. Martin. *"For Free India,"* in AXIS EUROPA, Bayside, 1998. Issue 14, Summer 1998. Page 4.

431 Gilbert, Martin. THE SECOND WORLD WAR – A COMPLETE HISTORY. Henry Holt & Co: New York, 1989. Page 278.

ABOVE: These two photographs were taken during a competition between the Indian volunteers and their German comrades. The game ended in a politically correct draw. *Bundesarchive & Museum of Modern History, Ljubljana, Slovenia.*

It was this "Indian National Army" that the 950th Indian Infantry Regiment was officially and ceremoniously inducted in early 1944. However this move, obviously geared for its propaganda purposes and possibly to raise the morale of the volunteers did not have the desired effect. By 1944 it was apparent to the whole world that the Axis were going to lose the war. German propaganda photographs of Indian volunteers in German uniform brought little hope to ordinary Indians that Germany would free them from British rule. As a result, the reason why the Germans had allowed the regiment to be raised- for propaganda purposes no longer existed. There were no plans to transfer the regiment to Burma, where the Indian National Army was fighting. It had taken special preparations just to carry Subhas Chandra Bose and a small staff by submarine to Japanese held territory. There was no question that a surface vessel could make it past Allied fleets. By 1944 the German submarine force was also in retreat. It was thus decided that the regiment had to remain in Europe. To the Germans, disbanding a full strength combat unit in 1944 seemed heretical. In addition, the ever present chance of an Allied invasion seemed to loom ever closer, and the German Army in France needed every man possible to man the Atlantic Wall.

The spring of 1944 proved uneventful for the men of the 950th Infantry Regiment. However one particularly motivated company within the Regiment, the 9th Company, requested to be posted to the Italian front lines in early May 1944. Surprisingly, the commander of the Regiment, *Oberstleutnant* Kurt Krappe approved the transfer, believing that the unit was the best and most motivated company in the Legion. Three officers, two of whom were German and one Indian officer, Leutnant Jaswat Singh Bindra, led it. One of the German officers was named *Leutnant* A. Opitz.[432] The Company had an authorized strength of 199 NCO's and enlisted men, which was almost double the principle strength of a German front-line company by 1944 standards. By May 26th 1944 the 9th Company was located in the Mailla Mountain range, just south of Chieti. It later moved to Pescara where it was attached to the Fusilier Battalion of the 278th Infantry Division.[433]

The company was employed against the British 5th Corps and Polish 2nd Corps. Specifically, Bindra requested that the unit be placed against any British and Indian allied formation. It eventually confronted and fought a British formation and elements of the 8th Indian and later the 4th Indian Division. This occurred in late May and throughout June 1944.

ABOVE & BELOW: Before the Allied invasion of France in the summer of 1944, the Indian volunteers had the opportunity to go on leave. Below they are seen at the German travel bureau in Paris. *US National Archives.*

[432] Hartog, Rudolf. IM ZEICHEN DES TIGERS. DIE INDISCHE LEGION AUF DEUTSCHER SEITE 1941-1945. Busse Seewald: Herford, 1991. Page 155.
[433] ibid. Page 156.

Towards the end of June the unit was pulled from the front lines and used for anti-partisan sweeps in and around the rear area of the German Gothic Line. During these operations, the company lost no men. In July the unit withdrew to Pesaro, south of Rimini, then to Pistoia and La Spezia. It remained in Ravenna in the fall of 1944 performing security duty between the Ravenna-Ferrara road and rail line until April 1945 when the front line collapsed. In this month 8-10 Indian volunteers in the 9th Company were wounded near Comacchio due to an enemy strafing attack. Shortly afterwards the company was caught by advancing allied forces and forced to surrender.

Meanwhile, garrison duty in France had proved relatively easy for the Legion's volunteers, and many of the men had the opportunity of going on small forloughs to Paris and other parts of France. This included scenic tours and the chance to meet or purchase female companionship and drink- things that were very important for soldiers. This all changed however, when the Allies landed on Normandy on June 6th 1944 and began the invasion of France. Acting on the orders of British SOE operatives, the French partisans, or *Maquisards* went into action all across France. The region of Bordeaux was no exception. It was in June that the first Indian volunteers from the Regiment lost to French guerrilla forces. In July 1944 the Indian Legion was finally ordered withdrawn from France. It was decided not to commit the regiment since the consensus within the German cadre staff was that the regiment would collapse from desertions and low morale.

The withdrawal of the Regiment finally cost about 40 Indian lives to French guerrilla attacks before they reached Dijon, a staging area on their withdrawal into Germany. The Free French Forces of General DeGaulle took Dijon itself in early September 1944. Worse still for the Regiment, during the withdrawal from France, about 250 Indian volunteers had either surrendered or deserted to the French guerrillas. The morale of the Indian Legion was at an all time low. Defeat loomed in the background and the volunteers knew it. For those men who surrendered, their pragmatism proved fatal to some of the Indian turncoats. Of the 250 who tried their lot with the French, some 29 were shot outright,[434] while the rest were handed over to the British Army for punishment.

On August 8th 1944 at Heuberg, the Indian Legion was transferred into the ranks of the Waffen-SS. Like the Cossacks of the German Army, this transfer proved to be a "paper" formality. Heinrich Himmler had been placed in charge of the Replacement Army after the attempt on Hitler's life on July 20th 1944. This allowed him the added leverage to acquire almost all of the Army's foreign volunteer formations into his private SS kingdom. The title of the Regiment changed one more time. The unit was now to be known as *Indische Legion der SS*.[435] Some SS officers were indeed assigned to the Regiment, but Heer officers and Army uniforms remained in use, with the exception of the SS officers now placed on staff. The officer roster for the Legion looked as follows on March 6th 1945:

---

434 Neulen, Hans Werner. AN DEUTSCHER SEITE: INTERNATIONALE FREIWILLIGE VON WEHRMACHT UND WAFFEN-SS. Universitas: Munich, 1985. Page 357.
435 NARS Microfilm Series T-175, Roll 191, Frame 2729186.

I. Commander: *SS-Standartenführer* Kurt Krappe, born on July 15th 1899, and promoted to his SS rank on November 1st 1944.
II. IIa (Operations Officer): *SS-Obersturmführer* Hellmuth Starcke, born on October 28th 1905, and promoted to current rank on October 1st 1942.
III. 1st Battalion CO: *Hauptmann* Adolf Scharwachter, born on December 3rd 1914, and promoted to current rank on February 1st 1944.
IV. 2nd Battalion CO: *Hauptmann* Karl Hamerl, born on October 24th 1917, and promoted to current rank on December 1st 1944.
V. 3rd Battalion CO: *Hauptmann* Hans Kutscher, born on December 14th 1911, and promoted to current rank on August 1st 1944.
VI. Reserve/Replacement Battalion CO: *Hauptmann* Theodor Glodig, born on May 27th 1895, and promoted to current rank on November 22nd 1940.[436]

The SS High Command had plans to eventually outfit the entire unit in SS uniforms. In fact, proof that this even began to take shape did not come out into the public eye until the summer of 1995, when Dr. David Littlejohn published a small but important article regarding this matter.[437] In it he revealed for the first time that indeed at least one SS officer in the Indian Legion had worn a right

ABOVE: Extreme left- Colonel Kurt Krappe; behind Krappe- an unknown Indian adjutant to Subhas Chandra Bose; Colonel Yamamoto (Japanese Army legation); unknown Officer with binoculars; Extreeme right with rain jacket and holding binoculars- "Netaji" Subhas Chandra Bose, the political leader of the pro-Axis Indian volunteers. *Rudolf Hartog Collection.*

---

[436] Ibid. Frame 2729186.

[437] Littlejohn, Dr. David. "The Indian Legion," in THE MILITARY ADVISOR: Bender Publications: San Jose. Volume 6, Number 3, Summer 1995. Pages 28-33.

collar tab that had been designed by the Waffen-SS specifically for the Indian Legion of the SS. It was the head of a Tiger on silver thread, with the characteristic black cloth background that was so typical of the collar tabs of all Waffen-SS units.[438]

The Indian Legion of the SS went into relative obscurity from the fall of 1944 until it was brought out in a conversation, which occurred at Hitler's Headquarters during a conference held on March 24th 1945. This was about six weeks before the end of the war. During this palaver Hitler became frustrated when told that not enough weapons were available for the new units that were being formed. When told that some foreign units had been armed before German ones, he complained that certain foreign formations were "resting all the time and never fighting!" The transcript of the conversation is, in my opinion, a fitting end-piece to the story of the Indian volunteers:[439]

Hitler: *"...I can't raise German divisions because I don't have any weapons. I'd rather just raise a German division and give it all those weapons."*
General Burgdorff: *"The Indian Legion!"*
Hitler: *"The Indian Legion is a joke. There are Indians who can't kill a louse, who'd rather let them be eaten up. They won't kill and Englishman either. I consider it nonsense purposely to put them opposite the English. Why should the Indians be braver in our service than they were under Bose in India? They used Indian units under Bose's leadership in Burma for the purpose of freeing India from the British. They ran away like a bunch of sheep!*

Why should they be braver here? I think that if we used the Indians to turn prayer mills or for something of that sort, they would be the most indefatigable soldiers in the world. But to use them for a real death struggle is ridiculous. How strong are the Indians? But it's all nonsense. If you have the surplus of weapons, such jokes for propaganda purposes are entirely irresponsible."
SS-Sturmbannfuehrer Goehler: *"The Indian Legion has a strength of 2,300 men."*
Hitler: *"We would be doing them the greatest favor if we told them that they don't have to fight anymore."*
Goehler: *"They have 1,468 rifles, 550 pistols, 420 submachine-guns, 200 light machine-pistols..."*
Hitler: *"Just imagine, they have more weapons than men. Some of their people must carry two weapons."*
Goehler: *"...Twenty four heavy machine guns, 20 medium mortars, 4 light howitzers, 6 light infantry howitzers, 6 anti-tank guns, it doesn't say what kind, 700 horses, 81 vehicles, 61 passenger cars, 5 motorcycles, 12 prime movers, of which 11 are ready for use."*
Hitler: *"What is the Indian Legion supposed to be doing?"*
Goehler: *"I can't say. They've been resting for quite some time."*

---

[438] With the exception of the *Ostturkischer-Waffen-Verband der-SS*, which had the individual honor of having a green background cloth for their cuff band and collar tabs.
[439] With the exception of the highly motivated 9th Company

Hitler: *"But they've never been in battle!"*
Goehler: *"No."*
Hitler: *"A unit which is in a rest area should, in my opinion, be a unit that has seen heavy fighting and is being refreshed. These outfits of yours are always refreshing and never fighting!"*

Indeed, the unit was considered such a joke, that when *SS-Oberfuehrer* Heinz Bertling was appointed to lead the Indian Legion of the SS in August 1944,[440] he failed to show up for his command for lack of interest! In the end, *Oberstleutnant* Kurt Krappe was given the rank of *SS-Standartenfuehrer* and continued to command the unit. In May 1945, after a failed attempt to cross over into neutral Switzerland, the Indian volunteers and German cadre staff quietly turned themselves over to US Army and French units. It was during this time that apparently some Indian volunteers were shot by French Army forces for having committed some crimes in France. The rest were eventually turned over to the British for punishment.

ABOVE: Volunteers from the Indian province of Punjab. The regiment contained Sikh, Hindus, and Muslims volunteers. *Museum of Modern History, Ljubljana, Slovenia.*

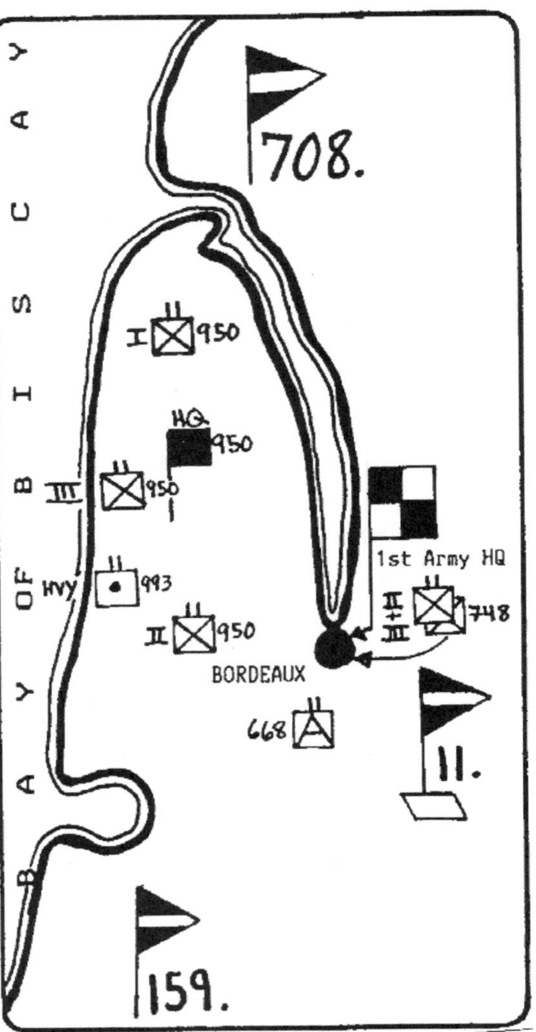

RIGHT: Location of the 950th Infantry Regiment (Indian) as of June 6th, 1944. The unit's neighbors included the 708th Division and 159th Division, as well as the 11th Panzer Division.

[440] Plans were already in effect during the late summer of 1944 to incorporate

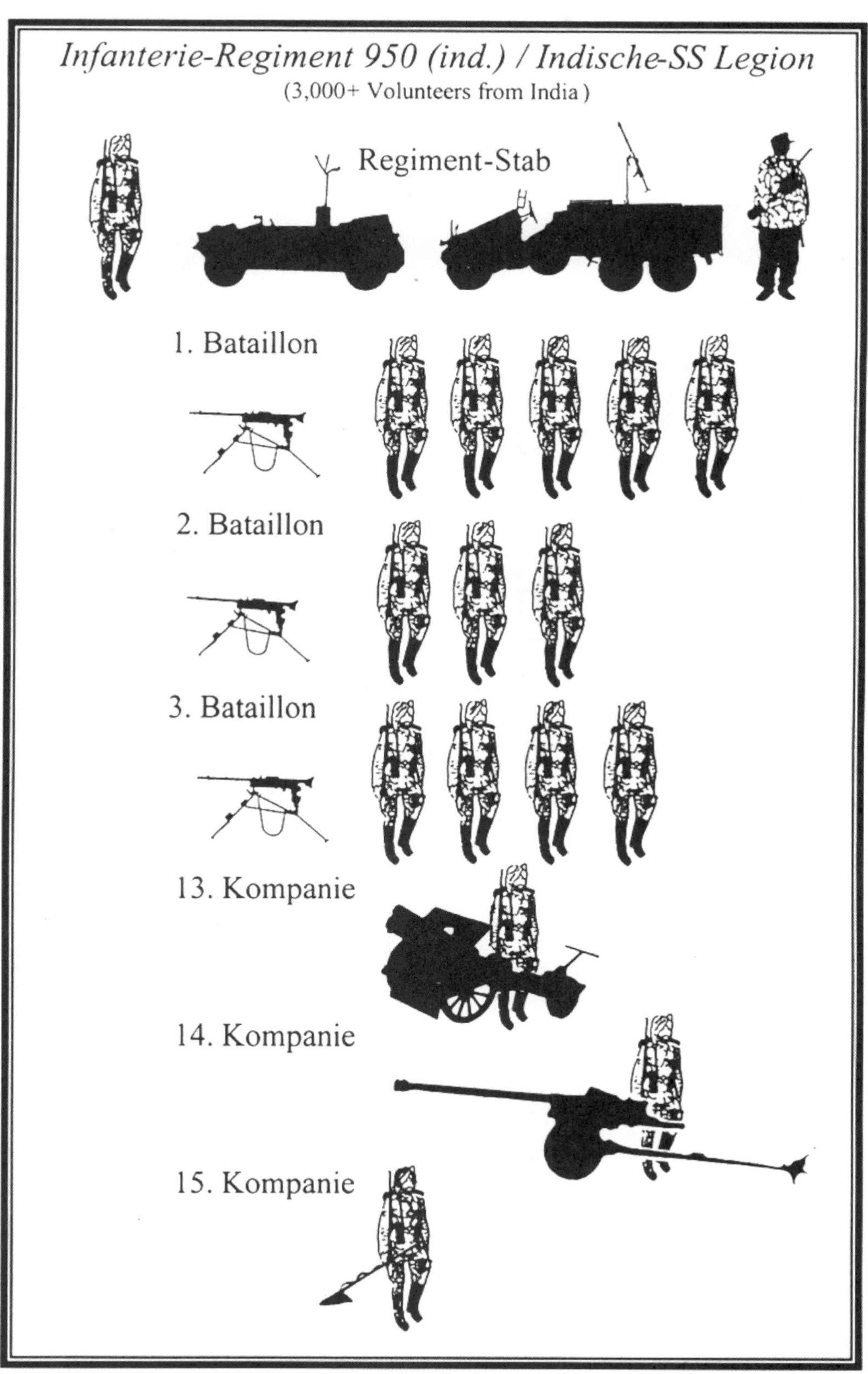
Infanterie-Regiment 950 (ind.) / Indische-SS Legion
(3,000+ Volunteers from India)
Regiment-Stab
1. Bataillon
2. Bataillon
3. Bataillon
13. Kompanie
14. Kompanie
15. Kompanie

ABOVE LEFT: Photo of a Sikh volunteer of the 950th Infantry Regiment, circa 1943.
He seems to be wearing a light tropical tunic and is also wearing shorts- obviously a summer uniform.
ABOVE RIGHT: Another photograph of a Sikh volunteer of the Indian Legion. The Springing Tiger arm patch is clearly seen.
RIGHT: Battle flag of the Indian Legion. There were two versions of the Indian Legion battle flag. This flag shown here is the second version. The Indian colors of Orange, White and Green were superimposed on the flag with a springing tiger emblem in balck and white.

CHAPTER 7
Indochinese Volunteers
In the German Army, 1944

By Antonio J. Munoz

In the summer of 1944, as the western Allies were already on French soil, the Chief of the *SS-Hauptamt* (SS Main Office), *SS-Obergruppenfuehrer* Gottlob Berger met with *Reichfuehrer-SS* Heinrich Himmler. Himmler had recently been appointed to the post of Chief of the Replacement Army,[441] and as such he was in a position to expand his SS Empire by including what were formerly Army foreign volunteer units into the Waffen-SS and SS/Police units. On the agenda was the possibility of recruiting North Africans, Senegalese, and even Indochinese men into the ranks of the SS and police forces. The plan was to use these men in the police battalions and regiments. The meeting took place on Julky 14th 1944 and figures of as many as 370,000 potential recruits were thrown speculatively.

In reality, the Germans had captured about 35,000 men from Senegal, North Africa, and Indochina during the French campaign in the summer of 1940. Of this number, about 20,000 had eventually been turned over to the Vichy Government, who used them mostly in construction battalions. The Vichy Government however, used several hundred for police duties within un-occupied France. The manner in which the Germans were to appeal to this group of foreign personnel was to try and appeal to their nationalistic tendencies. A university professor with experience in dealing with Thai, Vietnamese, Laotian, and Cambodian peoples was "hired" by the *SS-Hauptamt* and used to give "history" classes to those men still in German control. After the fall of the Vichy French government and the subsequent German occupation of what had up until then been un-occupied France in November 1942, most of these Indochinese men had fallen into German hands.

The German Army had either placed them working in French factories, or as helpers and even "Hiwis" (*Hilfswillige,* or volunteers) within some of the German occupation divisions in southern France. The "history" classes stressed freedom for the local population from French or British colonial rule. Undoubtedly the professor would point out that it was Germany that was fighting their colonial masters, and therefore Germany was to be considered a partner in the "fight against colonialism". No mention was made of course, of Imperial Germany's colonial rule up until World War One, and that most assuredly the lives of these Asian peoples would have remained the same or worsened in case of an Axis victory.

Eventually, enough volunteers from Thailand, Vietnam and Laos were recruited to form a small infantry force under the control of the German 19th

---

441 This was one of many "hats" which he was to wear. Another was head of Army Group Upper Rhine in 1944-45, while keeping his title of head of the SS & Police forces.

Army in southern France. On the night of August 21st 1944 as the withdrawal of the German Army from France was taking place; an eyewitness to this strange foreign formation observed their withdrawal northwards. *Luftwaffe* (Air Force) officer Georg Pemler stated that he came upon Indochinese volunteers in German uniform moving northwards. He said that it was an entire battalion of them, and that they camped along the road in rucksacks, packs, and even had women and children with them. There were approximately 20 eastern battalions in the region of the 19th German Army at this time. It could be possible that this *Luftwaffe* officer could have been mistaken, and that he was actually seeing Asiatic men from the far eastern parts of the Soviet Union. Whether Pemler was mistaken is really irrelevant, for at least one photographic evidence exists that these men did serve in the ranks of the German Army, although their number remains a mystery. The SS and Police forces never absorbed these Indochinese volunteers. If they remained in action into 1945 they were most probably split up and used as Hiwis within units of the German 19th Army in Colmar.

RIGHT: The only known photograph of an Indochinese volunteer in the service of the Wehrmacht (German Army). This photo was taken in southern France in the summer of 1944.

Part - III

The East Came West: Muslim, Hindu and Buddhist Volunteers In the German Army and Waffen-SS, 1942-1945

CHAPTER 8
Followers of "The Greater Way": Kalmuck Volunteers in the German Army 1942-1945

By Antonio J. Munoz

In the snowy expanses of Siberia
Large trees grow
And exiled Kalmyks
Suffer from the
-
Balakaev
[On Life in Siberia]

During the German invasion of the Soviet Union and subsequent occupation of captured territories, the German Army encouraged the establishment of some type of auxiliary police or self-defense formation raised from the local indigenous population. The minority non-Russian groups, especially the Kalmucks, Cossacks and Tartars, were given special consideration and treatment by the Germans and were permitted to establish self-defense units. One of the most interesting would eventually become known as the Kalmuck Cavalry Corps. This formation would become one of the most exotic foreign volunteer units in the Wehrmacht.

The Kalmucks[442] was a Mongolian race of people, scattered throughout Central Asia, and extending westward into southern Russia. The name was not used by the people themselves, but by Turkic races of Asia and the Russians to designate the allied tribes of the Zungars, Torgod (Keraits or Eleuths), Khoshod, and Doerboed. These tribes lived in Zungaria; around Koko-nor in northeastern Tibet; in the district called Ordus, within the great loop of the Yellow River of China; on the western slopes of the Altai; and in the steppes between the Don and the Volga Rivers and Caspian Sea. They were nomads, possessing herds of horses, cattle, and sheep.[443]

The Kalmucks migrated to the Volga Steppes, a little before 1700, and then again in response to a Chinese "invitation" seventy-one years later (1771). The resistance of the Kazaks on the northern steppe was greatly weakened by this Kalmuck migration. The story of the Kalmucks has been forever immortalized in De Quincy's classic essay, "Revolt of the Tartars."[444] The word "Kalmuck" literally means, "to remain" in the Turkish language. The Kalmuck people were a remnant of the Oirat Mongol Confederacy, which had stubbornly fought over

---

[442] Also sometimes spelled "Kalmyks".
[443] Vizetelly, Dr. Frank H., Editor. FUNK & WAGNALLS NEW STANDARD ENCYCLOPEDIA. Funk & Wagnalls Company: New York, 1931. Volume17, pages 20-21
[444] Caroe, Olaf. SOVIET EMPIRE: THE TURKS OF CENTRAL ASIA AND STALINISM. MacMillan & Co. Ltd.: London, 1954. Page 71.

control of Peking between 1450 and 1650. Later they were used as pawns in the inevitable power struggles between China and Russia. Surprisingly, the Kalmucks were never absorbed into Turkdom, nor did they embrace the Islamic faith. They were in fact, the only German Army military unit made up completely of Buddhists of the "Greater Way!"

Like all peoples under Stalinist rule, the Kalmuck way of life was turned upside down by the Communist lack in a belief in any God, collectivization methods, and other restrictions on the lives of these and other peoples. During the Russian Civil War, Lenin had promised the Kalmucks and other Asiatic races in Russia more freedom from the central government in Moscow in exchange for their help in defeating the Czarist armies. Instead, the Kalmucks and other peoples had formed "republics" which the Bolshevik Government quickly crushed. Resistance to Communist rule quickly followed. It wasn't until the summer of 1941 that the NKVD, the Soviet Secret Police had finally been able to gain the upper hand in the Kalmuck Steppes. But this guerrilla war had caused the population to be reduced to some 80-90,000 people.[445] This was in stark contrast to a population that had reached 190,600 people by 1887. In 1959, 72 years after this census, the Kalmuck nation only had 106,100 souls.[446] It seems that decades of fighting Moscow, famines caused by collectivization methods or purposeful acts, and deportation to Siberia as punishment for having assisted the Germans had taken a heavy toll.

The summer of 1942 brought the German invasion to the Kalmucks when Hitler's panzers roared towards Stalingrad on the Volga and the moved against the Caucasus. The farther Army Group's "A" and "B" advanced between the Caucasus and Stalingrad in those fall days of 1942, the wider grew the gap between their offensive spearheads in the Kalmuck Steppe. By August and September 1942 the front lines between those Axis units fighting in and around Stalingrad and the Axis forces fighting in the Caucasus was stretched to the breaking point. The German 16th Motorized Infantry Division had taken Elista, the capital of the "Kalmuck Autonomous Soviet Socialist Republic" which Joseph Stalin had established in 1935. The unit was now assigned the task of keeping a link between both army groups. The division quickly set up shop in the Kalmuck city of Elista and began sending long-range reconnaissance patrols from Uta, a staging town east of Elista.[447] It wasn't long before the Russians began partisan operations inside the Kalmuck ASSR, which included the entire expanse of the Kalmuck Steppe. At its height in November-December 1942, these Communist destruction units numbered nine (the 50th, 51st, 53rd, 55th, 57th, 59th, 71st, 73rd, and 74th Partisan Battalions).[448]

---

[445] Anders, Lt. Gen. Wladyslaw. HITLER'S DEFEAT IN RUSSIA. Henry Regnery Company: Chicago, 1953. Page 177.

[446] Pohl, Otto J. ETHNIC CLEANSING IN THE USSR, 1937-1949. Greenwood Press: Westport, 1999. Page 62.

[447] Carell, Paul. HITLER MOVES EAST 1941-1943. Little, Brown And Company: Boston, 1964. Page 507.

[448] Hoffmann, Joachim. DEUTSCHE UND KALMYKEN 1942 BIS 1945. Verlag Rombach: Frieburg, 1986. Pages 100-101.

In August 1942 the German 16th Motorized Infantry Division was beginning to experience guerrilla attacks and harassing raids on their line of communication. Major Poltermann, the Ic of the Division, requested permission from the divisional commander to raise a local volunteer militia from the nomadic Kalmuck tribes that would help them to guard the flanks. In peacetime Poltermann had been an industrialist in the Ruhr. The Soviets had organized a local militia in the Kalmyck ASSR that on July 30th 1941 amounted to 8,664 men. It would be these militiamen who would begin to harass the Germans as "destruction battalions" when the Germans reached the region.[449] Lieutenant-Colonel von Freytag-Loringhoven in Poltava quickly made some phone calls and located an interpreter for him who had knowledge of the Kalmuck people and best of all, could speak their language fluently.[450]

ABOVE: The winter of 1942-1943. The Germans began their withdrawal from the Caucasus and Volga Steppe. The Kalmyck Cavalry Corps played an important role in the withdrawal. In many instances the formation helped hold off the Soviet forces long enough to allow German units time to withdraw. *Bundesarchiv.*

This officer turned out to be *Sonderfuehrer* Dr. Otto Doll, whose real name was Otmar Werva. Another source states that his real name was Rudolf Vrba.[451] Whichever was the case, what is known is that "Dr. Doll" had been born in Russia before the First World War, and had served as a White Russian officer during the Russian Civil War.[452] After the war he had immigrated to the Sudeten land and had joined the German Army Secret Service (the *Abwehr*), in 1938. When summoned to 16th Motorized Infantry Division he had been working in the *Abwehr* offices in Feodosia, in the Crimea. His present rank was that of Lance

---

449 Pohl, op cit. Page 64.

450 Thorwald, Juergen. THE ILLUSION: SOVIET SOLDIERS IN HITLER'S ARMIES. Harcourt Brace Jovanovich: New York, 1975. Pages 70-71.

451 Piekalkiewicz, Janusz. THE CAVALRY OF WORLD WAR II. Stein And Day: New York, 1980. Page 218.

452 Nafziger, George F. THE GERMAN ORDER OF BATTLE: WAFFEN-SS AND OTHER UNITS IN WORLD WAR II. Combined Publishing: Pennsylvania, 2001. Page 217.

Corporal, but because he was the only individual which the Army could find that spoke Tibetan (the language of the Kalmucks), he was initially promoted to *"Sonderfuehrer"* and eventually reached the rank of Major or Colonel.[453] Because of his genuine concern for them, "Dr. Doll" came to be much admired and loved by the people whom he would share the next two years with. He immediately set about organizaing the Kalmucks, raising the first unit titled *Abwehrtrupp 103* in the middle of August 1942.[454] This force included an initial strength of two cavalry squadrons with about 150 horsemen in each unit.

BELOW: An NCO attached to the Kalmyck Cavalry Corps pets his camel. The unit contained horses and camels and was one of the most exotic formations in the German Army. *Bundesarchiv.*

Unlike other parts of the Soviet Union, the Germans actually made an attempt at granting semi-autonomous rights to the Kalmucks and other Caucasian peoples. Buddhist temples were reopened and local indigenous authorities were chosen, which enjoyed great autonomy. In December 1942 agrarian reforms started and the lands began to be restored to the Kalmuck people.[455] The Caucasian peoples had suffered greatly under Communist rule. For example, of the 4,000 mosques, 2,000 *meddressahs* (religious schools), and 10,000 *mullahs* (religious leaders)

[453] Littlejohn, Dr. David. THE PATRIOTIC TRAITORS. THE HISTORY OF COLLABORATION IN GERMAN-OCCUPIED EUROPE, 1940-45. Doubleday & Company, Inc.: Garden City, 1972. Page 363.

[454] Hoffmann, op cit. Page 20.

[455] Mulligan, Timothy Patrick. THE POLITICS OF ILLUSION AND EMPIRE: GERMAN OCCUPATION POLICY IN THE SOVIET UNION, 1942-1943. Praeger Publishers: New York, 1988. Page 128.

that existed in the region in 1920, only 150 mosques and 150 *mullahs* remained by 1939.[456] The religious buildings had simply been destroyed, and the Islamic leaders killed, or sent to a Siberian Gulag. In return for their newfound freedoms at the hands of the Germans, the Kalmucks and other peoples of the Caucasus reacted extremely favorably to the Axis occupation. For their support of the Germans, the entire Kalmuck population would eventually be exiled in 1946. This support is borne out by several accounts, including some Russian and German post-war histories: *"The situation was particularly bad in the Caucasus region, where the Kalmyks and a number of the Caucasian peoples, including the Chechens, Ingush, and some other peoples, served the Germans willingly."*[457]

ABOVE: A typical Kalmyck volunteer. The Mongolian features are undeniable! He is wearing a Cossack style cover with the German national eagle. *Bundesarchiv.*

And from the German point of view, the same results were seen: *"In some areas, such as the Cossack and Kalmyk lands in the North and in the Muslim areas, the welcome was truly enthusiastic."*[458]

This assistance to the German military initially began with the selection of a number of *Panje* Horses, small but sturdy Russian mounts to replace the losses of European horses that the Germans had lost by the tens of thousands. Of the total

[456] Alexiev, Alex. SOVIET NATIONALITIES IN GERMAN WARTIME STRATEGY, 1941-1945. Rand Corporation: Santa Monica, 1982. Page 21.
[457] Grenkevich, Leonid. THE SOVIET PARTISAN MOVEMENT 1941-1944. Frank Cass: London, 1999. Page 132.
[458] Alexiev, op cit. Page 23.

number of horses used by the Germans in the Russian campaign, 17% died of heart failure brought about by the exertion of towing guns or vehicles stuck in the *rasputitsa* (mud), as well as other cases causing lameness and stomach ulcers. On the open steppe, the European horses would die if the temperature fell to minus 4° degrees or less. The *Panje* horses used by the Kalmucks however, survived in these temperatures and seemed to have as much if not more stamina and energy than their larger, European counterparts.[459] These Kalmuck cavalrymen also used Bactrian camels, though the *Panje* horse was preferred.

The success of cooperation between the Germans and their benevolent policies netted great accomplishments in recruiting these native nomadic horsemen into more squadrons. In September 1942 25 defense units of 100 men each were organized throughout the Kalmuck region.[460] The mission of these units was to protect the Kalmuck settlements and help fight the guerrillas. This they did, as well as to cover the extended flanks of the 16th Motorized Infantry Division. They operated with swiftness and stealth. The partisan bands often did not know that they were being attacked until the Kalmucks were in their midst. Having an intimate knowledge of the countryside, and being accustomed to the harsh weather, the Kalmuck cavalry would seek their revenge on their tormentors. One author attested to their prowess as horsemen and guerrilla fighters: *"These masters of small-scale cavalry warfare soon proved themselves to be of inestimable value with their cavalry raids and reconnaissance expeditions into the Soviet interior."*[461]

Moreover, the Kalmuck squadrons protected the exposed flanks of the German troops concentrated at Utta, Chalkuta, and Justa, on both sides of the Elista-Astrakhan road. They were also excellent fighters not only against Soviet partisans, but regular Russian forces, and excelled as scouts. In fact, this reconnaissance and scout work was so invaluable that the commander of the 16th Motorized Infantry Division, General Graf von Schwerin said that the duties taken on by his division would have proved impossible to accomplish had it not been for the reliable assistance and cooperation given to his unit by the Kalmucks. That help was often passionate. The Kalmucks, long oppressed by the Communists, set about eliminating their enemy with a willingness and vengeance that even appalled some of the German officers. Although the Germans considered them as undisciplined fighters, they nevertheless respected their fighting competence. There was never any doubt about their effectives and zeal as attested to by this remark: *"Though the Kalmucks were totally without discipline in the western sense, they launched themselves passionately into their work. Indeed, they set about wiping out groups of Russians in the Steppes with such ardour that the German Army at times had to intervene to prevent atrocities."*[462]

---

[459] Lucas, James. WAR ON THE EASTERN FRONT 1941-1945. Janes Publishing Company: London, 1979. Pages 114-115.

[460] Pronin, Alexander. GUERRILLA WARFARE IN THE GERMAN OCCUPIED SOVIET TERRITORIES 1941-1945. Georgtown University Graduate School: Georgetown, 1965. Page 219.

[461] Piekalkiewicz, op cit. Page 218.

[462] Piekalkiewicz, ibid. Page 218.

This enthusiasm was, as stated earlier, brought about by the benevolent administration, which the German command wisely chose to follow. In fact, the initial speech made to the Kalmuck leaders was short and simple: *"The land is yours. You are free from the oppression of the Tsars and Bolsheviks...In order to keep power you must fight against the Soviet authority and its supporters."*[463]

LEFT: A German liaison officer is on a reviewing stand while a Kalmyck volunteer officer on horseback also reviews the cavalry squadrons, some time in 1943. *Bundesarchiv.*

Fight they did. In fact, soon after the last Soviet NKVD units had left Elista, five units of 30-40 men each had been independently raised by the Kalmucks at their own initiative. By December 1942 the Germans had recruited no less than 3,000 men[464] with a German cadre staff of 75 officers and NCO's. Most of the Germans were located in the principal headquarters staff. There were forty German officers and NCO's there, but an equal number of Kalmucks.[465] Unfortunately this German benevolence did not extend to all the people living in the Kalmuck ASSR. One source reported that *Einsatzkommando 11a* sent an *SD-Teilkommando* to Elista and before the end of 1942, 93 Jewish families had been rounded up and killed. The body count was around 300.[466] What would have been the reaction of the Kalmucks, one wonders, if they had known that these men who belonged to *Einsatzgruppe D,* had proudly recorded that in the first twelve months of the Russian campaign, the unit had *"liquidated at least 90,000 Asiatics, commissars, and Jews."*[467]

Meanwhile "Dr. Doll" had begun to lead the unit, while his Chief of Staff was a Kalmuck leader named Baldan Metabon.[468] At least one of the soon to be organized battalions was led by Major Abushinov.[469] In Elista, *Ortskommandantur I/649* provided support and weapons (mostly captured arms) to the Kalmuck squadrons. In Decemer 1942 a squadron of Kalmucks attacked a battalion (the 59th Destruction) of Russian partisans and achieved their single greatest victory to date- the destruction of half of the guerrilla battalion near Ulan

[463] Pronin, op cit. Page 227.
[464] Mulligan, op cit. Page 128.
[465] Pronin, op cit. Page 230.
[466] Hoffmann, op cit. Page 104n.
[467] Thorwald, op cit. Page 230.
[468] Laandwehr, Richard. *"The Kalmucken-Verband Dr. Doll, 1942-1945,"* in SIEGRUNEN. Brookings, 1994. Number 56, Spring 1994. Page 17.
[469] Carell, Paul. SCORCHED EARTH: THE RUSSO-GERMAN WAR, 1943-1944. Little, Brown And Company: Boston, 1970. Page 385.

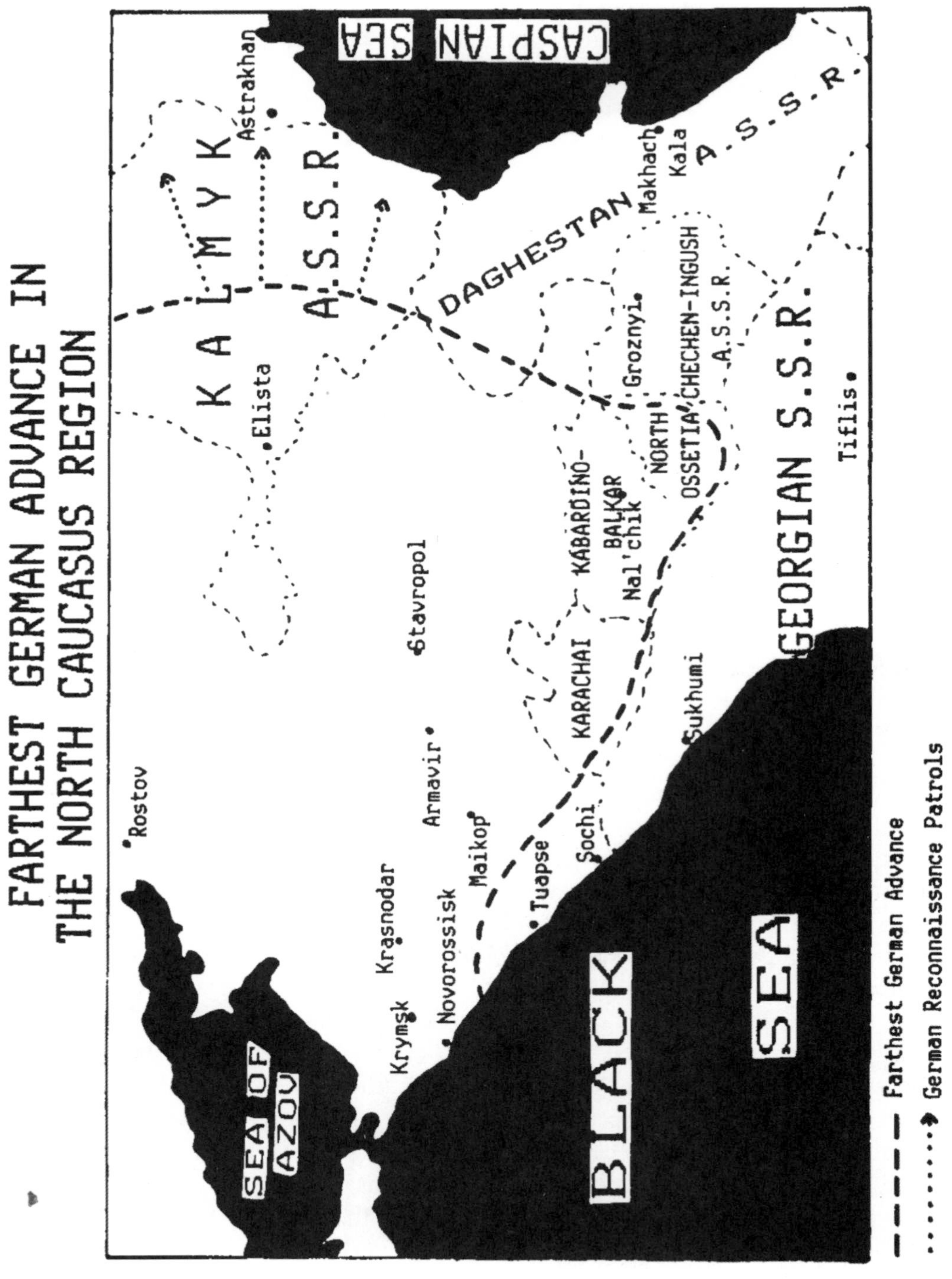

Tug, south of Utta.[470] The arrival of the Soviet winter offensive in and around Stalingrad however, begun on November 19th 1942, would eventually bring a halt to the German occupation of the Kalmuck region. By January 1943 the German

---

470 Piekalkiewicz, op cit. Page 218.

16th Motorized Infantry Division was in retreat, as well as the rest of Army Group's "A" and "B".

With them left countless tens of thousands of Caucasian peoples who had collaborated with the Axis forces, as well as their dependents. Dr. Doll, together with his assistants, tried to explain the situation to the Kalmuck leadership after assembling all of the tribes. It was a low point in morale: *"[The Kalmucks] at first refused to believe that their trust in the Germans had plunged them into an adventure that might mean the end of their existence as a people. In long columns, including women, children, herds, they made their way towards the Ukraine."*[471]

The Kalmucks counted on 10,000-15,000 people altogether. This left about 75-80,000 people who chose to stay behind for one reason or another. The decision was made to leave several cavalry squadrons in order to harass the advancing Russians. Those who did not wish to leave with the Germans and wanted to try their luck by staying were chosen. One "Division," which was equivalent to a reinforced battalion in strength, contained five cavalry squadrons (the 9th, 10th, 11th, 15th, and 16th). It remained behind to continue the fight using

BELOW: German cadre personnel of the Kalmucken Cavalry Corps in the summer of 1944. The unit remained active until January 1945 when it was overrun by Soviet armored forces and virtually destroyed. The remnants were sent to join Vlasov's Russian Army of Liberation at Münsingen Training Camp. *Museum of Modern History, Ljubljana, Slovenia.*

[471] Thorwald, op cit. Page 78.

guerrilla warfare. Soon after the Reds arrived, the region was flooded with NKVD forces looking for these cavalrymen.[1] It is quite certain that by the end of 1943 the NKVD had eliminated these Kalmuck squadrons. Hitler had stated flatly that he trusted the Muslim population of the Caucasus. He said so in December 1942 during a military conference: *"For the time being I consider the formation of these battalions of purely Caucasian peoples as very risky, while I don't see any danger in the establishment of purely Moslem units...In spite of all the declarations from Rosenberg and the military, I don't trust the Armenians either.*[2]

If Hitler considered the Moslems to be reliable, Stalin found them to be fittingly untrustworthy enough to eliminate their national "republics" and exile entire races of them. Based on their support for the Germans, Moscow made sure that the Kalmuck people were included in this group.[3] On December 27th 1943 the Presidium of the Supreme Soviet issued a decree which liquidated the Kalmyck ASSR, and listed a series of crimes against the state which the Kalmuck people had committed:

"...I don't know about these Georgians. They do not belong to the Turkic peoples...I consider only the Moslems to be reliable....All the others I deem unreliable."

"Taking into consideration that in the period of occupation by German-Fascist invaders of the Kalmyk ASSR many Kalmyks betrayed the motherland, joined organized German military detachments to fight against the Red Army, handed over to the Germans honest Soviet citizens, seized and handed over to the Germans kolhoz livestock evacuated from Rostov Oblast and Ukraine, and after the expulsion of the occupation by the Red Army organized bands and actively opposed organs of Soviet power so as to restore their destroyed German masters, commit bandit raids on kolhozes and terrorize the surrounding population..."[4]

BELOW: Arm Patch of the Kalmuck Cavalry Corps. It was a dark red design on a blue background. Another example existed in dark brown on a blue background. Both examples contained a yellow surround with the words in Tibetan and German reading "Kalmuck Formation Dr. Doll."

In the beginning of 1943, and in the midst of the withdrawal, "Dr. Doll" (a.k.a. Otmar Werva) was able to create a Kalmuck Cavalry Regiment based on a three-battalion

---

[1] Munoz, Antonio J. *"German SS, Police & Auxiliary Forces in Poland – Part V – 1944 and the Warsaw Uprising"* in AXIS EUROPA Bayside, New York 1998. Issue 15, Fall 1998. Pages 32-33

[2] FHQ, *'Lagesbesprechung,'* December 12, 1942.

[3] Dallin, Alexander. GERMAN RULE IN RUSSIA 1941-1945. MacMillan & Co. Ltd.: New York, 1957. Page 251.

[4] Pohl, op cit. Page 64.

unit. As stated earlier, each battalion was named a "Division," and contained around 750 men and a HQ's Staff of six officers and NCO's. This was equivalent to a reinforced battalion. In January Dr. Doll organized three such "Divisions" but one month later he had four. In each "Division" there were five (5) cavalry squadrons of 150 mean each plus a Squadron HQ's Staff of 5 officers and NCO's. Each Squadron contained three *Vzvod,* which were the equivalent of a cavalry platoon, and had a compliment of 48 men each plus a Platoon Staff of three officers and NCO's.[476]

On January 18th 1943 ten cavalry squadrons of the Kalmuck Legion were located just east of Salsk.[477] The unit was withdrawing right alongside *Kosaken-Regiment von Jungschultz* (Cossack Cavalry Regiment 'von Jungschultz'). This had been done for protection against attacks by superior enemy forces. The withdrawal followed the route of the Manych River all the way to Rostov. Since the unit had been officially formed on October 17th 1942, it had been referred to by the Germans as the *"Kalmuecken-Legion,"*[478] although the Kalmucks themselves referred to their formation as the *"Kalmyckij Kavalerijskij Korpus"* (Kalmuck Cavalry Corps).[479] In February 1943 the Germans changed the title of the unit and called it *"Kalmuecken-Verband Dr. Doll"* (Kalmuck Formation Dr. Doll).[480]

In February "Kalmuck Formation Dr. Doll" and "Cossack Cavalry Regiment von Jungschultz" withdrew alongside the 3rd Panzer Division until they reached Taganrog, where they were then attached to *Feldkommandantur 200.* Both units were now assigned to coastal guard duty by the Sea of Azov.[481] In early March 1943, while the Kalmuck formation was under the control of the 444th Security Division, Field Marshal von Kleist ordered that all Cossack units be sent to Kherson in the Ukraine with the objective of merging

RIGHT: A German liaison officer congratulates a Kalmyck volunteer after receiving an award for bravery. *Bundesarchiv.*

[476] Pronin, op cit. Page 230.
[477] Hoffmann, op cit. Page 193.
[478] Nafziger, op cit. Page 217.
[479] Hoffmann, op cit. Page 115.
[480] Nafziger, op cit. Page 217.
[481] Hoffmann, op cit. Page 115.

them all together into a larger armed and therefore more effective fighting force. The ignorance of higher authorities, who believed that if you were opposed to Stalin and rode a horse, you must be a "Cossack," caused the Kalmuck cavalry formation to be sent there as well.[482] However, it soon became evident to the German commanders at Kherson that "there had been a mistake." How could one supervise a volunteer from Smolensk and a Kalmuck horseman who had spent all his life on the Steppe using the same rules? This question was too problematic for the Germans and the Kalmuck formation was separated from the Cossacks and withdrawn.[483]

It was in March 1943 that the Kalmucks received their first arms since being withdrawn from their lands. It included 1,000 Dutch rifles and 35,000 rounds for these weapons.[484] Before this, the units had been armed with sabers and mostly Russian rifles. They were the first of what would be a plethora of various weapons from half a dozen different nationalities. By April 18th the strength of the unit was some 2,200 men. On April 28th there were 79 Kalmuck officers, 353 NCO's, and 2,029 men plus 2,030 horses and camels.[485] By the end of April 1943 the unit was still under 6th Army and performing coastal guard duty by Mariupol, 100 miles west of Taganrog. The unit next moved to Zaporozhye on the lower Dnieper River and placed under the control of *Oberfeldkommanten 397.* On May 23rd there were 67 Kalmuck officers, 374 NCO's, and 2,917 men. The formation had also "acquired" an amazing 4,600 horses and camels. By August 1943 the title of the *Kalmuecken Verband Dr. Doll* was changed to the *"Kalmucken Kavallerie Korps"* (Kalmuck Cavalry Corps). It was at this time that the order of battle for the unit was organized as follows:

CO: Major Ottmar Rudolf Werba (a.k.a. Dr. Doll)
Adjutant: Major Eduard Bataev[486]
Ia: Major Baldan Metabon
Liaison: Major Kallmeyer[487]

1. 1st Battalion – CO: Major Lukyanov Cilgirov
2. 1st, 4th, 7th, 8th, 18th Squadrons
3. 2nd Battalion – CO: Major Boldyrev Mukubenov
4. 5th, 6th, 12th, 20th, 23rd Squadrons
5. 3rd Battalion – CO: Major Abushinov Cilgirov
6. 3rd, 14th, 17th, 21st, 25th Squadrons
7. 4th Battalion – CO: Major Konokov Savkaev
8. 2nd, 13th, 19th, 22nd, 24th Squadrons

---

[482] Littlejohn, op cit. Page 319.
[483] Newland, Samuel J. COSSACKS IN THE GERMAN ARMY 1941-1945. Frank Cass: Portland, 1991. Page 38.
[484] Hoffmann, op cit. Page 116.
[485] Hoffmann, ibid. Page 136.
[486] Eduard Bataev was a pseudonym. His real name was Erdne Dordziev.
[487] By August 1944 *Hauptmann* Baron von Kutzschenbach had assumed this post.

It should be noted that the Chief of Staff, Baldan Metabon, was a non-Kalmuck Mongol. He held the post of Chief of Staff from June 1943 until March 1944. Metabon had previously been a member of the Soviet 110th Cavalry Division. From May until July 1944 Kalmuck Major Mukeben Chachlysev assumed this post. When Chachlysev and Dr. Doll were killed in battle in July 1944, Captain Dordzi Arbakov assumed the post of Chief of Staff. Another valuable officer, Lieutenant Kuskin, the Chief of the Kalmuck Field Police Troop, died in September 1944. Colonel Eduard Bataev would assume command of the Kalmuck formation upon the death of Doll.[488] The strength of the unit on July 21st 1943 was as follows:

GERMAN STAFF	KALMUCKS	GRAND TOTAL	
71 + 68[489]	3,000	3,139	
HORSES/CAMELS	RIFLES	PISTOLS	MACHINE PISTOLS
4,600	2,000	85	61
LIGHT MACHINE GUNS	HEAVY MACHINE GUN	LIGHT MORTARS (62mm)	HORSES AND CAMELS
5	1	14	1,800

The KKK continued to serve behind the lines throughout 1943. In July 1943 it was listed under *"Kommandeur der Osttruppen z.b.V. 721"* (Commander of Eastern Troops 721) by Krivoi-Rog.[490] By the end of 1943 the unit was under 4th Panzer Army and charged with guarding the rear of the German divisions in the Nikopol bridgehead. It was here that once again the Kalmucks proved their worth. The defensive positions of the Germans at the Nikopol bridgehead were in the shape of an arc seventy-five miles long. The depth of the combat area was no more than 6-9 miles from the eastern bank of the Dniper River. The *Plavna,* an extensive, swampy area also lay in this region. The area was ideal for Soviet guerrillas and indeed was swarming with guerrillas. The Germans had one ace in the hole- the Kalmuck Cavalry Formation. One author described very succinctly just how much the German *Landser* appreciated them:

"These clandestine forces in the inaccessible hiding places of the swamps would have been a serious danger to the German lines but for Senior Sergeant Willi Lilienthal. This man from Hamburg turned up at the end of November 1943 with the Kalmyk Major Abushinov. With him came five cavalry squadrons- 1,200 Klamyk volunteers from the yurt villages of the Kalmyk Steppe. These mortal enemies of the Russians had been fighting on the German side since the summer of 1942. With their wives and families they had followed 16th Panzer Grenadier Division from the wide-open spaces around Elista all the way to the west. There were no better scouts and no better hunters of partisans. They kept the franc-tireurs of the Plavna in check."[491]

[488] Hoffmann, op cit. Pages 132-133.
[489] Sixty-eight Germans were attached from *Landeschutzen Bataillon 917*, while an additional 71 were on staff on a regular basis.
[490] Hoffmann, op cit. Page 138.
[491] Carell, op cit. Page 385.

In fact this was one the of the Kalmuck battalions (the 3rd).[492] The rest were performing security duty up and down the length of the Nikopol bridgehead on both sides of the Dnieper River.[493] The unit was executing rear area security and anti-partisan duty for the 40th Panzer Corps. This duty was not without losses however, for by December 2nd the 3rd Battalion under Major Abushinov had lost 200 men killed or wounded. The 1st Battalion of the *Kalmyken Verband Dr. Doll* was under the command of Major Cilgirov. Together with Major Abushinov's 3rd Battalion and Hauptmann Munster and his *Geheim Feldpolizei Trupp 721,* these three units would take part in an anti-guerrilla sweep in late December 1943. *Abwehrtrupp 201* would also participate in an ancillary role. The aim of the operation was the destruction of Russian Major Kirpa's partisan band in the *Plavna* swamps. The operation netted 50 guerrillas killed and 32 captured. More importantly, it kept the partisans from the backs of the German defenders at the Nikopol bridgehead.

As good as they performed their missions in fighting their hated enemy, the Kalmuck nation experienced lack of understanding from many German commands that they were forced to come under. Having Asiatic features, they were not treated like the Cossacks, who it was thought, were transplanted Aryans. As a result, and in spite of their extreme value to the German command, they even experienced some bigotry:

"They carried out their task to the best of their ability. But the consequences of their transplantation into an alien world soon began to show up. Doll had never tried to convert Kalmucks into soldiers in the Western sense. He knew that it couldn't be done. The result was that they now became an endless nuisance to the German military authorites. Soon one headquarters or another was demanding that they be disarmed. It was mandatory that they be separated from their wives and children. The Kalmucks, for their part reacted, as they could not help reacting- like up-rooted, homeless, misunderstood, and unjustly attacked individuals. And what the Germans refused to give them they took for themselves."[494]

The next area of operations for the *Kalmucken Verband Dr. Doll* was in the Dnepropetrovsk-Dievka region in January 1944. It then moved on and crossed the Hungarian frontier in February 1944. It was in February that Gottlob Berger, the head of the SS Recruiting Office, had requested the Gestapo's consent to do away with the national insignias of peoples of the Caucasus that had been recruited to work in Germany. This request only covered the Tartars, Cossacks and Kalmyks, while the other Slavic peoples were still deemed too unreliable and needed to be easily recognized.[495]

---

[492] Hoffmann, op cit. Page 120.
[493] Hoffmann, op cit. Page 118.
[494] Thorwald, op cit. Page 78.
[495] Dallin, op cit. Pages 447-448.

At this time the *Kalmucken Kavallerie Korps* came under the control of *Oberfeldkommandatur 372*[496] in Lublin, Poland. In February 1944 the KKK was attached to the 213th Security Division for operational purposes.[497] The Kalmuck volunteers were now relegated to performing anti-guerrilla operations against the Polish underground army. In this new environment the Kalmucks encountered a different climate and fauna. The dry, wide-open steppes were long gone- replaced by woods, marshes, and hills that were unfamiliar to the Kalmucks. Their employment in these new surroundings would lower the effectiveness of the Kalmuck units, although alongside their beloved commander, Dr. Doll, they continued to do their best. In June 1944 the unit was still in the Lublin District where a large anti-partisan operation was launched against guerrillas entrenched in the Bilgoraj Forest. The Germans had amassed a sizable force for the drive and included the following formations:

GROUND UNITS:

1. Sonderdienst-Bataillon
2. CO: *SS-Sturmbannfuehrer* Helmut Pfaffenroth.
3. Sonderdienst-Bataillon
4. CO: *Rechtsrat* Dr. Jaensch.
5. 154. Reserve-Division
6. CO: *Generalleutnant* Altrichter
7. 174. Reserve-Division
8. CO: *Generalleutnant* Eberhardt
9. 213. Security-Division
10. CO: *Generalleutnant* Lendle
11. Kalmuck Cavalry Corps (attached to 213th Security Division)
12. CO: *Oberst* Dr. Doll
13. *Landschutzen-Bataillon 115* (Regional Defense Battalion 115)
14. *1.(mot.) Gendarmerie-Bataillon* (1st Motorized Gendarmerie Battalion)
15. 5th Hungarian Infantry Division (only parts, the bulk of the unit was at Kobrin).[498]

AIR UNITS:

1. *1. Staffel der Luftwaffe-Fliegergruppe 7*[499]

The Germans listed Polish Home Army losses as 898 killed, while *"193 bandits and 531 bandit helpers"* were apprehended. Axis losses were placed at 102 killed and 202 wounded. Captured equipment included 2 radio sets, 8 light machine guns, 3 anti-tank weapons (bazookas), 24 machine pistols, 2 mortars, 40 rifles, 230 hand grenades, 22,000 rounds of rifle ammunition, 2,500 rounds of

---

[496] Munoz, op cit. Page 33.
[497] Hoffmann, op cit. Page 143.
[498] Niehorster, Dr. Leo W.G. THE ROYAL HUNGARIAN ARMY, 1920-1945. Axis Europa Books: Bayside, 1998. Page 167.
[499] Munoz, op cit. Page 33.

machine pistol ammunition, 400 kg of explosives and 370 fuses.[500] There the KKK performed all too well, eliminating any guerrillas they found but their behaivior did not change and they continued to be misunderstood. The Germans always failed to understand how the Kalmucks felt. These people who had been uprooted from their ancestral home, had basically given everything up for the Germans, and felt that the Third Reich was indebted to them.

BELOW: Parade of the Kalmyken-Kavallerie-Korps (Kalmyk Cavalry Corps). The command staff sees the Kalmyk Squadrons parade past the German & Kalmyk officers. *Bundesarchiv.*

Therefore it was felt that the responsibility of the Germans was to supply the Kalmucks with their every need. If those needs were not met, then they felt justified in removing the property and livestock of the local peasants, as they needed it. Pretty soon the local German authorities were complaining about the formation once again. In a way, you couldn't blame the Kalmucks for taking this attitude, but it made them seem more and more like free-booters of the Thiry Years War. It was in July that the KKK was committed to fighting on the front lines against regular Russian units. Tragedy befell the unit when its beloved and much admired commander, Major Doll and some other Kalmuck leaders were killed. The loss of their German commander was so great that the unit became demoralized for a time and had to be withdrawn for several weeks. The interim commander was now to be Oberstleutnant Bergen.[501] Slowly, the unit's morale was once again raised, but not to the level at which it had been before the death of their beloved commander. On July 6th 1944 the KKK could count on the following forces and arms at its disposal:

[500] Gruenthal, Heide-Marie. NACHT UEBER EUROPA: DIE FASCHISTISCHE OKKUPATIONSPOLITIK IN POLEN (1939-1945). Pahl-Rugenstein Verlag: Koeln, 1989. Page 300.
[501] Hoffmann, op cit. Page 144.

OFFICERS	NCO'S	ENLISTED MEN	GRAND TOTAL
147	374	2,917	3,438
HORSES/CAMELS	RIFLES	PISTOLS	MACHINE PISTOLS
4,600	2,166[502]	246	163[503]
LIGHT MACHINE GUNS	LIGHT MORTARS	WAGENS	PKW and LKW light trucks
21	9	@ 500	8

In the fall and autumn the unit was stationed in the Radom district. The KKK was still there when in January 1945 the Soviet winter offensive began. The German front line cracked all across the front. It was during this chaotic period in the war that the Red Army forces finally trapped and conclusively defeated the Kalmuck Cavalry Corps near Kielce.[504] It was eventually decided that Colonel Eduard Bataev would assume command. What remnants remained of the KKK after the Soviet January 1945 offensive withdrew into Austria in February 1945. It is interesting to note that shortly before the Soviet offensive in January 1945, the strength of the KKK had been increased to around 5,000 men. This had been done by the ruthless conscription of all available manpower. Kalmuck men older than 45 years of age and younger than 18 had not been drafted into the Corps before 1944.[505]

Fascinatingly enough, it appears that plans had been in the works to include the KKK into the forming *Kaukasicher-Waffen-Verband der-SS*. One un-comfirmed report states that the *SS Hauptamt* (SS Main Office), had on January 8th 1945 authorized the transfer of the Kalmuck Cavalry Corps into the newly organized Caucasian SS Cavalry formation.[506 and 507] It would appear that the idea was dropped either because of the Soviet winter offensive, which began a few days later, or on account of the fact that the KKK had already been earmarked for the Vlasov Army. Perhaps it was on account of both, but in any case, we shall never really know. In late 1944, as General Andrei Andreivich Vlasov was attempting to gather all of the peoples of the USSR together against Stalin, most of the non-Russian peoples fighting alongside the Germans chose not to join his "Russian Army of Liberation." The small and greatly reduced Kalmuck Cavalry Corps, which had a "national committee" since as early as 1942, was one of the few non-Russian groups to decide to join the Vlasov movement.[508] This political decision was insignificant and without importance however.

The remnants of the Kalmuck Cavalry Corps withdrew through Silesia and eventually reached Austria in March 1945 when it was finally dissolved and its

---

502 Of this number, 1,092 were German manufactured, 1,025 were Russian Negat rifles, and 43 were Dutch. The 43 Dutch rifles were all that remained of the approximately 1,000 Dutch rifles that were given to the men in the Corps in early 1943. Perhaps they had been withdrawn because only 35,000 rounds of ammunition had been distributed for them.

503 Of this figure, 33 were German MP-40's and 135 were the popular Russian made PPS's.

504 Hoffmann, op cit. Page 153.

505 Hoffmann, ibid. Page 136.

506 Landwehr, op cit. Page 16.

507 Hoffmann, op cit. Page 152.

508 Dallin, op cit. Page 634.

survivors were used in the 600th and 650th Russian ROA Infantry Divisions.[509] This occurred at Troop Training Ground *"Neuhammer."*[510] The Kalmuck people experienced the same fate that awaited tens of thousands of other Soviet citizens who had chosen to cast their lot with the Germans. It was their sad fate in life to have put their trust in one dictatorial regime in order to get rid of an equally despotic power. In the end author Olaf Caroe put it quite justly when he said of them: *"It was their tragedy that, like the Kalmucks in the XVIIIth Century, they were used as pawns in the struggle of two contending empires on the chess-board of power-politics. In such a contest their own aims, however noble, could not be realized."*

ABOVE: Two Kalmyck volunteers, circa 1943. The unit wore Eastern Legion insignia. *Private American Collector.*

[509] Pronin, op cit. Page 229.
[510] Thorwald, op cit. Page 78.

Kalmuck Volunteers in German Service 1942-45

Abwehrtrupp 103 (August 1942)

Kalmücken-Legion (December 1942)

Kalmücken Verband Dr. Doll (January 1943)

Kalmuck Volunteers in German Service 1942-45

Kalmücken-Kavallerie-Korps (August 1943)

Kalmücken-Kavallerie-Korps (June 1944)

Kalmücken-Kavallerie-Korps (January 1945)

CHAPTER 9
The *Kaukasicher-Waffen-Verband der-SS* (1944-1945)

By Antonio J. Munoz

The origins of the *Kaukasicher-Waffen-Verband der SS* date back to the Volunteer Cadre Division made up of people from the USSR, which were initially located in France in 1944. This was the unit, which supplied trained volunteers to the eastern volunteer battalions, Russian and Cossack units, and even the 162nd Turkic-German Infantry Division. The division was a conglomeration of several training regiments that were merged together in early 1944 and stationed in France. The divisional headquarters was raised on February 1st 1944 and stationed in the French City of Lyon. This headquarters would administer the various regiments. There were five regiments in all, made up of differing nationalities. The regiments were split up along these racial and national lines. The order of battle for the Volunteer Cadre Division and its regiments was as follows:[511]

LOCATION	FORMATION	NATIONALITY
Lyon	Divisional Headquarters	Various ethnic groups
Lyon	*Schule der Freiwilligen Verbaende*[512]	Various ethnic groups
Castres	*Freiwilligen-Stamm Regiment 1*	Turkestani, Georgians, and North Caucasians
Mende	*Freiwilligen-Stamm Regiment 2*[513]	Volga Tartars, Azerbaijanis, and Armenians
Mende	*Freiwilligen-Stamm Regiment 2*[514]	AFTER April 1944: Ukrainians and Russians
Macon	*Freiwilligen-Stamm Regiment 3*	Turkestani Volunteers for the 162nd Infantry Division[515]
Namur	*Freiwilligen-Stamm Regiment 4*	Russian and Ukrainian Volunteers[516]
Langres	*Freiwilligen-Stamm Regiment 5*	Supplied Cossack volunteers.

511 Munoz, Antonio J. HITLER'S EASTERN LEGIONS, Volume II – THE OSTTRUPPEN. Axis Europa Books: Bayside, 1997. Page 24.

512 School of Volunteer Formations.

513 *"Freiwilligen-Stamm Regiment 2"* (Volunteer Cadre Regiment No.2).

514 The Division's 2nd Cadre Regiment went through reorganization several times. First it was purged of all Volga Tartars, Aserbaijanis, and Armenians in April 1944. The unit was now filled with Russian and Ukrainian volunteers. Two months later, in June the regiment was once again purged, this time of Ukrainians who were transferred out and the unit became a purely Russian formation.

At the end of 1944 General Andrei Andreyvich Vlasov, the head of the ROA, or Russian Army of Liberation, attempted to assert control over all of the peoples of the USSR that were fighting on the German side. The leaders of the Caucasian peoples protested bitterly about this. They were said to accept Vlasov as the head of a liberation movement against Stalin, but his control should be kept strictly to the Russian peoples. The importance of the document for our purposes lies in the fact that the Caucasian SS Cavalry formation was mentioned, alongside other Caucasian units:

ETHNIC GROUP	NUMBER	GRAND TOTAL
In Legion and Reinforcement battalions:		
Armenians	11,000	
Azerbaijanis	13,600	
Georgians	14,000	
North Caucasians	10,000	
TOTAL		48,600
In Construction and Supply units:		
Armenians	7,000	
Azerbaijanis	4,795	
Georgians	6,800	
North Caucasians	3,000	
TOTAL		21,595
In German units:		
Heer	25,000	25,000
In the *Waffen-SS* and *Luftwaffe*		
Waffen-SS	4,800	
Luftwaffe	2,200	
TOTAL		7,000
GRAND TOTAL		77,195

In addition, their comments specifically mentioned the Caucasian SS formation:

"In 1942 almost all the battalions were committed to fornt-line service. In spite of errors and abuses, they served well and frequently earned recognition from the highest German command headquarters. There are engaged in battle in Croatia at the present time: I. Georgian Mountaineers Battalion. II. North Caucasian Mountaineers Battalion and North Caucasian Battalions 842 and 843. The above-mentioned units participated in the difficult withdrawals from Greece. In Italy there are the Azerbaijanian regiment of the 162nd Infantry Division, Georgian Battalion II/198, and the Caucasian SS cavalry formation presently being organized."[517]

---

[515] After June 1944, the regiment was supplied purely Ukrainian volunteers.
[516] After June 1944, the regiment was supplied purely Ukrainian volunteers.
[517] Thorwald, Juergen. THE ILLUSION: SOVIET SOLDIERS IN HITLER'S ARMIES. Harcourt Brace Jovanovich: New York, 1975. Page 233.

The commander assigned to this new SS cavalry force was *SS-Standartenführer der Reserve* Arved Theurmann. Theurmann was born to a German family on August 4th 1892 in Zabela, Czarist Russia. His SS Personnel File at the Berlin Document Center states that his SS number was Nr. 273 804. This SS number was dated October 10th 1935. Before joining the SS, he had served in the SA from 1930 until 1935. Strangely enough, below this listing, his file also had another SS number for him, Nr. 273 509 and dated July 1st 1930.[518] His Nazi Party number was 3 703 – a very low Party number. The file states he received his promotion to *SS-Obersturmbannführer* on October 10th 1935. Apparently he was married on July 16th 1927. His wife was born in Pforzheim on July 26th 1903. He had four children, three girls and a boy. The first was a girl born on October 6th 1928. The next two were also girls, born on March 4th 1932 and August 3rd 1935. The last child was the boy, who was born on September 25th 1937.[519] It seems that he was trying very hard to raise a large family as the *Reichfuehrer-SS* Heinrich Himmler had requested.

Theurmann's career ran as follows: After graduating from High School, he attended a "higher education" in Hannover. After school he attended the SS Officer's Academy at Bad Tolz, he was assigned to *SS-Oberabschnitt West* from May 1st to October 1st 1937. He next served on the staff of SS Military District

ABOVE: A member of a North Caucasian volunteer stands alongside a German Order Police officer who seems to be looking at the harness of the horse hitched to a wagon. The arm patch of the Auxiliary Security Police can be clearly seen on the left arm of the volunteer above. *Museum of Modern History, Ljubljana, Slovenia.*

[518] Berlin Document Center file (hereafter referred to as BDC) – *SS-Standartenfuehrer der Reserve* Arved Theurmann.
[519] BDC, ibid.

XX (Kiel) from October 1st 1937 until April 1st 1940. His next tour of duty was on under *Kommando Stab Ost* from June 27th 1941 until April 1st 1942. His next assignment was as an officer of the Legion Nederland from April 1st until July 11th 1942. He was next placed on the Personal Staff of the *Reichfuehrer-SS (Persönlichen-Stab Reichführer-SS)* for one month, while being attached to SS-Ersatz-Abteilung Ost between July 11th and August 12th 1942. It was then that Theurmann was assigned to the staff of the Higher SS & Police Command "Caucasus" *(Hoehere SS und Polizeifuehrer Kaukasien)*.[520]

Theurmann held this post from December 1st 1942 until April 9th 1943. His next post was on the cadre staff of the forming Latvian volunteer SS division. He held this position from April 9th until November 1st 1943. His next assignment was on the reserve list of the *SS-Fuehrungshauptamt* (SS High Command) from November 1st 1943 until December 20th 1944. He was then posted to the local SS leader at Bad Saarow from December 20th 1944 until January 1st 1945, when he was assigned as commander of the forming Caucasian SS cavalry formation. The actual order sending him to command the unit was dated January 25th 1945, although the "official" date of his posting was December 20th 1944.[521]

Theurmann's service in the Czarist Army had included a stint with the Russian 16th Hussar Regiment during the First World War. During the Russian Civil War he had served in Lithuania from 1919 until 1920 as a member of the Baltic *Landwehr Division.* His military awards then had included the Baltic Cross 1st and 2nd Class, the Maltese cross and Russian Order Cross. In his years in the service of the Reich, Theurmann was holder of the "SS Death's Head Ring," "Honor Dagger" and also had the "Reich Sports Medal". [522] Preparations for the organisation for the Caucasian SS Cavalry Formation however, had begun even earlier. *SS-Obersturmbannfuehrer* Walter Blume, of the *SS-Fuehrungshauptamt* was

ABOVE: Two volunteers from the North Caucasus region. The man on the right side still seems to be wearing a civilian cap. *Antonio J. Munoz Collection.*

[520] Yerger, Mark C. ALLGEMEINE-SS. Schiffer Publishing: Atglen, 1997. Page 69.
[521] BDC, op cit.
[522] BDC, ibid.

assigned to help organize the *Kaukasicher Waffenverbande der SS.*[523] Records show that as early as October 31st 1944 the regimental commanders for the unit had been chosen. These were:

I. *Oberst* (Colonel) Israfil Bey
II. *Oberst* (Colonel) Kutschuk Ulagaj
III. *Oberst (Colonel) V. Sarkisjan*
IV. *Oberst* (Colonel) Michael Pridon Zulukidse[524]

Colonel Israfil Bey, as well as the other regimental officers was offered the rank of *Waffen-Standartenfuehrer der-SS.* Bey was in charge of the Azerbaijani volunteers, while Ulagaj (also spelled Ulagay) was the assigned commander of the North Caucasian soldiers. *Waffen-Standartenfuehrer der-SS* Michael Pridon Zulukidse was to lead the Georgian contingent. Zulukidze was actually a Georgian prince. Each regiment would contain two cavalry battalions. The North Caucasian and Azerbaijani cavalry battalions were to be trained and organized by the Replacement Battalion of the 22nd SS Volunteer Cavalry Battalion, while the Replacement Battalion of the 8th SS Cavalry Battalion trained the two Georgian cavalry battalions. The first regiment to be ready for employment was the Georgian SS Cavalry regiment, which completed training in November 1944.[525] However, several battalions of

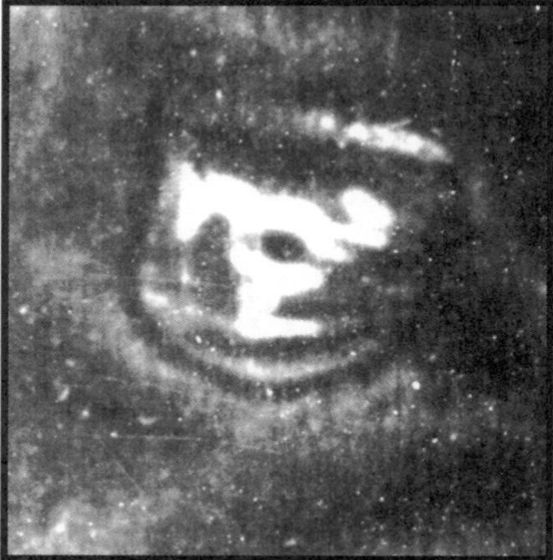

LEFT & ABOVE: A North Caucasian volunteer. The 2nd design of the *"Bergkaukasien"* arm patch can be seen on the right sleeve. *Museum of Modern History, Ljubljana, Slovenia.*

523 NARS Microfilm Series T-175, Roll 168, Frame 2700372.
524 NARS Microfilm Series T-175, Roll 168, Frame 2700380.
525 NARS Microfilm Series T-175, Roll 168, Frame 2700386.

Caucasian peoples were already assigned to the unit in September 1944. The North Caucasian 836th Infantry Battalion, who had 6-700 men left, after its withdrawal from France, was located in Belfort, France and was earmarked for the Caucasian SS Cavalry unit.

On January 1st 1945 *Stamm-Regiment 1* of the Volunteer Cadre Division- that is, the battalions containing the Turkestani, Georgians, and North Caucasian volunteers were at Neuhammer Training Camp, Germany as of January 20th 1945.[526] Unfortunately, the unit only had 375 men left- or barely a half a battalion sized unit of men to work with. The head of the North Caucasian people, Kasi Kasbek was located in Paluzza, northern Italy. It was there that he had a *Lehr-Schule* (Leadership School) plus a hospital for wounded Caucasian volunteers, which was run by Professor Dr. Ketschkarov.[527] Paluzza was located just north of

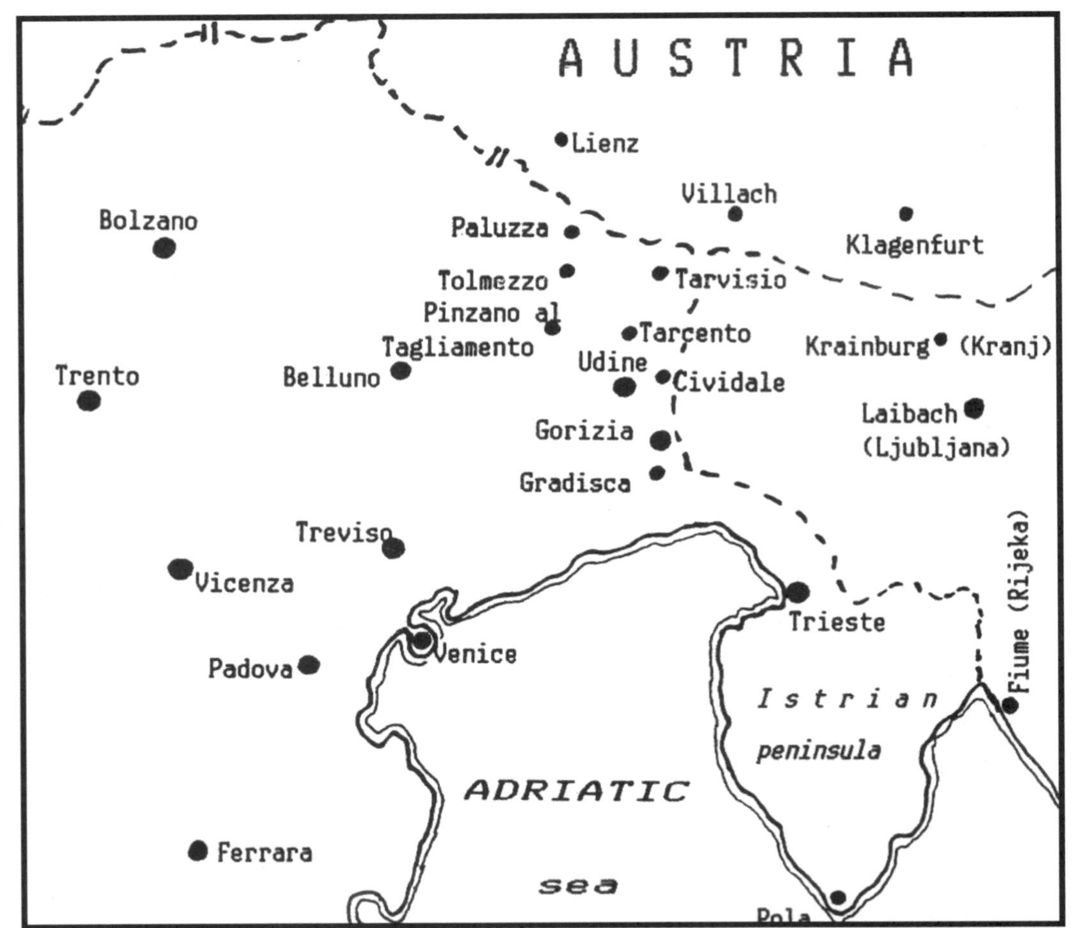

ABOVE: General reference map of the Italo-Austro-Slovene border region. This area is the region in northern Italy where the *Kaukasicher-Waffenverband der-SS* was stationed. General Domanov's Cossack Corps also operated in this region. This corps protected the family members of the Pannwitz Cossack Corps (15th SS Cossack Corps).

526 NARS Microfilm Series T-175, Roll 168, Frame 2700388-92.
527 NARS Microfilm Series T-175, Roll 168, Frame 2700459.

Tolmezzo, in northern Italy. The decision to send the forming SS cavalry unit to northern Italy was partly made by *SS-Standartenfuehrer* Fritz Arlt, the head of the *Leitstelle-Ost* staff, who was responsible for ethnic groups from the Soviet Union.[528]

A document dated "21 October 1944" and written by *SS-Standartenführer* Fritz Arlt of *Amtsgruppe D* of the *Leitstelle-Ost* staff listed the recruiting potential for the forming Caucasian SS cavalry unit. In the letter, Arlt stated that there he estimated to be 30,000 potential Caucasian volunteers in German-held POW camps, with an additional 10,100 more likely recruits in German work and construction units. Furthermore, his statistics showed that 60,000 more Caucasian recruits were already in the hands of the *Wehrmacht,* and that of this number perhaps 10-20,000 had already been either killed, wounded, captured, or had deserted. This still left a large pool of possible volunteers with which to raise the formation, a good number of which were in the Legion volunteer battalions.[529]

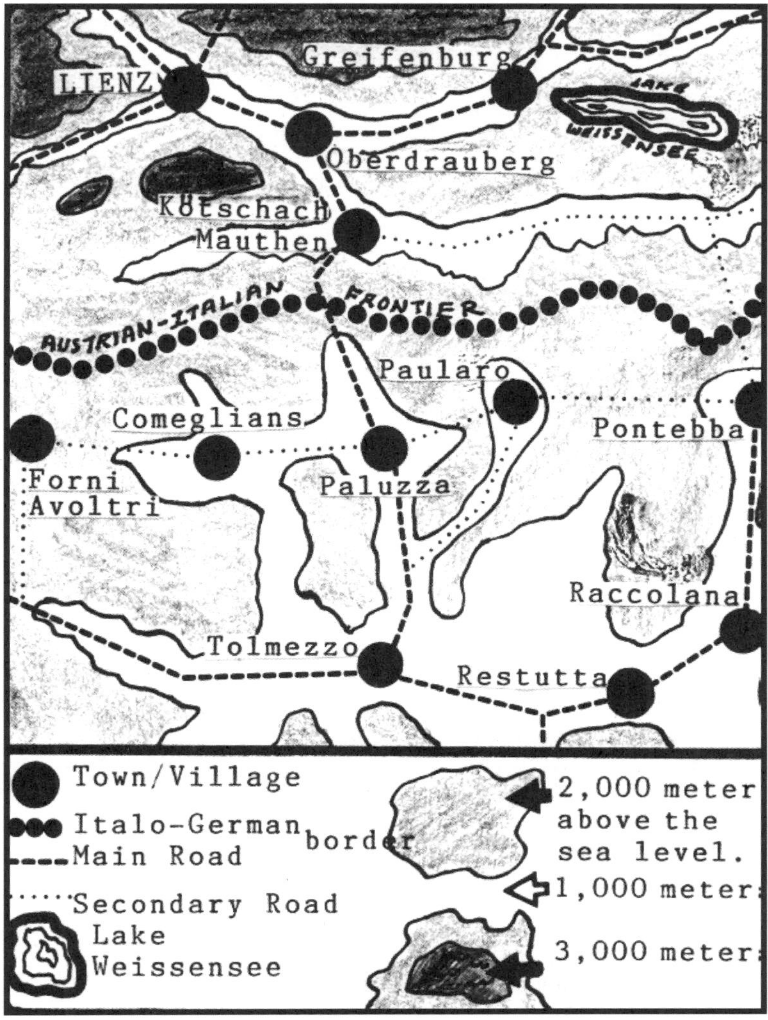

LEFT: The general area of operations of the Kaukasicher-Waffen-Verband der SS. The region between Tolmezzo – Paluzza – and the Austrian frontier by Lienz is shown.

Members of the Cossack exiles in Italy today swear that the Caucasian SS Cavalry Brigade should not be confused with the Volunteer Brigade "North Caucasian" *(Freiwilligen Brigade Nord-Kaukasien)* which arrived in Tolmezzo, northern Italy from Novogrudki, in Beloussia under Sultan Ghirey-Klitsch. They state that these two formations were separate and distinct. However, it may be possible that they

[528] Carnier, Dr. Pier Arrigo. L'ARMATA COSACCA IN ITALIA 1944-1945. Grupo Ugo Mursia Editore, 1990. Page 27.

[529] NARS Microfilm Series T-175, Roll 168, Frame 2700388.

simply could wish to eliminate all reference or affiliation to the SS from their history, or it just could be that indeed two separate units existed. However, German author Joachim Hoffman, who is an expert on the Russian volunteer movement, gives us a clue. He stated clearly that the Armenian, Aserbaijani, Georgian, North Caucasian, and Turkestani volunteers were earmarked for the Caucasian and Eastern Turkic SS formations.[530] This means that any units made up of these people in late 1944-45 were earmarked for these two SS brigades.

However there were always exceptions and reasons why some of these units never made it to their assigned formation(s). For example, as late as March 15th 1945 Ukrainian Guard Company 644 and 1/825 Volga Tartar Company was performing railroad security duty under the 2nd Army in Prussia.[531] Another example was the revolt of the 822nd Georgian Infantry Battalion, stationed on Texel Island off the coast of Holland. It mutinied on April 6th 1945 and killed all 400 Germans of its 1,600-man strength. It took the Germans a week of hard fighting before they finally put the revolt down.[532] Specific units that have been tentatively identified as having helped to form the Caucasian SS Cavalry Brigade included the following units:[533]

1. 835th North Caucasian Construction Battalion (?)[534]
2. 837th Volga Finnish Battalion
3. 781st Turkestani Battalion
4. 783rd Turkestani Battalion
5. 786th Turkestani Battalion
6. 789th Turkestani Battalion (?)
7. 795th Georgian Battalion
8. 797th Georgian Battalion (?)
9. 799th Georgian Battalion (?)
10. 815th Armenian Battalion

In addition, there were several battalions, which were dissolved, in early 1944. The personnel from these units were transferred to other battalions, which were still active. It may well be that these men were processed through the newly created Volunteer Cadre Division in France. Those battalions included the following formations:

1. 792nd Turkestani Battalion
2. 793rd Turkestani Battalion

---

[530] Hoffman, Joachim. DIE OSTLEGIONEN 1941-1943. Verlag Rombach Freiburg, 1986. Page 164.
[531] NARS Microfilm T-78, Roll 645, Frame 000778.
[532] Littlejohn, David. THE PATRIOTIC TRAITORS. THE HISTORY OF COLLABORATION IN GERMAN-OCCUPIED EUROPE, 1940-45. Doubleday & Company, Inc.: Garden City, New York, 1972. Page 365
[533] Tessin, Georg. VERBAENDE UND TRUPPEN DER DEUTSCHEN WEHRMACHT UND WAFFEN-SS 1939-1945. Biblio Verlag: Osnabrueck1975-1999. 18 Volumes. Volumes 12 & 13, various pages.
[534] A "(?)" mark indicates that this unit was "possibly" used, but there is no definitive proof.

3. 794th Turkestani Battalion
4. 820th Azerbaijani Battalion
5. 839th Turkestani Battalion
6. 840th Turkestani Battalion
7. 841st Turkestani Battalion
8. 842nd Turkestani Battalion

As stated earlier, the Caucasian SS Cavalry Brigade was formed with the remnants of the 1st Volunteer Cadre Regiment. The Volunteer Cadre Division was raised from the following battalions:

1. Volunteer Cadre Regiment No.1
2. I/370th Turkestani Battalion
3. II/4th Georgian Battalion
4. I/9th Georgian Battalion
5. II/4th North Caucasian Battalion

These battalions were all disbanded and sent to Castres, southern France in February 1944.

6. Volunteer Cadre Regiment No.2
7. 804th Azerbaijani Battalion
8. 806th Azerbaijani Battalion[535]
9. II/9th Armenian Battalion[536]
10. 832nd Volga-Tartar Battalion
11. 833rd Volga-Tartar Battalion
12. 834th Volga-Tartar Battalion

These battalions were all disbanded and sent to Mende, southern France in February 1944.

1. Volunteer Cadre Regiment No.3
2. 792nd Turkestani Battalion
3. 794th Turkestani Battalion
4. 839th Turkestani Battalion
5. 841st Turkestani Battalion
6. 842nd Turkestani Battalion

These battalions were all disbanded and sent to Macon, southern France in February 1944. The regiment was to provide replacements for the 162nd (Turkic) Infantry Division.

---

[535] The 804th and 806th Azerbaijani Battalions were later saent to reinforce the 162nd (Turkic) Infantry Division.

[536] In May 1944 the men from this unit were withdrawn from the 2nd Volunteer Cadre Regiment and became the 4th Battalion of Grenadier Regiment 917 of the 242nd Static Infantry Division.

Volunteer Cadre Regiment No.4

This regiment was formed in March from Ukrainian and Russian volunteers. The regiment was to serve replacements for units made up of these two Soviet peoples.

Total strength of the *Freiwilligen Brigade Nordkaukasien* was around 5,000 men and 2,000 dependents. The Caucasian SS Cavalry Brigade was forming in Paluzza, just north of Tolmezzo. Many times both units have been confused, but one wonders if indeed they were distinct and separate formations. Just notice that the strength of the Caucasian SS Cavalry Brigade had 4,800 men (according to one source), while the Volunteer Brigade North Caucasus had 5,000. This and other similarities like their apparent location make us wonder. Another similarity is that the German liaison for the *Freiwilligen Brigade Nord-Kaukasien* was *Hauptmann der Schutzpolizei* Paul Theurer, while the commander of the SS cavalry brigade was Arved Theurmann- similar names.[537] In addition, some of the officers like Colonel Kutschuk Ulagaj were mentioned as being an officer in both formations. This too, is an indication that the formations were one and the same.

On November 24th 1944 *SS-Hauptsturmfuehrer* Dr. Rainer Olzscha, of *Amtsgruppe D* of the *SS-Hauptamt* submitted a report detailing the insignia to be worn by the men in each regiment of the Caucasian SS Cavalry Brigade. The *Waffengruppe "Georgien"* would continue to wear the national insignia on their left sleeve. The other *Waffengruppe's- "Armenien," "Nordkaukasien," and "Aserbeidschan"* would also do as well. In addition, each *"Waffengruppe,"* would be entitled to wear a black cuffband on the lower left sleeve. The cuff band would have the title of the regiment with silver thread lettering.[538] Each *"Waffengruppe"* was the equivalent of a regiment in size and contained two cavalry battalions. Each cavalry battalion contained four cavalry squadrons, one of, which was considered a "heavy" squadron because they had more machine guns and mortars. A German *"Kriegsgliederung"* for 1944 contained a detailed outline of how the SS cavalry brigade was organized:[539]

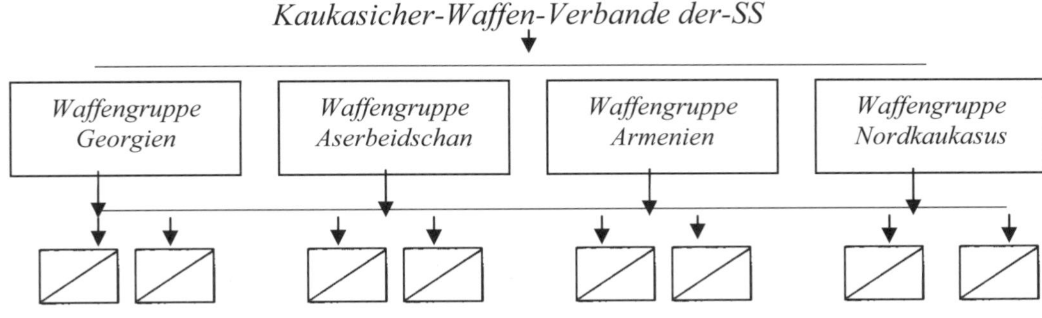

[537] According to German sources, Paul Theurer was in reality the liaison officer to Cossack General Domanov and his Special Armed Cossack Corps stationed in northeastern Italy.

[538] NARS Microfilm Series T-175, Roll 168, Frame 2700321.

[539] NARS Microfilm Series T-175, Roll 140, Frame 2668442.

It appears that the main reason why Arved Theurmann had been chosen to command the Caucasian SS Cavalry Brigade was (1) his knowledge of the Russian language and (2) his service on the staff of the *Hoehere SS und Polizeifuehrer "Kaukasien"* (Higher SS & Police Command "Caucasus"). This tour of duty in the Caucasus however, had been brief. Other officers who had served with Theurmann in that command included:

I. *SS-Sturmbannfuehrer* Otto Boettcher
II. *SS-Hauptsturmfuehrer* Otto Krumbein
III. *SS-Hauptsturmfuehrer* Willi Krueger
IV. *SS-Hauptsturmfuehrer* Otto Thorbeck
V. *SS-Obersturmfuehrer* Hans-Otto Jaeger
VI. *SS-Untersturmfuehrer* Werner Schmidt
VII. *SS-Untersturmfuehrer* Hugo Isebarth[540]

While Theurmann was the typical ethnic German from Russia, the regimental commanders of the brigade had some interesting careers and similar backgrounds together. Kutschuk Ulagaj for example, who was the commander of the *Waffengruppe Nordkaukasien* had been married in 1932. He had been born a Circassian and was a Muslim by faith and had a wife. He had graduated from an academic school in Krasnodar and on August 6th 1913 had graduated from the Czarist Army Cavalry School at Yelissavetgrad. Ulagaj had served in the Czarist army and had won numerous medals, including the Dagger of St. George, which had an inscription describing his bravery in combat.[541]

He had served as a cavalry officer while in the Czarist army and by 1917 had been promoted to Captain. He returned to the North Caucasus Mountains in 1917 and helped to organize a White Russian cavalry formation. He and his family then immigrated to Poland after losing the civil war. His cavalry unit fought in the North Caucasus Mountains until October 1st 1920 at which time they withdrew and fought their way to the Crimea where he

LEFT: Kutschuk Ulagaj as he appeared in late 1944. *Berlin Document Center.*

[540] BDC – Personnel Folder of Arved Theurmann.
[541] BDC – Personnel Folder of Kutschuk Ulagaj.

joined Wrangel's White Russian forces. He served there as commander of the 3rd Kuban Cossack Cavalry Regiment. He ended the war as a colonel.

Ulagaj left the Soviet Union at the end of the Russian Civil War. He continued his activities in the cavalry by next serving as an officer of the Polish Army. When the Bolshevik government tried to take lands that belonged to Poland a war broke out between the USSR and Poland in the early 1920's. In this short-lived war, Ulagaj served with distinction. In 1924 Kutschuk Ulagaj and his family had moved to Albania where Ulagaj was able to obtain a commission in the Albanian Army as a cavalry officer. He served in the Albanian Army from 1924 until 1937. Ulagaj's father was a career public advisor who spoke Russian, Albanian, Italian, and Croatian. The first mention of Kutschuk Ulagaj serving in the German Army was a note in his personnel file that stated he had been on the staff of the German command in Belgrade, Yugoslavia in 1942. It is likely that he might have served initially in the Russian Guard Corps[542] and then been placed on the permanent staff of the German command in Belgrade.

On December 12th 1944 Kutschuk Ulagaj was inducted into the *Waffen-SS* and sent to *SS-Panzergrenadier Ersatz und Ausbildungs Abteilung 1* (SS Armored Infantry Training and Replacement Battalion No.1) where he would be clothed and outfitted. On the same date he was given the rank of *Waffen-Standartenfuehrer der-SS.*[543] At this time, his wife and children were staying at the Hotel Aschgan in Villach Eck am See, in southern Austria. This town was actually just across the border from Slovenia. What is fascinating about Ulagaj's history towards the end of 1944 is his connection to *Waffen-Obersturmfuehrer der-SS* Tscherim Soobzokov.

RIGHT: Photograph of Pridon Zulukidse as he appeared in late 1944. *Berlin Document Center.*

Soobzokov was a Circassian whose affiliation with the Germans had begun in 1942. He had actually gotten into trouble in 1941 when he had struck the judge who had sentenced his brother to a term in a Soviet prison. He had hence been placed in a Red Army penal battalion and had been wounded in the shoulder in 1941. After this, he was sent to rehabilitate in a military hospital in his home region, although he stated that he received little medicine or treatment. When the Germans arrived in July 1942 it wasn't

[542] Munoz, Antonio J. FOR CZAR AND COUNTRY: A HISTORY OF THE RUSSIAN GUARD CORPS, 1941-1945. Axis Europa Books: Bayside, 1999. Page 13.
[543] BDC – Personnel file of Kutschuk Ulagaj.

long before the 18 year-old Soobzokov volunteered for service. He became a junior clerk in the local police department in August. He won the disfavour of the local German officer so in the fall of 1942 he joined a front line unit:

"The Germans had formed a battalion, the 800th Battalion, of our people to fight with their army. I don't know where they got all the people. Some were probably prisoners of war who joined to keep from starving. In late September, this battalion passed through our town to fight the Red Army 30 miles away, and I asked to go with them. To me were given two carts and horses, and my job was to supply the battalion horses with hay. I was only in one fight- some Red Army troops attacked us once from the forest and I didn't run away. I deserted from the battalion in February of 1943 and lived with a group of refugees. In June of 1943, in the town of Partizani, in the Ukraine, one person who is now living here in New Jersey pointed me out to the Germans. I was picked up by the German military police and they told me I would be shot within 48 hours. But some of our elders talked them out of it, and I was taken back into the armed forces and sent to the front in the Kuban sector."[544]

Soobzokov managed to get himself out of the battalion by claiming that his shoulder wound was giving him trouble. He was sent to a Legion hospital in Poland where he says he received little medical care- much like he had experienced while under the Red Army! He managed to escape from Poland and was in Hungary in 1944 when the German Military Field Police *(Feldpolizei)* caught up to him:

BELOW: A pre-war photograph of SS-Standartenführer Arved Theurmann. *Berlin Document Center.*

"In November 1944, I was taken into custody again in Hungary and accused of hiding Soviet partisans, which was totally untrue. They put me through a tough interrogation...they beat me around the head a lot, on and off, for about two weeks. I was released with the help of an elderly man who was an officer with Vlasov. He was able to talk the Feldgendarmerie [German Military Field Police] out of shooting me. By this time the

[544] Interview of the late Tscherim Soobzokov.

land was shrinking, you could not move around anymore.[545] *I told the whole truth to a professor I knew, and he took me to meet General Kutschuk Ulagaj, who was recruiting Circassians for the Germans. He had been a Colonel in the Czarist army, and his name was known to all Circassians. My wife's grandfather had once hid him from the communists, around 1920. He escaped from the Russians and had been living in Berlin. He told me that I was in a lot of trouble but that he would try and help me."*[546]

It was in this way that Tscherim Soobzokov came to be posted to the *Kaukasicher Waffenverbande der-SS* on January 4th 1945. He thus saved himself from a Red Army or German firing squad, or at the very least, from a Soviet Gulag or German concentration camp. The commander of the *Waffengruppe Georgien* was Michael Pridon Zulukidse, who was a Georgian prince who was born on October 8th 1894 in Tiflis, Georgia. He had served in the Georgian Army and had earned the Kaiser Wilhelm Order of Anna medal (3rd and 4th class); the Stanislaus Medal (3rd and 4th class) with laurel crowns. He had graduated from High School in Elisaethpol inn 1912. He then attended the Czarist cavalry school in St. Petersburg. He received his commission as a 2nd Lieutenant in October 1914. He was assigned to the Russian 7th Ulahn Regiment. He later attended Law School at St. Petersburg but only completed three semesters. On April 8th 1922 his wife gave birth to a son, Konstantine Gleimuras Zulukidse.

Zulukidse served on the Rumanian front as a battalion commander in the Czarist 7th Cavalry Division. This Russian division was decimated and Zulukidse was captured, along with other members of the division. He and eight other Georgian officers and 120 other ranks in the division decided, with the help of the Austro-Hungarian military, to form a Georgian cavalry regiment which would help form the core of a Georgian army that would help give Georgia its independence. It was in Georgia that his unit was merged with the Georgian 2nd Hussar Regiment on March 28th 1918. His cavalry formation was a part of the White Russian forces and as a result, was instrumental in helping top defeat the Red Army holding Achalziche. His regiment was later sent to Tiflis to assist the city commandant in clearing the capital of *"Bolshevist-Anarchists."*[547] Zulukidse described quite fully his service in those days:

"With my same two squadrons I was ordered to Letschmum under General Shobataschvilli to fight the rebels. After this operation on July 28th 1918 I received the order to free the town of Abastumani which was being held by the Turks. Besides my two squadrons I was given an infantry battalion. After the battle of Sekari Pass on August 4th I occupied the town the next day and was commandant until August 15th. By the outbreak of the Georgian-Armenian war I was called to Tiflis and named the commander of the 2nd Hussar Regiment after which we were sent to the Armenian front. Here I was a group commander to the

545 Soobzokov means by this that Axis held territory was shrinking.
546 Interview of the late Tscherim Soobzokov.
547 BDC – Personnel file of Kutschuk Ulagaj.

left flank. The war ended with the destruction of the Armenian troops and I successfully took part in all the operations."

"On January 5th 1919 I was promoted to colonel. On May 1st I was sent to Ossetia to put down a Bolshevist rebellion. After clearing this place of the Bolshevist bandits on May 27th I was named commandant of the government district of Arthvili. I remained here until the Bolshevist army invaded Georgia, upon which I formed a special cavalry formation to be used on the Tiflis front. On February 25th 1921 Tiflis fell and my unit was sent to defend the town of Batum from the Turks. With my cavalry unit and a few infantry units under my orders, the town was freed of the Turks, who lost 2,000 men and 60 officers. After the full occupation of Georgia by the Bolshevists I began my illegal actions, which were carried on in contact with Colonel Kaichorso, the famous leader of the Georgian rebellion of 1924. In 1923 I had to break off my fight against the Bolshevists under special circumstances and flee to Turkey."[548]

From Turkey Michael Pridon Zulukidse immigrated to France where he made his living by first being a factory hand and then working as a truck driver. His days as an officer and prince were now behind him. For many years he worked in these low paying jobs while attending French language High School at night. In 1936 he volunteered to join the Spanish *Falange* to fight the Spanish government which was partly controlled by the Communists, Socialists, Anarchists, and other left leaning or liberal groups. Even after so many years, the resentment he held over the loss of his country to the Bolshevik revolution was deep enough in his convictions to want to oppose it.

When the Vichy French government was formed, its army had to be reorganized. Zulukidse was approached and asked if he would accept a commission in the Vichy French Army in Syria. He was told that in the future there might be a chance that the French Army might enter the Caucasus against the Russians and the French General Staff needed officers who knew the countryside and its people. Zulukidse accepted but things did not develop as he thought. His regiment in Syria was sent against British forces that were advancing from Palestine. On January 1st 1941 he had been made commander of a Vichy French cavalry in the Saphis Regiment in Algiers, where on January 25th 1941 he and his squadron put down what he termed as a *"communist inspired rebellion in a Vichy French infantry regiment."* From March through September 1941 he took part in Vichy French army maneuvers in North Africa.

In September 1941 some comrades who told him that the French were forming a regiment of volunteers to fight in the Soviet Union contacted him. With forty other ex-Czarist officers he travelled to Versailles, the home base of the French Legion in order to join. He and his comrades remained in the regiment for three weeks until the German command told them that they had to be withdrawn because they were not French born. In those heady days of late 1941 the Germans were still arrogant and full of bluster. They felt that these Czarist-era officers were not needed. However, in October 1942 he and others like him were recalled to

[548] BDC – Personnel file of Kutschuk Ulagaj.

Germany. They were sent to the Reich Ministry for Eastern Affairs and offered the opportunity to fight in Russia. He was sent to Kielce, Poland to a Russian POW camp that was run by *SS-Sturmbannfuehrer* Geibel. There he was entrusted with forming a Caucasian formation from Soviet POW's. He served in this unit all through 1943 as guard personnel in other camps. The men also took part in anti-partisan operations. In 1944 the formation was disbanded and he and 100 other men were sent to France where they served as Waffen-SS guard personnel.[549]

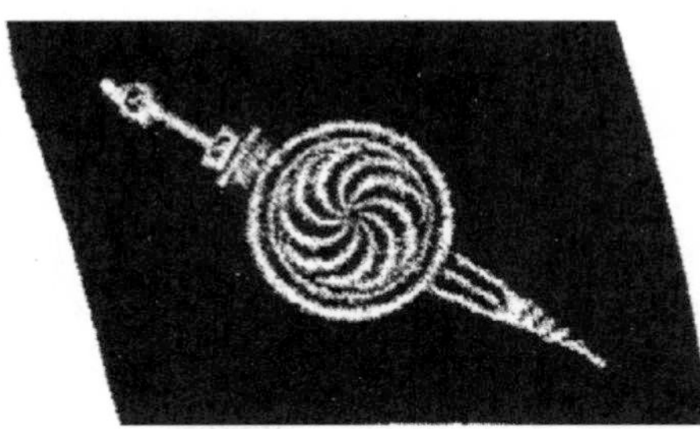

ABOVE: The right collar tab of the *Kaukasicher-Waffenverband der-SS*. It sported a Muslim sword and shield.

BELOW: Another member of the Caucasian SS Formation in Paluzza, Italy, summer of 1944. *Museum of Modern History, Ljubljana, Slovenia.*

Between August 1st 1944 and February 1st 1945 Colonel Michael Pridon Zulukidse served as a reserve officer in *SS-Kavallerie Ausbildungs und Ersatz Abteilung 8* (SS Reserve and Replacement Cavalry Battalion No.8). From February 1st 1945 he was under the *Kaukasicher Waffen-Verband der-SS*. It was the *SS-Kavallerie Ausbildungs und Ersatz Abteilung 8* that helped to train and organize the *Waffengruppe Georgien* and its two-cavalry battalions. *SS-Kavallerie Ausbildungs und Ersatz Abteilung 22* (SS Reserve and Replacement Cavalry Battalion No.22) helped to train and organize *Waffengruppe Nordkaukasus and Waffengruppe Aserbeidschan.*

The personnel file that remains for Muhammed Israfil Bey is quite small. In it it states that Bey had a wife and was named Fatima Beyraschenska, who had been born in Slovenia on October 15th 1907. He and his wife had two children. His daughter was born in 1929 and his son in 1932. In 1944 the boy was aged 12 and daughter was 15. Ulagaj had been born in Bsebai on January 25th 1893. He

[549] BDC – Personnel file of Kutschuk Ulagaj.

spoke many languages: Aserbaijani, Russian, Polish, and French. Like the other officers assigned to command the *Waffengruppen* (regiments) in the Caucasian SS Cavalry Brigade, Bey was promoted to *Waffen-Standartenfuehrer der-SS* on December 12th 1944. The following officers were in command of the brigade as of March 6th 1945:[550]

CO	*Standartenfuehrer der Reserve*	Theuermann, Arved
Ia	*Obersturmbannfuehrer*	Aichinger, Hubert Ritter von
Ic	*Hauptsturmfuehrer der Reserve*	Jaskiewicz, Emanuel von
CO – *SS Waffengruppe "Armenien"*	*Waffen-Standartenführer der SS*	V. Sarkisjan
CO – *I. Abteilung/ SS Waffengruppe "Armenien"*		
CO – *II. Abteilung/ SS Waffengruppe "Armenien"*		
CO – *SS Waffengruppe "Aserbeid-schan"*	*Waffen-Standartenfuehrer der SS*	Bey, Muhamed Israfil
CO – *I. Abteilung/ SS Waffengruppe "Aserbeidschen"*		
CO – *II. Abteilung/ SS Waffengruppe "Aserbeidschen"*		
CO – *SS Waffengruppe "Georgien"*	*Waffen-Standartenfuehrer der SS*	Zulukidse, Pridon
CO – *I. Abteilung/ SS Waffengruppe "Georgien"*		
CO – *II. Abteilung/ SS Waffengruppe "Georgien"*		
CO – *SS Waffengruppe "Nordkaukasien"*	*Waffen-Standartenfuehrer der SS*	Kutschuk, Ulagaj
CO – *I. Abteilung/ SS Waffengruppe "Nordkaukasien"*		
CO – *II. Abteilung/ SS Waffengruppe "Nordkaukasien"*		
Other officers in the *Kaukasicher Waffen-Verband der SS:*		
	Waffen-Hauptsturmfuehrer der SS	Barkalaja, Akaki
	Waffen-Obersturmfuehrer der SS	Abubakarov, Abdul
	Waffen-Obersturmfuehrer der SS	Dzhido, Misost
	Waffen-Obersturmfuehrer der SS	Dujakulov, Ramasan
	Waffen-Obersturmfuehrer der SS	Magomayev, Chaibulla
	Waffen-Obersturmfuehrer der SS	Schakmann, Anatolie
	Waffen-Obersturmfuehrer der SS	Soobzokov, Tscherim
	Waffen-Obersturmfuehrer der SS	Uschano, Magomed
	Waffen-Untersturmfuehrer der SS	Dikayev, Achmet

[550] Munoz, Antonio J. THE LAST LEVY: WAFFEN-SS OFFICER ROSTER, MARCH 1st 1945. Axis Europa Books: Bayside, 2001. Pages 96-97.

	Waffen-Untersturmfuehrer der SS	Dscharimov, Ismail
	Waffen-Untersturmfuehrer der SS	Kordsachia, Georg
	Waffen-Untersturmfuehrer der SS	Magomayev, Harun-Raschid

On November 3rd 1944 the actual Waffengruppen were in various stages of development. While each group was to contain about 1,200 men each, some were overstrengthed. One of these was the *Waffengruppe Nordkaukasus*, which had a strength of 1,538 officers and men.[551] The full distribution of officers and men in this group as of November 3rd 1944 was as follows:

Formation	Officers	NCO's	Men	Total
Regimental Staff	20	15	12	47
1st Cavalry Battalion Staff	16	8	21	45
1st Cavalry Squadron	7	17	64	88
2nd Cavalry Squadron	8	18	60	86
3rd Cavalry Squadron	10	20	97	127
4th Cavalry Squadron	6	17	72	95
Total:	47	80	314	441
2nd Cavalry Battalion Staff	5	6	3	14
5th Cavalry Squadron	5	12	79	96
6th Cavalry Squadron	4	13	57	74
7th Cavalry Squadron	4	13	44	91
8th Cavalry Squadron	4	10	69	83
Total:	22	54	282	358
3rd Cavalry Battalion Staff	6	15	38	59
9th Cavalry Squadron	3	18	131	152
10th Cavalry Squadron	3	17	101	121
11th Cavalry Squadron	1	17	93	111
12th Cavalry Squadron	1	24	119	144
Total:	14	91	482	587
13th Cavalry Squadron	5	15	72	92
14th Cavalry Squadron	-	-	-	-
GRAND TOTAL	108	255	1,162	1,525

The commander of *SS Waffengruppe "Armenien"* was a certain *Waffen-Standartenführer der-SS V. Sarkisjan.* No data is available on this officer. The fascinating thing about this order of battle is that the unit contained three battalions instead of the authorized two. We do not know whether this organization remained unchanged until the end of the war, or if the regiment was reduced to the requested two-battalion regiment. What is known is that the unit remained stationed in northern Italy for the rest of the war. The actual transfer of the unit from Neuhammer Training Camp to Paluzza in northern Italy occurred in early January 1945. The actual order was dated December 30th 1944.[552] The

---

551 NARS Microfilm T-175, Roll 168, Frame 2700458.

552 Landwehr, Richard. THE KAUKASICHER WAFFENVERBANDE DER-SS. Siegrunen Magazine: Brookings, No. 56, Spring 1994. Page 11.

German field post numbers were finally assigned to the formation in February 1945 and were the following:

FORMATION	FIELD POST NO.
Brigade Staff – *Kaukasicher-Waffen-Verbande der-SS*	13360
Regimental Staff – *Waffengruppe Nordkaukasien*	02439
I. Bataillon / *Waffengruppe Nordkaukasien*	20358
II. Bataillon / *Waffengruppe Nordkaukasien*	15518
Regimental Staff – *Waffengruppe Armenien*	12443
I. Bataillon / *Waffengruppe Armenien*	19309
II. Bataillon / *Waffengruppe Armenien*	16927
Regimental Staff – *Waffengruppe Georgien*	21345
I. Bataillon / *Waffengruppe Georgien*	23251
II. Bataillon / *Waffengruppe Georgien*	00628
Regimental Staff – *Waffengruppe Aserbeidschan*	21771
I. Bataillon / *Waffengruppe Aserbeidschan*	22213
II. Bataillon / *Waffengruppe Aserbeidschan*	01793

In late April 1945 a Cossack officer reported to the combined Cossack-German headquarters of General Krassnoff in Tolmezzo. He announced that the Catholic[553] "Osoppo" Partisan Brigade had captured Georgian Prince Michael Pridon Zulukidse, and his 3rd Detachment. In reality, he had surrendered his command after the guerrillas had promised to spare him and his men. Krassnoff was now offered the same choice, but he chose to move his men and horses to southern Austria.[554] In the beginning of 1945 the *Kaukasicher-Waffenverbande der-SS* was still located in northern Italy. It was not used against the Red Army or the western Allies but continued to

LEFT: A member of the *Kaukasicher-Waffen-Verband der-SS* in northern Italy, in late 1944. *Bundesarchiv.*

[553] And therefore, non-communist guerrilla formation.
[554] Carnier, op cit. Pages 159-160.

remain "forming" until it meekly surrendered to British forces in early May 1945. Tscherim Soobzokov's interview described the attitude he had while in the forming SS cavalry formation. While it may or may not be prevalent throughout the unit, it is nonetheless very poignant and a fitting end to the story of this Caucasian SS Cavalry Brigade:

"I never had anything to do with fighting in the SS, because this division had not completed its formation. Actually, I think the idea was to keep POW's out of combat and out of the hands of the Russians. We were almost disconnected from Berlin. Nobody was under my command, and I wasn't under anybody's command. What stupid person is going to join the SS at the end of 1944?"

It should be noted that at the time of this interview, Soobzokov was under investigation by the Office of Special Investigations for crimes against the Jewish population in the Caucasus region, so he may have been trying to over-simplify the matter in order to put an innocent spin on his actions. But it appears from all available data that he did not join the Waffen-SS until December 1944 and that the *Kaukasicher Waffen-Verband der-SS* committed no crimes against the Soviet Army or western Allies, basically because it was never committed; let alone the partisans or civilian population in Italy. However, by his own admission he did serve in one capacity or another under the SS & Police Command in the Caucasus and that is the basis for the charges made against him.

BELOW: Two members of the *Kaukasicher-Waffen-Verband der SS.* The insignia they are wearing indicates that they are from the Gendarmerie unit. Notice the SS style shield on the left sleeve. *Museum of Modern His-tory, Ljubljana, Slovenia.*

LEFT: Two members of the *Kaukasicher-Waffen-verband der-SS* in northern Italy. This formation was a cavalry unit that contained two cavalry battalions in each regiment. *Museum of Modern His-tory, Ljubljana, Slovenia.*

BELOW: Map of the upper Caucasus region and Volga Steppe. The region shows the areas where the German SS *Einsatzgruppen* murdered 3,800 Caucasian Jews in September 1942.

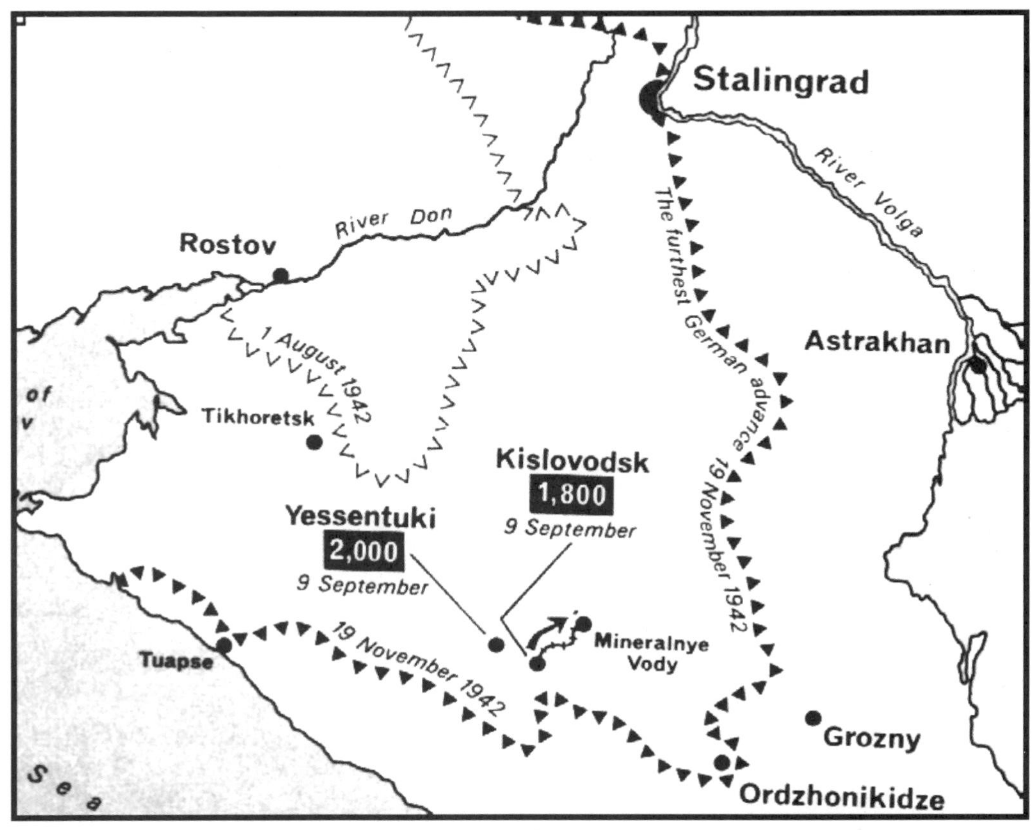

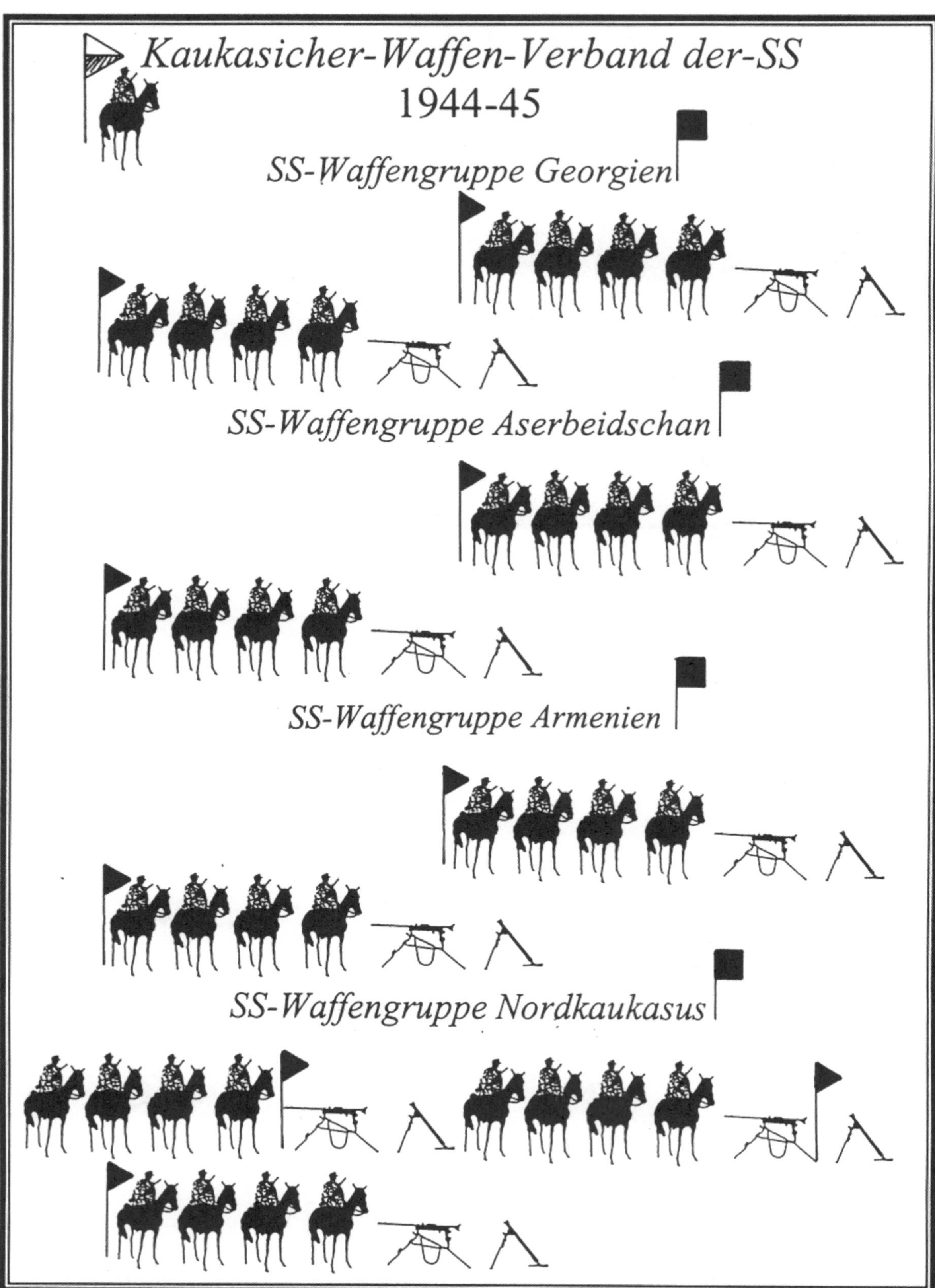
Kaukasicher-Waffen-Verband der-SS
1944-45
SS-Waffengruppe Georgien
SS-Waffengruppe Aserbeidschan
SS-Waffengruppe Armenien
SS-Waffengruppe Nordkaukasus

The Soviet Republics of the Caucasus Region

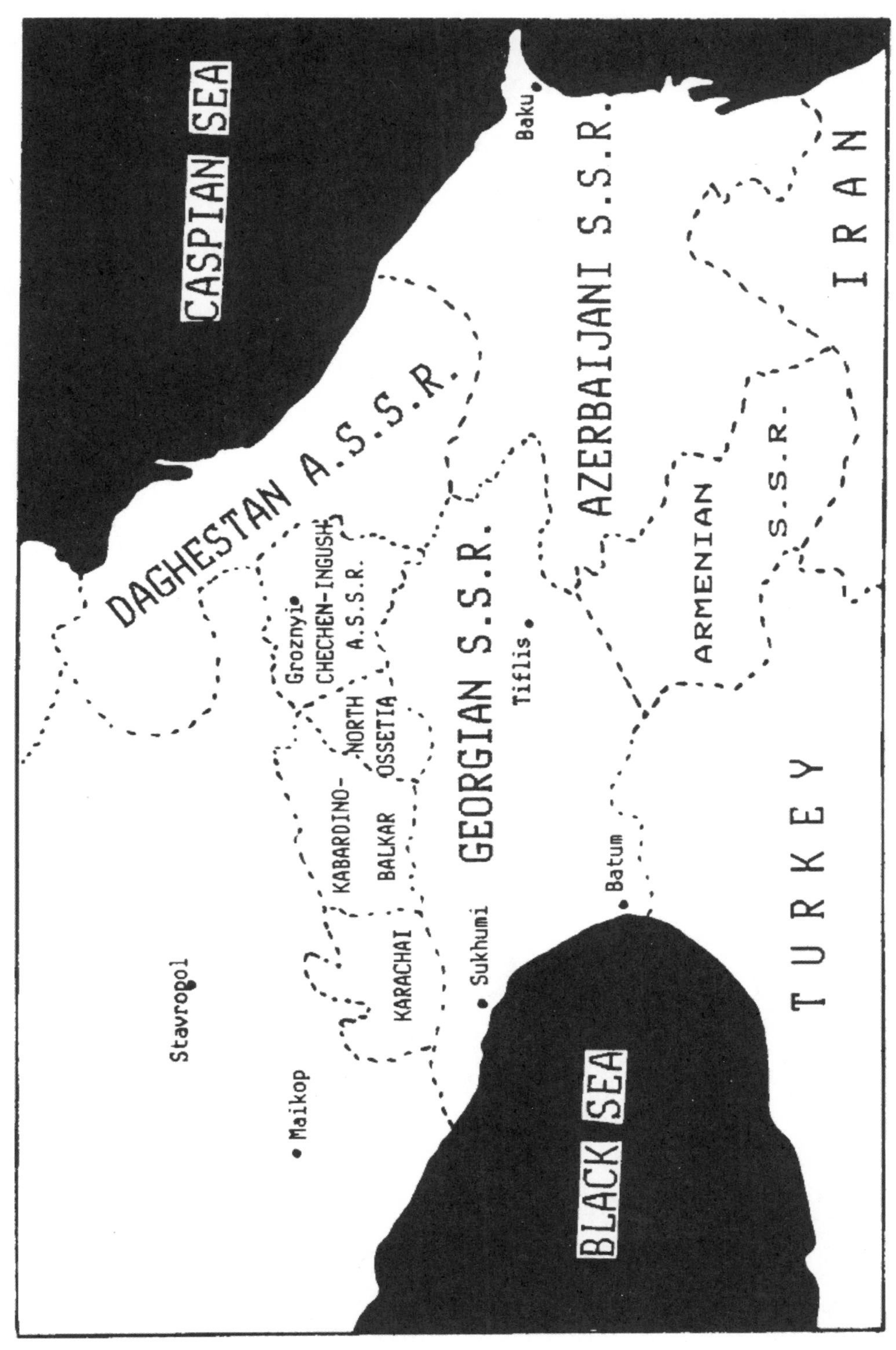

CHAPTER 10
The *Waffen-Gebirgs-Brigade der-SS (tar. Nr.1)* 1944-1945

By Antonio J. Munoz

The origins of the *Waffen-Gebirgs-Tartar-Brigade der-SS* goes back to the initial batch of Crimean Tartar volunteer auxiliary companies that began to be raised in the Crimean peninsula in the fall of 1941. Even before the German invasion of the Soviet Union in 1941, there were groups and individuals the mostly Moslem areas of the country that opposed the communist system. These came from the various races such as the Uzbeks, Kazaks, Kirghiz, Tajiks and Turkmen, as well as Crimean Tartars, and the peoples of the Caucasus: the Kalmucks of the Volga Steppe, the Azerbaijanis, Georgians, Armenians, and North Caucasians. Most of these émigré refugees had escaped the USSR before 1923. After this year it became increasingly difficult for those people who opposed the Bolsheviks to escape the Soviet Union.[555]

Most of the refugees were of the older generation like Mustafa Chokai, Osman Khoja (also called Togan), as well as younger men like Kayum Khan, who would become one of the leading proponents of a Turkestan free of Russian or

ABOVE: In the beginning the Crimean Tartar villagers were given second-hand weapons, given a white arm patch that read "Im Dienst der Deutschen Wehrmacht" ("In the Service of theGerman Armed Forces") and attached to local German garrisons. This photograph was takern in the winter of 1941-42. *Bundesarchiv.*

[555] Caroe, Olaf. SOVIET EMPIRE: THE TURKS OF CENTRAL ASIA AND STALINISM. MacMillan & Co. Ltd.: London, 1954. Page 243.

Turkish control. Two of these exiles were a Crimean intellectual leader named Jafar Krimer and Cafar Seydahmet. They too, like the others, were hoping not for the restoration of the Romanov monarchy like the White Russian exiles, but sought independence for their region. They basically distrusted any Russian government, whether it was Communist, monarchist, or even democratic. The attitude of the White Russian armies during the Russian civil war had borne this out. These leaders sought no less than complete independence from Moscow. Nothing less would suffice. This attitude lasted even through the Second World War. While General Andrei Andreyvich Vlasov sought to gain the control of all anti-Stalinist forces, these leaders did their best to oppose this plan. In fact, even though a special effort was made in late 1944 to find non-Russian peoples to join Vlasov's KONR movement, of those that accepted, most were figureheads without political clout. In fact, of all the committees formed by Rosenberg for the non-Russian peoples of the USSR, only the Kalmucks actually merged with the KONR units.[556]

RIGHT: The first Tartar battalions are formed during the summer of 1942. Initially, these units were not clothed in proper military attire. Their volunteers wore civilian clothes and were armed with hand-me-down weapons. *Antonio J. Munoz Collection.,*

It was therefore not strange that when the Germans reached some of the regions where these peoples lived, they would be stirred to action by German promises of self-determination and independence. Former émigrés who were aided in forming so-called independence committees under the guidance of Alfred Rosenberg and his *Ostministerium* (Ministry for the East) backed up these promises. Of course, the Germans were giving false hopes and aspirations when in fact they had no desire to free the people of the Soviet Union and establish independent

[556] Dallin, Alexander. GERMAN RULE IN RUSSIA 1941-1945. A STUDY OF OCCUPATION POLICIES. MacMillan & Co. Ltd.: London, 1957. Page 635.

states. In fact, on July 16th 1941 Adolf Hitler himself had declared that the Crimea was to be emptied of its entire people and populated by transplanted Rumanian ethnic Germans from Transnistria.[557] *Reichfuehrer-SS* Heinrich Himmler convinced Hitler however, that the current military situation called for this plan to be postponed until after the war was over. He stated clearly that: *"For the duration of the war, touching on the question of the Tatars and their transfer to consolidated areas by all means must be avoided. We must not bring the least unrest to these people who incline towards us and have faith in us. This would be a catastrophic error."*[558]

Actually, the very first Crimean volunteers were formed in October 1941 under the auspices of the German 22nd Infantry Division. This German unit organized a militia unit that was armed with rifles but initially did carry any ammunition. The militia was to act as the local police in the villages and towns in the region of the 22nd Division. Things began to get more organized in January 1942 when the German SD, or *Sicherheitsdienst* (SS Security Service) began raising Tartar Self-Defense companies: *"A Tartar Self-Defense Company about 100 strong, will be formed by the SD for the fight against partisans in the following localities: (1) Karassubasar, (2) Bacht-schissaraj, (3) Simferopol, (4) Yalta, (5) Aluschta, (6) Sudak, (7) St. Krim, and (8) Evpatoria."*[559]

ABOVE: In the beginning, the Tartar recruits wore ragged civilian attire. Arms were mostly second-hand Russian weapons. Initially, German clothing began to be issued in early 1942 and included a variety of attire. By the fall of 1942, the Germans had begun to arm and properly clothe their Crimean Tartar allies with proper German clothing and weapons. *Bundesarchiv.*

Eventually, these SD-sponsored companies were expanded into six battalions. *Einsatzgruppe D,* which had units operating in the Crimea basically, supplied the officers and direction, as well as the logistics to arm and clothe these Crimean Tartar volunteers. That the SD was directly involved in the creation of these Tartar units is

[557] Dallin, ibid. Pages 254 and 256.
[558] Dallin, ibid. Page 257.
[559] Heilbrunn, Otto and Aubrey Dixon. COMMUNIST GUERRILLA WARFARE. George Allen & Unwin Ltd.: London, 1954. Page 129.

borne out by another account:

"Six Crimean Tatar battalions were recruited for police and anti-partisan duties largely under the direction of the SD. While the German command found them helpful, the extreme nationalists looked upon them as the nucleus of a future 'Crimean Army'. Among the rank and file their formation appears to have evoked neither enthusiasm nor violent hostility."[560]

However, although six battalions were originally raised, the eventual number would reach eight. These battalions were listed as the following:

I. *Schutzmannschaft Bataillon 147*
II. *Schutzmannschaft Bataillon 148*
III. *Schutzmannschaft Bataillon 149*
IV. *Schutzmannschaft Bataillon 150*
V. *Schutzmannschaft Bataillon 151*
VI. *Schutzmannschaft Bataillon 152*
VII. *Schutzmannschaft Bataillon 153*
VIII. *Schutzmannschaft Bataillon 154*[561]

BELOW: By the fall of 1942 some of the Crimean Tartar battalions were more organized and better clothed. Here a Crimean Tartar company parades past its German commander. *Museum of Modern History, Ljubljana, Slovenia.*

[560] Dallin, op cit. Pages 258-259.
[561] Tessin, Georg and Norbert Kannapin. WAFFEN-SS UND ORDNUNGSPOLIZEI IM KRIEGSEINSATZ 1939-1945. Biblio Verlag: Osnabrueck, 2000. Page 595.

The initial creation of a Tartar Mountain Regiment was made in late March, early April 1944, when the German Order Police Command in Crimea gathered what effective Tartar battalions still remained and merged them into a three-battalion Tartar Mountain Regiment. This unit took part in the German defense of the Crimea and was withdrawn shortly before the fall of the peninsula. The first instance of the regiment being employed against the Russians was on April 11th, 1944 when the unit was situated in Dzahankoy and used to bolster the Rumanian defenses of that Crimean city.[562]

The regiment's main line of resistance was in the city itself, while the Rumanian 10th Infantry Division, with about 4,500 men covered its left flank, and the Rumanian 19th Infantry Division, with about an equal number of troops, covered its right flank. Unfortunately, by April 14th the combined German, Rumanian, and Tartar forces had been pushed back south, halfway to Simferepol. The unit was now holding the town of Barangar[563] The Tartar Mountain Regiment next served north of Simferepol, and again, was located between the trenches of 10th and 19th Rumanian Infantry Divisions. The unit was withdrawn to Rumania in the beginning of May 1944. In fact, the Germans managed to evacuate 36,000 Germans, 3,800 enemy POW's, 16,000 Russian volunteers of the "Eastern Legions", 1,600 Crimean civilians, and 9,600 Rumanians.[564]

Reichführer-SS Heinrich Himmler instructed the commander of the Higher SS & Police Command "Black Sea" *(Höheren-SS und Polizeiführer "Schwarzes Meer"), SS-Brigadeführer und Generalmajor der Polizei* Konrad Hitschler to supply 200 ethnic-German men of the *Ordnungspolizei* (Order Police) for the forming Tartar SS brigade.[565] Hitschler had previously held the command of SS Police Cadre Regiment *"Oranienburg."*[566] Later in the war, Hitschler would be posted as Commander of the Order Police in Hungary.[567]

The Germans assigned a brigade medical officer for the unit. This turned out to be *SS-Sturmbannführer* Dr. Heinz Thumstäder. Born on April 26th 1907, Thumstäder's SS number was 314179. He was later promoted to *SS-Obersturmbannführer* four months after the brigade was disbanded. The actual date of promotion was April 30th 1945.[568] According to one source, the unit was to contain about 600+ auxiliary "hilfswilliger" who were not actual combat troops but support personnel. The actual strength of the brigade on September 20th 1944 is hereby compared with its authorized strength:[569]

---

562 Hinze, Rolf. RÜCKZUGKÄMPF IN DER UKRAINE 1943/44. Verlag Dr. Rolf Hinze: Neustadt, 1991. Page 545.

563 Hillgruber, Andreas. DIE RÄUMUNG DER KRIM 1944. Verlag E. S. Mittler & Sohn: Berlin, 1959. Page

564 Hillgruber, ibid. Page 40 and Hinze, op cit. Page 565.

565 Kleitmann, K. G. DIE WAFFEN-SS – EINE DOKUMENTATION. Verlag Der Freiwillige: Osnabrück, 1965. Page 513

566 Mehner, Kurt. DIE WAFFEN-SS UND POLIZEI 1939-1945. Militär-Verlag Klaus D. Patzwall: Norderstedt, 1995. Page 325.

567 SS-Hauptamt. DIENSTALTERLISTE DER SCHUTZSTAFFEL DER NSDAP. STAND VON 9. NOVEMBER 1944. Gedruckt in Reichsdruckerei: Berlin 1944.

568 NARS Microfilm T-175, Roll 77, Frame 2593584.

569 Kleitmann, op cit., page 379.

	Officers	NCO's	Men	Auxiliaries	Grand Total
Authorized	67	440	2,927	614	3,434
Actual	11	191	2,219	-	2,421

Of the above number of 2,421 men, exactly 1,097 men were *Volk-deutsche.* The morale of the unit was low, given that they had been withdrawn from the Crimea and all of the volunteers knew that Germany was on the defensive and losing ground. In addition, the poor and lack-luster administration and management of the Tartars at the hands of their German masters had a permanent negative and demoralizing effect on the volunteers.[570] This was borne out by the defection of men from the Tartar battalions beginning in late 1942.

The unit had received the remnants of the *Ostmuselmanische-SS Regiment* (Eastern Muslim SS Regiment), a unit that had operated in Belorussia and had taken part in the crushing of the Warsaw uprising.[571] At the end of 1944, the decision was made to disband the SS brigade and reform the Tartar volunteers into a two-battalion regiment that would become part of the *Östturkischer-Waffenverband der-SS* (Eastern Turkic Moslem SS Brigade). An attempt had been made earlier in the summer to absorb the Kalmuck Cavalry Corps, but this move was opposed by the German officers and Kalmucks in the unit and they were eventually transferred into the Cossack Cavalry Corps in 1945.[572] The Tartar volunteers now became part of *SS-Waffengruppe Krim.* The group had two infantry battalions of four companies each, plus a separate anti-tank company and infantry gun company attached to the regimental *(Waffengruppe)* headquarters.[573]

LEFT: Variations of the Emblem of the Crimean Tartars – the "Tamga." Please refer to page 18 in this book for a full color illustration of both variants.

[570] Dallin, Alexander. GERMAN RULE IN RUSSIA: A STUDY OF OCCUPATION POLICIES 1941-1945. MacMillan & Co. Ltd.: London, 1957. Pages 260-265.

[571] Littlejohn, David. FOREIGN LEGIONS OF THE THIRD REICH, Vol.4. J.R. Bender Publishing: San Josre, 1987. Page 253.

[572] Littlejohn, David. THE PATRIOTIC TRAITORS: THE HISTORY OF COLLABORATION IN GERMAN-OCCUPIED EUROPE, 1940-45. Doubleday & Company: Garden City, 1972. Page 325.

[573] Munoz, Antonio. FORGOTTEN LEGIONS: OBSCURE COMBAT FORMATIONS OF THE WAFFEN-SS 1943-1945. Paladin Press: Boulder, 1991. Page 180.

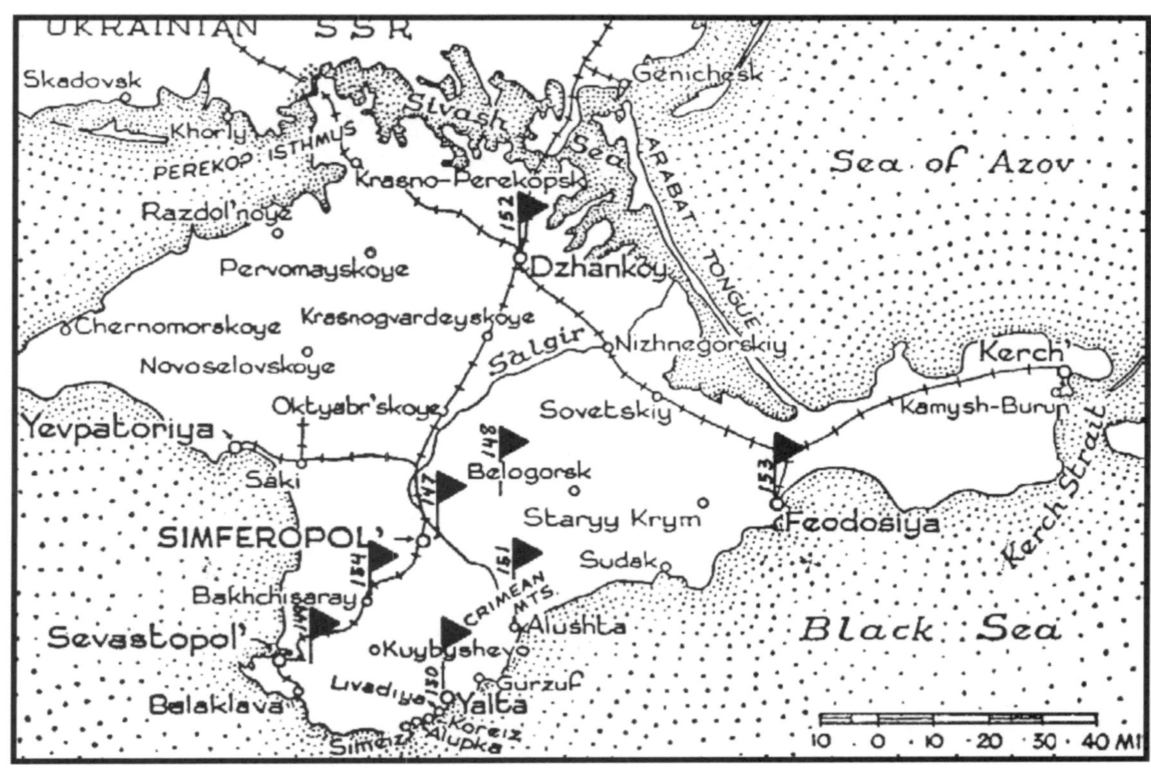

ABOVE: The Crimea in 1943. The Crimean Tartar battalions are listed in their respective area of operations.
LEFT: Two Tartar volunteers of the Schuma battalions, in the spring of 1942. They are wearing a mixture of German uniforms- Black General-SS trousers and light summer tunics and caps. The weapons they carried were initially just as varied.
BELOW CENTER: Right collar tab attributed to the Tartar SS Brigade. *Keith Williams Collection.*

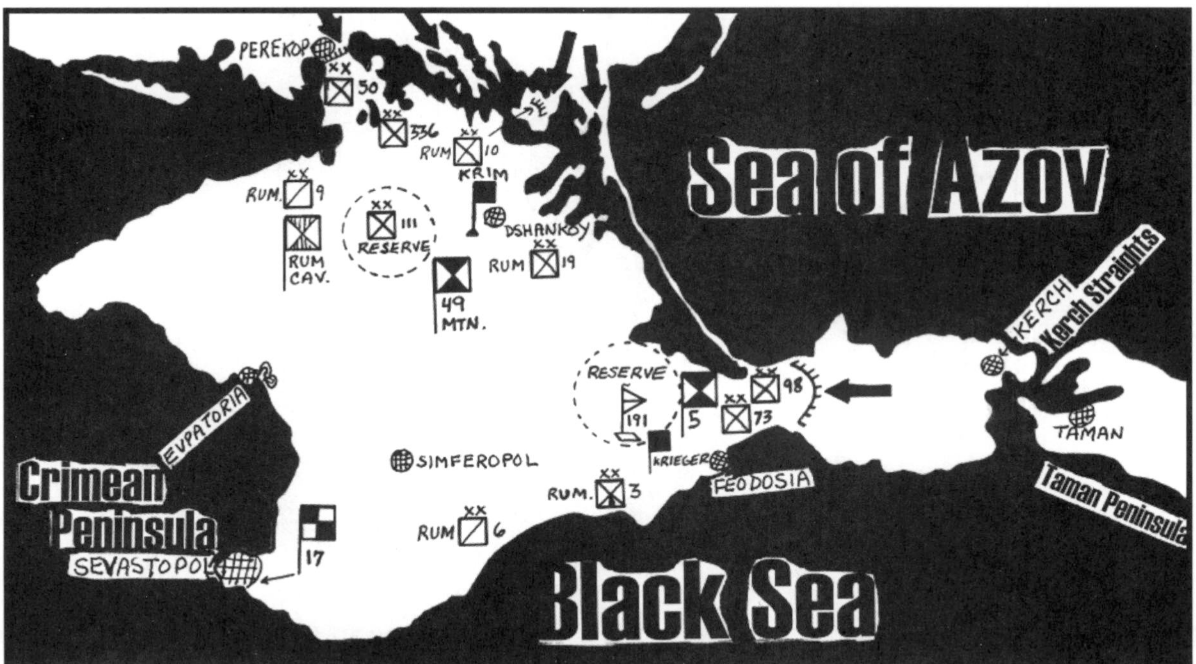

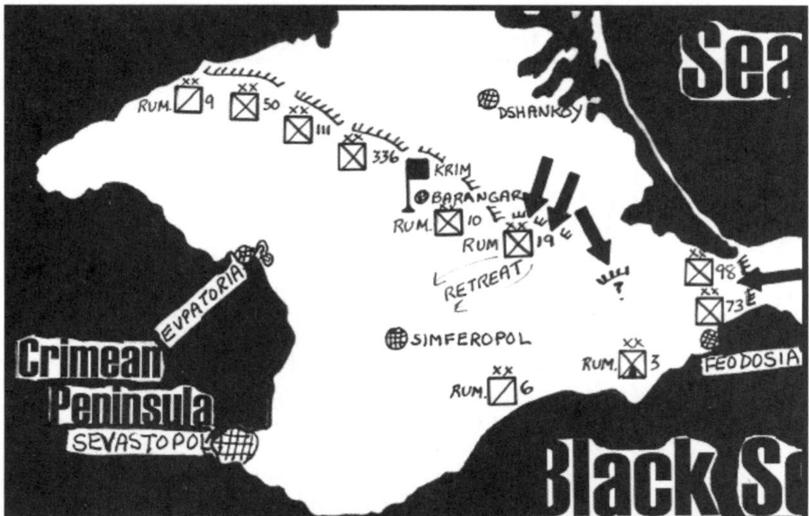

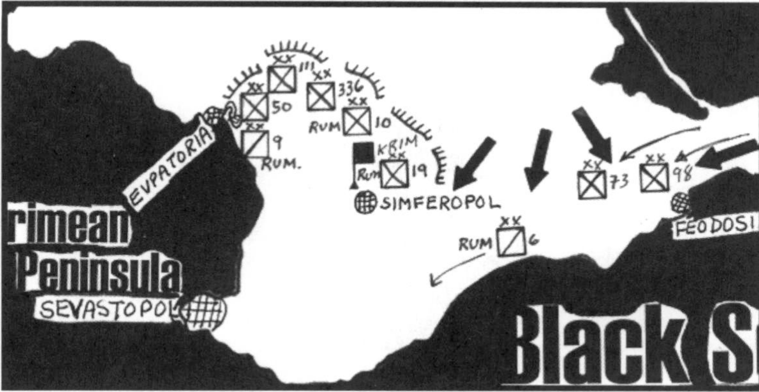

ABOVE, LEFT & BELOW LEFT: The Tartar Schuma battalions became increasingly ineffective as the Red Army began its return into the Crimean peninsula. Defections became common and the reliability of the Tartar battalions questionable. As a result of this, and the ever present demands for more units on the front lines, the decision was made by the local SS & Police Leader command to merge all reliable and still combat effective companies into a Crimean Tartar Mountain Regiment which would then be employed at the front. These three maps show the position of this Tartar Mountain Regiment during the defense of the Crimean from April – May 1944.

Evacuated before the Axis collapse, the Tartar unit was sent by sea, first to Rumania, and later reinforced with more German Order Police reinforcements-mainly Volkdeutsche (ethnic Germans) before being officially expanded into the SS Tartar Mountain Brigade.

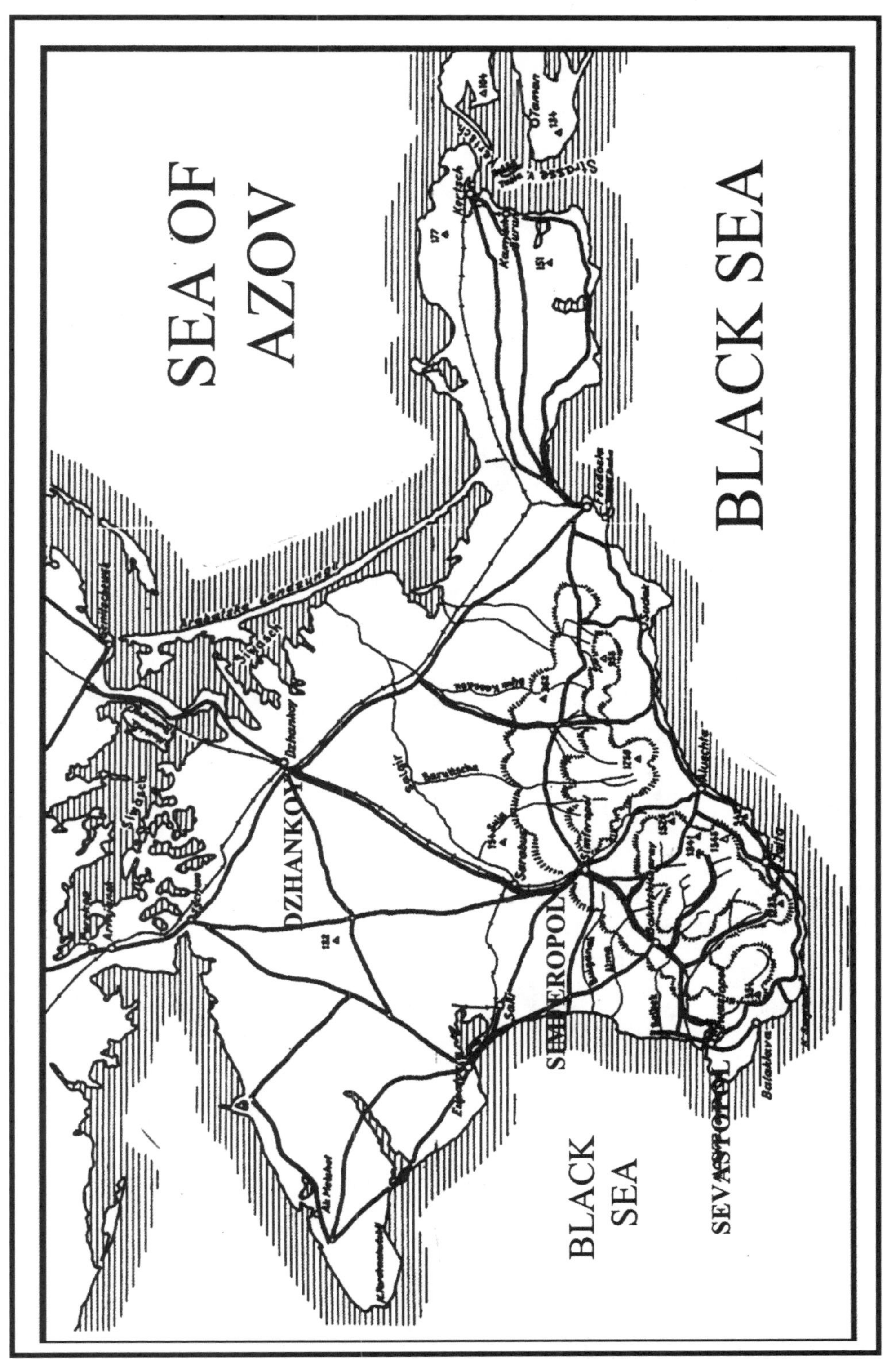

Main Road & Rail Lines in the Crimea, 1941-1944

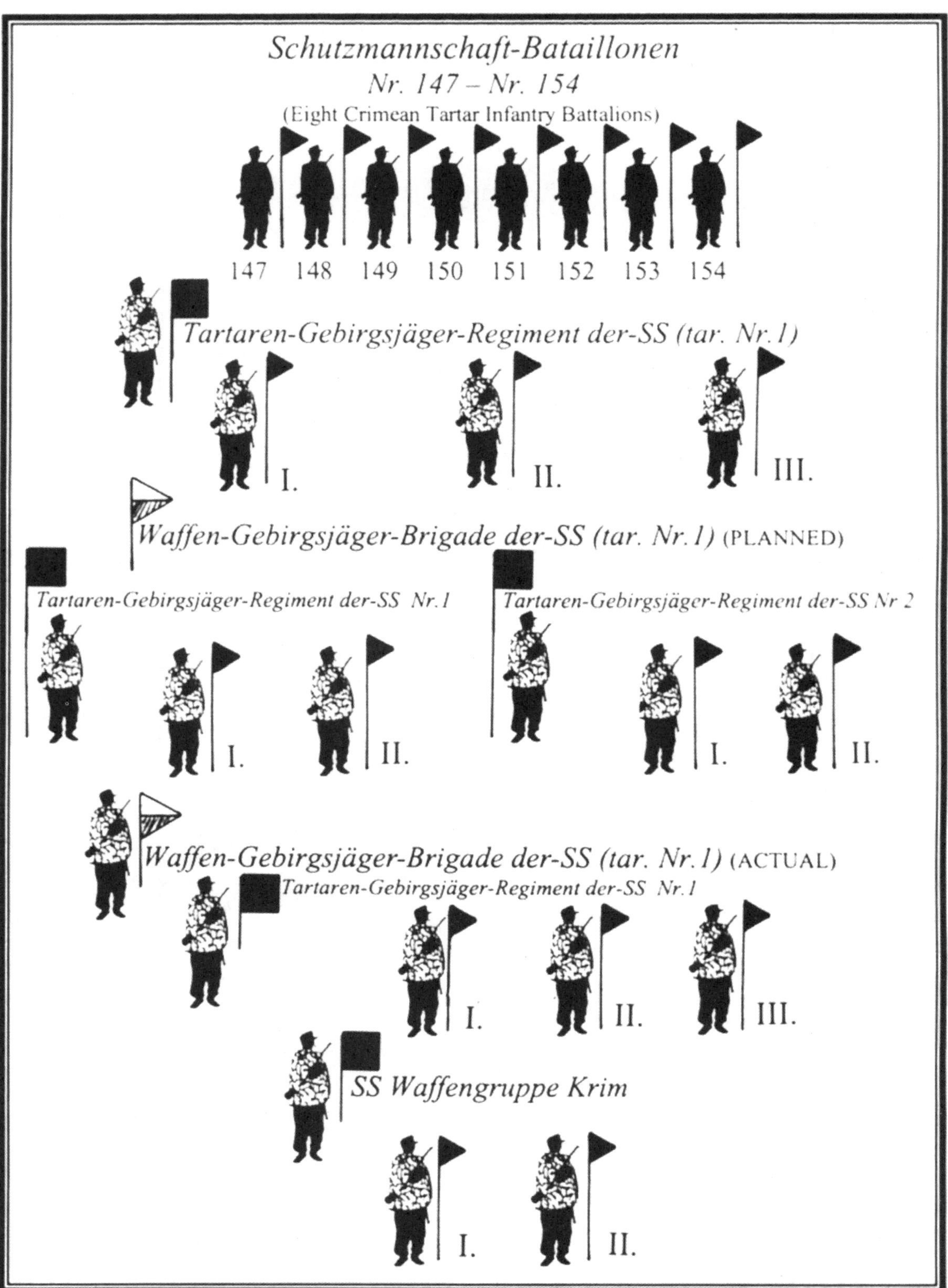
Schutzmannschaft-Bataillonen
Nr. 147 – Nr. 154
(Eight Crimean Tartar Infantry Battalions)
147 148 149 150 151 152 153 154
Tartaren-Gebirgsjäger-Regiment der-SS (tar. Nr. 1)
I.
II.
III.
Waffen-Gebirgsjäger-Brigade der-SS (tar. Nr. 1) (PLANNED)
Tartaren-Gebirgsjäger-Regiment der-SS Nr. 1
I.
II.
Tartaren-Gebirgsjäger-Regiment der-SS Nr 2
I.
II.
Waffen-Gebirgsjäger-Brigade der-SS (tar. Nr. 1) (ACTUAL)
Tartaren-Gebirgsjäger-Regiment der-SS Nr. 1
I.
II.
III.
SS Waffengruppe Krim
I.
II.

CHAPTER 11
Lions of the Desert:
Arab Volunteers in the German Army
1941-1945

By Antonio J. Munoz

INTRODUCTION

The origins of the Arab volunteer movement in the German Army date back to the failed Iraqi Army uprising of May 1941. Hitler had always expended too little interest on the political currents that moved the Arab world. This explains why German intelligence was inadequately prepared in an area which presented favorable opportunities because of long standing friendly contacts and what appeared to be several similar goals on the part of Nazi Germany and the Arab world.

The Supreme Command of the German Armed Forces (OKW) was taken by surprise by the anti-British uprising in Iraq. In the diplomatic, propaganda, and military fields Germany had neglected to prepare for just such an eventuality. Having no outside support, the Iraqi Army uprising failed. The opprotunity to exploit the Iraqi unrest therefore quickly slipped away from the Germans- much to their dismay. An attempt to send aid and support to the Iraqi's was begun during those hectic days in May 1941 when the Germans established a command staff under *Flieger a. D.* Helmuth Felmy. The headquarters staff was called *"Sonderstab F"* (Special Staff F), where "F" stood for Felmy. The best that this quickly organized staff could do was to make last-minute plans and half-boiled improvisations, which could only give token and therefore inadequate aid to the Iraqi insurgents.

After the collapse of the uprising, the decision to keep the staff active was made since the incident had proven Germany's inadequacies and lack of preparedness when it came to Arab matters, not to mention an total absence of a firm Arab policy. A solid policy towards the Arab world would elude the Germans, mainly because they had no desire to give the Arab world independence. The Third Reich had envisioned occupying the Middle East as a means by which they could control this oil rich region, but aside from evicting the French and British from the area, they had no intentions to allow the Arab countries their independence. Aspirations by Arab leaders in the region, coupled by false promises of independence after a Nazi victory, were the most the Germans were to give the Arab world. But these promises would prove to be a chimera.

Since the Germans had no firm policy in place and their goals in this region were rather limited to control and exploitation of the natural resources, the special staff formed under General Felmy had no political importance whatsoever.

LEFT: A German officer of Sonderstab F (Special Staff "F", for Felmy). Addressing Arab volunteers in North Africa. Notice the special arm patch of Staff "F" being worn on his right arm. *Museum of Modern History, Ljubljana, Slovenia.*

It was eventually relegated to helping to form volunteer units made up of peoples from the Arab world who believed that a Nazi victory would aid their cause. There were many that wished their region to be free of European rule; those who thought that evicting the French and English would lead to self-rule. Then there were those who also wished to see the complete elimination of Jews from the region and therefore backed the Nazis fervently. There were also those who sought both of these goals. Indeed, the Mufti of Jerusalem[574], Hadji Muhammed Amin Al-Hussein, and the Iraqi leader, Prime Minister Rashid Ali Al-Gailani both sought to use the Arab volunteers raised by Staff "F" as the nucleus of a future Arab Army. In 1943, Al-Hussein was 46 years old while Al-Gailani was 50.[575]

The two men would vie for control of this "future" army for the rest of the war. This fued would sap the morale of the volunteers to a certain extent and proved counter-productive. In the end, the only good that *"Sonderstab F"* ever made of its contacts with Arab leaders and their followers was to count them as merely so many more men that could be used in battle. The German-Arab 845th Infantry Battalion was one such result.

SPECIAL STAFF "F"

The mission of *Soderstab "F"* therefore changed from a multi-purpose role that encompassed political and military objectives to that of a purely military mission. The initial political aims, however vague, deteriorated even more as the German options in the Arab world were diminished by the changing fortunes of

[574] The Germans gave him the title "Grand" Mufti, to elevate his importance in both the Arab and western world.

[575] Seidler, Franz W. DIE KOLLABORATION 1939-1945. F. A. Herbig Verlag: Muenchen, 1995. Pages 212 and 263.

war. Special Staff "F" was eventually relegated to being transformed into a regular army corps' headquarters, and its specialized Arab units were squandered in regular combat. Instead of forming the spearhead of a joint German-Arab alliance against England and France in the Middle East, these formations were used piecemeal in battle.

RIGHT: The special arm patch created for the Arab volunteers. The words "FREE ARABIA" was written in German and "The Arab Countries in Freedom" written in Arabic.

The ill-equipped and late blooming North African battalions that were formed by the Afrika Korps in Tunisia in early 1943 were destroyed by the Allied victory in that region, shortly after they had been raised. They briefly operated as coastal guard and rear area security and were armed with a variety of second hand clothing and weapons. The better trained German-Arab Training Battalion, which had been in existence since July 1941 suffered from a politically divisive power struggle between the Mufti of Jerusalem, Hadji Muhammed Amin Al-Hussein and the Iraqi leader, ex-Prime Minister Rashid Ali Al-Gailani. In this struggle there was even a third Arab faction that emerged and supported Fauzi Kaikyi, the former Syrian military commander.

The conspiratorial intrigues of these three factions did much to sap whatever cohesiveness the Germans were trying to instill in this training battalion of Arabs from diverse parts of the Middle East. It wasn't until the Germans expunged the most fervent, and therefore, most troublesome supporters of these three "cliques" that the Arab Training Battalion began to function as a proper military unit. Again, lack of a proper German policy had also allowed these various groups, each with their own personal goals, to subvert the very military unit, which had been organized to represent the pro-Axis Arab world.

The cadre of the German-Arab Training Battalion was established in the town of Sunium, on the southernmost tip of the Greek region of Attica. There, permanent quarters were established using the weekend villas of wealthy Greek Athenians, although the majority of the personnel ended up living in tents. The climate there was subtropical and the initial batch of Arab volunteers had no problems with this, since they had been raised and lived in a similar climate.

ABOVE: A Stöwer 40 light vehicle of *Sonderstab "F"* (Special Staff Felmy). This vehicle was the precursor of the German Volkswagen. Its German Army designation was Kfz.2 and began production in 1936. The Staff insignia was painted on the side of the vehicle.

Training of the battalion began immediately. The following statement describes the initial stages of the training:

"Special Staff F and the Arab volunteers gathered at Sunium in July 1941. Training of the Moslems began almost immediately. The Arabs had a fair knowledge of German and showed themselves willing to learn. Unfortunately, they lacked imagination and this made it difficult for them to understand the significance of the individual phases of a military operation. Quite a number of volunteers could not understand why they should have to go through a toughening up process, although this is an integral part of military training everywhere in the world. The Arab attitude was that it was unnecessary to make a serious effort."[576]

Another problem that quickly surfaced and showed its ugly head was the mistake of using German instructors who had formerly lived in Arab countries. While at first glance these Germans, almost all of them quite knowledgeable in the language of the recruits, seemed the perfect candidates to train and become the German cadre of this Arab battalion, further experience showed that they had preconceived ideas about Arab recruits. These ideas were that Arabs were a race of menials and shirkers. Soon this attitude crept up into the ranks and was detrimental to morale and training. Another unit, which was under the command

---

[576] Felmy, General der Flieger Hellmuth. GERMAN EXPLOITATION OF ARAB NATIONALIST MOVEMENTS IN WORLD WAR II. U.S. Army Study: Europe, 1946. MS # P-207, page 13.

of Special Staff "F," was the all-German *Sonderverband 288,* which had begun training on July 24th 1941 in Potsdam. It was geared for desert warfare.

The structure of this unit was specifically geared for mobile desert warfare. Many of its German personnel had prior experience in the deserts of the Middle East and North Africa. Many had seen prior service in the French Foreign Legion. This unit was soon despatched to North Africa, as a support for Rommel's Afrika Korps. It was flown to Benghazi as a blocking force. It never returned to the control of Special Staff "F", as it was eventually redesignated as *Panzergrenadier-Regiment "Afrika"* and became an integral part of Rommel's army on October 31st 1942.[577] The table of organization for the unit on July 24th 1941 looked as follows:

Sonderverband 288:
Staff Company & Armored Car Platoon
1) Special Company
2) Mountain Climbing Company
3) Rifle Company
4) Machine-Gun Company
5) Anti-Tank Company
6) Anti-Aircraft Company
7) Engineer Company
8) Signals Company

ABOVE: A German member of *Sonderverband 287.* Notice the Special Staff "F" arm patch on his right sleeve. *Signal Magazine.*

On January 26th 1942 a Captain Schober assumed command of the German-Arab Training Battalion. The Arab volunteers were now issued with a specially manufactured cloth arm patch with the Muslim colors of Red, Green, White, and Black and the words "FREE ARABIA" written in German underneath, and the Arabic translation written on top. By April 1942 the Arab contingent in the battalion stood at 133. Quite a number of them had been former POW's who had served in either the French or British forces. They came from Syria, Saudi Arabia, Egypt, Trans-Jordan, Palestine, Lebanon, and Iraq. There was also a separate company which had been formed from former German members of the French Foreign Legion and was under the direct control of Special Staff "F." This company proved hard to control and was soon disbanded and its men dispersed within the German-Arab Training Battalion. The original 30 Arab volunteers were not grouped together with the new batch of 103 Arab recruits, but formed a separate company, which also contained Germans.

There was another German special formation *Sonderverband 287* formed a year later on August 4th, 1942. This unit contained Arab volunteers as well as a

[577] Tessin, Georg. VERBAND UND TRUPPEN DER DEUTSCHEN WEHRMACHT UND WAFFEN-SS 1939-1945. Biblio Verlag: Osnabrueck, 1973-1996. Volume 9, page 23.

German cadre staff. This unit was also referred to as the German-Arab Legion. The formation contained three battalions. The 1st and 2nd Battalions were motorized and had four companies apiece. The German-Arab Training Battalion at Sinium, Greece was designated as the unit's 3rd Battalion. The organisation was as follows:

Sonderverband 287:
Staff Company
I. Panzergrenadier Battalion
1st Company
2nd Company
3rd Company
4th Company
Independent Companies-
5th Anti-Tank Company
6th Armored Car Company
Light Engineer Company
Assault Gun Battery
Rocket Launcher Battery
II. Panzergrenadier Battalion[578]
7th Company
8th Company
III. Panzergrenadier Battalion[579]
9th Company
10th Company
11th Company
12th Company
Signals Battalion 287
1st Communications Company
2nd Communications Company

ABOVE: A Black member of the North African Arab battalions.

The German-Arab Training Battalion *(a.k.a. – 3rd Panzergrenadier Bataillon/ Sonderverband 287)* had three companies made up of Arabs with German and a few Arab officers,[580] and one company made up purely of Germans. The 9th, 10th, and 11th Company were mainly Arab manned, while the 12th (heavy weapons) Company was purely German. The total number of Arabs in the 3rd Battalion was only 392 volunteers. On the whole, Special Staff "F" had a total of 5,931 officers, NCO's and enlisted men. This included the units attached to it as well as the permanent Staff personnel. When the Special Staff "F" was re-designated as the 68th Army Corps on April 9th 1943 the unit contained the following Corps troops:[581]

578 This battalion was established on October 22nd 1942.
579 This was the German-Arab Training Battalion.
580 Of the original 30 Arab volunteers, fifteen had recently been promoted to the rank of 2nd Lieutenant.
581 Tessin, op cit. Volume 5, page 278.

1. *Arko 168*[582]
2. *Korps-Nachrichten Abteilung 468*
3. *Korps-Nachschubtruppen 468*
4. *Panzer-Spähkompanie 468*

1943	June-August	Army Group "E" & "F"	Athens
	September	11th Italian Army	Athens
	October-December	Army Group "E" & "F"	Athens
1944	January-October	Army Group "E" & "F"	Athens
	November-December	2nd Panzer Army/ AG "F"	Serbia & Hungary
1945	January-April	2nd Panzer Army/ AG "South"	Hungary (Drava)
	May	2nd Panzer Army/ AG "Southeast"	Styria (Slovenia)

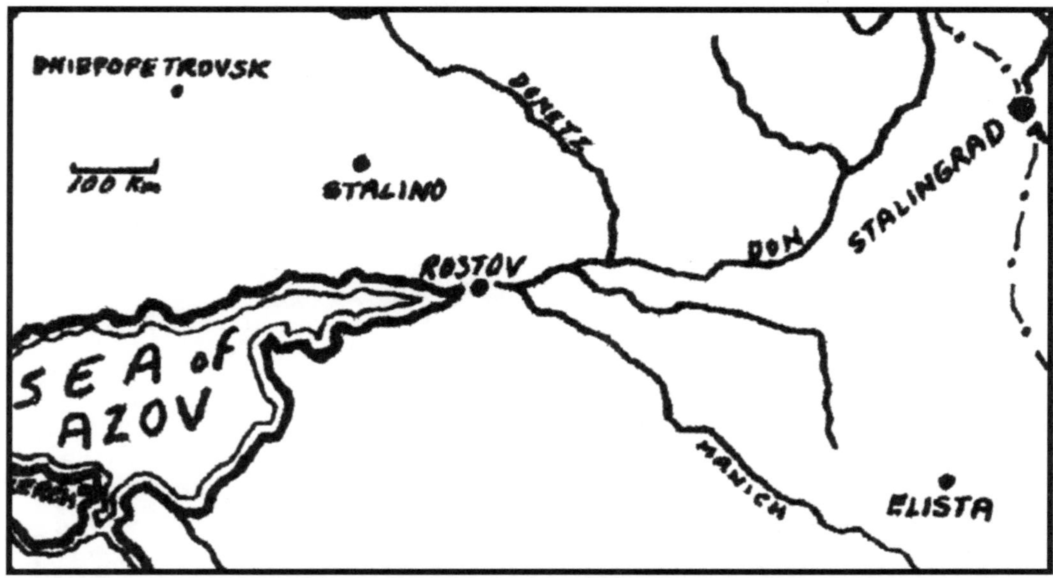

ABOVE: General reference map of the area between Rostov – Stalingrad – Elista.

EMPLOYMENT IN RUSSIA

On June 28th 1942 the Germans launched their summer offensive in the southern regions of the Soviet Union. By August 9th 1942 the first Soviet oil fields had been captured near Maikop at the beginning of the Caucasus Mountains. Having never been employed as a corps-sized unit, Special Staff "F" suggested

[582] "Arko" stood for "Artillerie-Kommandeur", or Artillery Commander. This staff controlled all of the artillery units directly attached to the corps headquarters.

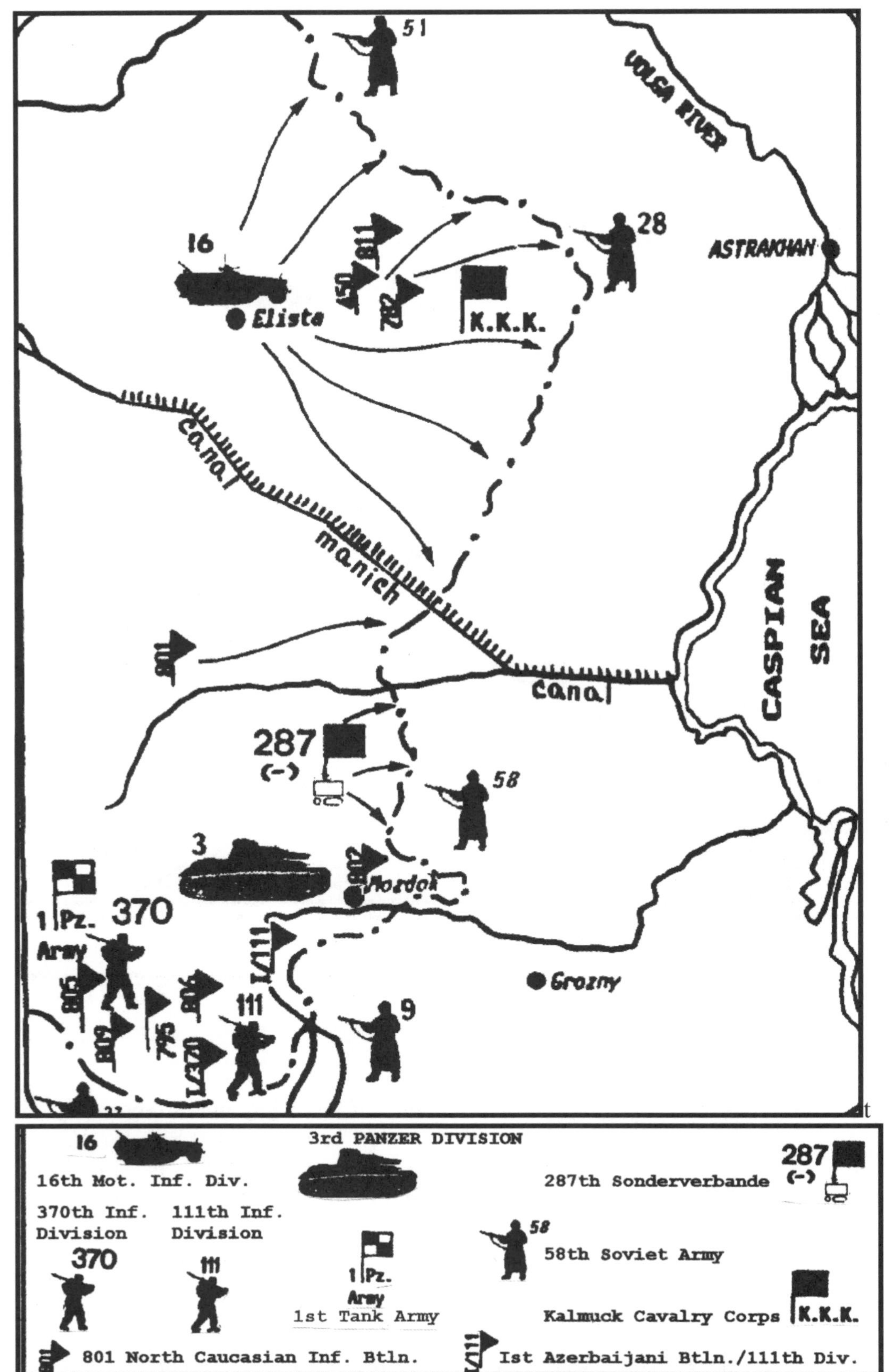
51
VOLGA RIVER
28
ASTRAKHAN
16
Elista
811
450
782
K.K.K.
canal
manich
canal
CASPIAN SEA
801
287
(-)
58
3
Mozdok
1 Pz. Army
370
I/111
805
806
809
795
111
9
Grozny
16
3rd PANZER DIVISION
287
(-)
16th Mot. Inf. Div.
287th Sonderverbande
370th Inf. Division
111th Inf. Division
370
111
58
58th Soviet Army
1 Pz. Army
1st Tank Army
Kalmuck Cavalry Corps
K.K.K.
801 North Caucasian Inf. Btln.
Ist Azerbaijani Btln./111th Div.

hat it be employed in the Caucasus region with the hope that once the German Army crossed this last mountainous barrier, they would be in a position to strike at British forces in Iraq, Syria and Iran. The Arab elements in *Sonderstab F* could therefore be employed in the region in which they were intended- the Middle East. *Sonderverband 287* was the first unit of Special Staff "F" which was sent directly to Stalino in southern Russia. It was transferred directly from the Doberitz Training Ground. The unit moved to Stalino with its 1st and 2nd Battalions. The 3rd (German-Arab Training) Battalion was not yet in Russia, as it was coming from Sinium, Greece alongside the headquarters of Special Staff "F." Events in North Africa eventually required the employment of *Sonderverband 288* in North Africa.

Sonderstab "F" arrived at Stalino in September 1942. It was at this time that the unit was redesignated *Generalkommando z.b.V.* (Corps Headquarters for Special Employment). Its members were allowed to wear a special corps arm patch worn on the middle of the right arm sleeve. This patch was machine woven and depicted a tilted swastika at its base, with an oval wreath of palm leaves surrounding a palm tree and a rising sun behind it. The new designation was in line with its new assignment at Stalino, which included among other things, a directive, which outlined a training program that was, geared specifically form desert warfare. The directive stressed that the individual soldier had to learn to fight independently, and that training should include live fire practice with various types of weapons. This would make the individual volunteers able to employ various weapons, including captured enemy arms. The program also included reconnaissance, observation, and orientation by use of a compass. The Arab language was to be confined to phrases for everyday use and the essentials of military terminology.

It was clear that the corps command still believed that it was going to be employed in the Middle East, by way of the Caucasus Mountains. This plan was soon placed in jeopardy when Army Group "A" began to be bogged down in late September- early October 1942. The difficult and mountainous terrain, coupled by stiffening Red Army resistance and reinforcements finally halted the German panzers short of their objective. The line separating Army Group "A" in the Caucasus and Army Group "B" in Stalingrad and the Volga River bend now became increasingly stretched. Soon it was necessary to send additional German forces to help cover this exposed and vital link in the Axis front line.

The only unit which was not committed in early October 1942 that could conceivably perform the mission of screening this exposed and weak link was *Sonderverband 287*, which had been kept in Stalino and uncommitted after its arrival in southern Russia. The order to move the 287th Special Purpose Regiment to the southern regions of the Kalmyk A.S.S.R. arrived on October 5th 1942. A day later the two battalions moved out of Stalino and were officially attached to the German 1st Panzer Army. For operational purposes, *Generalkommando z.b.V.* was detached from the control of OKW and assigned to Army Group "A". The plan was now to insert the 287th on the left flank of 1st Panzer Army in the area of Kuma between Niny-Stepnoe (40th Panzer Corps) and the Manich Canal, where

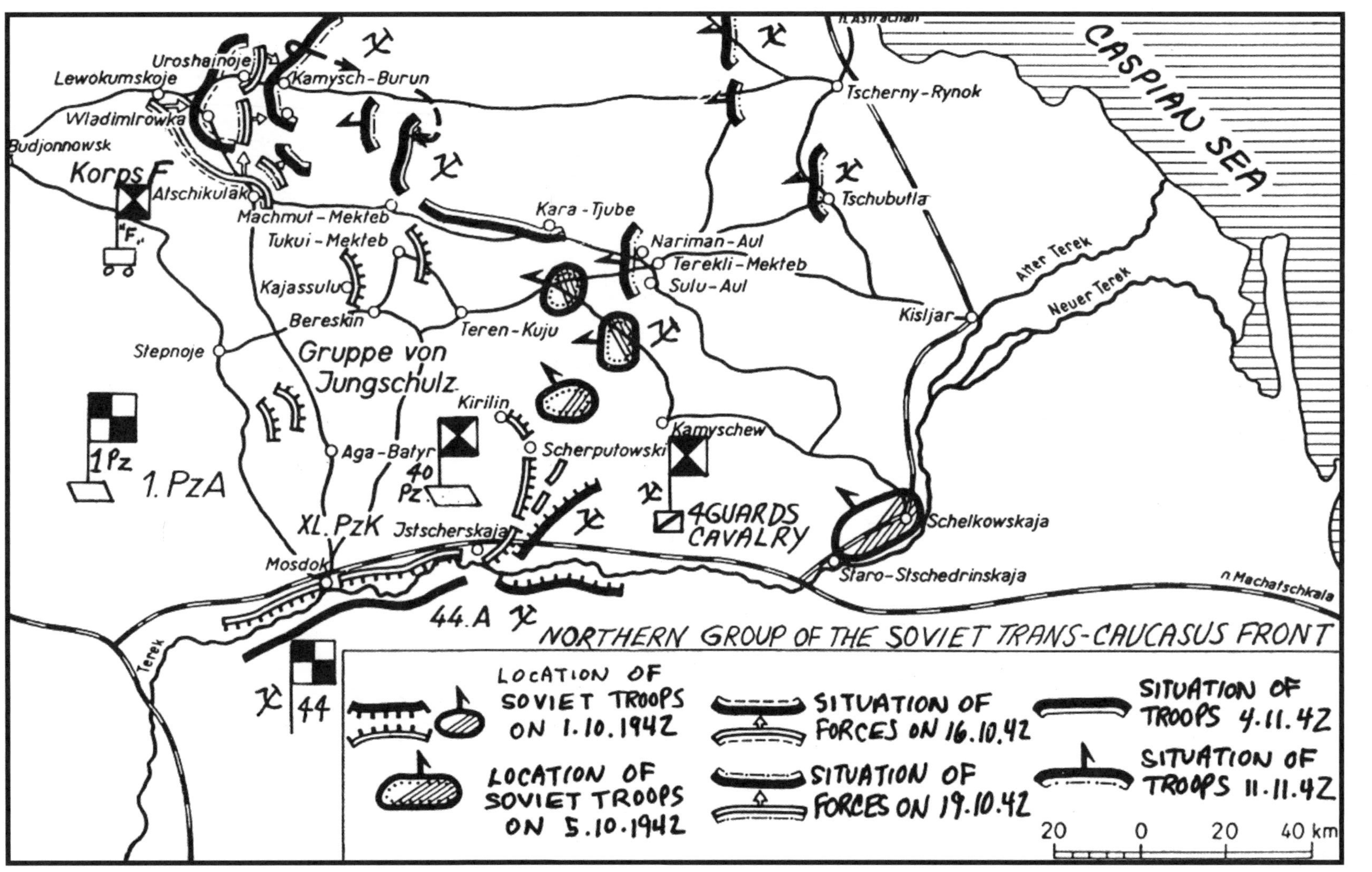
CASPIAN SEA
n. Astrachan
Uroshainoje
Lewokumskoje
Kamysch-Burun
Wladimirowka
Budjonnowsk
Korps F
"F"
Alschikulak
Machmut-Mekteb
Tukui-Mekteb
Kajassulu
Bereskin
Stepnoje
Kara-Tjube
Nariman-Aul
Terekli-Mekteb
Sulu-Aul
Tscherny-Rynok
Tschubutla
Kisljar
Alter Terek
Neuer Terek
Teren-Kuju
Gruppe von Jungschulz
Kirilin
Scherputowski
Kamyschew
Aga-Batyr
40 Pz
1 Pz
1. PzA
XL. PzK
Jstscherskaja
Mosdok
4 GUARDS CAVALRY
Schelkowskaja
Staro-Stschedrinskaja
n. Machatschkala
44.A
44
Terek
NORTHERN GROUP OF THE SOVIET TRANS-CAUCASUS FRONT
LOCATION OF SOVIET TROOPS ON 1.10.1942
LOCATION OF SOVIET TROOPS ON 5.10.1942
SITUATION OF FORCES ON 16.10.42
SITUATION OF FORCES ON 19.10.42
SITUATION OF TROOPS 4.11.42
SITUATION OF TROOPS 11.11.42
20 0 20 40 km

the 16th Motorized Infantry Division's southern-most mobile defense ended. The 16th Division was based in the capital of the Kalmyk A.S.S.R.- Elista. From there, the division would send out deep reconnaissance forces in a wide arc. The German motorized unit was assisted in this mission by cavalry squadrons of Kalmuck volunteers who opposed the Soviet regime.

The main defense points for the 287th Regiment turned out to be Acikulak and Urozayne on the Nogayer Steppe. The regiment had arrived in its new positions with 720 Ukrainian *Hilfswilliger* (auxiliary volunteers), which had been recruited mainly in Stalino. Felmy's corps headquarters also recruited hundreds of these auxiliary volunteers before the corps withdrew from the USSR. The employment of the 287th Special Purpose Regiment in regular front line fighting signaled a new chapter and changing mission for the specialized units of Corps Felmy. The requirements of the Russian Front now took precedence over the need to keep these particular and unique units uncommitted. Those who understood the initial reasons why these formations were created also comprehended that it was a crime to send them into the Russian "meat grinder," which tended to chew up units and spit them out with amazing speed and volume.

In order to help accomplish its new mission, the 287th Special Purpose Regiment was temporarily assigned the 801st North Caucasian Infantry Battalion, which was led by German Captain Burkhardt. Other units assigned to the regiment included Infantry Battalion *"Bergmann,"* under Dr. Theodor Oberlander, and Cossack Cavalry Regiment *"von Jungschultz."* It is interesting to note that the Teletype assigning Generalkommando z.b.V. to Army Group "A" specifically stated that the German-Arab Training Battalion was not to be committed to combat north of the Caucasus Mountains. As the 287th Special Purpose Regiment was about to move to the front a number of the Arab volunteers came down with the flu or other ailments. This was attributed by the Germans to the continued intrigues of the diverse opposing political groups within the battalion. The problem became so severe that General Felmy himself paid a visit to the unit on October 5th 1942 and addressed the Arab volunteers:

"I have received a report from your battalion commander, Captain Schober, that there is dissension and division among your ranks. This disturbs me greatly, as I have nothing but admiration for the fighting qualities of the Arabs. I remember specifically one attack which I witnessed while serving under the Turkish Army, of an Arab unit at the battle of Gaza in 1917 which greatly impressed me. Their courage was noteworthy. Unfortunately, I am at a loss for words to understand the courage which I saw then, with the defeatism and dissension which I have heard is going on among your ranks. I am not here to urge you to fight for your Arab countries if you yourselves refuse to do so. All Muslim volunteers requesting to be separated from German military service will not be impeded, but I promise you that your names will be given to the Grand Mufti. He can deal with you as he sees fit. Furthermore your permits to reside in the Reich shall be revoked, and you will be asked to leave national territory immediately. I am going to allow you all to think over your decision until 1800 hours today, at which time every man here will be asked a simple 'yes' or 'no.'

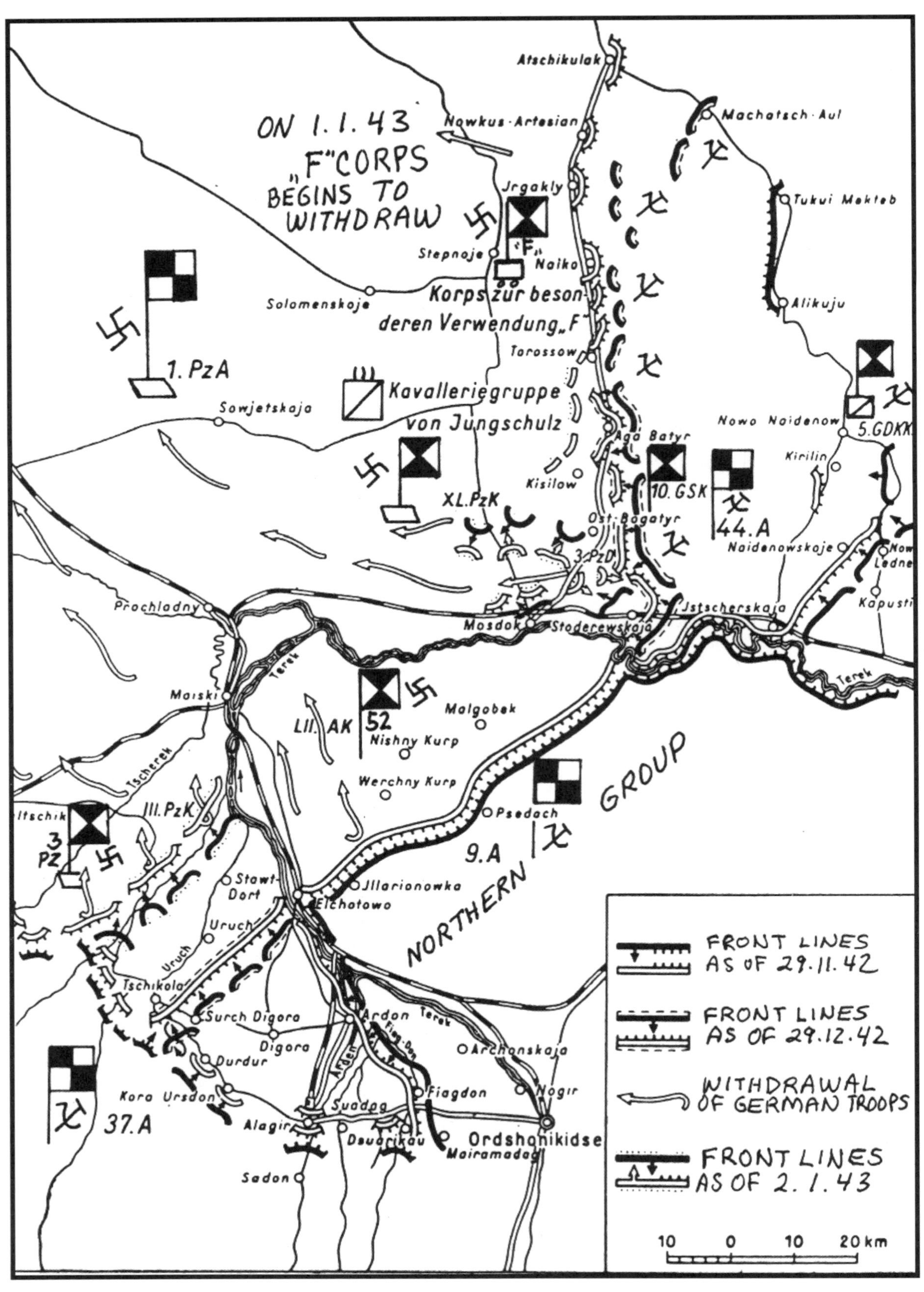

ON 1.1.43 „F"CORPS BEGINS TO WITHDRAW
Korps zur besonderen Verwendung „F"
1. PzA
Kavalleriegruppe von Jungschulz
XL.PzK
3.PzD
10.GSK
44.A
5.GDKK
LII. AK
52
III. PzK
3 PZ
9.A
NORTHERN GROUP
37.A
Atschikulak
Nowkus-Artesian
Machatsch-Aul
Tukui Mekteb
Alikuju
Jrgakly
Stepnoje
Naiko
Solomenskoje
Torossow
Sowjetskaja
Aga Batyr
Kisilow
Nowo Naidenow
Kirilin
Ost-Bogatyr
Naidenowskaja
Prochladny
Mosdok
Stoderewskaja
Jstscherskaja
Kapusti
Terek
Maiski
Malgobek
Nishny Kurp
Werchny Kurp
Tscherek
Psedach
Stawt-Dort
Jllarionowka
Elchotowo
Uruch
Tschikola
Surch Digora
Digora
Ardon
Durdur
Archonskaja
Kora Ursdon
Fiagdon
Nogir
Suadag
Alagir
Dsuarikau
Ordshonikidse
Mairamadag
Sadon
FRONT LINES AS OF 29.11.42
FRONT LINES AS OF 29.12.42
WITHDRAWAL OF GERMAN TROOPS
FRONT LINES AS OF 2.1.43
10 0 10 20 km

ABOVE: Photograph showing North African Arab volunteers with their battalion battle flag. Notice that they are dressed in a variety of Vichy French and German Army clothing and equipment. *Museum of Modern History, Ljubljana, Slovenia.*
BELOW: A column of Arab volunteers and their German cadre personnel. Most volunteers carry the white arm band with the words "In the Service of the German Army" printed on it. *Museum of Modern History, Ljubljana, Slovenia.*

Your battalion commander, Captain Schober will report the results to me personally, that is all."[583]

---

[583] Felmy, General der Flieger Hellmuth, op cit. Pages 22-24.

Reports indicate that aside from those Arabs who were willing to quit at any price, most of the volunteers opted to remain in the battalion. The disgruntled elements in the battalion were sent to the German Armed Forces High Command Counterintelligence Division under guard. Thereafter the battalion returned to normal. In October, the 1st and 2nd Battalions had been dispatched to Budenovsk and assigned patrol duty between the left wing of 1st Panzer Army and the southernmost element of the 4th Panzer Army- 16th Motorized Infantry Division. The 16th Motorized Division had its headquarters in the city of Elista, which was the capital of the Kalmuck ASSR.

As soon as the 287th Special Purpose Regiment arrived at Budenovsk, it helped to repel a thrust by the Soviet 4th Cavalry Corps. The expected breakthrough by Army Group South into Iran never materialized but the Russians did launch a massive winter counterattack that began on November 19th 1942 and did not end until the German 6th Army was destroyed and the threat to the Caucasus oil fields was averted in the spring of 1943. Events in the Mediterranean were also developing in November 1942. On the 8th of this month, a large American and force landed on the Atlantic coast of Morocco and Algeria and was threatening to cut off Rommel's *Afrika Korps* from its bases in Tripolitania, Libya.

The decision to transfer the desert trained Generalkommando z.b.V. and its specialized units to North Africa were soon reached and the corps headquarters and its sub-units were withdrawn from the Soviet Union. However, due to the serious nature of the military situation facing the Germans in southern Russia, only the 3rd (German-Arab Training) Battalion was immediately shifted to Palermo, Italy in anticipation of its employment in North Africa. It wasn't until January 1943 that the *III. Bataillon/ Sonderverband 287* was actually sent across the Mediterranean Sea and landed in Tunisia. In order to retain some sort of control over the battalion, the Generalkommando z.b.V. sent a representative along to Army Group South in Italy, Lieutenant-Colonel Meyer-Ricks[584]. This occurred on December 7th 1942. As it turned out, Meyer-Ricks and Captain Schober would prove quite instrumental in helping to raise several volunteer Muslim battalions for the Axis cause in Tunisia.

THE GERMAN-ARAB TRAINING BATTALION IN THE MEDITERRANEAN

A special recruiting organ was established called the *Kommando deutsche-arabische Truppen*, or *Kodat*. In Vichy French Tunisia, the DAL (*Deutsche-Arabische Lehr Abteilung,* or German Arab Training Battalion) began to recruit hundreds of unemployed Muslims from various tribes into Arab auxiliary battalions. While the Vichy French government of Laval recruited Arab labor battalions to build fortifications, the Germans armed and clothed their Arab auxiliaries and gave them the less hazardous duty of coastal defense and rear area guard and security duties. The *"Freies Arabien"* arm patch mentioned earlier,

[584] Meyer-Ricks was the Chief of Staff of the Generalkommando z.b.V.

was freely distributed. Among the ranks of these Arab volunteers were numerous men of obvious Black extraction, which no doubt reminded some of the older German officers of the Black *Askari* soldiers which served the Kaiser under von Lettow-Vorbeck in German East Africa during the First World War.

The sight of Arabs in German uniform, wearing sleeve bands with the words "Free Arabia" embroidered on them, had an excellent effect on the number of new enlistments. Soon numerous companies had been raised. They were separated by region, so there were companies made up of Moroccans, Tunisians, and Algerians. These were manned by Arabs from those regions and were led by German officers and Sergeants. Approximately five German ex-Foreign Legionaries were attached to each company as NCO's. There was a lack of supplies due to the stranglehold which the Allies had on Axis supply ships moving from Italy to North Africa. It was thus that many of these new volunteers had to make do with Vichy French army uniforms and worn out French rifles. One source states that as many as 6,300 Arabs were recruited this way.[585]

The two major drawbacks of these new Arab battalions were (1) the inadequate quantities of uniforms, equipment, and arms and (2) the very limited amount of time which the Germans had to train these new battalions. Eventually,

ABOVE: An Arab flag bearer is flanked by two German cadre NCO's. The Arab battalions contained a German cadre staff that controlled and led the battalions and line companies. *Museum of Modern History, Ljubljana, Slovenia.*

[585] Caballero-Jurado, Carlos. LA ESPADA DEL ISLAM: VOLUNTARIOS ARABES EN EL EJERCITO ALEMAN 1941-1945. Garcia Hispan, Editor, 1990. Page 175.

the Vichy French government raised a combat unit made up of Arabs. This was actually a formation made up of Arabs and Frenchmen who had been living in North Africa. The battalion was dubbed the *"Phalange Africaine"* (African Phlanx). Command of this mixed Arab/French unit was given to a Corsican Captain in the service of Vichy France. His name was Pierre-Simon Ange Cristofini. The *"Phalange Africaine"* only managed to recruit 406 men, of which only 132 were local Arabs. The men in this battalion wore French colonial uniforms with German helmets. The decal on the German helmet sported a rectangle with the French tricolor (blue/white/red).

RIGHT: Arm Patch of the *"Phalange Africaine."* It sported a gold surround shield, and gold double headed battle axe on a black back-ground. *Author's Collection.*

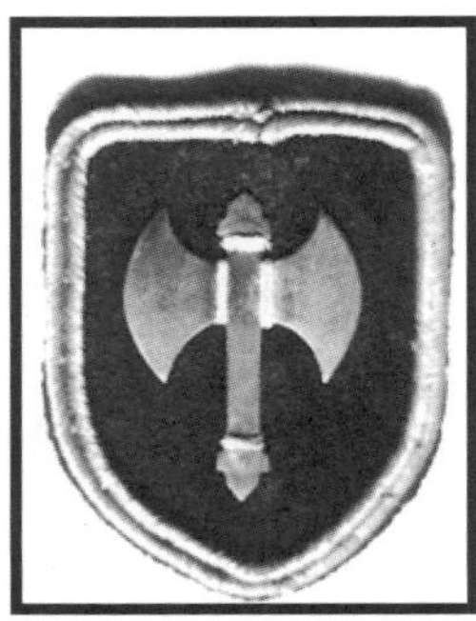

LEFT: Notice that the Arab soldier on the extreme right side of this photo, carrying the MG-34 machine gun is wearing a French-style uniform. Museum of Modern History, Lju-bljana, Slovenia.

On March 18th 1943 they swore allegiance to Marshal Petain and on April 25th they saw their first action against elements of the British 8th Army. The unit lost 70 dead. Still later in the month the *Phalange Africaine* fought against DeGaule's Free French forces. In this battle, 14 men were captured by the Free French, who instantly had them shot for treason.[586] Thereafter the unit disintegrated quickly. On February 13th 1943 the 132 Arabs of the *Phalange Africaine* had been absorbed into the DAL *(Deutsche-Arabische Lehr Abteilung).*

A total of two Tunisian, one Algerian, and one Moroccan battalion were organized. Although the four battalions were primarily composed of Tunisians, Algerians, and Moroccans, they also included small numbers of other Arabs. These included Egyptians, Syrians, Iraqis, Senussi, Tuaregs, and other desert Arabs. Each battalion consisted of three infantry companies armed with carbines and light machine guns, plus a heavy weapons company equipped with mortars

---

[586] Littlejohn, David. THE PATRIOTIC TRAITORS. THE HISTORY OF COLLABORATION IN GERMAN-OCCUPIED EUROPE, 1940-45. Doubleday & Company: Garden City, 1972. Page 255.

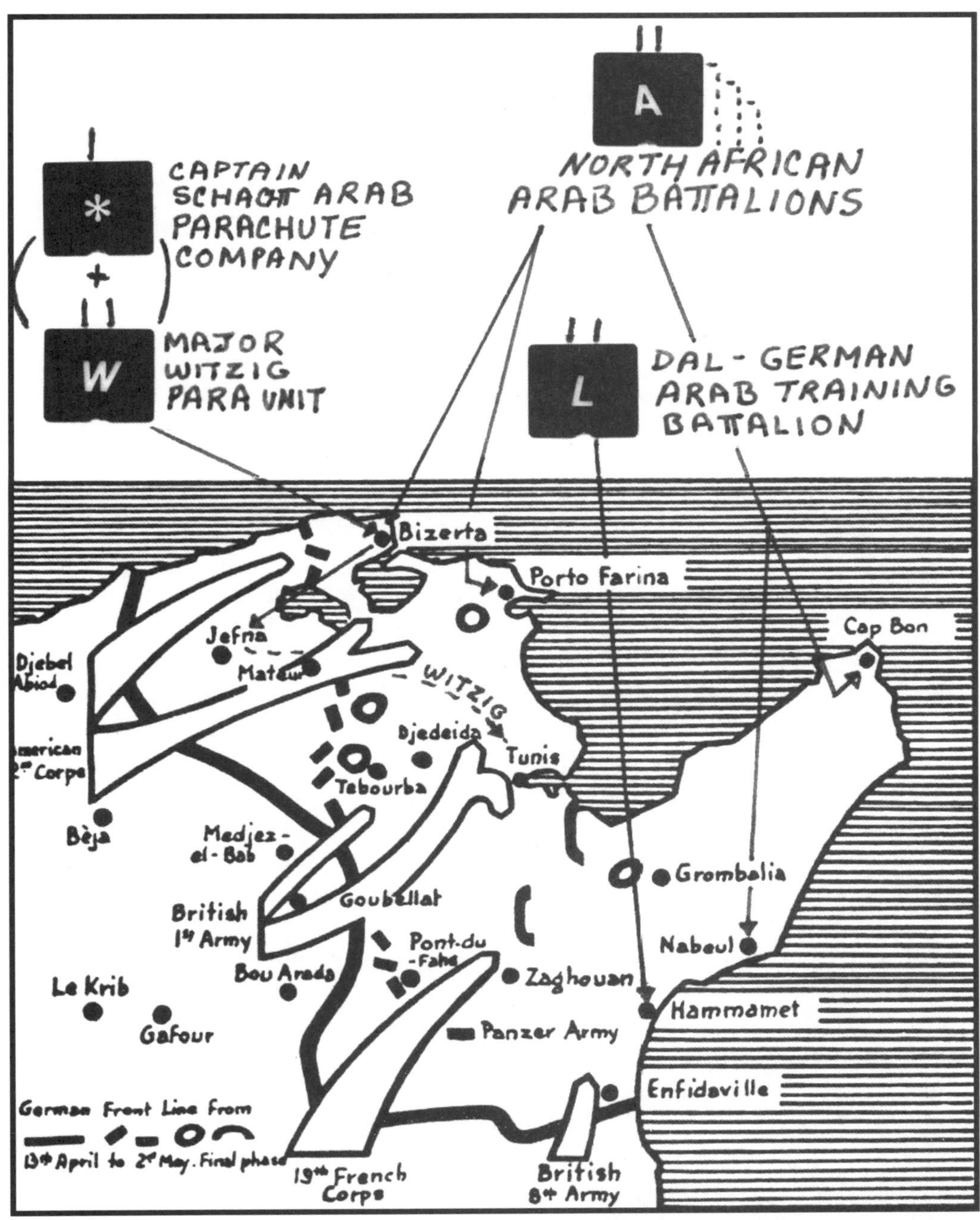

ABOVE: Map showing the areas in Tunisia where the Germans employed their Arab units. The arrows indicate the final Allied drives in May 1943 that caused the final defeat and surrender of *Panzerarmee Afrika*.

and heavy machine guns.[587] The infantry companies were all at full strength and had 150 men each, while the heavy weapons companies had around 200-220 men each. If we add up the totals for these four battalions raised we come up with a count of some 2,600-2,700 men- a far cry from the 6,300 quoted by another author. I am inclined to believe that perhaps no more than 3,000 were recruited

[587] Felmy, General der Flieger Hellmuth, op cit. Page 28.

and that the strength of the DAL and these Arab battalions in total only numbered some 3,500 men. On February 24th 1943 Lieutenant-Colonel Meyer-Ricks and Captain Schober were both killed during an Allied air attack. The loss of these two specialized officers severly crippled the training of these battalions and permanently disabled further effective recruitment of the local Arab population. Because the *Generalkommando z.b.V.* was still heavily engaged in southern Russia, no suitable replacements were on hand to assume the critical posts of these two officers:

"Although as a general rule the death of a commander did not result in the dissolution of a German military unit, in a case such as this where special conditions prevailed the loss could have serious consequences. Both dead officers had performed their duties well, and both spoke Arabic fluently. It was difficult to find other men who were as expert in the field of German-Arab relations. Finally, a Colonel von Hippel, who had seen service in the former German African colonies, was entrusted with the command of Kodat by the 5th Panzer Army."[588]

This was the same Colonel von Hippel who had been in command of the German-Arab Training Battalion which had captured the British commandos at Hammamet. Meanwhile, the *Generalkommando z.b.V.* had finally been withdrawn from Russia, but had left all of its sub units to the 24th Panzer Corps. The order for the transfer arrived on February 24th 1943. When the corps was transferred to Reggio in southern Italy, General Felmy flatly stated that he could not employ his command in North Africa because his corps lacked all support units, including the basic communications battalion which every corps needed. This fact saved the men in the headquarters from ending up as prisoners of war when *Panzerarmee Afrika* surrendered in May 1943.

There were two types of Arab formations that were raised- those for combat and guard duty and those which were to serve under the supervision of German engineers as construction workers. The Arabs that were to serve as engineers wore a white brassard on the right sleeve of their jacket with the inscription *"In Dienste der Deutschen Wehrmacht"* (In the Service of the German Armed Forces). Those who were earmarked for the combat battalions wore the *"Freies Arabien"* arm patch. While the North African Arab battalions were being organized by the men of the German-Arab Training Battalion (a.k.a. - the 3rd Battalion/ 287th Special Purpose Regiment), the unit was also charged with the coastal defense of the Gulf of Hammamet from Cape Bon to Susa.

During one night in the spring of 1943 the British landed an eight-man commando team by submarine at Hammamet in order to blow up the headquarters of Captain Fritz von Koenen's Brandenburg commando unit. Von Koene's commandos had led numerous successful sorties behind the Allied lines in Tunis and Algeria. The attempt by the small British commando force was unsuccessful. Within 48 hours the entire eight man team was caught by the Brandenburgers acting in conjunction with the Arabs of the 3rd Battalion/ 287th Special Purpose Regiment. The commander of the small British force, a captain, was drowned

---

[588] Felmy, General der Flieger Hellmuth, ibid. Page 29.

while attempting to return to the submarine from whence they had disembarked. There were other instances when other German commands tried to make use of Arab volunteers. For example the German 1st Parachute Regiment recruited 80-100 Arabs and gave them parachute training with the hope of uding them behind the lines. Similarly, Otto Skorzeny, Hitler's leading commando employed Arab volunteers, but these shall be discussed later on.

By mid-March the British 8th Army reached the Mareth line in southern Tunisia. The situation became so critical that the Germans sent in one of the Tunisian battalions to the front lines. However this move proved disastrous as the Arabs lit fires to stay warm when they reached the front. Unaware that this new battalion had arrived, the Germans in the local region fired on their positions. The British forces in front of the Arabs were thus able to see the Arab positions and immediately attacked the Tunisians. The battalion collapsed and was overrun. The 5th Panzer Army concluded from this brief but bloody engagement that it would be better if the Arab battalions were kept behind the lines performing security and coastal guard duty. Another use of the Arabs came in April 1943:

"In mid-April 1943 some of the German personnel in the German-Arab Training Battalion, and all Moslems who had finished their training, reinforced by ex-Foreign Legion troops, were consolidated into a 'task force' near Ferryville in Tunisia. This group included two infantry companies and one heavy company, the latter composed of one heavy infantry howitzer platoon, one 20mm anti-aircraft platoon, one anti-tank platoon, and one heavy machine gun platoon. During the following weeks this task force was employed in the northern sector of the front, southwest of Matör and in the Sedyenane Valley. It served as the tactical reserve of an Austrian division, and later with the 999th Light Afrika Division."[589]

Few details are known about this unit but it is known that it was employed next to Major Witzig's parachute battalion. On May 1st the combined German-Arab unit relieved a battalion from the Hermann Göring Panzer Division. That same day the unit succeeded in repelling a US attack. On May 3rd the battalion performed rearguard duty for an infantry regiment and on the 6th it was placed as the reserve battalion for a *Luftwaffe* (Air Force) regiment that had recently been formed for infantry duty from ground crews and staff. The final end of this ad-hoc German-Arab battalion was as follows:

"On the afternoon of May 7th the group was to have assumed responsibility for the protection of an anti-aircraft unit established along the Bizerta-Tunis railroad. As the task force was about to move into position the antiaircraft unit was overrun by American tanks. The following day the supply trains of the task force were disbanded, its records destroyed, and the remnants of of the group, less than 100 men, assembled at Porto Farina, north of Tunis. Here from 4-5,000 other Axis soldiers waited in well disciplined ranks for ferries to

---

[589] Felmy, General der Flieger Hellmuth, ibid. Page 31.

evacuate them. The majority of the Arab soldiers in the task force remained with German troops and went voluntarily into captivity with them."[590]

US records state that about 2,000 Arab prisoners were stationed in US POW camps in Opaluka, Alabama as of April 10th, 1946. This gives us an indication of the size of the German recruitment of Arabs in North Africa in just a few months' time. It confirms the estimate of around 2,700 total recruits, not including the German-Arab Training Battalion. In some instances, Arabs were executed individually for treason- as happened in 1944 and reported in the British newspaper, the "Daily Mail." A small one paragraph story appeared on the bottom of the front page of the April 1st 1944 issue in which it was reported that: *"DEATH FOR NAZI ARAB: Algiers, Friday. – Sentence of death for treason was passed by a French military court to-day on an Arab, Kaci Djilali, who fought in Russia against the Red Army and in Tunisia against the Allies.- Reuter."*[591]

ARAB PARACHUTISTS AND COMMANDOS

During the period in which the German-Arab Training Battalion was stationed in the Gulf of Hammamet, a certain Captain Schacht of the German 1st Parachute Regiment was appointed by Army Group South (Italy) to train between

ABOVE: Fawzi el Kotub as he appeared in 1948. *Author's Collection.*

[590] Felmy, General der Flieger Hellmuth, ibid. Pages 31-32.
[591] Daily Mail, Saturday, April 1st 1944, bottom of front page.

80-100 Arabs from the German-Arab Command *(Kodat)* for instructions in demolition and engineering work. For this reason they were transferred to the Wittstock Parachute School near Berlin, Germany. There were others in the German camp who took an interest in the Arab volunteers and their potential as saboteurs and commandos.

Otto Skorzeny was one such German who between November 1943 and June 1944 trained 60-75 Italians, 20 Serbians, 15 Frenchmen, and 25 Arabs in the *A-Schule* (A School) established by the Abwehr in a country estate between The Hague and Schevenningen in Holland. These Arabs had come from the now dissolved Italian-Arab (parachute) legion. In addition, a W/T course, lasting several months, was begun in December 1943. The technical direction was in the hands of a pro-German Dutch engineer. The course was conducted by a German technician from the Havel Institute. The students included two Italians, four Frenchmen and Belgians, and two Arabs.[592] One such Arab commando was a Palestinian Arab named Fawzi el Kutub. Kotub had escaped Palestine in 1943 after getting into trouble with the British authorities. The then twenty-five year old Kotub was a follower of the Mufti of Jerusalem, who managed to get him posted to Skorzeny's commando and sabotage school in Holland.[593]

After a year's training in the most refined techniques of sabotage and commando operations, he was ordered to lead a four-man team of German saboteurs into Palestine. He refused and was immediately handcuffed and sent to a prison camp in Silesia, where he lingered for three months until the Mufti of Jerusalem was able to get him out, offering to give him a job in Berlin preparing Arabic propaganda for the Germans. In 1945 he was caught by the Soviet attack on the German capital and only managed to escape by dressing himself up as a wounded German soldier.

He was caught by US troops near Salzburg, Austria and placed in a POW camp. Later he was allowed to return to Palestine. His most notable "achievement" would be the destruction by bombing of the Palestinian Post building on February 1st, 1948. His expertise in explosives, learned while serving under the Germans, was finally put to use. He figured slightly in the Arab-Israeli bombings and counter-bombings while the British still held a mandate over Palestine.

But what of the 80-100 Arabs who went to Wittstock for parachute and demolitions training? Apparently his small Arab parachute company was used behind the Allied lines in North Africa with good results. Major Witzig's exploits included the delay of US forces by blocking the Jefna tunnel pass, then advancing on to Sadjenane, further west. The Arab Parachute Company under Captain Schacht was used by Witzig's Parachute Engineer Battalion.[594] These Arab

[592] Mendelsohn, John – Editor. COVERT WARFARE: INTELLIGENCE, COUNTER-INTELLIGENCE, AND MILITARY DECEPTION DURING THE WORLD WAR II ERA. Garland Publishing, Inc.: New York, 1979. Volume 13 – THE FINAL SOLUTION OF THE WEHRMACHT. USFET Interrogation Center, CIR/4 – Excerpts from a report on the German Sabotage System, 23 July 1945, page 7.
[593] Munoz, Antonio J. LIONS OF THE DESERT: ARAB VOLUNTEERS IN THE GERMAN ARMY 1941-1945. Axis Europa: Bayside, 1996. Page 18.
[594] The Parachute Engineer Battalion was later expanded to the 21st Parachute Engineer Regiment.

parachutists had first to prove that (1) they had two years prior service in the army, and (2) that they had the stamina to complete the rigorous paratroop training given. Captain Schacht noted:

"The command (Kodat) was composed of Moroccans, Algerians, Tunisians, Senussi, Tuaregs, Syrians, Egyptians, Iraqi, and desert Arabs. Volunteers had to provide proof of two years of service in the army of their own country before they were accepted. Former French colonial troops mixed with Italian Sahara veterans, British trained colonial fighters of the Middle East countries, and Foreign Legion soldiers. One old sergeant had even served in the Turkish Army in World War I."[595]

LEFT: Major Schacht as he appeared in 1944. In 1945 his Arab paratroopers would rally to his new command, a parachute regiment, and would serve in front of Berlin. About 100 Arabs would therefore serve in the battle for Berlin. *Bundesarchiv.*

THE GERMAN-ARAB 845th INFANTRY BATTALION

After the Germans lost the swamp positions positions in Tunisia, there was no longer any opportunity to employ the *Generalkommando z.b.V.,* which had been withdrawn from Russia. It was therefore decided that the corps' command would be redesignated as a motorized corps headquarters and on April 8th 1943 it was redesignated as the *Generalkommando z.b.V. 68 (mot.).* The corps had no units of its own, save the 287th Special Purpose Regiment, and that unit was itself withdrawn and sent to southern France on March 15th 1943 where it became *Grenadier Regiment 92 (mot.).* This regiment became active on May 2nd 1943 and was then sent to act as part of the occupation force in Serbia. In October 1944 it suffered heavy losses during the battle for Belgrade in October 1944, and was reformed on January 11th 1945 as a motorized brigade by the expansion of the engineer company and artillery battery into battalions, plus the addition of an anti-tank battalion.[596]

With the departure of the 287th Special Purpose Regiment, the corps command was once again left without any unit of its own. The German-Arab Training Battalion (a.k.a.- 3rd Battalion/ 287th Special Purpose Regiment) was in Tunisia and could not be used any time soon by the corps. Nevertheless a *Wehrmacht* (German Armed Forces) High Command order dated "29 March 1943" emphasized that the Generalkommando would continue to function as its

---

[595] Busch, Erich. DIE FALLSCHIRMJAEGER CHRONIK 1935-1945. Podzun Pallas Verlag: Friedberg, 1983. Page 165.

[596] Tessin, Georg. VERBANDE UND TRUPPEN DER DEUTSCHEN WEHRMACHT UND WAFFEN-SS 1939-1945. Biblio Verlag GmbH: Osnabrueck, 1973-1999. Volume 6, Page 122.

field agency for all Arab matters: *"The pertinent order contained a paragraph to the effect that the Special Corps was to organize a staff to deal with all political issues and propaganda connected with the Moslem world. This staff was to serve with the German-Arab battalion."*[597]

RIGHT: An Arab member of the 845th German-Arab Infantry Battalion sits down to read the Arabic language version of the German propaganda magazine, "Signal." *Museum of Modern History, Ljubljana, Slovenia.*

When the corps command finally left Russia, it was diverted to Greece where there was a need for a German corps command to control several small units. The corps arrived in Greece towards the end of May 1943. Meanwhile elements of the German-Arab Training Battalion which had remained at Palermo, Italy while the bulk of the Battalion was employed in Tunisia were ordered incorporated into a new Arab unit: the 845th German-Arab Infantry Battalion, a unit which was organized at Dõllersheim Training Camp. Dõllersheim Training Camp was located north and northeast of Linz, Austria. The main camp was about 12 miles east of Zwettl, which was itself north of Linz and was an annex to the larger camp. Initially the new Arab battalion contained four companies. It was in the summer of 1943 that the 845th German-Arab Infantry Battalion was assigned to the *Generalkommando 68 Armeekorps (mot.)*. The corps quickly issued a training directive for the unit on June 30th 1943: *"1. The Battalion is under the direct command of the Generalkommando. Initially it will organize into units all Arabs ready to serve the German cause and will train them in guerrilla tactics.*

2. For this purpose it will give the Arabs:

---

[597] Felmy, General der Flieger Hellmuth. Op cit. Page 33

a. Basic infantry training.

b. Training in teamwork for surprise raids be carried out by squads and half-squad sized units.

c. Training in demolition techniques (ranger type training).

3. If possible, squads should be composed of men from the same locality.

4. ...

5. ...

6. ...

7. The Battalion's 5th Company will be a parachute company. Lieutenant Rolf is appointed commander of this company.

8. ...

9. Also attached to the Generalkommando is the Arab Recruiting Center (Westa) in Paris. At present this agency is mainly an intelligence unit.

10. After its transfer to the zone of O.B. ***Süd*** *the battalion will be employed for guard duties in addition to its normal training routine."*[598]

LEFT: A squad of Arab volunteers and their German NCO go over a maneuver. This photograph was taken in Greece in 1944. *Museum of Modern History, Ljubljana, Slovenia.*

What is very interesting about this document relating the training and organizational layout of the 845th Battalion is that for the first time since Tunis, it mentions the Arab Parachute Company that had attached itself to Major Witzig's

[598] Felmy, General der Flieger Hellmuth. ibid. Pages 33-34.

Parachute Engineer Battalion. It had been withdrawn to the Italian capital just before the collapse of Axis resistance in North Africa. It shows that this company was attached to the 845th German-Arab Infantry Battalion while in Greece. Another aspect which becomes clear is that the new Arab battalion would still continue to train in what were obviously unorthodox and unconventional warfare

ABOVE: During their spare time, the Arab volunteers liked to indulge in games of sport. One of their favorite was blind wrestling, where each opponent was blindfolded and placed in a circle. The men were to find each other and wrestle the other to the ground. *Museum of Modern History, Ljubljana, Slovenia.*

techniques. This type of training would later prove to be instrumental in allowing the Arab battalion to operate against the Greek ELAS (Communist) guerrillas with great effectiveness. The very nature of the Arab soldier allows for a terrific guerrilla fighter- one that is adept at using all of the tricks that other partisan movements employ. In the unconventional fight that the Greek guerrillas waged, the Arab volunteers of the 845th Infantry Battalion surpassed their Greek opponents at every turn.

The 845th German-Arab Infantry Battalion completed its training in November 1943 and was posted to the *Generalkommando 68 Armeekorps* in the Pelopenesus region of Greece. There it came under the control of the German 41st Fortress Division. This division controlled numerous static, fortress, and garrison battalions and brigades, many of which were formed from the penal battalions of the German Army. There were small cases of desertion, as in the case which happened on November 19th 1943 when three Arab members of the deserted with their weapons, but overall the battalion did not suffer from high desertions.

One source states that the 845th (German-Arab) Infantry Battalion did not come under the control of the 41st Fortress Division until the spring of 1944, when it was transferred to the Lani region, with its base headquarters in Anfiklia, just west of Thebes. Its first large-scale anti-partisan operation occurred on April 7th

ABOVE: An excellent photograph of two Arab volunteers of the 845th German-Arab Infantry Battalion while undergoing an operation in the field. The Arabs were famous for being able to employ concealment techniques. In this photograph, the "Freies Arabien" arm patch is clearly seen being worn on the right sleeve of the soldier on the left. *Museum of Modern History, Ljubljana, Slovenia.*

1944 when the battalion plus around 3-4,000 other German troops were employed against the 2nd ELAS Division, then operating in the Helicon mountain range, by the Gulf of Corinth.

One reliable source states that when the 845th Battalion arrived in Greece, it was initially given the responsibility for railroad security protection north of Salonika, under the 91st Army Corps, Army Group "E." The battalion stayed in this region near the Aegean Sea until its move to the Pelopennesus in the spring of 1944. It was in the Helicon mountain range of southern Greece that the 845th Battalion proved its worth. As stated earlier, guerrilla warfare was a form of combat which seemed to suit the Arab mentality. A few typical examples from the experiences of Captain von Voss, the commander of the 1st Company/ 845th German-Arab Infantry Battalion, show the type of situation frequently encountered by German officers in their dealings with the Arab volunteers:

BELOW: While the Greek mountains are seen in the near distance, a platoon of Arab volunteers from the 845th German-Arab Infantry Battalion march past. The unit's performance far exceeded expectations when it was pitted against the Greek, and later, the Yugoslav guerrillas. The irregular warfare that characterizes partisan conflict was ideal for the Arab style of combat. They were masters of stealth and ambush. *Museum of Modern History, Ljubljana, Slovenia.*

229

"One day, Ali ben Mohammed reported to the medical officer and requested to be hospitalized. The officer examined Ali and found him in excellent health. Why do you want to be hospitalized? He said. You're not sick. Others get into the hospital, why can't I? You are healthy and you're not going into a hospital! Ali turned to the door, which had a glass panel, and pushed his head through it. Covered with blood, and with pieces of glass sticking into his scalp, he faced the doctor and asked: Am I sick now? On another day, the company was drilling. Everything seemed to be going well. Suddenly, one Machmut hurled his rifle away and flung himself on the ground. Ich nix soldat! (Me no soldiers!), he cried. His friend Mabruk was so ashamed at Machmut's behavior that he drew his bayonet and gave himself five or six blows over the head with it, exposing the bone under his scalp.

On another occasion two Arabs were teasing a soldier about his homosexual inclinations. That same night the soldier in question took his rifle, placed it behind the ear of one of his two tormentors, and pulled the trigger. During an action against partisans, Colonel von Eberlein, the commander of a security division, radioed that he was caught between two rivers. I told some of my Arabs, who were fond of the fierce old man with all his medals. All of them volunteered to go with me to the colonel's rescue. When we came to the river, they refused to let me wade across; they insisted on carrying me across on their shoulders. My Arabs never filched any of my personal belongings, though as a rule they stole like magpies. They liked to stuff themselves with good food, they liked to get drunk, to loot and rape; but they also knew how to die bravely, and they resisted pain remarkably well."[599]

The German-Arab 845th Infantry Battalion was also instrumental in capturing some Allied agents who were assisting the Greek guerrillas, among them being Captain McGregor, who was caught in Monte Parnasso. But it was the Greek Communist Major-General Stefanos Sarafis who paid them an unwitting praise, when he singled them out amongst what were 2,500-3,000 Axis troops attacking his 2nd ELAS Partisan Division in the region of Helicon in April 1944:

"Between April 7-11 a force of Germans, Battalionists, Italians, and Moroccans – about 2,500 men in all – tried to clear the Helicon district of ELAS troops. They landed from small craft in the Corinthian Gulf, in the Zaltsa and Ayii Saranda Bay, and after being reinforced from Thebes, Levadia and Amfissa, advanced towards Koukoura, Kyriaki, Distomo and Chostia. There was fierce fighting for four days at Kyriaki. Enemy dead and wounded: 250 including 45 Battalionists.[600] *In these operations they pillaged and burnt houses and raped girls."*[601]

---

599 Felmy, General der Flieger Hellmuth. ibid. Page 38.

600 General Sarafis used the term "Battalionists" to denote Greek collaborator units.

601 Sarafis, Major-General Stefanos. ELAS: GREEK RESISTANCE ARMY. Merlin Press: London, 1980. Page 441.

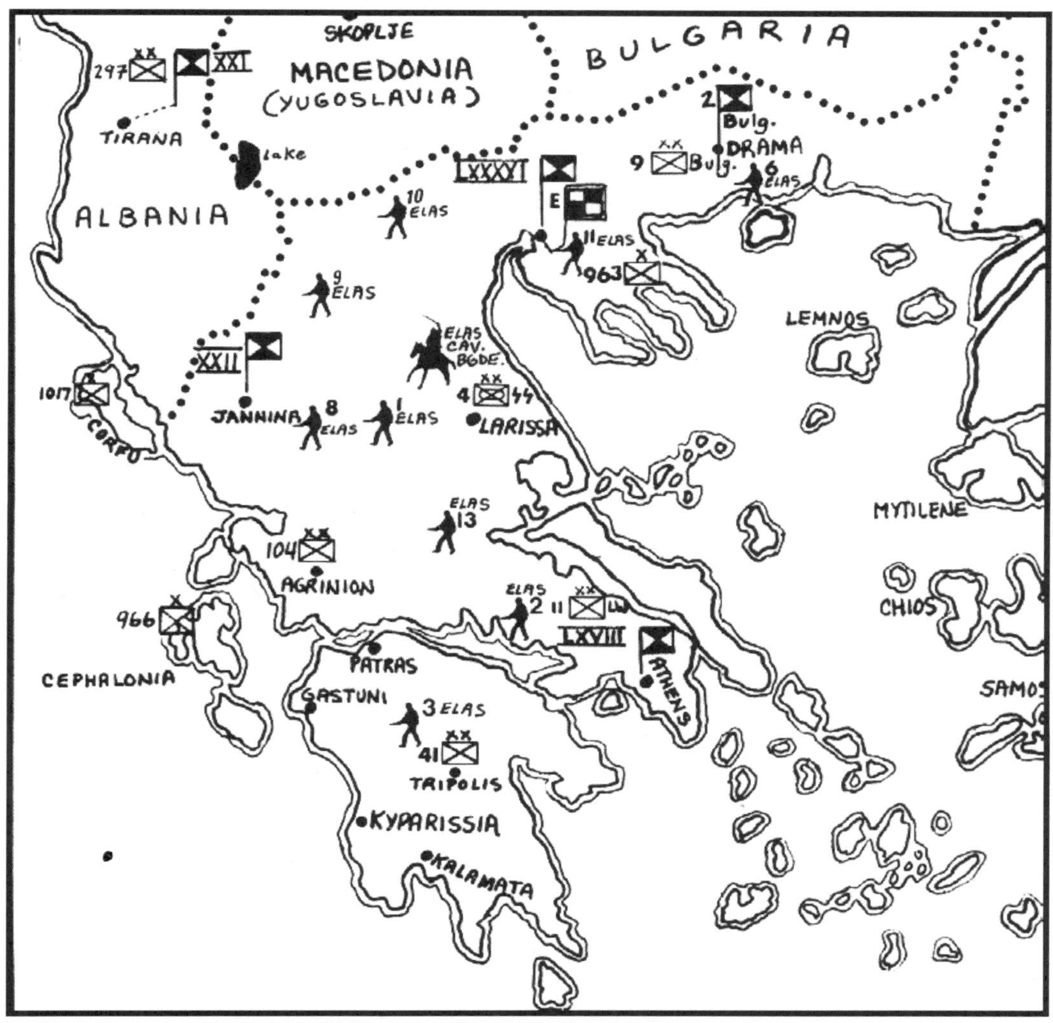

ABOVE: General location of the Greek ELAS guerrilla forces and major German divisional and corps headquarters. The 68th Army Corps, the former "Corps Felmy" was located in the Athens region.

No doubt, some of the raping and pillaging was done by the Arab soldiers in Captain von Voss's 1st Company and the rest of the 845th Battalion for that matter. The recruiting of more Arab volunteers had never ceased. Offices were set up all over Europe and by a careful review of Allied POW's; many more Arabs came forward and joined the German Army. It was in this way that a second battalion of Arabs was raised at Zwetll, near the Doellersheim Training Camp on September 1st 1944. The training of this second Arab battalion began that very month. The unit was designated as *"II/ Deutsch-Arabische Infanterie-Bataillon 845"* (2nd Battalion/ German-Arab Infantry Battalion845).

During October and November 1944, as the second battalion was undergoing training, the original 845th Battalion made a fighting withdrawal from Greece during the general German retreat from that country. Although they were employed as part of the rear guard, the morale of the battalion did not waver, in

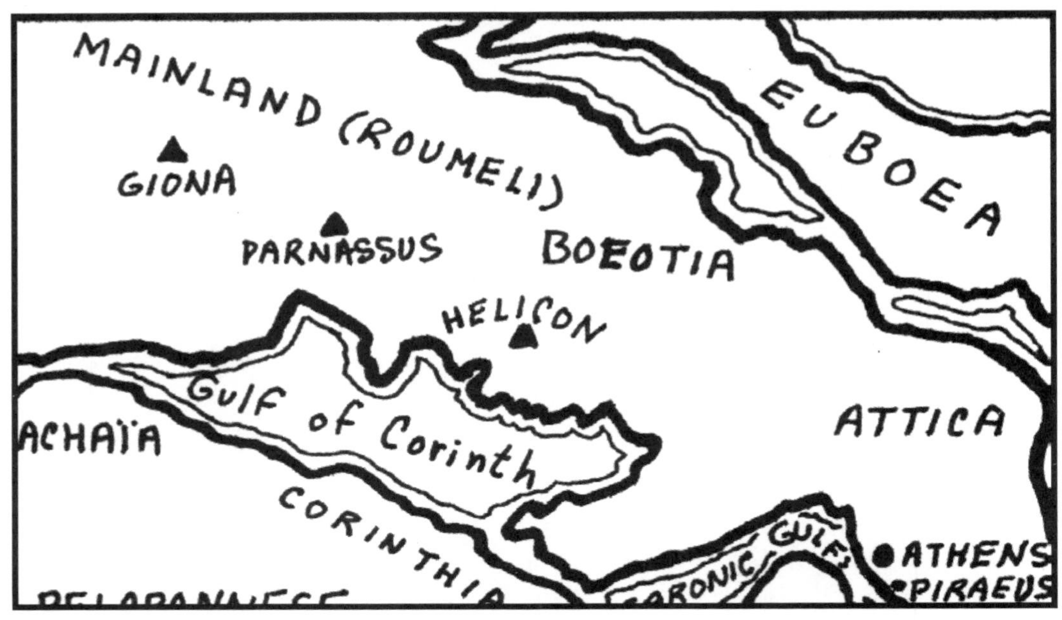

ABOVE: Athens and Attica Region. This area was patrolled by the 68th Army Corps and its sub-units, including the German-Arab 845th Infantry Battalion.

fact, if anything it got better. An example of their bravery is given by General Felmy while the battalion was in Bosnia-Herzegovina:

"When the German Army evacuated southern Greece in October 1944, and retreated northward through the Balkans, the 845th German-Arab Battalion usually furnished the rear guard. Remarkably, enough the Moslem troops soon became accustomed to the severe cold and even though they suffered high losses they remained effective. The German forces retreated from Greece into Yugoslavia, frequently delayed by air raids and partisans. Throughout the withdrawal the Arabs gave a good account of themselves. Towards the end of November, the 1st Company/ 845th German-Arab Infantry Battalion attacked Hill 734 at Uzice four times in succession despite the bitter cold and deep snow. A fifth attack was successful."[602]

Due to heavy losses, it was decided on January 10th 1945 to disband the existing 2nd Battalion, which had been training at Zwetll, Czech Protectorate, and to distribute the men of this unit into the depleted line companies of the original 845th German-Arab Infantry Battalion. The German cadre personnel of this 2nd Battalion did not follow the Arab recruits into Yugoslavia however. Instead, the Germans were transferred into the 48th *Volksgrenadier* Division that had been reforming at this time. Another blow to the strength of the original 845th Battalion had come in November 1944 when about 100 of the remaining Arabs in the 5th Company- the one that was parachute trained, deserted en-masse from the unit

[602] Felmy, General der Flieger Hellmuth. Op cit. Pages 36-37.

and elected to join their old German paratroop commander from their battles in North Africa, Captain Schacht, who they learned was organizing a special parachute regiment for action on the eastern front. This new unit, led by the now promoted Major i.G. Schacht, would eventually become the 25th Parachute Regiment of the 9th Parachute Division. This division would fight in front of Berlin during the final weeks of the war. Major Schacht mentioned "his" Arab volunteers in a personal letter in which he wrote:

ABOVE: Parade for inspection. The men of the battalion developed a high *"sprit d'corps."* Notice that many are wearing tropical trousers and summer tunics- very necessary items of light clothing for the tropical weather of Greece. *Museum of Modern History, Ljubljana, Slovenia.*

"...In November 1944, word got around that I had been entrusted with the activation of a parachute regiment for special employment. Before this month was over approximately 100 Arabs had deserted from their jobs with various staffs to volunteer for service in the new regiment. Under the leadership of officers who had commanded them during the Tunisian campaign, they formed an extra company for the regiment. During the fighting in March and April 1945 in Pommerania and on the Oder marshes the Arab Company fully proved its effectiveness. In at least two instances I owed my life to the Arabs. Their losses were in proportion to their courage."[603]

[603] Felmy, General der Flieger Hellmuth. Ibid. Page 39.

But what of the original 845th German-Arab Infantry Battalion that was fighting in Bosnia-Herzegovina in the fall of 1944? It was withdrawn from Greece and followed the 41st Fortress Division as it moved from Larissa, Greece through Bitolj and Skoplje, Macedonia, and then on to Kraljevo. From Kraljevo, the Arab battalion moved on towards Uzice, and from there it headed towards the Sarajevo area in Bosnia where it ended the year refreshing: *"In February 1945, after an interval for rest and rehabilitation, the Arab battalion was employed between the Danube and Sava Rivers.*[604]

In March and April 1945 it was still fighting under the 41st Division, just southeast of Vinkovci in Syrmia. Its higher corps command was the *Generalkommando 34* (34th Army Corps). The 41st Division had by then been re-designated as an infantry formation. In late April the battalion had been pushed back to Vukovar and ended up under the 104th Jaeger Division of 15th Mountain Corps. Later, the unit was shifted to Zagreb: *"In April it participated in the retreat that brought General Hauser's 41st Fortress Division to positions west of Zagreb, in Croatia. Here the battalion was captured. As far as can be ascertained the Arabs were concentrated in special prisoner of war camps and released after about one year of captivity."*[605]

BELOW: Morning roll call in Croatia, early 1945. Snow can be seen covering part of the ground. Although winter is apparent, the men were still wearing summer clothing. German officers in the battalion noted that the Arab volunteers adapted to the changing weather of Yugoslavia versus the warmer climate of southern Greece. *Museum of Modern History, Ljubljana, Slovenia.*

[604] Felmy, General der Flieger Hellmuth. Ibid. Page 37.
[605] Felmy, General der Flieger Hellmuth. Ibid. Page 37.

ABOVE: The company bugler. The German-Arab 845th Infantry Battalion's effectiveness against the Greek and later, the Yugoslavian guerrillas grew until the unit became known for its effectiveness by the German command. *Museum of Modern History, Ljubljana, Slovenia.*

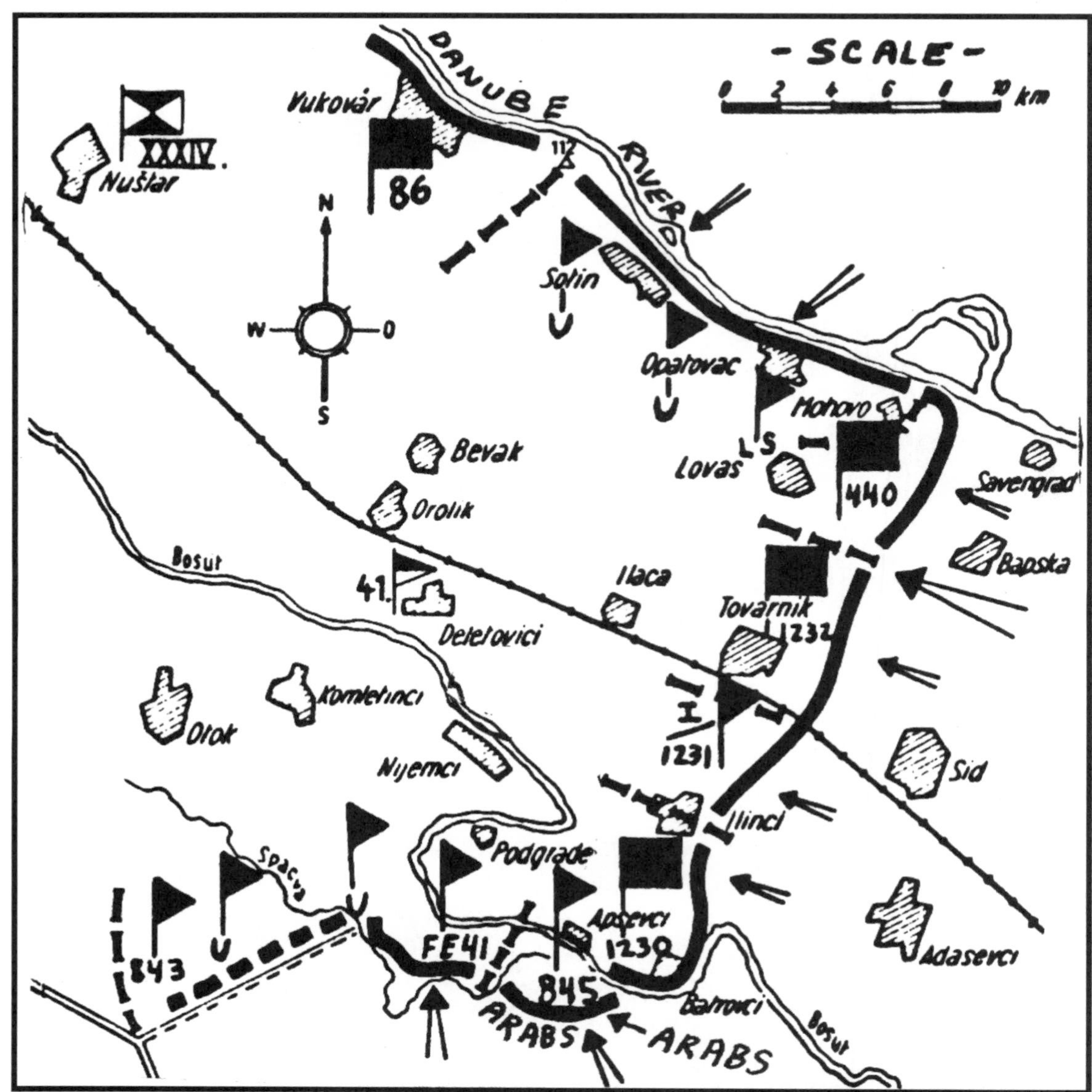

ABOVE: April, 1945. The Arab 845th Battalion was attached to the German 41st Infantry Division. Other non-German units which were attached to the 41st Division (formerly the 41st Fortress Division) was the 843rd North Caucasian Infantry Battalion; As well as four Croatian Ustashe (U) battalions. There was also one "LS" - *Landeschutzen Bataillon* (Regional Defense Battalion) within the Division.

An estimated 500 Syrians, 150-200 Palestinians, 450 Iraqis, 150-200 Lebanese, and perhaps 5-6,000 Moroccans, Tunisians, Algerians, Egyptians, Lybians, and desert Arabs joined the Axis forces between 1941 and 1945. About 6,000 of this number passed through the various German military organizations, while the rest served in the forces of Vichy France. They were a minute, though important political contribution to the German war effort simply because they were Arabs in German uniform and furbished rolls upon rolls of propaganda photographs and films to support the German war effort. Their military contribution can be said to have been insignificant.

This was basically because the purpose for which they were raised never came- the expected takeover by Axis forces of the Middle Eastern counties from the British and the use of these microscopic Arab forces as the basis for a future pro-Axis Arab army. There is one instance in which the Axis did begin full-cale recruitment of the local Arabs. This was the occupation of Tunisia when *Panzerarmee Afrika* was forced out of Tripolitania, Libya by the British 8th Army. During the brief time that the Germans recruited in Tunisia, they managed to raise five battalions- about a small brigade in size of Arab volunteers- and all of it while fighting on two fronts, the Americans in Algeria and the British coming from Lybia. They also created these battalions with extreme shortages of all kinds. We can only assume that more recruits and units would have been forthcoming if the Axis were not preoccupied with fighting on two fronts.

At the beginning of the Second World War, the Germans had an absence of any organized or pre-determined policy towards the Arab world. This situation pretty much remained unchanged throughout the war. Aside from vague promises of independence and a shared hatred of Jewry, Nazi Germany had very little to offer the Arab world by way of a concrete policy of self-determination and self-rule to the Arab peoples that had up until then been ruled by either France or England. One would imagine that the Allies courted the Arab people a lot better, and obtained better results. Indeed this proved to be the case when American forces landed in Morocco and began to arm Arab units with US equipment on behalf of the Free French. But before this the Allied interest towards the Arabs was negligible.

Beginning in 1943 Arab participation on the Allied side proved to be a conscriptive affair- one that would send an Algerian infantry division to fight in Italy. This was the work of pre-war colonial conscription brought back to life. In actuality, there were far more "colonial" troops employed in the Far East than were used in the North African or European campaign. In fact, the Free French under General Charles DeGaulle employed around 400,000 colonial troops during World War Two. It is an interesting observation to make, that in November 1944 when the defeat of Nazi Germany was certain, and the Allied newspapers were reporting the first Allied divisions were entering the *Reich,* these same colonial conscripts were suddenly withdrawn from Europe and sent home.

One author has speculated that the French wished to rid themselves of these "colored" units in order to show that it had been European (French) soldiers who had delivered the final blows, but all of this is conjecture. Suffice it to say that once they were no longer needed, this substantial colonial force was reduced and sent home. At the end of the Second World War, many peoples from third world countries expressed their desire to expel their former colonial masters and achieve true self-government. Many of these were former members of the Allied colonial troops, who went on to take part in the struggle for their own country's independence.

True political freedom was one right which the Allies were to deny the Arab world, at least until the war was over, and then only grudgingly. For this reason, we can argue that the Allies did not have much more to offer to the Arab people. Many would counter by saying that the Nazis, having racist policies, offered the Arabs even less. But those who choose to see Arab involvement with the Nazis in the Second World War in this light fail to observe the primary reason for their participation with the Axis: For the Arabs, it wasn't so much what the Nazis had to offer them, as much as what would be destroyed as a result of that Nazi victory.

ABOVE: A Schematic diagram of the 845th German-Infantry Battalion as it appeared in 1944-1945.

CHAPTER 12
LEBANESE VOLUNTEERS IN THE GERMAN ARMY 1937-1941

By Moustafa Assad

The following is an account of his WW2 experiences as told by a Lebanese man who was in his 20's when he traveled to Germany in 1936. He was interested in business at the time, but one-day he happened to attend a political rally for the Nazis in Germany and everything changed for him. His name is Ahmed Al-Akhdary, originally descending from a family of merchants of whom traveling was a habit. He used to travel to Europe first with his father and then alone to pursue the family business. His third trip to Germany in 1936 and his first contact with Hitler at that rally touched him deeply, and he did not return as usual to his country but instead remained there in 1938.

He became a factory worker, but was denied membership in the Nazi party for racial reasons. Luckily for him the factory owner, a prominent Nazi, summoned him to ask about a certain issue. Immediately he took the initiative and asked the owner to help him to become a member of the party. Two days later he was a member, and possibly the first of Arab origin, possibly his blue eyes helped. He attended all the rallies that were held, meeting many important people in the Reich through the aid of his boss, and became very well known at his factory. Soon he was appointed as the official spokesman and representative of the Nazi party at this factory (chemical and agricultural products).

In 1937 he was introduced to the leading SS chief of the district in order to help organize a festival welcoming a senior Nazi leader on an inspection tour. He did what was expected and more, and the two men became friends. Later the men began to cooperate on more important issues. They organized a very successful attack at a Communist underground gathering and received great attention for their work. Later they were requested to organize a more "uniformed" para-military arm to control the district, and this they did. By the end of that year they had established a military militia about 60 strong and later supplied them with uniforms that were (as remembered) dark blue with a silver swastika embroidered on the collar for the soldiers, and with a golden one for the officers. The two commanders had their swastikas in red. He remembers wearing these uniforms for at least a year. Their weapons being six Lugers and all sorts of clubs, although no headgear were worn.

During 1937, a major street battle occurred, "anti-party" militants wildly named as Communists took to the streets only to be confronted by the local Nazi unit. The battle was bloody, Hansa (as he recalls his name, but with no last name) was killed in the action as well as 9 of the Nazi militia (or Marchers as they were called). Ahmed (now called "Dory" by his friends) was also wounded. He recovered from his wounds but he couldn't forget his dead friend so he decided that he should make a trip back to his country Lebanon. He arrived there during the second month of 1938, remained there for one month and then he wanted to go back to Germany again.

He contacted the German delegate to the Middle East who instructed him to remain in the region for another month in order to help promote Nazi thoughts, and because "something important" was going to happen soon, and *"we need good men like you to keep their eyes open"*. He was instructed too to organize a group of men, finance them and to have them ready for any shaky situation that might occur. He was supplied with money, and a Luger pistol (that he still treasures to this day). It took him 3 months to do this job but very few men were interested in his ideas. When he finished he had assembled 24 men.

His trips to the German embassy were very secret and quit regular. There was no other means of communication and a transmitter was not available. Eventually the French started to notice the organization when 3 members were found dropping off leaflets, the men were arrested and interrogated. None of them spoke at first but then they broke down and the organization was exposed. As soon as the French knew about the organization, the unit felt threatened. The Germans knew of this and the whole band was transferred at night to Beirut and then aboard a small boat who transferred them to a German ship waiting off the coast of Cyprus. Then a commercial ship took them to Germany where they were all sent to work in the same factory that Dory used to work in.

Upon his return Dory re-organized the marchers and arranged for the newcomers to join also. In 1939 the marchers were soon instructed to join the Army, however the Army refused to take the Arab marchers so Dory, now in a good position to bargain, decided that he should have the honor of organizing a force of non-Germans who would serve the Party. His request was approved after many setbacks, but his force was not to serve before having the permission of an Army official (his name could not be recalled).

They were trained extensively by a young Army officer called Shirach, and the small party grew and to number 300 hundred men, mostly Lebanese and Syrians with a minority of Egyptians. Dory became the actual commander of the force and he started to work on a suitable badge. He designed and redesigned until he got what he wanted; a Nazi Eagle wearing on its head the traditional (Bedouin) headgear. When his army observer saw the emblem he became furious but Dory got the blessings of his superiors. By the time the approval came through, the war began and Germany invaded Poland. The first objective given to Dory and his force was to establish contacts with people in Lebanon and Syria. This was done, but their links were minimal, until Germany invaded France and then everything changed from there on.

Suddenly Dory found himself with an immense quantity of interest and facilities. He was told that he and his force were to be dropped behind enemy lines in Lebanon to create underground cells and to recruit volunteers. At that time the French were still fighting, and when zero hour came the group was transferred to an airport where they took 8 planes (unknown, with no national identities), they flew for many hours then they landed. All windows were covered and passengers were not allowed to know exactly where they did land (a mystery to this date). The planes probably refueled and then took off again. This time they were given orders to jump and they jumped in a deserted area in the eastern part of the South Lebanon.

Fully armed but with no uniforms, they concealed their weapons and some went to their nearby homes while others hid in the mountains. Their first mission was to destroy the railway line that linked Palestine with Lebanon and Syria. The mission one was about to take place when an urgent message came from Berlin by German radio. The coded letter canceled the mission and instructed them to go on and create a popular unrest against the French. This was easy. Three men were dressed up in French uniforms and transported into a village near Sour (Tyr). The soldiers attacked civilians in the coastal city. They then left, leaving the city in turmoil. When a real French patrol came by the angry mob attacked and killed all the soldiers, and then the mob attacked the French HQ in the region killing two more soldiers.

Things led to more unrest and this time Dory and his men participated actively in the action. Soon the whole South was on fire. Berlin was so happy that a plane filled with arms was hurriedly sent to reinforce them. The French commander in the region declined attacking, as already the situation in France was bad, and he was afraid. He eventually decided to step down. By the time Dory got orders to attack and burn the main French HQ in the south, France had surrendered, and the mission was cancelled. Major Dory, as his men called him now, was ordered to report to the seaport of Beirut with 20 of his men so that they could look as though they were coming in as German observers. The rest of his men were to do the same also. After spending 5 months as German observers they were given the choice of staying or regrouping in Germany. Only 27 remained while the rest left for Germany.

Germany was again at war in the Balkans, and Major Dory was assigned to assemble his men and leave for (he can't remember) near the frontier in order to be a part of the invading force. They were to protect the rear flank of the invading force. Dory remembers that the area was very rocky and almost impassable by tanks. He recalls his first fight against Greek infantry, and also remembers the first man of his force to die and the tree they buried him under. The force attacked against by dug-in Greek infantry and one of the men immediately fell.

When the force went to the ground Dory decided that the only way to pass is to outflank the Greeks. He sent a group of 10, which were successful in routing out the Greeks and capturing them. Their next orders were to capture a village in the Greek countryside. When they arrived they found that forces of the British Expeditionary Force occupied the village. Stukas bombarded the village for two days, and when Dory and his men stormed the village the BEF[606] retreated. Hours later, the BEF attacked the village again and Dory's force was had to retreat again. The force requested artillery cover and Dory this time was determined to give a blow to the BEF and attacked again.

The BEF retreated again, but Dory did not enter the village, instead he ordered his men to form a semi-circle around the village, and he waited. It wasn't

[606] BEF stood for British Expeditionary Force- the Editor.

long before the BEF attacked the village again and entered, only to find it empty. Now Dory ordered the artillery to open fire and the circle to be closed. The BEF surrendered to Dory after 3 hours. Dory now had his first armored vehicle, a Universal Carrier, captured from the BEF, he painted his emblem along with a very large German Cross on the sides and the front. They continued their advance and then they were ordered to head back to the rear lines; as other plans had been prepared for Dory and his men.

It was to be Libya and the Afrika Korps who would now host Dory and his force. The command in Berlin thought that an Arabian contingent would sound good in Libya so Dory was sent to Libya by plane while his force was to follow him by ship. Dory's trip was quick but his troops were not. Their ship suffered a direct hit from a torpedo and capsized. Other ships in the convoy rescued the survivors but about 140 men had drowned. Only 100 reached North Africa but their fighting spirit was broken. Dory spread his men among the DAK battalions serving as translators or liaison officers.

While the men were organized in the various German battalions, Dory himself was given the opportunity of being a free advisor. He was to roam through the various battalions and help upon request. His men were integrated and given tanks, he went to see the "boys" when they received their first Panzer IIs and they were more than proud of them despite their being obsolete. When he returned to his base he heard that Rommel has chosen to attack immediately, even before regrouping. He decided that this man was either mad or a genius. He returned to the regiment that was attacking and joined his men. They were 20 men with three Panzer II tanks. He requested another one but was refused because there were none available.

During this battle he managed to capture a British tank slightly damaged but still OK. He is not sure what it was, but after some pictures were shown to him, it appears to have been a Vickers. The battle was raging and he only found time to put two large crosses on the sides. Soon afterwards his tank was hit and started to burn. He barely jumped out when it exploded from another hit. His German driver died instantly. His force now numbered about 70 men and they were given 3 more Panzer III tanks but they needed repairs. He remembers using all kinds of improvised spare parts from all nationalities. When the repair work was finished the three tanks were international by every sense of the meaning. Many modifications were applied even an up-armored front (bulldozer like). The unit's emblem was painted on the sides of the turret, and the first tank was named Marcher, the second Beiruth, and the third Dory.

He remembers the closing days when they started facing the then powerful Sherman tanks. He knew he had an excellent tank but the gun wasn't powerful enough, especially against the "pyramid" (Sherman). Then came the petrol shortage and he remembers many days when he simply parked his tanks because there were no fuel to move them. He remembers the destruction of his second Panzer III "Beiruth" when it hit a mine and exploded killing all the crew. He continued to fight with the Afrika Korps to the end, and when the Alamein battles came he knew in advance that they were going to lose. He saw that they were attacking with all their forces and had no reserves or reinforcements.

When the battle came he knew that he was going to die, he summoned his men and said a farewell speech and wished his men the best luck. When the battle started he was one of the first to attack. His force suffered a heavy defeat when a gun emplacement took the lives of all his tanks; four Panzer II's and two Panzer III's, including his tank. It was hit on the side and the shell didn't explode, but it destroyed his idler wheel and shattered the tracks. His crew left but he remained in his tank waiting for the next shot to take his life along with his tank, he waited but was slightly disappointed when he realized that the gun shooting at him had been destroyed and the Germans now controlled the emplacement.

He left the disabled tank and it was only then that he realized that he had been wounded. He was taken to a hospital behind the lines and the war for him was now over. The allies defeated the DAK evenually and Dory became Ahmed again. He came back to his country claiming that he had been a slave laborer in Germany. He never saw any of his men again, and assumes they are all dead. He destroyed all his papers before leaving the desert. He also destroyed his uniform and badge but kept his Luger and a Walther to this day. This story was only told to his "family" in 1963 when he returned to Egypt – to revisit Alamein - this time as a tourist.

-14 January, 1989
Moustafa Assad, Sidon, Lebanon

Retired Major Dory personally told me this story in 1989. I managed to see the Luger, a 1936 issue and the Walther pistol. The Luger had the unit's emblem engraved on it as well as the name *"Dory."* If anyone knows more about this unit I would like to hear from you.

POSTCRIPT-

It is possible that Major Dory actually had been assigned to the Brandenburg 287th Special Purpose (Commando) Regiment, which was composed of foreigners and was transferred to North Africa where it operated.

- Antonio J. Munoz

CHAPTER 13
THE SWORD OF ISLAM:
The History of the 13.Waffen-Gebirgs-Division der-SS "Handschar"

By Antonio J. Munoz

ABOVE: The "Handschar" Divisional emblem.

ABOVE: The right collar tab of the 13th SS (Bosnian Muslim) Division "Handschar"

"The Bosnian Muslims proved to be the most unfortunate group in Yugoslavia during World War Two. Ethnically Serbian and speaking Serbo-Croatian, they were despised by their Christian Serb neighbors, used by the Croatians to fight those Serbs, repudiated by the Albanian Moslems for being closet Serbs, and exploited by the German SS as a ready manpower source."

The above statement best describes the situation in which the Muslim community of Yugoslavia found itself in during the Second World War. Those citizens of Yugoslavia of the Muslim faith amounted to approximately 900,000 souls. They were mostly concentrated in the provinces of Bosnia and Herzegovina. This was roughly 6% of Yugoslavia's population as of 1941. According to the Austro-Hungarian Empire's census from 1910, Bosnia-Herzegovina contained 434,061 Croats, or 23% of the population of those provinces before World War I. Orthodox Serbs numbered 811,505 or 43% while Muslims numbered 603,910 or 32% of the population. This number apparently increased to 40% of the population in these two provinces by the start of World War II.

Bosnia had been an independent kingdom in medieval times, and had formed a very distinctive character under the Ottoman occupation, when a substantial portion of its inhabitants converted to the Islamic faith. These Muslim converts had once belonged to a much persecuted Christian sect known as the *Bogomils,* who had then converted to Islam in gratitude to the religious tolerance that the Ottoman Turks had extended to them. This was in direct contrast to their Serbian Orthodox brothers who, it seems, had persecuted them.

The Austro-Hungarian Empire had acquired Bosnia-Herzegovina in 1887 and quickly moved to incorporate her into the empire. One way to do this was to conscript the local male population and form infantry regiments. Four infantry regiments were raised from the Moslem population and were reported to be among the bravest of the Imperial Army. Muslim recruits were allowed to wear a red fez headdress. The four regiments raised were located as follows:

1. Bosnia-Herzegovina Regiment No.1 – Sarajevo
2. Bosnia-Herzegovina Regiment No.2 – Banja Luka
3. Bosnia-Herzegovina Regiment No.3 – Tuzla
4. Bosnia-Herzegovina Regiment No.4 – Mostar

Later on, when World War I broke out and the Austro-Hungarian Army moved against Serbia, these Muslim regiments were used against the Serbian army, adding to the already high enmity between the Serbian Orthodox and Muslim communities. The end of World War I saw the formation of the Yugoslav state- a by-product of the treaty of Versailles and a British-French invention. Now the provinces of Slovenia, Bosnia-Herzegovina, Montenegro, Serbia, Kosovo, Vojvodina, and Macedonia all came together with their ethnic and religiously diverse peoples to form the Kingdom of the Serbs, Croats, and Slovenes. The country was composed of the following ethnic and religiously varied people:

ETHNIC GROUP	POPULATION	% Of Population
[Orthodox] Serbians	6,500,000	41%
[Catholic] Croatians	3,500,000	22%
Slovenians*	1,500,000	9%
Macedonians**	900,000	6%
Moslem Slavs	900,000	6%
Montenegrins**	500,000	3%
Others: ethnic-German, Hungarians, Greeks, Albanians, Bulgarians, Italians, and Russian exiles!	2,200,000	13%

* Primarily Catholic ** Primarily Orthodox

By the time that Germany and her Axis partners invaded Yugoslavia, these different ethnic and religious groups were ready to fight each other for equally diverse reasons. The Yugoslav government had long been dominated and controlled by the majority Serbs, which of course, many non-Serbs resented. The king was Serb, and the Yugoslav Army's officer corps was overwhelmingly Serbian. In fact, it wasn't until April 3rd 1941, or three days before the German invasion of Yugoslavia began, that Serbian General Dusan Simovic invited Croatian leaders to join his newly formed government, which had recently toppled the regime of King Paul.[607]

The German invasion of Yugoslavia merely accelerated the breakup of the country. This inevitable break would be halted at the end of the Second World

[607] The Serbian General Staff, always anti-German, had done this because King Paul had signed a non-aggression treaty with Nazi Germany a few days before. In his place, another Serbian prince was placed on the thrown.

ABOVE & BELOW LEFT: German Order Police officers post recruiting posters announcing the raising of the "Handschar": Division. Please refer to page 18 in this book for a full color view of this recruiting poster. *U.S. National Archives*.

War and Yugoslavia would remain together under the strong hand of Communism. After the death of Marshal Tito and the coming of democracy, the breakup of Yugoslavia eventually began in 1991 and ended only nine years later after almost every province went through a bloody struggle to free itself from Belgrade's control.

The Serbian coup leaders in 1941 had immediately annulled the pact, which King Paul had signed with Germany. King Paul had requested one of the stipulations in that pact to be that German troops were not to use the sovereign territories of his kingdom (Yugoslavia) for any future invasions of any countries. Astonishingly, Hitler had granted this request and was one

BELOW: Five Bosnian Moslem brothers serving in the same platoon, somewhere in the 13th SS "Handschar" Division. *Bundesarchiv.*

that the minor Axis countries like Romania, Hungary, and Slovakia did not have. Even though this pact had included this and similar stipulations, helping Yugoslavia to keep her neutrality with its neighboring countries, it was not palatable to the Serbian generals in Belgrade who still remembered how Germany supported the Austro-Hungarian empire in World War I. Additionally, the Serbs were very pro-French and pro-British and therefore anti-German. It was natural for them to resent cohabitation and any form of collaboration with Germany. They also had a chauvinistic attitude towards the other ethnic groups that made up the Yugoslav kingdom.

It was only natural then, that the Germans would support opponents of the Serbian dominated Yugoslav government, such as the Croatians who had long sought their independence from Belgrade; or the Slovenians or Macedonians, or Muslims for much the same reason. The dislike between Macedonians and Serbs for example, who shared the same basic religion, was such that when Bulgarian troops entered that Yugoslav province, they were welcomed by most of the population.[608] Similar incidences occurred when German forces crossed into

[608] Of course, after tasting a few years of Bulgarian occupation the attitude altered, but initially the Macedonians welcomed the change from the Serbian dominated political scene. For a time the most pro-Bulgarian elements, including IMRO, or the Inner Macedonian Revolutionary Organization even hoped for a declaration of Macedonain independence and a rebirth of the Macedonian glory that was built by Alexander the Great, but the Bulgarians were never interested in Macedonian independence and only played this political card in order to help keep control of the region.

Croatia and when Italian troops entered Kosovo and were greeted by the Muslims there.

It wasn't until the fall of 1942 that *Reichsfuehrer-SS* (National SS Leader) Heinrich Himmler and SS-General Gottlob Berger, who headed the Waffen-SS Recruiting Office, approached Germany's dictator, Adolf Hitler with the proposal to raise a Bosnian Moslem SS division. This was a significant event, since up until then the Waffen-SS had only recruited German, Germanic, or ethnic German volunteers into their SS units. But the idea of a Moslem SS division was very appealing to Himmler, Berger, and finally to Hitler. For Himmler, it seemed that Moslem men would make the perfect SS soldier. He believed that they made the best soldiers in an ideological struggle against Judiasm and Communism.[609]

The Moslems, he articulated, were all opposed to Judiasm. Their religion taught them that if they died in battle, they would immediately be sent up to heaven where their needs would be taken care of by a harem of beautiful women. What better religion a soldier could have, he reasoned? For Gottlob Berger, recruiting Bosnian Moslems also made sense. The constantly high losses in men in battle kept him hard-pressed to find replacements for the expanding SS divisions. The Bosnian Moslems would be another ready source of recruits for him. Finally, Hitler agreed with both Himmler and Berger, and added that the Moslems would help the Germans to garrison Yugoslavia and would therefore spare a German division for employment in Russia or elsewhere where the need was greater.

RIGHT: On the left, the Mufti of Jerusalem visits the 13th SS "Handschar" Division. On his right is Karl Sauberzweig, the SS general in charge of the division. *U.S. National Archives.*

[609] The Germans often did not differentiate between Judiasm and Communism and called them by the collective title of "Bolshevism".

ABOVE: The Germans tried to inculcate a hatred of communism and anti-Semitism into the Bosnian Moslem volunteers by providing propaganda that suited that purpose. *Museum of Modern History, Ljubljana, Slovenia.*
BELOW: A Muslim volunteer reads the German made pamphlet titled "Islam & Judiasm" while his comrades listen. This was a well posed propaganda photo. *Bundesarchiv.*

LEFT: A Bosnian SS member of the 13th SS "Handschar" Division escorts a wounded partisan prisoner. *Museum of Modern History, Ljubljana, Slovenia.*

When Hitler gave his "blessing" to the project of raising a purely non-Germanic SS division, he forever left the recruiting door open for the so-called non-aryans and so-called *untermensche.* It would seem that the needs of total war were slowly but surely whittling away at German notions of superiority of the Germanic race.

Earlier in the year, the Germans had been successful in raising a volunteer mountain division from ethnic German Serbs from the Banat region of the Yugoslav province of Vojvodina. In fact, this ethnic German SS division, which contained 21,000+ men at its peak strength, was raised only by the forceful conscription of the ethnic German population. This was testified under oath by *SS-Obersturmbannfuehrer* Robert Brill, of the *SS-Hauptamt* (SS Main Office) during questioning at the Nuremberg War Crimes Trials:

Herr Pelckmann: *"Statistics for the earlier years, 1940, 1941, 1942, have not been compiled by the Commission. Perhaps you could give us examples of how non-volunteers were taken into the Waffen-SS at such an early period."*

Herr Brill: *"Yes, I have already mentioned that 36,000 men who were drafted by emergency decrees. In addition, in 1940 we drafted men from the police to set up our field Gendarmerie. We drafted men from the Reichpost to secure our army mail. We drafted the civilian employees of the SS-Verfugungstruppe. In 1941 we frequently drafted personnel from the Army for our cavalry units. I recall further that about 800 Army men were drafted into the Waffen-SS in the summer of 1941...In 1942 we deviated considerably from the volunteer basis. About 15,000 racial Germans were drafted into our Prinz Eugen Division."*

This was a true statement concerning *Waffen-SS* recruitment efforts. Regarding the recruitment of ethnic Germans, in many cases these men who lived outside the borders of the *Reich* were obtained under false pretenses. One example of this was the use of the local German Bund organization in a particular

ABOVE: A German *SS-Hauptsturmführer* speaks with some Bosnian Moslem men from his company in Brcko, sometime in 1944. *Museum of Modern History, Ljubljana, Slovenia.*

region or country, in order to obtain replacements for the *Waffen-SS*. These foreign-born ethnic Germans would be invited to Germany for what was billed as a "summer toughening up corse." Upon arrival in Germany the men would find out that they had joined the *Waffen-SS!* When the recruit would complain, he was put under tremendous mental strain to "accept" his new lot in life. This forceful recruitment of racial Germans outside the borders of the Reich helped to relieve somewhat the high casualty losses incurred by the *Waffen-SS* divisions, but the supply of manpower was neither inexhaustible nor enthusiastic and therefore mediocre in quality. This became so especially after many an ethnic German recruit would write home, bitterly warning his friends not to fall for the same trap. Soon Gottlob Berger was seeking other sources of manpower.

It was therefore hoped that the Muslim community of Bosnia and Herzegovina, which Himmler knew was fairly substantial, could be expected to raise another division for the Waffen-SS. Heinrich Himmler's knowledge of the Bosnian Muslims went back to World War I. Although he himself had very little war experience, having only been an officer candidate who never reached the front lines before the war ended. He did nevertheless get to hear about the "brave Mujos" from returning war veterans who had campaigned in the Balkans and had seen first hand the bravery and ferocity of the Muslim regiments of Emperor Franz-Joseph. Himmler would not forget these old war stories and would remember the Muslims from Bosnia and Herzegovina.

LEFT: A pre-war photograph of Albert Stenwedel, a *Reich* German who woul eventually become the commander of the 2nd Battalion/ 27th Mountain Infantry Regiment of the SS. Here he is seen as a member of the Leibstandarte Adolf Hitler in the rank of an SS 2nd Lieutenant. While serving with the SS "Handschar" Division, he would eventually hold the rank of SS-Sturmbannführer (SS Major). Photo courtesy of the *Justin Horgan Collection*.

The Croatian *Ustashe*[610] had already recruited the Muslim population of Bosnia-Herzegovina as had the Croatian Army. Now the Waffen-SS hoped to do the same. At this stage in the war, the majority of the Tito partisans were principally composed of Serbian volunteers, with Croatians in the minority. This fact was also taken into consideration by the SS, who hoped to take advantage of the mistrust and hatred between the Muslim and Serbian communities. Herein lies another reason why Hitler, Himmler and Berger wished to raise a Bosnian Muslim SS division. It was hoped that the natural animosity which existed between the Muslim and Christian Orthodox populations would make the unit an effective occupation force. The irony was that both the Muslims and Orthodox Serbs were from the same Slavic stock. They were two communities that should have lived side by side as brothers, for they come from the same family tree, but their religious zeal drove a wedge between them that even resurfaced fifty years later, in the 1990's and caused untold horrors and suffering on both sides.

On February 10th 1943 Adolf Hitler formally approved of the project and three days later Heinrich Himmler directed that the commander of the ethnic German *"Prinz Eugen"* SS Division, *SS-Gruppenfuehrer und Generalleutnant der Waffen-SS* Artur Phleps, himself a racial German from Rumania, would be charged with raising the division. The unit was initially referred to as the "Croatian SS Volunteer Division." On February 19th Artur Phleps set to work at establishing a formation staff that would form the basis of the new SS divisional

---

[610] The Ustashe were Croatian political troops much like the SS, of Croatian Fascist dictator, Ante Pavelic. While the Germans had initially wanted Croatia to be ruled by a moderate Croatian leader of the Croat Peasant Party, the Italians, who had backed the Croat extremists, insisted on Pavelic being made leader.

headquarters. Late in February a meeting was held between Ante Pavelic, the Croatian Fascist dictator and Artur Phleps and SS-Brigadefuehrer und Generalmajor der Polizei Konstantine Kammerhofer, who was the Higher SS & Police Leader in Croatia and therefore, Himmler's immediate representative.

ABOVE: Albert Stenwedel (at the head of the small table), with other German officers of the 13th SS "Handschar" Division, somewhere in Bosnia, 1944. Photo courtesy of the *Justin Horgan Collection.*

Kammerhofer represented Himmler in all matters. Pavelic was informed matter of factly that the decision had been taken to raise an SS division from what amounted to subjects of the Croatian state. Although Pavelic did not show any outward signs of surprise, anger or indignation, he was nevertheless furious that thousands of his subjects were to be recruited into what was a foreign military organization, without so much as a token request of permission from the Croatian government! Pavelic was teeming with anger at the Germans, who had arbitrarily decided to raise this unit without his consent or "blessing." Instead, they were telling the *Poglavnik*[611] of their decision as an afterthought. He resolved then and there to agree to the German *faít acomplí* for he was in no position to anger the Germans, since he was dependent on them for military support. Instead however, he decided he would do his best to undermine and torpedo the entire recruiting effort. German arrogance at not even consulting him prior to their final decision, on what was clearly a matter for the Croatian state to decide, was indicative that the Germans considered Pavelic and his Croatian government as nothing

[611] *"Poglavnik"* was the Croatian equivalent to *"Fuehrer."*

Zweitschrift

IM NAMEN DES FÜHRERS
VERLEIHE ICH
DEM

SS-Unterscharführer

Albert Beder

3./SS-Geb.Jg.Rgt.28

DAS

EISERNE KREUZ
2. KLASSE

H.Qu., 8. August 1944

Der Kommandierende General:

gez. A. Phleps
SS-Obergruppenführer
und General der Waffen-SS

(DIENSTGRAD UND DIENSTSTELLUNG)

ABOVE: Certificate awarding the German Iron Cross (2nd Class) to a German sergeant in the 3rd Company of the 28th SS Mountain Regiment of the "Handschar" Division. The award has been signed by SS General Artur Phleps, the commander of the 5th SS Volunteer Mountain Corps. *Author's Private Collection.*

ABOVE & BELOW: Parade of the 13th SS "Handschar" Division. The Mufti of Jerusalem gives the Nazi salute, as company after company of Bosnian Muslim SS men pass in review. *U.S. National Archives* and *Bundesarchiv*.

more than a puppet of the Reich. This move clearly infringed on Croatia's sovereignty and Ante Pavelic was hell bent on teaching the Germans a lesson.

SS formation be designated as the *"SS Ustashe Division Hrvatska"* (SS Ustashe Division Croatia). Both Kammerhofer and Phleps agreed to this request, only to get the formal approval from the Croatian Fascist leader. This was tantamount to a "rubber stamp" of approval and Ante Pavelic knew it. Both of Pavelic's requests were later ignored by the Germans. Ante Pavelic thereupon resorted to sabotage and subterfuge to cripple the SS recruiting drive from the very beginning. He did this by giving a strict, verbal and written warning that any Muslim who opted to join the Waffen-SS would either be drafted into the Croatian Army or be sent to a concentration camp. This campaign increased when the Croatian leader was told that many Muslims in the Croatian Army were deserting to join the new SS division.

The reasons for the desertions were many- an increase in pay, "prestige" of belonging to what was then considered an elite German military organization, better equipment, arms, and clothing, better leadership, not to mention having three good square meals a day and higher pay. A special diet was quickly established for the Muslim recruits who had to avoid pork and some other items. Yet in spite of all this, the number of Muslim recruits began to dwindle to almost nothing by March and April 1943. This had occurred in spite of Himmler's order to Gottlob Berger to send Kammerhofer about 2,000,000 *Reichmarks* to help finance the recruiting effort. It seems that the *Poglavnik* was getting his revenge. If things did not improve, the projected number of 26,000[612] Muslim recruits would not be reached by the target date of August 1st 1943. Additionally, Kammerhofer and Berger both feared that the entire project was now in jeopardy.

RIGHT: A cavalry troop of the 13th SS Division.

[612] One source states that the projected number was actually 20,000 Muslim recruits, out of which several hundreds were to be Albanian Muslims.

BELOW: Men of the 13th SS "Handschar" Division move through Bcko, by the Sava River in March 1944. *Museum of Modern History, Ljubljana, Slovenia.*

An investigation was launched by the staff under Artur Phleps to try and ascertain what the problem was causing the recruiting effort to falter. On April 19th 1943 the finding of the staff was that the reason for the failure of the recruiting endeavor lay squarely on the feet of the Pavelic regime, which was doing all it could to undermine the Muslim SS recruiting effort. Himmler was now the one to be outraged. He ordered Kammerhofer to remind the Poglavnik that Croatians were supposed to be puppets. The Croatians had few friends. The Serbian Chetniks were fighting the Croat state. The Tito partisans were fighting the Croat state, and the Italians who initially backed them, were now doing their best to destabilize the Croatian regime. The Croatians therefore, desperately needed continued German support in order to avoid being overrun by their enemies. For this reason Ante Pavelic could impede German interests just so far. The Poglavnik eventually relented and the recruiting campaign was allowed to proceed unimpeded.

But the damage had already been done and the number of Muslim recruits still remained below requirements. The Germans now put off all pretenses and began the forcible conscription of *"unsere Mujos"* (slang for "our Muslims"). The German NCO's which were assigned to accept and train these Muslim recruits had been the veterans of earlier German victories and were, for the most part, indoctrinated into the racist principals and ideals of National Socialism. These theoretical principals espoused the superiority of the *Herrenmensche* (superman) over the *Untermensche* (sub-human). For these German SS men, it was extremely difficult to accept these Slavic Muslim recruits, non-aryans to be sure, as their equals and partners in the struggle against the guerrillas. The military requirements and necessities of the day were fast superceding political dogma. As will be seen, this was a recipe for disaster and would cause a major problem.

By July 1943 enough recruits had been gathered so that the training of the division could officially begin. The SS-FHA, or *Führungshauptamt* (SS High Command) now gave the forming division its first title on July 2nd 1943: "Croatian SS Volunteer Mountain Division." Thirteen days later the divisional staff first mentioned the title *"Handschar"* (Scimitar) in its records, as the name that had been bestowed on the division. A Scimitar was an Arab sword and had a very distinctive look. The overwhelming majority of the Muslim recruits came from Bosnia, but the officer corps of the division was principally composed of German or ethnic German officers and NCO's. There were also numerous cases of racial Germans from Hungary also serving in the division. These served especially as interpreters between the German officers and their Serbo-Croatian speaking recruits. One such example was *SS-Unterscharfü- hrer* Franz Pakos, who began his military career in the Hungarian Army.

The German officers assigned to the division ran the gambit from previous serving police officers to even a former concentration camp commandant! One former police official, *SS-Sturmbannführer* (SS Major) Karl Liecke, had served in the German Order Police before the war. He later had been drafted into the SS Police Division and fought on the northern sector of the eastern front. He became the fourth officer to lead one of the Muslim SS regiments[613] in the Division, and

[613] Waffen-Gebirgsjaeger-Regiment der-SS No. 27.

was only relieved of this post late in the war. Another officer, SS Major Egon Zill, had the following "qualifications" before he was posted to the "Handschar" Muslim SS Division:

"Born in Plauen, 1906; Baker and janitor; joined the Nazi Party and SA in 1923, transferred to the SS, 1926; Promoted to SS Major, 1942; Service in Hohnstein, Sachsenburg, and Lichtenberg Concentration Camps, 1934-1937; Protective Custody Camp Leader at the Dachau Concentration Camp, 1937-1941; Staff member of the Concentration Camp Buchenwald, 1938, and Women's Concentration Camps Lichtenburg and Ravensbrueck, 1938-1939; Commandant of the Concentration Camp Hinzert, Natzweiler, and Flossenburg, 1942..."[614]

Egon Zill was listed as the commander of the 2nd Battalion in one of the regiments in the Division in July 1944; However an SS officer roster dated "1 October 1944" listed him as being transferred into the 23rd SS *"Kama"* Division. Although SS Major Egon Zill was the exception, his example nevertheless shows us that the Division's officer corps had officers that were not considered "ideal" and properly trained infantry officers. Many had been transferred over from the Order Police, and administrative posts. It can be said that the most qualified commanders were not sent to the Muslim SS Division, since they were kept for the truly elite SS formations. From all of this we can only surmise that the officer corps of the *"Handschar"* Division was composed of diversely qualified and unqualified officers which most likely would have produced mixed results.

This is after all quite understandable, given the fact that the Division was earmarked for occupation duty and anti-partisan operations and not the more strenuous front-line combat duty of other units. The Germans did try to raise the morale of the Muslim recruits. One way that this was achieved was to allow the Muslims in the Division to practice their Islamic faith. Special rations were also accorded the unit: *"Each battalion had its Iman, each regiment its Mullah, and with Hitler's consent, the Moslems were given the same privileges they had in the old Imperial Austro-Hungarian Army: special rations and permission to observe their religious rites en-masse."*

The Germans even went to the trouble of establishing two religious schools specifically geared for the Islamic faith in order to train the Imans and Mullahs of the Army and Waffen-SS. One was located in Göttingen and the other in Dresden. The Dresden School was intended primarily for Waffen-SS units, while the one at Göttingen trained religious pupils for the German Army, who also had a large number of Muslims from the Soviet Union in their ranks. The school in Dresden was given the official blessing of the Mufti of Jerusalem, whom the Germans had "elevated" by referring to him as the "Grand Mufti of Jerusalem". This Mufti from Jerusalem was El Hajj Amin Hussaini, who had fled Palestine after the British sought his capture. Himmler was reported to have viewed Islam in good graces, stating he had: *"...nothing against Islam because it educates the men in this division for me and promises them Heaven if they fight and are killed in action; A very practical and attractive religion for soldiers!"*

---

[614] Personnel File – Egon Zill, Berlin Document Center (now under Bundesarchiv).

In addition, special insignias were made specifically for the Muslim SS Division – one being the right collar tab which depicted a swastika and a hand holding a Scimitar, or curved sword which was favored by Turkish troops of the Ottoman Empire. The Muslim recruits were expected to take the oath of allegiance, like other Waffen-SS members. A special oath of allegiance had to be devised however, which would simultaneously make the Muslim SS recruits swear an oath of loyalty to Adolf Hitler and Ante Pavelic, placating the vanity and suspicions of the Croatian leader:

BELOW: The *"Handschar"* Division's supply officer during the spring and summer of 1944, the *Reich* German, *SS-Sturmbannführer* Albert Fassbender. When the 13th SS Division was disbanded, he did not remain with the rump of the Division but was transferred to the SS-FHA.

"I swear to the Führer, Adolf Hitler, as Supreme Commander of the German Armed Forces to be loyal and brave. I swear to the Führer and to the leaders whom he may designate, obedience unto death. I swear to God the Almighty, that I will always be loyal to the Croatian State and its authorized representative, the Poglavnik, that I will always maintain the best interests of the Croat people and always respect the state constitution and laws of the Croatian people."

On July 2nd 1943 the SS-FHA decided to shift the forming Moslem SS Division to southern France in order to avoid disruption of the unit's training schedule by the partisans, or further Croatian attempts to undermine the unit. The divisional headquarter's staff was now placed in the French town of Le Puy. The divisional forming staff was, as stated earlier, raised and led by SS General Artur Phleps. While he was in charge of the newly formed divisional staff, some proposals as to who would eventually lead this new division were circulated. One of the choices proposed which stuck initially was *SS-Standartenführer* (SS Colonel) Herbert von Obwurzer, who was indeed chosen and given control of the Division towards the end of April 1943. While some post-war historians have argued that von Obwurzer was mainly concerned with recruiting and as such cannot be considered as the first true divisional commander, two German authors (including SS General Paul Hausser) state clearly that until August 8th 1943, when Obwurzer was removed from command of the division, he was indeed the commander of the SS "Handscahr" Division. The fact that he was mainly concerned with the recruiting drive is understandable, given that during this early stage in a division's development, there's a need to recruit men to flesh out the unit!

Finally, on August 1st 1943 a German officer in the *Wehrmacht*, Major Karl Gustav Sauberzweig, was inducted into the Waffen-SS and given the rank of *SS-Oberführer*, which is the SS rank somewhere between Colonel and Major-General. This induction was voluntary and Sauberzweig did not oppose it at all. In fact, he volunteered. Eight days later, on August 9th he was given command of the Division, which had by then been taken from von Obwurzer because of apparently irreconcilable differences between himself and the Croatian regime. It seems that Obwurzer's recruiting campaign had taken an anti-Croatian stance which Himmler realized would be detrimental to the already strained German-Croat relations. He was removed from command to (1) placate the Croatian government and (2) allow the forming of the division to continue without further Croatian hindrance. Sauberzweig had served as an ordnance officer in the pre-war German Army, first in a cavalry regiment and then in an artillery regiment. Although he was born in Prussia, he later went on to serve in Austria, where he became a member of the General Staff of the 17th Army Corps in Linz, Austria. Later the headquarters of this corps was moved to Vienna. Earlier, Sauberzweig's military career had also included a stint with the 8th Prussian Infantry Regiment before becoming a general staff officer on October 1st 1930.

UNSERE MUJOS

As stated earlier, the placement of the Slavic Muslim SS recruits under the command of German SS NCO's and officers who were accustomed to treating so called "sub-humans" as their equals, led to incidents and bad feelings, misunderstandings, and insensibilities between the recruits and their SS cadre personnel. The Germans would sarcastically refer to the recruits as *Mujos* or *Muselgermanen,* and other insults and humiliations which were heaped on the Muslim men. To make matters worse for the Germans, the Muslim SS Division had been infiltrated by a communist cell that was bent on wrecking the training program and demoralize the unit as a whole.

In this the communists were in agreement with the Croatian Fascists – they both wanted to ruin the Division! They planned to do this by (1) Magnifying the racist incidents which the German training personnel themselves caused and (2) by a program of misinformation that was geared to confuse the recruits, deplete their morale, and cause as much friction between them and the Germans as was possible. One such example of misinformation was the rumor that circulated by this communist cell, that the Germans were planning to employ the Division against the western Allies, and this had been the reason why the unit had been shifted to France. Of course, such a move would have proved disastrous, since the Muslims of Yugoslavia had no quarrel with the western Allies and therefore no desire to fight against these countries.

The Germans understood this only too well. Unfortunately for the Germans, this rumor was reinforced when the Muslim recruits found themselves training in France and wondering what they were doing so far away from home. The Germans couldn't just explain that they had removed the unit from the Balkans because they feared that the partisans would disrupt the training. This would imply that the Germans were not in control of the countryside and the situation- furthering to demoralize the unit. Another "open wound" which the communist cell worked on was the compulsory service, that is, the outright forceful conscription of the Muslim men into a foreign army. Away from home, not knowing if their families were safe from communist or Chetnik attack, the recruits wondered just what they were doing in southern France.

Tensions continued to simmer just beneath the surface until the night of September 16th-17th 1943, when weeks of German insensibilities and communist agitation efforts finally boiled over and erupted into what was then thought to be unthinkable: the first ever mutiny within the ranks of the Waffen-SS! The mutiny occurred within the 1,000 men of the division's engineer battalion. The rebellion was led by *Waffen-Oberjunker der-SS* (SS Officer Candidate) Ferid Dzanic. The battalion was stationed in the village of Villefranche-de-Rouergue when it mutinied, killing most of the German officers and NCO's in the unit. One known ethnic German officer who was killed during the uprising was 38 year old *SS-Obersturmfuehrer* (SS 1st Lieutenant) Julius-Friedrich Galantha. There were other plotters in the mutiny, among which were *SS-Oberjunker* Eduard Matutinovic and Nikola Vukelic, and *Waffen-Oberscharführer der-SS* (Sergeant of the SS) Lutfija Dizdarevic.

These men, led by Dzanic and fourteen other enlisted men, went about systematically forcing each sentry and then each platoon to join the mutiny or die. They thereupon grabbed the Germans in the 1st Engineer Company and began to kill them. Dr. Scheiger, the Battalion medical officer was one of the many Germans caught by the mutineers. He personally begged Sergeant Dizdarevic to spare his life, quoting the numerous times he had shown sympathy for the Bosnian recruits. Temporarily, Dizdarevic relented, noting that he had no personal quarrel with the "good doctor", and that he was one of a few German officers who had treated the recruits with respect. Dr. Scheiger was placed in a room with *Waffen-Obersturmführer der-SS* Halim Malkoc, the Battalion's Iman. Both officers were used as hostages. In spite of this temporary reprieve, both Scheiger and Malkoc were later strangled by Dzanic and some other plotters.

By midday on September 17th the new divisional commander, *SS-Brigadeführer* Sauberzweig[615] had approached the division's communications battalion, which was the nearest unit to the engineer battalion, and headed towards the village of Villefranche-de-Rouergue and the mutineers in order to personally put down the revolt. Altogether 20 German NCO's and officers were killed by the mutineers. It was later learned that the plotters had been in contact with the local French *Marquisard* resistance cell. The chief instigator of the revolt, *Waffen-*

[615] Sauberzweig had recently been promoted to this rank.

Oberscharführer der-SS Lutfija Dizdarevic preferred to escape into the woods and join the French partisans rather than face the German attack as resistance quickly fell. In the preceding days to come, a court martial was convened and 50 Muslim recruits were condemned to death and shot by firing squad.

The mutiny caused the intended effect which the communists had desired. The rank and file soldiers of the Division were completely demoralized. The Imans and Mullahs tried to restore calm and order, and to reassure the Muslim recruits. The Germans even sent the Mufti of Jerusalem to the Division in the hope that his presence and words of encouragement would restore the morale of the men. In addition to the 50 recruits who were shot by firing squad, an additional 825 Muslim recruits of the engineer battalion were transferred to Dachau Concentration Camp on September 27th 1943. This transfer was done in secret, while the Division was en-route to Neuhammer Training Camp in Silesia. The Germans simply diverted the appropriate rail wagons to Dachau, much to the surprise of the 825 men who were expecting to arrive at Neuhammer. In effect, the engineer battalion was dissolved and later had to be rebuilt from scratch. Later on 536 men out of the 825 recruits sent to Dachau were deemed "rehabilitated" and sent to the Organization Todt. The remaining 289 men of the original engineer battalion were sent to an SS Penal Recruit Battalion stationed in Chlum, in the "Protectorate" of Bohemia and Moravia (Czech territory). Those unfortunate Bosnian Muslim recruits ended the war by serving in the infamous *"Dirlewanger"* SS Penal Brigade/Division. Soon after the revolt, the decision was made to transfer the Division closer to Yugoslavia. With this in mind, the entire 21,065 man force was sent to Silesia in September and October 1943. The Division was composed of the following numbers of men:

Officers	NCO's	Men	TOTAL
360	1,931	18,774	21,065

Instruction now resumed anew and the unit settled down to a daily routine of recruit training. On October 9th the Division was finally given its first official title: *13.SS-Freiwilligen-Bosnien-Herzegowinen-Gebirgs-Division [kroatien]* (13th SS Volunteer Bosnian-Herzegovinian Mountain Division [Croatia]). Up until then, the two Muslim SS mountain infantry regiments in the Division had been simply numbered "1" and "2". Later still, in June 1944 the title was changed so that the words "Bosnia-Herzegovina" was removed and the name "Handschar" (Scimitar) was added. The regiments were renamed in order to designate their non-Germanic status:

I. Waffen-Gebirgsjäger-Regiment der-SS No.27 (kroatische Nr.1)
II. Waffen-Gebirgsjäger-Regiment der-SS No.28 (kroatische Nr.2)

On January 12th 1944 a German press release stated that: *"in order to fight Bolshevism, a Bosnian volunteer formation had been raised from the Muslim faithful."* It further went on to state: *"The Grand Mufti of Jerusalem was spiritually backing the unit and its purpose."* Of course, no mention was made of the unit's mutiny in France and the delay in training and low morale that it caused on the "Muslim faithful." In the beginning of February 1944 110 trains carried around 20,000+ men and 8,000 mules of the Division to Bosnia-Herzegovina. The German 2nd Panzer Army, then operating in Yugoslavia, was to receive four divisions as reinforcements in that month:

1. *392. Kroatische-Deutsche Legions-Infanterie-Division*
2. *42. Jäger Division*
3. *"Brandenburg" Division*
4. *13.Waffen-Gebirgsjäger-Division der-SS "Handschar"*

The Muslim SS formation was moved through Vinkovci, Jarmina, Bacinci, Novo Selo, Bojagaci, Kukujevci, Mlasica, and Sid. One source states that the Moslem SS Division was placed under the 5th SS Volunteer Mountain Corps,

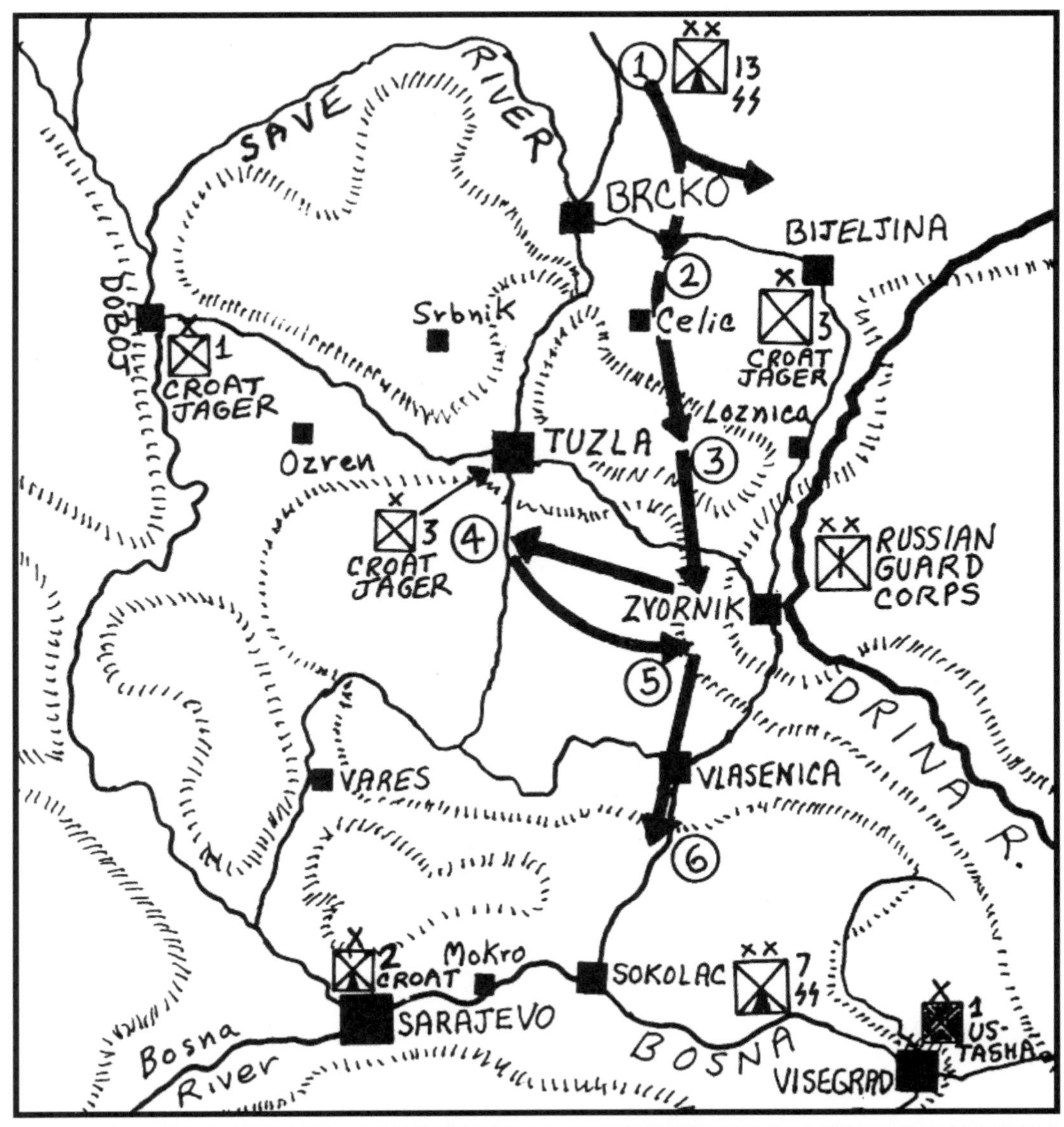

ABOVE: Area of Operations of the "Handschar" SS Division in 1944.

THE OTHER MUSLIM LEGIONS

There were other Muslim formations that were raised by the Croatians during the Second World War. The Croatian Ustashe, the political troops of Ante Pavelic raised units of Muslim volunteers. The Croatian Gendarmerie also had a Muslim Militia in Bosnia-Herzegovina that contained 7,500 members. Then there was the Husko Legion, raised in Cazinska Krajina in western Bosnia which contained 3,000 Muslim volunteers in 11 battalions. The Husko Legion was formed in the summer of 1943 but defected to the Tito Partisans in February of 1944 when it seemed that the war was now going in favor of the Allies. The commander was Husko Milijkovic, a pragmatic Muslim chieftan. Another Muslim commander by the name of Hadziefendic formed another Muslim legion in Northeastern Bosnia. That militia formation was later absorbed into more reliable Croatian forces so it would not defect like the Husko Legion. Its numbers were in the hundreds and remained under a thousand men.

BELOW: Muslim militiamen of the Husko Legion. The emblem worn was a Muslim crescent and star or double crescent facing away from each other inside a large crescent and a small star above (see below right).

Bosnia-Herzegovina and the Surrounding Regions

but another lists the unit as being at the disposal of the 2nd Panzer Army. The "Handschar" Divisional Headquarters was initially located in Vinkovci, Syrmia but was eventually shifted south of Brcko, in southeastern Bosnia in March 1944. On March 10th 1944 the two mountain infantry regiments were officially renumbered as the 27th and 28th Regiments. The Divisional Reconnaissance Battalion, *13.SS Aufklärungs-Abteilung* began their first anti-partisan operation when it took part in *Unternëhmen Wegweiser* (Operation Sign Post). The operation was aimed at clearing up the Bosut Forest and the area of Zupanje-Lipovac-Bosni Raca north of the Sava River, near Brcko.

Operation "Signpost" was conducted by the "Handschar" Division in the region marked "1" on the map. During this drive, the German *42nd Jäger Division* was also employed. By March 15th the Division's 27th SS Mountain Regiment was moving across the Sava River by Zupanja, while its sister regiment, the 28th, was located east of Brcko by Bosna Raca. Bijeljina was reached on the 16th. There followed a period of rest where the Division established itself mainly in the area bordering Brcko-Celic-Bijeljina.

The next operation to be launched by the Division against the partisans began on April 11th 1944. This drive is listed on the preceding map as region "2." This maneuver was code-named *"Osterei"* (Easter Egg). While this operation was in progress, the 1st Battalion of the 28th SS Mountain Regiment, which was made up purely of Albanian Muslim recruits, was withdrawn from the Division and sent to Albania where the Germans were raising an Albanian SS mountain division called "Skanderbeg." This Albanian unit would contain a mixture of Albanian Moslems and Catholics. Operation Easter Egg was quickly followed by *Unternëhmen Maibaum I* (Operation May Pole I), which ran from April 26th until May 5th. The area of operations for the Division in this action is labeled "3" on the previous map. The heart of this drive was the attempted destruction of the Partisan 3rd Proletarian Corps, that comprised the 16th, 17th, and 36th Partisan Divisions. The corps was located between Vlasenica and Srebrenica.

The Partisan 27th Infantry Division, which was located in the region of Romanja-Plannina, was also earmarked for elimination in order to wipe it out as a possible support for the 3rd Proletarian Corps. The SS *"Handschar"* Division was now under the operational control of the *5. SS Freiwilligen-Gebirgs-Armeekorps* (5th SS Volunteer Mountain Corps). This corps also controlled the *7. SS Freiwilligen-Gebirgs-Division "Prinz Eugen"* (7th SS Volunteer Mountain Division "Prince Eugene"). The 5th SS Corps ordered the SS *"Handschar"* Division to concentrate in the region between Tuzla and Rosanj, while the SS Division "Prince Eugene" would be employed further south in a line between Rogatica and Sokolac.

By May 1st the Partisan 16th Division, which contained around 2,000 men, had been chased southeast and out of Vlasenica by elements of the SS *"Prinz Eugen"* Division. Meanwhile, the Partisan 36th Division was in the process of Operation "Signpost" was conducted by the "Handschar" Division in the region being pushed into the mountain region northwest of Drinjaca by the SS *"Handschar"* Division. The operation ended on May 5th and was considered a success. Operation May Pole II began on May 14th and ran only until May 18th. In this action the *"Handschar"* Division was not directly involved and only the SS *"Prinz Eugen"* Division took part. The main point of this short operation was to clean out pockets of resistance from the remnants of the Partisan 17th Division just northeast of Sarajevo, around Kladanj. It was during this period in time that the 7th SS Division was accused of killing innocent civilians while searching for members of the Partisan 17th Division. One brigade of the 17th Division managed to make a run for it and escaped by moving through the region east of Sarajevo, and then south to Dobropolje, where elements of the *"Prinz Eugen"* Division caught up to it and engaged this guerrilla brigade.

The month of June 1944 was spent by the Moslems in the "Handschar" Division regrouping and resting. The decision to raise a second Moslem SS division had been made early in the summer. Another locally raised corps headquarters was now organized that would in theory control both Moslem divisions. This was the *9. Waffen-Gebirgs-Armeekorps der-SS* (9th Armed Mountain Corps of the SS). The title clearly showed its non-Germanic status, since all German or Germanic units were prefixed with the title "SS," whereas the non-Germanic formations of the Waffen-SS were always referred to as "Armed unit of the SS."

The second Muslim SS division was soon titled *"Kama,"* even before the official order came through to form the unit. That occurred on June 17th 1944. Seven days prior, on June 10th a large batch of Moslems from the SS "Handschar" Division were ordered transferred over to *"Kama"* in order to form its divisional cadre. Trying to raise this second Moslem SS division outside of Yugoslavia might have proven ruinous as had already been shown by the mutiny that had occurred in the SS *"Handschar"* Division. Besides, the borders of the *Reich* were quickly shrinking in the summer of 1944, so the decision was made to begin training and forming the unit in the region bordering the Sava River – Spreca and Drina Rivers. The entire formation however was soon sent to the province of Vojvodina, which was considered relatively free of partisan guerrillas. The division was specifically sent to the Batschka (Banat) region of Vojvodina, which included a sizable population of racial German Serbs.

One sub-unit of the "Handschar" SS Division was now transferred en-masse to the "Kama" SS Di-vision. This was the *13. SS Au-fklärungs-bteilung* (13th SS Reconnaissance Battalion) that was now rede-signnated as the *23. SS Aufklä-rungs-Abteilung* (23rd SS Reconnaissance Battalion).[616] This was ordered by the *SS-Führungshauptamt*, SS-FHA (SS High Command). Another unit to be de-tached from the Division was the *13. SS Flak Bataillon* (13th SS Anti-Aircraft Ba-ttalion). This unit was redesignated as *SS-Flak-Abteilung 509* and given over to the forming 9th Mountain Corps of the SS. The next anti-partisan drive in which the 13th SS Mountain Division *"Handschar"* took part in was nicknamed *"Vollmond"* (Full Moon), and began on July 7th 1944. It centered on the area between Priboj-Loznica. This area is marked as "6" in the previous map. This

---

[616] The SS "Kama" Division had been assigned the ancillary number "23." In the Waffen-SS Battle Order, it was the 23rd Division, and following custom, its battalion-sized units were all numbered "23." The two SS mountain infantry regiments were numbered "55" and "56."

drive was intended to eliminate the newly reconstituted 16th "Vojvodina" Partisan Division, as well as the 38th "Bosnian" Partisan Division.

These units were reported to have been defeated by the *"Handschar"* Division, but remnants managed to withdraw across the Drina River. Next came operation *"Fliegenfänger"* (Fly Trap) that began on July 14th and centered on the region south of Tuzla. This operation is labeled "4" in the previous map. Later still, on August 4th the Division took part in *Unternehmen Hackflesich* (Operation Ground Meat). In the first days of September 1944 the unit was ordered by the 5th SS Volunteer Mountain Corps to move to the region of Vukovije, Osmaci, and Srebrenica. It was in this area that the 13th SS Mountain Division battled the 6th "Vojvodina" Partisan Brigade.

These constant maneuvers and movements were not without losses. Although the Division had begun operations with an effective strength of over 21,000 men but by September 20th 1944 the Division had an effective strength of 14,263 men. This meant that between March and September 1944, the *"Handschar"* Division had lost 7,000 men killed, wounded, and missing. The numbers of men missing also included deserters which amounted to a significant amount of men. Since the divisional records indicate that during these seven

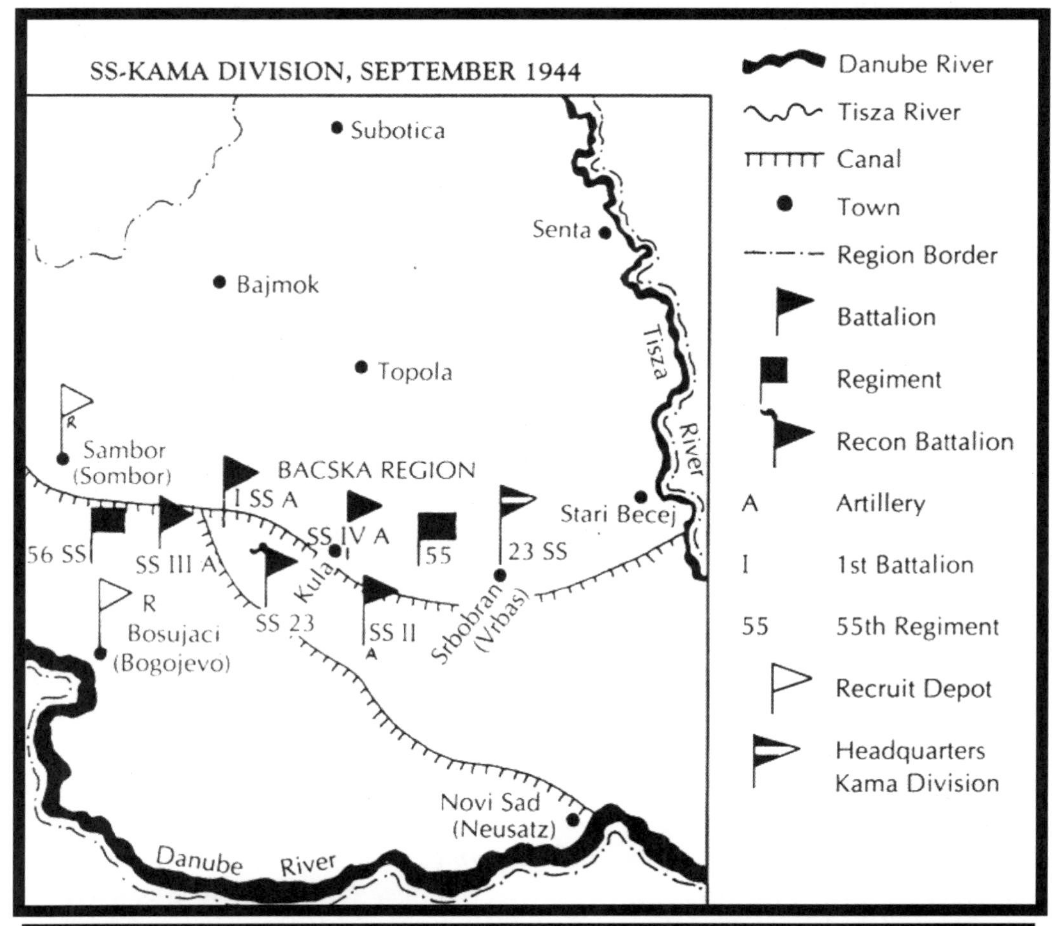

ABOVE: Location on the Hungarian-Yugoslav border region where the 23rd SS Mountain Division "Kama" was forming in September 1944.

months of fighting, about 3,000 Muslim soldiers deserted from the unit. It also shows that the unit took about 4,000 casulaties. This averages out to about 571 men killed and wounded, with an additional 428 men deserting per month! Added together these two figures average about 1,000 men per month. If these losses would have been allowed to continue, the unit would have ceased to exist within the year!

These losses indicate several things. First, it shows that the Division was either heavily engaged and/or was roughly handled by its own officers, thus incurring these high casualty rates. This supposition is certainly quite plausible, especially in light of the fact that the Division's officer corps contained a goodly number of officers with little or no infantry experience. Secondly, it shows us that a large percentage of the Muslim soldiers in the Division had no desire to fight for the Germans. This may have been as a result of their mistreatment at the hands of their German training officers, or the communist inspired revolt which demoralized the unit, or both.

The Germans were hoping that the Muslims would fight well to defend their homes in Bosnia and Herzegovina and this was a belief that should have proved correct, and yet the unit performed mediocre to poor. Perhaps the forced conscription of these men also played a role in the low effectiveness of the unit. Conscripted men mainly fight with less enthusiasm than real volunteers. Finally, the efforts by Ante Pavelic to torpedo the recruiting effort probably also played a part. When the Germans began to recruit Muslims for the 23rd SS *"Kama"* Division they were met with a dismal recruiting effort. The manner in which the Division was brought together, made all of these causes and effects:

"Problems arose in handling of men who formed the ethnically mixed detachments and purely 'volkish' units of completely foreign origin. On top of this, these foreign volunteers were motivated to fight for different reasons than their Reich German counterparts. The result of this was that often their deployment could only occur in certain areas and only against certain enemies...These and similar difficulties considerably reduced the military quality of these units. Therefore cases of mutinies, or refusals to fight appeared even within Waffen-SS formations. This was the case in the SS Divisions 'Handschar' and 'Skanderbeg' as early as the period of basic training."

Yet, in spite of all of these apparent shortcomings, the Germans had decided as early as the beginning of the summer of 1944 to raise a second Muslim SS division. There is a consensus among general historians that the *"Handschar"* Division was not really worth the trouble to form, and that all of the "pampering" and special attention bestowed to it by Himmler and the *Waffen-SS* – which included special Muslim diets, special religious schools, special insignia and clothing[617] was a wasted effort in a poor investment. I tend to agree with this hypothesis: *"Despite elaborate uniforms and the spiritual ministrations of the pro-Nazi Grand Mufti of Jerusalem, Haj Amin el Hussein, the Moslems never seem to have repaid the attention lavished on them."*

---

[617] The men of the division wore a special red Fez with SS insignia.

Ethnic & German Officers	Ethnic & German NCO's	Ethnic & German Men	TOTAL GERMANS
279	1,611	4,125	6,015
Muslim Officers	Muslim NCO's	Muslim Men	TOTAL MUSLIMS
67	339	7,842	8,248
Grand Total Officers	Grand Total NCO's	Grand Total Men	GRAND TOTAL
346	1,950	11,967	14,263

The above table lists the numbers of men in the Division in September 1944. The list is split up by ethnic background and by rank. Although the Germans had been working on raising a second SS Moslem division that eventually reached the stages of early development, that unit had to be aborted for lack of recruits. The decision to disband the *"Handschar"* Division soon followed in late September, early October 1944. Heinrich Himmler was reported to have realized that the unit's performance, even under the most favorable of conditions, had been mediocre at best and lamentable at worst. The Division actually began to lose units and men even before it was disbanded. This was because it was used as a source of recruits for other SS formations like the *"Skanderbeg"* and *"Kama"* Divisions. When the "Handschar" Division was finally disbanded, the following divisional elements were also assigned to the *9. Waffen-Gebirgs-Armeekorps der-SS:*

1. *13. SS Panzerjäger-Bataillon*
2. *13. SS Aufklärungs-Abteilung*
3. *13. Waffen-Gebirgs-Artillerie-Regiment der-SS*
4. *13. SS Pionier-Bataillon*

These units now became the following corps troops:

1. *SS-Panzerjäger-Abteilung 509*
2. *SS- Aufklärungs-Abteilung 509*
3. *SS- Waffen-Gebirgs-Artillerie-Regiment der-SS 509*
4. *SS Pionier-Bataillon 509*

What remained of the *"Handschar"* Division was turned into a battle group in the first week of October 1944. The commander of Army Group "Southeast" requested Himmler's permission to transfer the Moslem SS division from Bosnia to southern Hungary, but apparently the Moslems in the Division were unwilling to take any action beyond their native region. The remaining Moslems in the *"Handschar"* were therefore ordered released from service. The heavy casualties and desertions, low morale and poor fighting quality, coupled by large transfers of units from the Division in an attempt to form further questionable SS formations, all came together to destroy the "Handschar" Division: *"The local Bosnians were officially allowed to revert to civilian status –*

possibly in order to prevent them from doing so unofficially (taking their weapons with them!"

This statement pretty much explains the German attitude towards the Muslim soldiers by late 1944. In fact, in October 1944 an additional 1,000 Muslims deserted the division. The estimated 6,000+ German and ethnic-German personnel of the now disbanded division were grouped under a reinforced regimental battle group. Although there were enough men in this group equal to a brigade in strength, the unit remained categorized as a battlegroup. In October and November 1944 *Kampfgruppe "Handschar"* (Battlegroup "Handschar") received a reinforcement of 3,000 German sailors who had served aboard vessels operating in the Aegean and Mediterranean Sea, mainly from Greek ports. In addition, the decision to transfer back to the *kampfgruppe* all of the battalions and the artillery regiment that had been made corps units of the 9th Mountain Corps of the SS was made in December 1944. Perhaps the German command was hoping to reform the division.

It is reported that *SS-Standartenführer* Desiderius Hampel, who was an ethnic-German Croatian, and had previously led the 27th Regiment in the Division and was later given control of the entire division when he was promoted. However, another documentary source states that *SS-Sturmbannführer* Hans Hanke, who initially led the 13th SS Communications Battalion, and later led the Division's 28th Regiment, effectively led the "Handschar" Battlegroup in the last months of the war. German sources list Hanke as having been promoted to SS-Obersturmbannführer on January 30th 1945. Still another fountain of information lists Desiderius Hampel as the commander of the *"Handschar"* unit until the end of the war. This apparent confusion has been caused by the fact that Hans Hanke led a battlegroup[618] of the *"Handschar"* Division that had been detached for duty with Army Group "South" in Hungary in the middle of October 1944, while the remainder of the Division (what was left) was either in the process of being deactivated or regrouped.

In December 1944 the *"Handschar"* Battlegroup, minus the reconnaissance battalion which was already in Hungary was located in the town of Barcs on the Drava River under the 68th Army Corps/ 2nd Panzer Army. Sauberzweig's command of the 9th Armed Mountain Corps of the SS lasted only until December 1944 when he was replaced by *SS-Obergruppenführer* Karl von Pfeffer-Wildenbruch. This corps was located in Budapest in December, where it was encircled late that month by Soviet mobile forces and eventually destroyed in February 1945. It was in this month that SS-Flak-Abteilung 509 (i.e.- 13.SS Flak Battalion) rejoined the "Handschar" Battlegroup and placed around the towns of Kaposvar and Nagykaniza near Lake Balaton in Hungary. The battalion was relegated to the dual role of anti-tank and anti-aircraft defense.

In fact, during its brief history, this SS Flak battalion was responsible for shooting down 54 bombers, 5 fighters, seven tanks, two guns, 40 vehicles, plus numerous other smaller enemy military equipment. SS Reconnaissance Battalion 509 had also rejoined the battlegroup in December 1944 when Hanke and his men returned from the front. In January 1945 the "Handschar" Division was deemed

618 The battlegroup was composed of the reconnaissance battalion of the division.

fit enough to be activated as a division-sized formation once again. This time it lacked any Moslem soldiers and was purely an ethnic German and German formation. As such, its effectiveness increased dramatically. On March 5th 1945 just a day before the German "Spring Awakening" offensive against Soviet forces in Hungary, the *"Handschar"* Division was listed as follows:

1. Two strong infantry battalions
2. Four medium strength infantry battalions
3. Three average strength infantry battalions

TOTAL: Nine (9) infantry battalions

1. Armored Train No.64 and Armored Train No.79 attached to the Division as defensive support.
2. Anti-tank guns available: 10
3. Artillery Support: six light and two heavy artillery batteries

TOTAL GUNS: 10 anti-tank and 32 artillery barrels.

1. Motorization: 70%
2. Combat Readiness Status: Category No. 3 – (Capable of full defense).

A further troop report for the Division dated March 17th 1945 showed that through the use of an influx of personnel from the German Army and Air Force rear area units, the *"Handschar"* Division was able to obtain a strength of 9,228, of which 3,601 were combat troops. The combat troops were referred to as the "bayonet" strength, since these were the actual number of men manning the line companies and other combat units in the division. By 1945 German standards, the Division was magnificently manned. The unit remained under the 68th Army Corps of 2nd Panzer Army for the rest of the war. It withdrew from the region south of Lake Balaton in mid-April 1945 in order to avoid being encircled by Soviet and Yugoslav forces. Its line of retreat placed the Division in the province of *Untersteiermark* (Lower Styria), which was in reality part of Slovenia. The area it was then located in in Lower Styria was around the city of Marburg (Maribor), on the Drava River.

Actual capitulation of the unit did not occur until May 7th 1945 in the region just south of St. Vieth, on the Glau River to members of the British Army. The men of the Division hoped that their surrender to Allied troops would prevent their capture by the Tito partisans, who were surely going to judge them for their actions in Yugoslavia. The *"Handschar"* Division operated in Bosnia, Yugoslavia between March and October 1944. This was a span of only 8 months. During this period some of its German and Moslem members committed atrocities. A total of 38 German nationals who served in the Division were extradicted to Yugoslavia after the war. These included mainly the leadership of the Division, such as the divisional, regimental and battalion commanders.

The final military analysis of the SS *"Handschar"* Division was that it was not worth forming and could be considered a failure of the Germans to exploit the manpower resources of the Moslem population in Yugoslavia. There had been various reasons why this had occurred, some of which had been outside of the control of the Germans, like (1) Ante Pavelik's successful undermining of the German recruiting drive, and (2) the communist cell which initiated the revolt of the division while in France. However the German SS command was also at fault for (3) supplying the division with officers who lacked proper combat experience and mediocre leadership, and (4) the arrogance of the German training officers and NCO's towards their Muslim recruits. The use of the Mufti of Jerusalem in order to try and play the religious card with the recruits was lukewarm at best. This was because the Moslem recruits from Bosnia considered themselves Europeans first and Moslems second. The history of the 13th SS *"Handschar"* Division then is a perfect example of everything that was wrong with the manner in which Germany often attempted to exploit foreign manpower resources.

A. The Husko Legion-

In 1943 Husko Miljkovic created a legion in Cazin Region. It was officially called the 'Moslem Militia' *(Muslimanska milicija)* and consisted of 11 battalions. In February 1944 the Husko Legion deserted to the Partizans and was redesignated as the 1st Moslem Brigade of the Una Operational Group, 4th Croatian Partisan Corps. Legion personnel had no special uniforms and wore a mixture of former Croatian Ustashe, and Domobran uniforms with the crescent and star shown on pages 271, 278 and 279 as badges on their fez covers. Special rank insignia was worn on the sleeves.

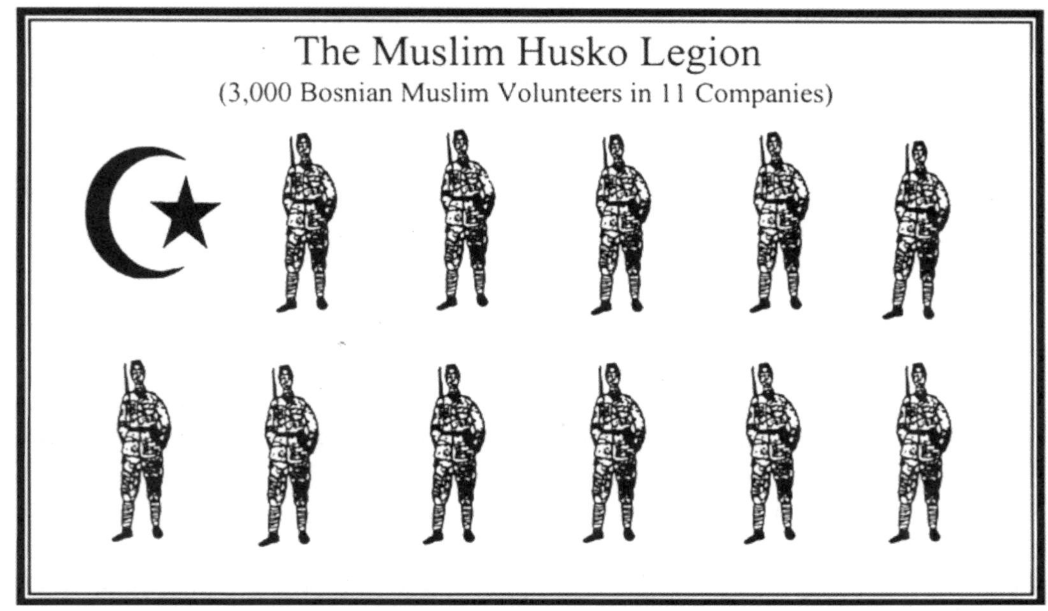

B. The Hadziefendic Legion-

In 1941 Major Muhamed Hadziefendic proposed to Field-Marshal Kvaternik, the Croatian Defense Minister, about the establishment of a volunteer Moslem militia to be raised in the Northeast Bosnia. His plan was quickly approved and in late 1941 Hadziefendic had formed the People's Uprising Volunteer Brigade (Dobrovoljacki zdrug narodnog ustanka), unofficially called the 'Hadziefendic Legion'. It comprised at least 4-5 "People's Uprising Volunteer Detachments", each divided into several companies.

The officers and some of the NCOs of the Legion wore standard Croatian Army uniforms and insignia, whilst the volunteers wore civilian clothes. Many NCOs attached Army rank insignia to the collars of their civilian jackets and some companies were equipped with ex-Yugoslav helmets of the French Adrian model. In December 1942 the German Plenipotentiary in Croatia, General Glaise von Horstenau, demanded that the personnel of the Legion be disciplined and uniformed but it is not known if that order was carried out.

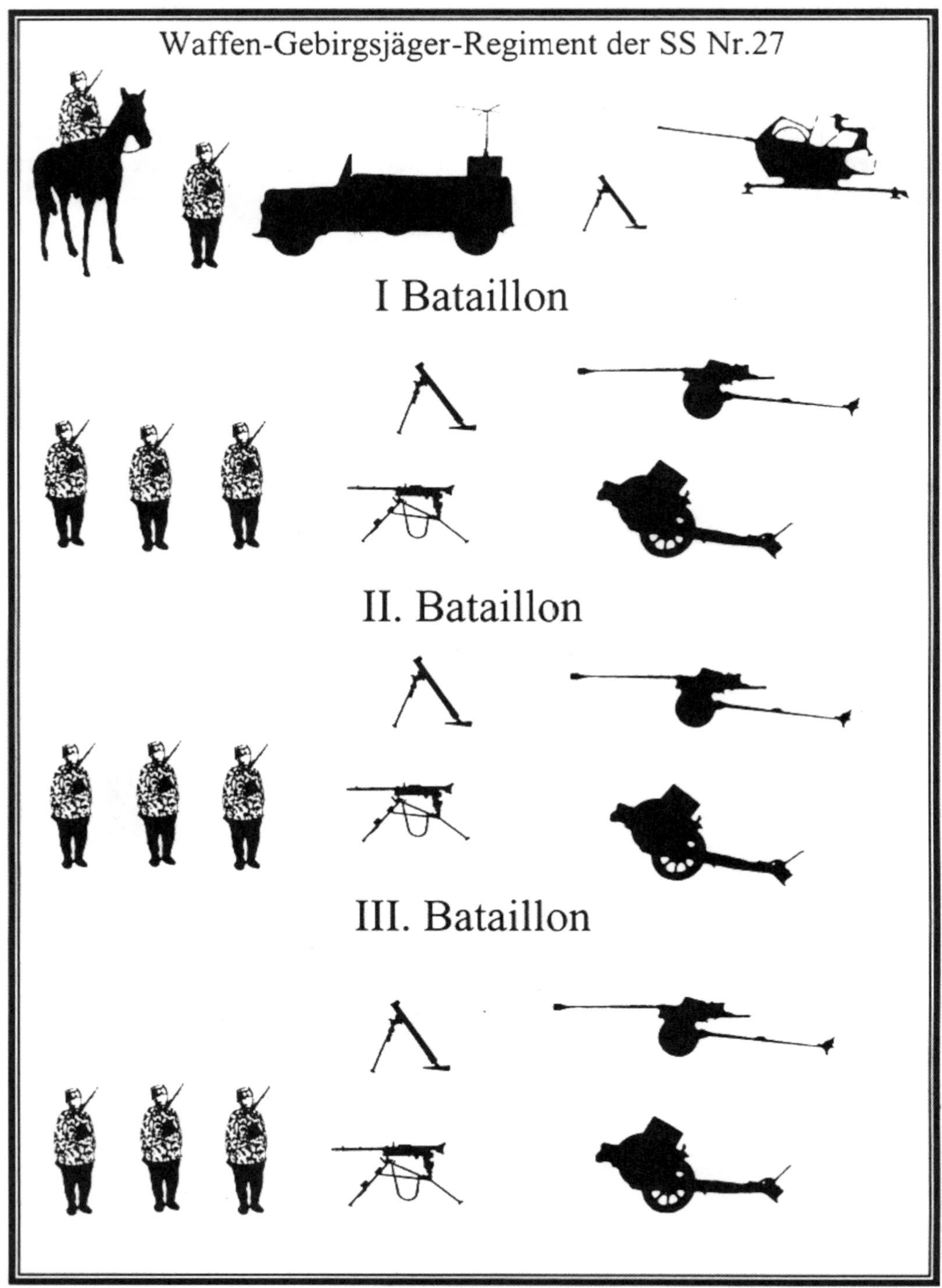
Waffen-Gebirgsjäger-Regiment der SS Nr.27
I Bataillon
II. Bataillon
III. Bataillon

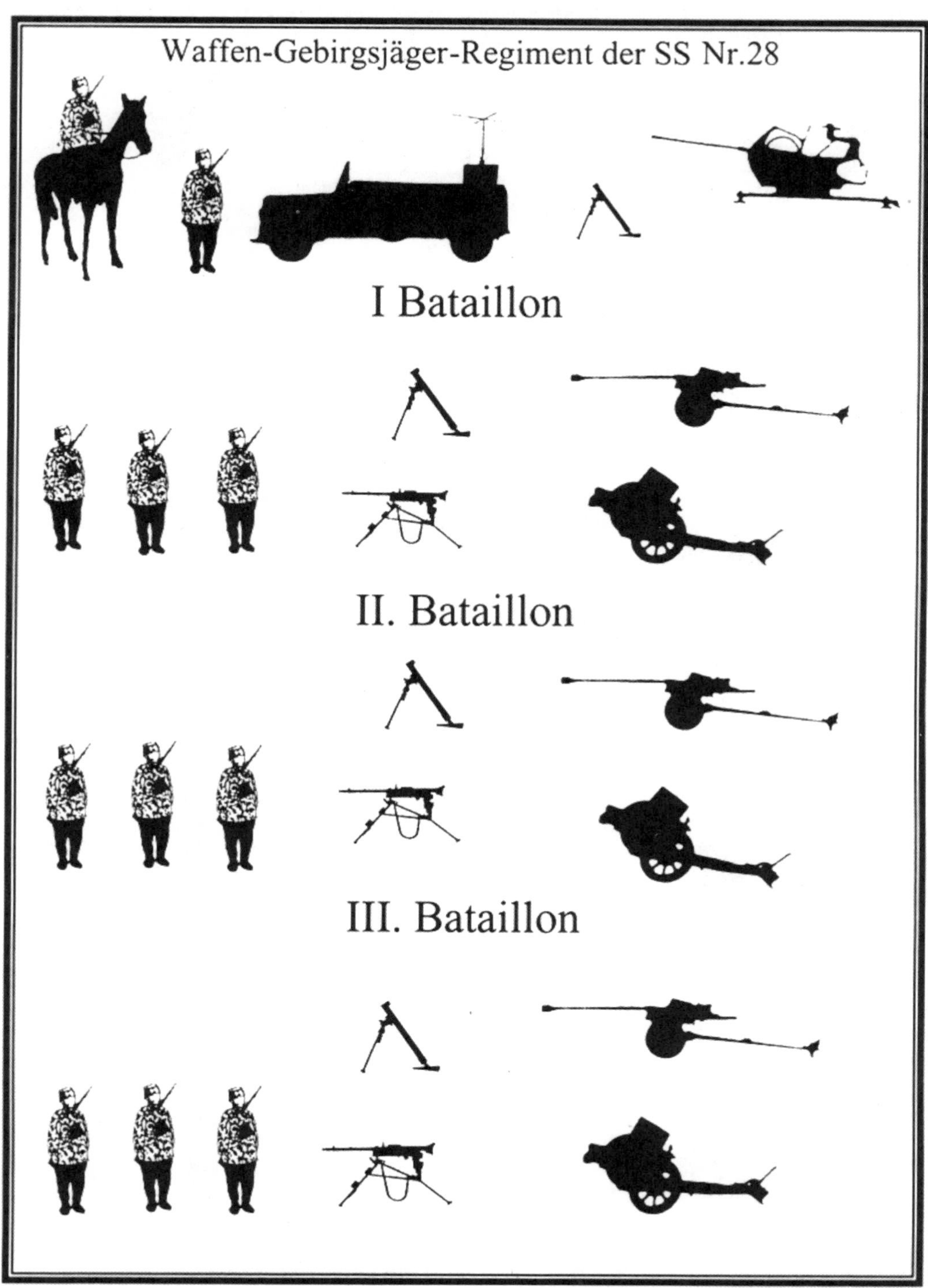
Waffen-Gebirgsjäger-Regiment der SS Nr.28
I Bataillon
II. Bataillon
III. Bataillon

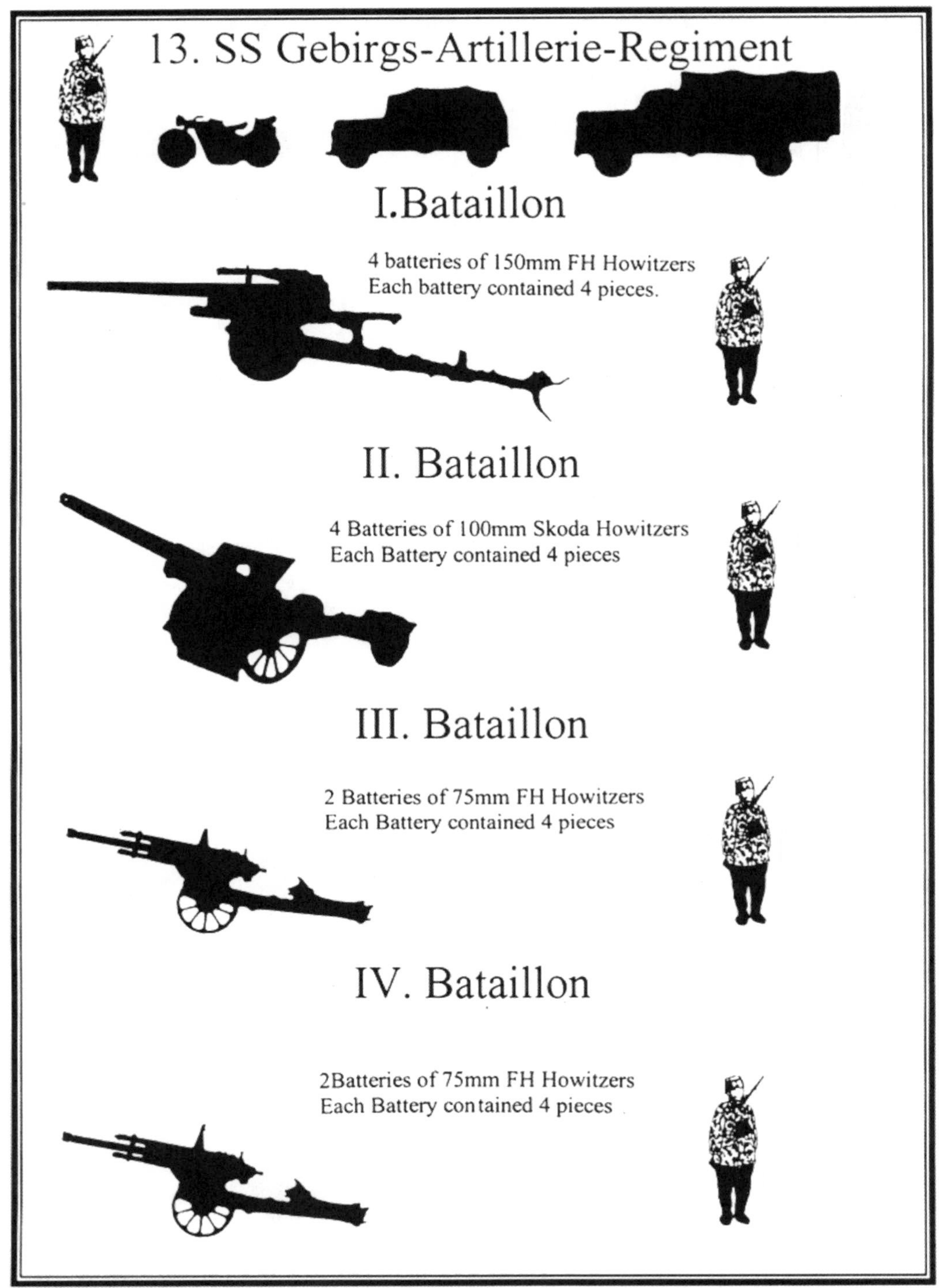
13. SS Gebirgs-Artillerie-Regiment
I.Bataillon
4 batteries of 150mm FH Howitzers
Each battery contained 4 pieces.
II. Bataillon
4 Batteries of 100mm Skoda Howitzers
Each Battery contained 4 pieces
III. Bataillon
2 Batteries of 75mm FH Howitzers
Each Battery contained 4 pieces
IV. Bataillon
2Batteries of 75mm FH Howitzers
Each Battery contained 4 pieces

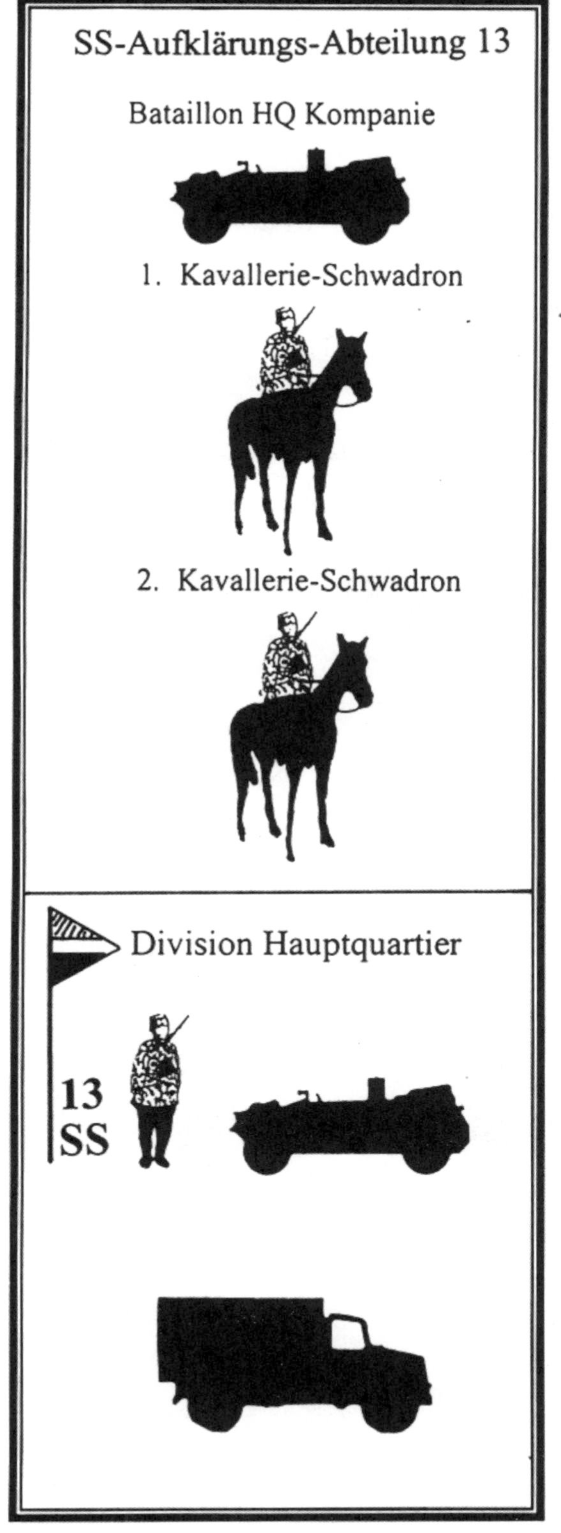
SS-Aufklärungs-Abteilung 13
Bataillon HQ Kompanie
1. Kavallerie-Schwadron
2. Kavallerie-Schwadron
Division Hauptquartier
13
SS

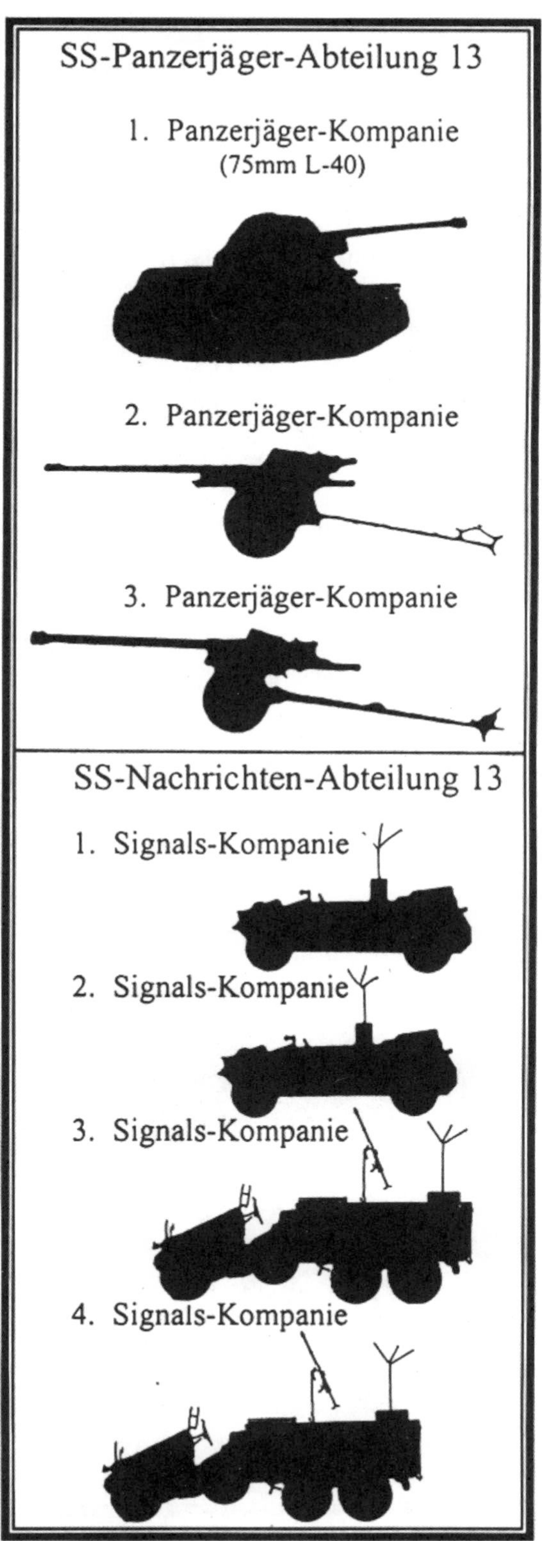
SS-Panzerjäger-Abteilung 13
1. Panzerjäger-Kompanie
(75mm L-40)
2. Panzerjäger-Kompanie
3. Panzerjäger-Kompanie
SS-Nachrichten-Abteilung 13
1. Signals-Kompanie
2. Signals-Kompanie
3. Signals-Kompanie
4. Signals-Kompanie

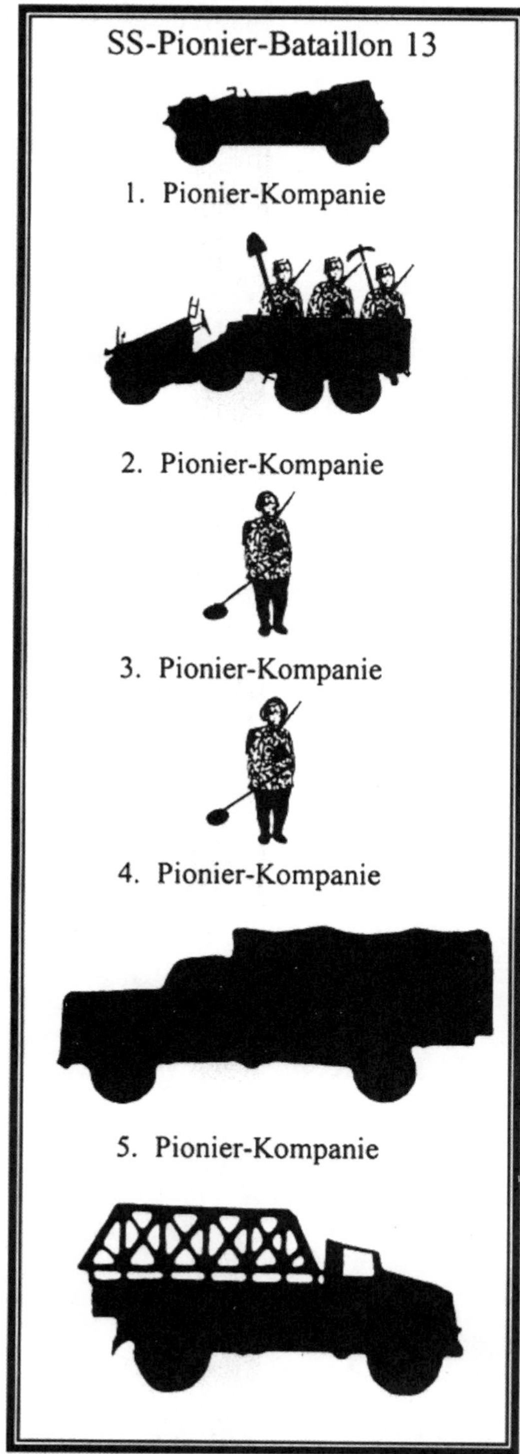
SS-Pionier-Bataillon 13
1. Pionier-Kompanie
2. Pionier-Kompanie
3. Pionier-Kompanie
4. Pionier-Kompanie
5. Pionier-Kompanie

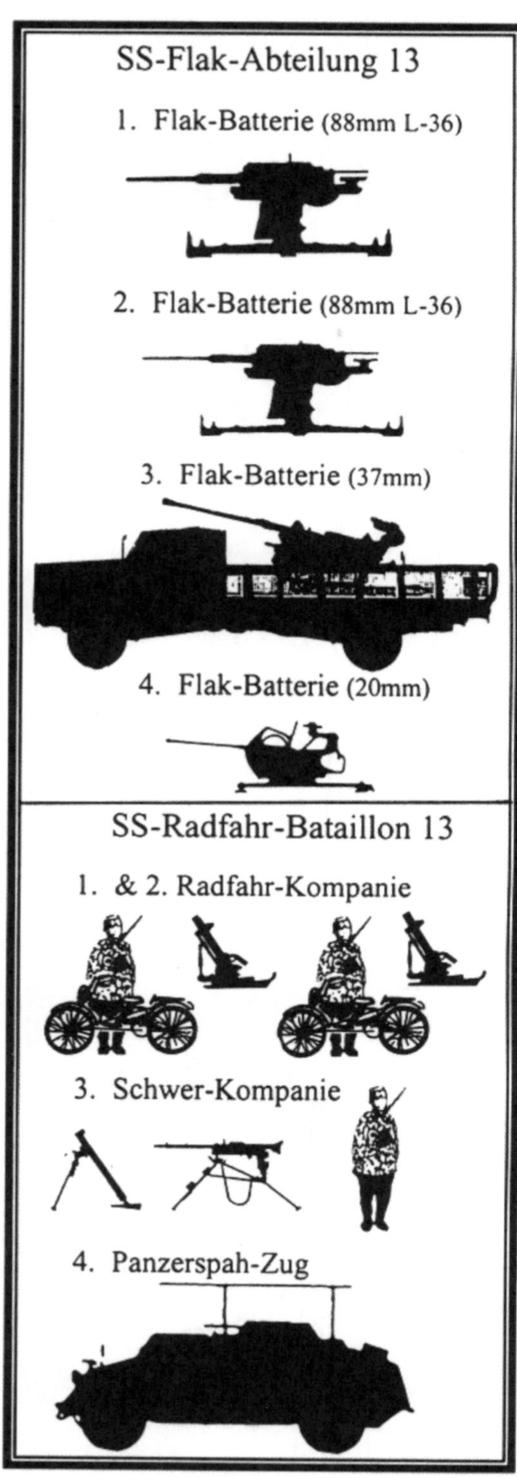
SS-Flak-Abteilung 13
1. Flak-Batterie (88mm L-36)
2. Flak-Batterie (88mm L-36)
3. Flak-Batterie (37mm)
4. Flak-Batterie (20mm)
SS-Radfahr-Bataillon 13
1. & 2. Radfahr-Kompanie
3. Schwer-Kompanie
4. Panzerspah-Zug

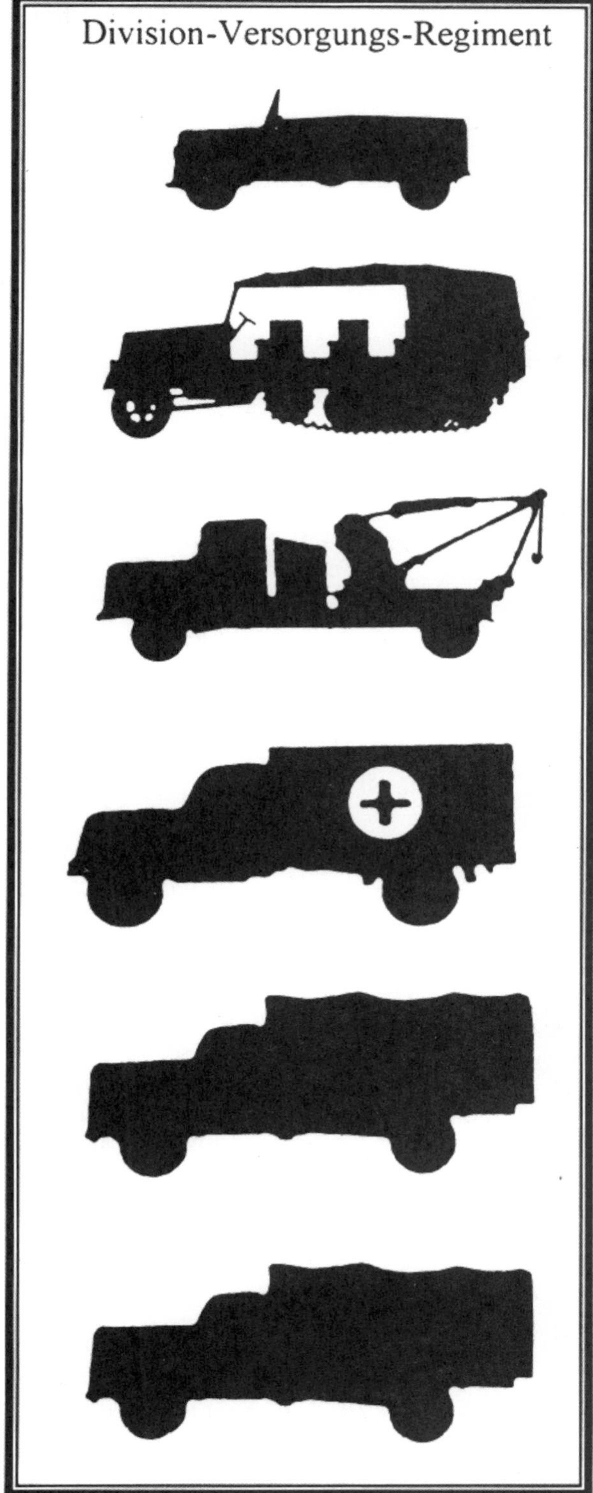

ABOVE: The right collar tab of the aborted SS Kama Bosnian SS Division. *Author's Collection*

CHAPTER 14
The Moslem Militia And Legion of the Sandjak 1943-1945

It is generally agreed that among those countries either allied with or occupied by Germany during World War II, none produced a greater variety of hodgepodge military and paramilitary formations than did the former Soviet Union and the former Yugoslavia usually based on some ethnic differentiation these almost always took the form of legion, militia, guard, police or auxiliary police units and, more often than not, had a German commander and a small German cadre. This article is an attempt to put the pieces together on what may have been one of the most obscure of the irregular units formed in Yugoslavia: the Moslem Militia of the Sandjak. Although it is occasionally mentioned in the literature, few details concerning it survived the war. Sandjak (Sandzak in Serbo-Croatian and Sandschak in German) is a mountainous region in eastern Montenegro with a large Moslem population that dates back to the conquest and occupation of much of Yugoslavia by the Ottoman Turks nearly five centuries ago. Hated, frequently harassed and occasionally attacked by their Serbian Orthodox neighbors, the Sandjak Moslems had usually found it necessary to maintain some sort of a community protective association to keep watch over their villages and safeguard their property.

Immediately following the Blitzkrieg invasion of Yugoslavia on 6 April 1941 by German and Italian armies[619] and the country's defeat and capitulation barely 12 days later, the Sandjak Moslems strengthened their protective organization because of the growing Chetnik and Communist Partisan threat in eastern Montenegro. Discarded Yugoslav weapons and equipment left over from the war in April, a few Italian rifles and numerous volunteers transformed the protective association by the end of 1941 into something more akin to a village guard or militia.

In February 1942 the Militia was used offensively for what is believed to be the first time, and is credited with helping to drive the Partisans out of Sandjak. On 1 February Moslem Militia from Sjenica and villages in the Pester Mountains to the south of Sjenica, together with Chetniks and Nedic collaborator troops from Serbia, attacked Partisan units in Nova Varos (see map on page 4) but were thrown back. A week later on 7th February, Moslem Militia from the village of Komarani near Nova Varos that were operating with elements of the Italian 19th Division "Venezia" from Prijepolje, engaged in a running fire fight with Partisan units withdrawing across the Lim River into western Sandjak.[620] By the end of

---

[619] The Hungarian Army also took part in the invasion, as well as the Bulgarian Army which occupied Yugoslavian Macedonia after the Yugoslav Army capitulated.

[620] Vojnoistorijski intitut. *Oslobodilacki rat naroda Jugoslavije 1941-1945*. Vol.1 Belgrade: 1963. Pages 199-200. Hereafter referred to as VIII, v.1 & VII, v.2. and

Maletic, Mihailo. *Yugoslavia in the Second World War*. Belgrade, 1977. Pages 54 and 76.

February the Partisans had cleared eastern Sandjak and the region remained relatively peaceful until the beginning of 1943. A completely unexpected horror befell the Sandjak Moslems between 5 January and 7 February 1943. Acting on a carefully prepared plan to seize the Sandjak for them by cleansing it of its Moslems, strong Chetnik forces descended on the area in two separate actions and massacred in the most bestial fashion all those they could lay hold of in the districts of Prijepolje, Plevlja, Priboj and Cajnice -no one was spared. The Chetnik report also stated that around 500 armed Moslem self-defense militiamen were encountered during the raid on 5 January and some 1,200 during the second action on February 7th. The Moslem Militia killed or wounded 94 Chetniks, according to the after-action report.[621]

ABOVE: The Sandjak (Sandzak) Region

[621] NARS Microfilm T-501, roll 249, Frame 000338. and

Tomasevich, Jozo. *The Chetniks: War and Revolution in Yugoslavia, 1941-1945*. Stanford University Press: Stanford, 1975. Pages 258-259. and

Dedijer, Vladimir and Antun Miletic. *Genocid nad Muslimanima, 1941-1945*. Sarajevo, 1990. Pages 378-381.

Recovering from the battering and heavy losses suffered during January and early February, the Sandjak Militia did not actively participate in the second largest anti-Partisan operation conducted by the Axis occupiers in Yugoslavia during the war, even though much of the action occurred in the Sandjak. This was Operation *"Schwarz,"* which was also known to the partisans as the Fifth Enemy Offensive. The total number of victims ran between 5,000 and 10,000, mostly

ABOVE: Moslem militiamen from the Sandjak. In some instances, a small white cap is seen being worn, while in other instances, a white turban covers the head. Their home village lies in the background. *Bundesarchiv.*

women and children. The lower figure is from postwar Moslem sources and is probably closer to the true Offensive in Yugoslav history, pitted 127,000 Axis troops against the weakened remnants of Tito's main line divisions that numbered around 19,700 men.

The operation ran from 15 May to 15 June and two units, the 724th Infantry Regiment of the German 104th *Jaeger* Division and the Italian "Venezia" Division, held positions for more than two weeks right in the heart of the Sandjak Militia's home territory, yet they were not employed in closing the ring around Tito's forces even though they were reported to be in considerable strength. In a top secret *(Geheimkommandosache -Chefsachen)* operations order dated 25 April 1943, just a few weeks before *"Schwarz"* was scheduled to begin division commanders and chiefs of staff were instructed: *"They* [the Moslems] *are to be treated as allies and are not to be disarmed. The Moslems in Sandjak have formed a Moslem self-defense militia, which is essentially an armed village guard. It supposedly comprises 8,000-10,000 men.* "[622]

---

[622] NARS Microfilm T-501, roll 249, frame 000338. and

ABOVE: *SS-Standartenführer der Reserve* Karl von Krempler, the portly German who would lead the Sandjak Militia for most of its existence. According to an SS roster for November 1944, von Kremplerwas promoted to this rank on March 1st 1944. *Museum of Modern History, Ljubljana, Slovenia.*

On 9 September 1943, the date Italy capitulated, the German 118th *Jaeger* Division handed over the town of Pljevlja to the Sandjak Militia. The Division CO, *Generalmajor* Josef Kuebler, wanted to maintain the Militia at strength of around 5,000 because his own troop strength was too weak to fight both the Partisans and the Chetniks and keep the supply roads open at the same time. Kuebler viewed the Sandjak Militia as a local defense force and as a counterweight against the Partisan and Chetnik bands in the region. However, he did not feel that he could supply and equip them, and wrote to higher headquarters for their immediate assistance.[623] Meanwhile, strong Chetnik forces began concentrating in the area for a planned assault on Pljevlja. To prevent the town from falling into the hands of the Chetniks, the Partisan 2nd Proletarian Division opened an offensive against them on 20 September and then entered Pljevlja on 22 September without any opposition from the Militia. In wartime Yugoslavia, towns changed hands frequently and it was more the norm than the exception for the defenders to strike an agreement with the attacking force that left the town unharmed with few if any casualties on either side.[624]

VII, v.1, op cit. Pages 425-465. and

Colic, Mladenko. Pregled operacija na Jugoslavenskumratistu 1941-1945. Belgrade, 1988. Pages 113-126.

623 NARS Microfilm T-314, roll 661, Frame 000439.

624 SS-Personnel Hauptamt. Dienstalterliste der Schutzstaffel der NSDAP. SS-Oberstgruppenführer bis SS-Standartenführer, Stand von 9. November 1944. Gedruckt in der Reichsdruckerei: Berlin, 1944. and

BELOW: A Moslem fighter of the Moslem Militia of the Sandjak, some time in 1943. *Bundesarchiv.*

About five weeks later, on 30 October, the Sandjak Militia is mentioned for the first time in connection with a German officer named von Krempler, being referred to in an operations order as Moslem Group von Krempler ("Muselmanengruppe von Krempler"). *Oberst der Polizei und SS-Sturmbannführer der Waffen-SS* Karl von Krempler was considered something of an authority on the Moslems of Yugoslavia, having been involved in recruiting large numbers of them in East Bos nia for the 13th SS Mountain Division *"Handschar"* during the spring and summer of 1943.

In a rare photo taken during the summer of 1944, von Krempler is shown as a portly, sloppily dressed older officer of average height with the *Edelweiss* sleeve insignia on his right sleeve, above which is sewn the special badge for single handed destruction of a tank. Where he managed to destroy a tank is unknown, but he may have been in Russia prior to being reassigned to Yugoslavia. In any case, he was sent to Sandjak in early October 1943 and given the task of rebuilding the Militia into what the Germans hoped would eventually be a legion.[625] Sjenica, now the principal seat of German authority in Sandjak and headquarters of Krempler's Militia and other units, became a target of the

---

VII, v.1, op cit., Pages 562-566.

[625] NARS Microfilm T-314, roll 661, Frame 001119. and
NARS Microfilm T-501, roll 256, Frame 000374 and 000777. and
NARS Microfilm T-311, roll 286, Frame 000125. and
Kumm, Otto. 7.SS-Gebirgs-Division "Prinz Eugen" im Bild. Munin Verlag: Osnabrück, 1983. Page 159.

Partisans and the 2nd Proletarian Division began assembling forces in the area on 10 November 1943 for a planned assault on the town.

But before it could be launched, some five (5) battalions of German troops, supported by Krempler's Militia, counterattacked over the next two days and forced the Partisans to withdraw from the area.[626] Later in the month, as the Germans made preparations for a major anti-Partisan operation *("Kugelblitz")* that was to take place to the south of Tuzla in East Bosnia, agreements were signed with most Chetnik units whereby they promised to cease hostilities against all German-allied forces throughout Yugoslavia with effect from 21 November 1943. The Sandjak Moslem Militia was specifically named in at least several of these agreements. On the same date, 2nd Panzer Army issued orders that Group *"Siegfried"* (2nd Regiment *"Brandenburg,"* 524th Grenadier Regiment, Moslem Legion von Krempler, and a battery of artillery and platoon of tanks) was to secure the Sjenica area to allow for the unhindered movement of 1st Mountain Division, which was to pass through Sjenica en-route from Greece to East Bosnia for *"Kugelblitz."*[627]

ABOVE: After the Germans assumed control of the Moslem Legion of Sandjak (Sandzak), they tried to organize the unit along company and battalion lines. Here a platoon of Moslem militiamen undergoes inspection by a German SS NCO. *Bundesarchiv.*

By the end of 1943 Krempler's Moslems were beginning to take shape along more formal (and more German) lines, although even their kindest critics could never in practice consider them a legion. Then and later, they remained simple peasants who disappeared for days and weeks without notice to till or harvest their land. German plans to provide uniformed and other equipment were never completed, and only a handful received *Wehrmacht* alpine trousers, tunics and boots. Nearly all of them however wore a fez, some of which were Red while others were White. Drill, discipline and training were sadly deficient, no matter

[626] VII, v.1, op cit. Pages 626-627.

[627] Tomasevich, op cit. Pages 321, 328, and 331. and NARS Microfilm T-313, Roll 194, Frame 7454441.

how hard Krempler and his team tried. These were the same problems the Germans were faced six months later in their mistaken attempt to form and train the 21st SS Mountain Division *"Skanderbeg"* in nearby Kosovo using Albanian Moslems. Finally, the Moslem commander and leader of the Sandjak Militia Hafiz Sulejman Pacariz, is identified in the literature for the first time. How long he had held that position is not known. Described as a colorful character and a respected religious figure, Pacariz is said to have led his men while riding a Black stallion.[628]

In January 1944 the war resumed in Sandjak following a prolonged lull. On 16-17 January the Militia supported a local offensive by German and Chetnik forces southwest of Sjenica against the Partisan 7th Brigade and 4th Proletarian Brigade that was aimed at opening up the north-south roads through central Montenegro which was firmly held by Tito's rapidly growing and increasingly well-armed forces. The effort proved unsuccessful and the Militia returned to Sjenica.[629] In February another attempt was made between the 6th and the 8th of the month by the Germans, Chetniks and Moslem Militia to open a road or two through Central Montenegro, but this too failed even though some headway was made and the town of Meljak was taken from the Partisan 4th Sandjak Brigade. The lack of progress, the strength of the enemy and the weather forced a halt to further efforts until reinforcements could be brought up, and a general lull again fell over Sandjak for the next month and a half.

Meanwhile, the Sandjak Moslems were granted a certain degree of autonomy by the Germans, and Krempler helped them set up an administration in Sjenica. On 21 February 1944 in response to an inquiry, the Higher-SS and Police Commander in Serbia *(HSSPF Serbien), SS-Gruppenführer* August Meyszner,

THE SANDJAK MOSLEMS IN ITALIAN SERVICE

The Sandjak Moslems had an earlier sponsor before their collaboration with the Germans. While Italy still maintained control of Montenegro, an all-Moslem legion was formed for service in the Sandjak under the sponsorship of the Italian MVAC (Milizia Voluntare Anti-Comunista), or Anti-Communist Volunteer Militia. As of February 28th, 1943 the total number of Moslems from the Sandjak who were serving in this legion was 780 men. It is ironic to note that the same Chetnik forces that launched a series of punitive expeditions in the Sandjak in January and February 1943 - expeditions whose purpose was to kill all Moslems, also belonged to the Italian MVAC. So during February, 1943 you had MVAC Chetniks killing MVAC Moslems. This blood fued between the Orthodox Serbians and Moslems never ended, and explains what the Germans called a "pointless gun battle" between the Serbian State Guard and about 200 Moslem militiamen near the town of Ivanjica Gust across the border from Sandjak and Montenegro on July 15th, 1943.*

- Antonio J. Munoz

---

*Axis Europa Magazine, Vol.I, No.l, "The Serbian State and Frontier Guard. 1941-45 (part 1)." page 9, column one.

---

[628] Private conversation with author, Profesor Nigel Thomas, March 1984.
[629] VII, v.2, Belgrade, 1965. Page 211.

informed the Military Commander Southeast *(Militärbefehlshaber Südost), General der Infanterie* Hans Felber, that Krempler's forces in Sandjak consisted of two battalions of Moslems totalling around 800 men.

But this seems to be in conflict with or at least an element of confusion is present, a message sent by the Military Commander Southeast to 2nd Panzer Army on 28 February stated that from Krempler's force of around 4,000 to 5,000 Moslem Militia, 2,000 were to be taken away to provide for the organizing of a Moslem Legion. The Legion, it continued, was to be similar in type and manner to the 13th SS Mountain Division *"Handschar,"* and was to be uniformed, equipped and supplied by the Germans. Further, the legion would be provided with a scale of rations identical to that for German troops.[630]

March 1944 brought further fighting and clarification of the Militia's chain of command. On March 18th Militia forces from around Priboj, German troops and Chetniks garrisoned in the town and elements of 4th Regiment *Brandenburg* from Prijepolje, fought an 8-hour battle with elements of the Partisan 4th Border (Krajiski) and 2nd Proletarian (Proleterski) Brigades that had been threatening Priboj and the immediate area.

ABOVE: After Italy's surrender, the Moslem Militia was amply armed with heavier Italian weapons supplied to them by the Germans. *Bundesarchiv*.

The enemy was driven off and the town held, but the Germans were forced to strengthen its garrison. On the 26th Military Commander "Southeast" cabled the *Reichführer-SS* in Berlin stating that Krempler's Moslem Militia together with elements of the Moslem Legion then forming in Sandjak were to be immediately

---

[630] NARS Microfilm T-501, Roll 256, Frames 000006, 000089, 000142, 000314, 000318, 000352, 000550-59, 000777-78. and
NARS Microfilm T-311, Roll 286, Frame 000125.

subordinate to 2nd Panzer Army (headquarters in Niska Banja near Nis, in Serbia) and for troop services to *HSSPF "Serbien."* This proposed chain of command was approved by Himmler on 30 March, who at the same time appointed von Krempler SS Commander in the Sandjak Region *(SS-Führer im Gebiet Sandschak).*[631] Beginning in April, Krempler's Moslems in whole or in part in almost continous anti-partisan operations over the next five months.

From their base camps in large "liberated" areas of central and parts of eastern Montenegro guerrilla forces were ordered by Tito to begin moving into Serbia, which until the spring of 1944 had been relatively free of them. The Germans of course, wanted to block this movement and keep the enemy bottled up in Montenegro. On 4 April Krempler's Militia was alerted for the first of these large, coordinated anti-Partisan operations, *"Kammerjäger"* (Exterminator), which continued for nearly 7 weeks. On 11 April Krempler's men moved along the Brodarevo-Bijelo Polje road around 25-40 kilometers southwest of Sjenica against the Partisan 37th Division, together with thousands of Germans and Chetniks. The fighting see-sawed back and forth for weeks up and down the Tara and Lim Valleys with town and villages in many cases changing hands several times.

ABOVE: Sandjak militiamen, circa 1944. Notice the extremely young age of some of these village militiamen. *Bundesarchiv.*

The breakout into Serbia eventually failed, and Tito ordered his divisions to pull back into their Montenegro-Sandjak bastion, regroup and then initiate a buildup of forces pending a second attempt.[632] By the end of May most of

---

[631] NARS Microfilm T-501, Roll 256, Frames 000352 and 000374. and
VII, v.2, op cit. Page 229.

[632] NARS Microfilm T-501, Roll 256, Frame 000414. and
Tomasevich, op cit. Pages 407-408. and
VII, v.2, op cit., Pages 218-224. and

Krempler's Sandjak Moslems had returned to Sjenica to rest and refit. Between 18 and 24 June 1944 two battalions of German troops supported by 400 Sandjak militiamen began an advance along a narrow dirt track toward Bijelo Polje, about 50 to 60 kilometers distance as it wound its way across the Pester Mountains. But unexpectedly strong resistance from elements of the Partisan "Garibaldi" Division[633] and several brigades from other divisions prevented the column from reaching Bijelo Polje after a week of fighting that cost each side around 150 casualties.[634]

A week later, Krempler's Legion carried out a night attack on 1/2 July across the Lim River near the village of Stitari, just east of Bijelo Polje. A small bridgehead was gained on the west bank, but formations of Tito's 2nd Division held good positions and Krempler's men could go no farther. The bridgehead was eventually given up because it was difficult to supply and there were inadequate fresh troops necessary to expand it. The legionaries were therefore forced to pull back across the river to their prepared positions on the east bank.[635] After the beginning of Operation *"Kammerjäger"* and before the second of the major anti-Partisan operations in eastern Montenegro commenced on July 18th 1944, Krempler's forces underwent reorganization. On 28 April *HSSPF Serbien* (now *SS-Gruppenführer* Hermann Behrends) in Belgrade reported to *Reichsfuehrer-SS* Himmler in Berlin that the formation of supply and there were inadequate fresh troops necessary to expand it. The legionaries were therefore forced to pull back across the river to their prepared positions on the east bank.

After the beginning of Operation *"Kammerjaeger"* and before the second of the major anti-Partisan operations in eastern Montenegro commenced on 18 July 1944, Krempler's forces underwent reorganization. On 28 April *HSSPF Serbien* (now *SS-Gruppenfuehrer* Hermann Behrends) in Belgrade reported to *Reichsfuehrer-SS* Himmler in Berlin that the formation of Legion Krempler was in the process of being completed, and that Hauptamt Orpo[636] in Berlin had been most helpful in the effort. In July 1944 the Legion was formalized and redesignated as “Police Self-Defense Regiment Sandjak” *(Polizei-Selbstschutz-Regiment Sandschak).*Its field post numbers were as follows:

1. Regimental Staff Company – 21 095
2. 1st Battalion – 22 118
3. 2nd Battalion – 23 051
4. 3rd Battalion – 24 125
5. 4th Battalion – 24 983

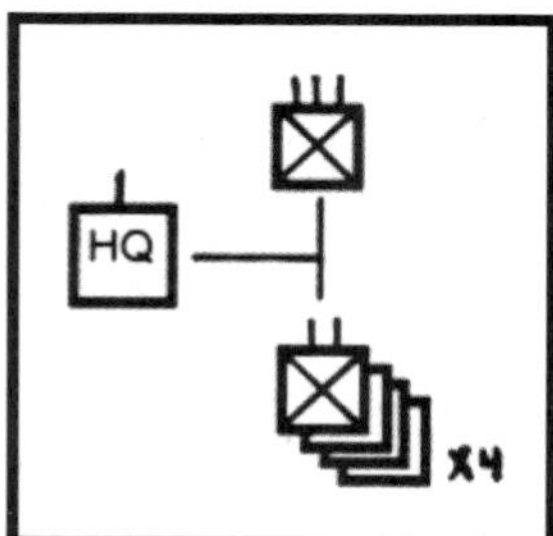

Postwar Yugoslav sources, based on P/W interrogations, maintain that three of these four battalions were in existence at the end of July 1944, and

Strugar, Vlado. Jugoslavija 1941-1945. Belgrade, 1969. Pages 243-244.

633 This unit was made up of Italians who had decided to join the Yugoslav guerrillas.

634 VII, v.2, op cit. Pages 224-225.

635 Ibid., page 225.

636 Headquarters of the German Order police.

together with the remaining Sandjak Moslem Militia, not included in the Regiment (formerly Legion), the total strength ran around 4,000 men – all of which came under Oberst der Polizei von Krempler. Yet a carefully constructed order of battle layout of all German forces in the Balkans that was prepared by Commander-in-Chief "Southeast" *(Oberbefehlshaber Südost/ Heeresgruppe F)* and forwarded to OKH in Berlin, shows the new Regiment as only having a headquarters staff and the 1st Battalion, with 1st-4th Companies, the latter marked "in training."

ABOVE: A closer look at some of the Sandjak (Sandzak) village militiamen of "Legion Krempler". *Bundesarchiv.*

So it would appear likely that Police Self-Defense Regiment Sandjak never matured past a single battalion, and the remaining Moslem forces under Krempler were all Militia. It may be as stated earlier, that the Germans at this point in the war simply could not provide the uniforms and equipment to outfit more than one battalion. There were just too many new units in formation in Germany and outside Germany competing for too few resources.[637] The second major anti-Partisan operation, *"Daufgänger"* (Daredevil), began on 18 July and ran to 28 July 1944. Intended to smash Tito's second breakout attempt from Montenegro into Serbia, it only succeeded in slowing down three of his divisions, but they eventually forced their way through into western Serbia. By 2 August,

---

[637] NARS Microfilm T-311, Roll 286, Frame 000125. and
NARS Microfilm T-78, Roll 410, Frames 6378310-72. and
VII, v.2, op cit., page 254. and
Neufeldt, Hans-Joachim, Jürgen Huck and Georg Tessin. Zur Geschichte der Ordnungspolizei 1936-1945. Schriften des Bundesarchiv: Boppard-am-Rhein, 1957. Part 2, Page 71. and
Hnilicka, Karl. Das Ende auf dem Balkan 1944/45. Musterschmidt – Göttingen Verlag: Zürich, 1970.

the 2nd Proletarian, 5th Shock and 17th Divisions had evaded the German net and crossed over the Ibar River, which forms the border between Montenegro and Serbia.

The operation involved a large mixed force of German, Bulgarian, Serbian collaborator, Chetnik, Albanian, and Sandjak Moslem troops spread over a large area. Krempler's men were deployed around Bioca on the east bank of the Lim between Bijelo Polje and Berane (today, Ivangrad). Holding this sector, they were instrumental in delaying for 11 days the movement of the 5th Shock and 17th Division across the Pester Mountains toward the Ibar.[638] The Germans now directed their efforts toward preventing the three remaining divisions in Montenegro, the 1st Proletarian, 3rd Shock, and 37th Division, from following the same course. If these forces, which comprised the Partisan 1st Corps, could be sealed off between the Tara and Piva rivers, they could be crushed on the field of battle and their infiltration into Serbia prevented.

This, the third of the large anti-Partisan operations, was called *"Ruebezahl,"* and began on 12 August and concluded on 30 August 1944. It involved elements of the 7th SS Volunteer Mountain Division "Prinz Eugen," 21st Mountain Division of the SS *"Skanderbeg,"* 1st Mountain Division, Albanian Army units, Chetniks and numerous other formations. Krempler's Legion/Regiment/ Militia began playing their role on 14 August when, in company with 14th Regiment/ 7th SS Volunteer Mountain Division *"Prinz Eugen,"* and 2nd Regiment Brandenburg, they attacked toward Bijelo Polje and then along the road toward Prijepolje, forcing back elements of the 1st Proletarian and 37th Divisions. In the intense fighting that ensued, the Partisans suffered heavy losses, even though they had been ordered by Tito to avoid contact with the enemy and move to the southeast. By the last week of August the weakened, but still intact divisions of the Partisan 1st Corps broke out of Montenegro and pushed into southwestern Serbia. A large-scale linkup with the oncoming Soviet forces was now inevitable.[639]

At the beginning of September 1944 the main body of Krempler's Legion/Regiment was deployed along the line Priboj-Prijepolje-Pester Mountains-Rozaj, and attached to *Kampfgruppe "Bendel"*. This battlegroup contained two battalions of Moslem light infantry from the rapidly dissolving Albanian Army, with German officers and trainers in overall command. During the first half of the month many of the better German formations throughout central Yugoslavia were rushed to take up defensive positions in the Banat and along the Serbian-Bulgarian border to block the Red Army's rapidly moving spearheads through western Romania, and so prevent these from cutting off *Heeresgruppe E's* line of withdrawal from Greece. In consequence, Krempler's forces found them overextended and were forced to pull back to Sjenica. Aware of Army Group E's planned withdrawal from Greece and the Aegean through Macedonia, Kosovo, Sandjak into Bosnia, the Partisan 2nd Corps in Montenegro issued orders on 9

[638] Tomasevich, op cit. Pages 409-411. and VII, v.2, op cit. Pages 266-268.

[639] Tomasevich, ibid. Page 410. and VII, v.2, ibid., pages 266-268.

October for the 7th Brigade/ 3rd Division, and two battalions from the 3rd and 5th Brigades/ 37th Division to move on Sjenica and either take the town and hold it, or destroy all communications targets (i.e., bridges, telephone lines, rail lines, etc.) leading into and out of the town.

The Partisan force arrived in the area on 14 October and that night launched a strong attack on Sjenica and its garrison, Police Self-Defense Regiment Sandjak. Krempler's Moslems were taken by surprise and forced back to Duga Poljana, 23 kilometers to the east. Although German forces retook Sjenica on 25 October, this was the end of Krempler's Moslem Militia forces in the Sandjak. Now scattered and demoralized, with many of their villages in Partisan hands, nearly all of the older militiamen deserted or simply went into hiding. Tito had issued a general amnesty in September and many collaborator personnel were able to safely switch sides.[640]

The several hundred younger men who remained in uniform and managed to evade Tito's Partisans arrived in Sarajevo at the beginning of November 1944 well-armed and in good order, with Hafiz Sulejman Pacariz and his Chief of Staff, Major Ramiz Sipilovic, at their head. Here they rested and refitted for several months before being placed under the authority of *Ustashe* General Vjekoslav "Maks" Luburic, who had been sent to Sarajevo by Croatian *Poglavnik* (i.e.-*Fuehrer,* or Leader) Dr. Ante Pavelic, to take command of *Ustashe* forces in East Bosnia and Herzegovina and to round up and impress the small bands of Moslem and non-Moslem militia withdrawing to the Sarajevo area.The Sandjak Militia (and ex-Legion Krempler, ex-Police Self-Defense Regiment Sandjak) was allowed to retain its identity and Pacariz was given the rank of *Ustashe Pukovnik* (Colonel in the *Ustashe* Militia). In the meantime, *SS-Standartenführer der Reserve und Oberst der Polizei* Karl von Krempler and the German training cadre who had severed all contact with the Militia after it departed the Sandjak, were reassigned and Police Self-Defense Regiment Sandjak was formally disbanded in Graz, Austria in the beginning of 1945. In early March 1945 after five months of inactivity, the Sandjak Militia was ordered to the front along the Ivan Sedlo (Ivan Saddle), just 25 kilometers southwest of Sarajevo, through which the road from Mostar ran (and still does to this day). Heavy fighting prevailed here over the next month, but the German-Croatian defenders could not hold out and Sarajevo fell to the Partisans on April 6th 1945.

RIGHT: Albanian Muslim men enlist in the German 21st SS "Skanderbeg" Division, some time in the summer of 1944. *U.S. National Archives.*

[640] VII, v.2, op cit. Pages 395-396.

Of the militiamen from the Sandjak, some were killed in the defense of Sarajevo, some were captured in the city itself and then executed by the Partisans, but the majority made their way to Sisak, southeast of Zagreb, where they were incorporated into General Luburic's *"Obrana"* Brigade, considered by many Croatians to have been their most elite World War II combat unit. In mid-April the Brigade was reorganized and renamed the 30th Assault Regiment and became part of the newly formed Croatian 18th Assault Division, then stationed and undergoing training in Sisak. The Partisan offensive to end the war moved very rapidly during the second half of April 1945 and the component elements of the new 18th Croatian Assault Division were forced to retreat toward Austria before the formation of the Division could be completed. Only a handful of the Sandjak Moslems were able to reach safety. The others were hunted down and murdered in Zagreb after the city fell to the Partisans on 8 May 1945. Some also fell in battle along the route of withdrawal into Austria, or were handed over to Tito after the war by the British and subsequently perished on forced death marches, or in death camps.

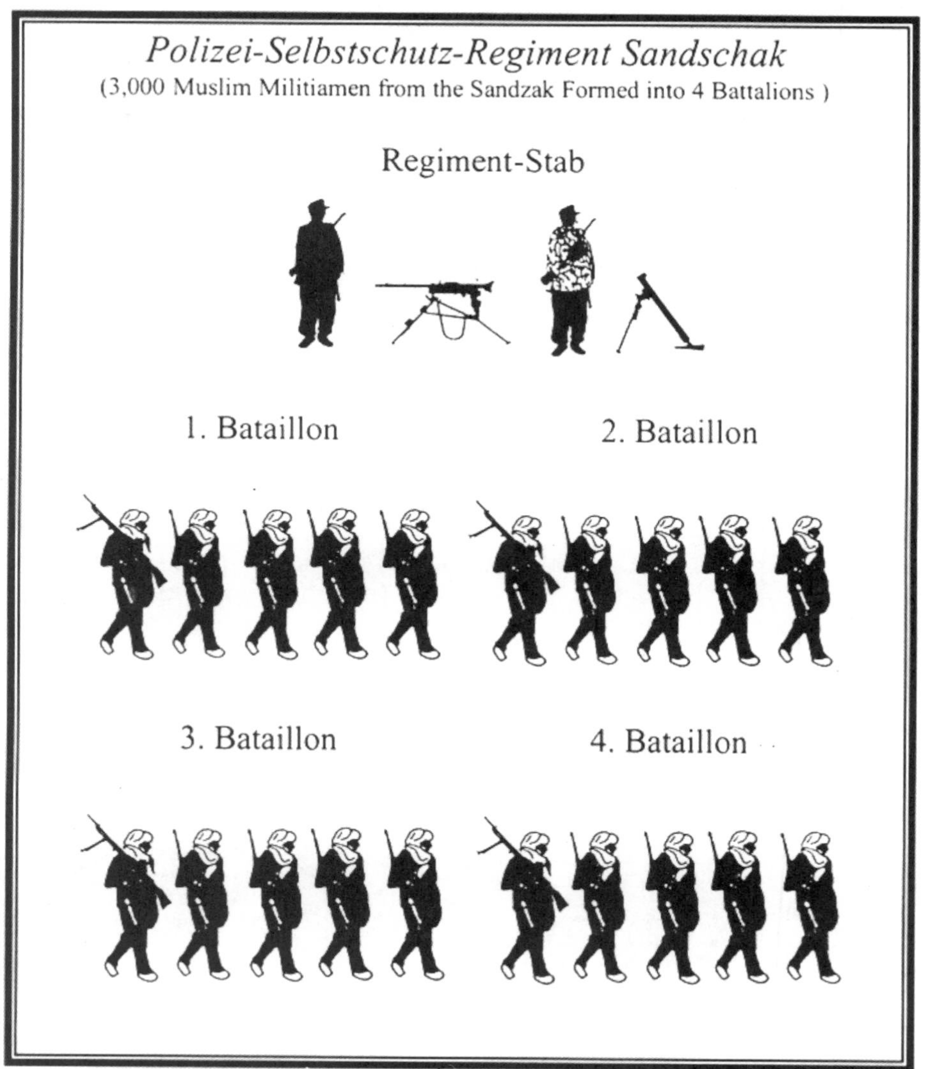

CHAPTER 15
Albanian Collaborationist Militia
1943-1944

By Antonio J. Munoz

INTRODUCTION

On April 7th 1939 Italy invaded Albania and defeated the small and inadequate Albanian Army in a matter of days. They then deposed King Zog and Albania was taken into the Italian Empire.[641] A puppet, "autonomous" government was established and a new Albanian Army and Fascist Party were formed. This new Albanian Army was first tested in October 1940, when Italy invaded Greece. The performance of the Italian-sponsored Albanian battalions was lamentable. For example, on November 4th, 1940 the *"Tomor"* Battalion, which was considered to be one of the best units of the 7,000-man Albanian Army, was ordered to attack a hill in the Lapishtit Mountain range on the Albanian-Greek border region. The hill was captured but the Greek Army counterattacked and under the shock of this attack, the "elite" Albanian battalion fell back in disarray.

Efforts by the Italian military police to stop the rout were met by rifle fire from the Albanian soldiers! Out of about 1,000 men in the *"Tomor"* Battalion, only 120 could later be found, including the Battalion's discomposed commander.[642] Total Albanian contribution to the Italian war effort had come in the form of 6 infantry, 6 mobile territorial and 2 garrison battalions. This did not include the Albanian Fascist Militia and Gendarmerie. During the campaign the Albanian battalions simply disintegrated. In fact, the entire Albanian loss in men during the war was a mere 59 killed and 68 wounded![643] After the war between Greece and Italy came to an end, it was decided that the remnants of the Albanian Army, about 2,500-3,000 men would be reorganized and led only by Italian officers.[644] Eventually, four rifle regiments and four Black Shirt (Fascist Party) battalions were raised for the new Albanian Army units under Italian control.[645]

When the war with Greece was concluded, most Albanians were happy to see those areas that had held Albanians in Greece (mainly on the Albanian-Greek border) become a part of "Greater Albania." Similarly, the Kosovo area, which

---

[641] Ready, J. Lee. *World War Two Nation by Nation*. Arms & Armor Press: London, 1995. Page 17.
[642] Cervi, Mario. *The Hollow Legions: Mussolini's Blunder in Greece 1940-1941*. Doubleday & Company: New York, 1971. Page 133.
[643] Cervi, ibid., page 308.
[644] Ibid., page 323.
[645] Ready, J. Lee. *The Forgotten Axis: Germany's Partners and Foreign Volunteers in World War II*. MacFarland & Company: Jefferson, 1987. Page 408.

ABOVE: King Zog of Albania. In the background are his three nieces and nephew- all of them were colonels in the Albanian Army! Notice the metallic emblem on the front of their uniform head cover. It is the emblem helmet of Prince Skanderbeg. *Author's Private Collection.*

had been a part of pre-war Yugoslavia, was annexed and given to Albania. Yet, in spite of these aggrandizements, there remained certain sections of Albanian society that resisted the Italian annexation of their country and fought the occupation through guerrilla warfare. These groups not only included the Zogists, who wanted to see King Zog return to the throne but the Communists, headed by Enver Hoxha, and several nationalist or secular groups. Albania was still very much a backwards and clannish country, with most people owing allegiances to one leader or another, and blood fueds that could last for decades.

1943

By the time that the Italian armistice was declared in September, 1943 the Albanian guerrillas, whose numbers had risen to around 20,000 (Communist and nationalist), controlled most of the countryside, while the Italian Army and its collaborationist Albanian forces were confined to garrisons in the larger towns, cities, and the Albanian coast.[646] The Germans had few friends in Albania. The Zogists were pro-British and so were the Moslem *Balisti,* a Moslem political movement with strong backing in northern Albania and the Kosovo which Italy

---

[646] Munoz, Antonio. *Forgotten Legions: Obscure Combat Formations of the Waffen-SS 1943-1945*. Paladin Press: Boulder, 1991. Page 227.

had annexed from Yugoslavia. Eventually, these Balisti would be courted by the Germans and when they realized that no British or American landing would take place in Albania, they would throw their support on the German side and against the Communists, whom they viewed as a greater threat.[647]

Author Rex Trye, who is much of an authority on the Italian Army, stated in his book, *"Mussilini's Soldiers"* that all of the officers in these Albanian Fascist battalions were Italian, while the NCO's were a mixture of Albanians and Italians. He also went on to describe how the 1st Legion (a battalion in size) was stationed in the capital of Tirana, while the 2nd was at Coritza, the 3rd at Valona, while the 4th was located at Scutari. He states that all were dissolved in 1943, but one photograph from the A. E. Barrows collection raises the question as to whether these Fascist volunteers continued to serve in some other units under German command after these Fascist battalions were dissolved. This German propaganda photograph came with a rather interesting caption: *"Ein albanischer Freiwilliger der sich zum Kampf gegen die Anhaenger der Badoglio-Clique und die kommunistischen Banden gemeldet hat. -PK- Kriegsberichter Przibilla 25.9.1943"* Translation: "An Albanian volunteer, who has responded to the fight against the followers of the Badoglio clique and the Communist bands - War Correspondent Przibilla 25.9.43"

ABOVE: The Italian M33 helmet used by Albanian Fascist Militia battalions. Notice the "Skanderbeg" emblem painted on the left front-side of the helmet. Below the emblem is an Italian fascist V symbol. *Rudy D'Angelo Collection.*

Obviously this picture is of an Albanian volunteer in the service of the Germans, shortly after Italy's surrender. There are some circumstantial evidence from the photograph which leads me to suspect that this particular group of Albanians (for this man seems to be standing in a group), is an ex-Albanian Fascist militiaman. Notice first of all, the helmet. It is an Italian made Ml6 helmet, issued to the Italian Fascist Public Security Police in the 1920's. This item was probably brought over and put into Albanian service after the Italians retired the model from service in their security forces; or perhaps it was a hangover from that earlier period. Whichever is the case, we now have photographic proof that it was still in use by late 1943, and that Albanian units serving under the Germans were using them. The second noticeable item on the photograph (and more telling), is the *Fiamme* which was a cloth collar tab device which resembled flames (therefore its name).

[647] NARS Microfilm T-501, Roll 258, Frame 000628.

This particular item was used by Fascist Militia units. The emblem on the cloth collar *"Fiamme"* seems to be either a goat's head or ram's head emblem although close examination through a magnifying glass could not positively establish this. There were some warlords who were nationalists and anti-Communist but refused to join the Germans. One of these was Abas Kopi and his guerrillas. Kopi continued to have British advisers in his command, just like there were advisers in Enver Hoxha's headquarters. The only difference between these two guerrilla groups was that most of the British officers assigned to support and help direct Albanian resistance to Axis rule were pro-Communist As a result, few supplies if any, ever reached the nationalist guerrillas.

BELOW: An Albanian Fascist militiaman serving as a volunteer with the German military, September 1943. The man is wearing Albanian Fascist collar tabs, a French-style helmet, and Italian military blouse. *Al Barrows Collection.*

The Albanian *Gendarmerie* and collaborationist civil government, that is, those segments of the Albanian society who had already been backing the Italians, readily welcomed German intervenetion in Albania. After all, they had backed the Fascists since 1939 and they would have had to pay the ultimate price for their collaboration either from the nationalists or the Communists. Initially, the only forces which the Germans sent to Albania in September, 1943 were the 100th *Jaeger* Division, which took control of the capital, Tirana; and the 92nd Independent Motorized Grenadier Regiment[648]. One year later, in September 1944 the larger units which the Germans would have garrisoning Albania would be the (1) 181st Infantry Division, (2) 297th Infantry Division and the (3) newly forming 21st Armed Mountain Division of the SS *"Skanderbeg."* Other German formations included the headquarters of the 21st Mountain Corps.

[648] This was an expanded *Sonderverband 287* which, if we will recall, was connected to the Arab Axis movement and had also served under *Sonderstab F* (Felmy).

ABOVE: In an Albanian Moslem town, the local militia and Albanian Gendarmerie patrolled the streets together. Notice the swastika symbol on the wall of the building in the background. The tower of the local Mosque can be seen behind the building. *Antonio Munoz Collection.*

In October 1943 the Germans sent three *"Feldkommandanturen,"* numbered 1030, 1039, and 1040. These were distributed respectively to Tirana, Prizren, and Struga. A "German Plenipotentiary in Albania" (or DGA) was set up and the post given to *Oberrat* Dr. Westphal, whose job it was to coordinate

German military moves in the country with those of the Albanian collaborationist civil and military authorities.

ABOVE: A parade of Muslim clergymen, escorted by an Albanian *Ushtar* (Gendarmerie). The collar tabs of the Albanian Gendarmerie were red, while the uniform was green in color. The emblem on the cover is the metallic "Rams Head" helmet emblem which was made famous by George Kastriotis (who wore it). He was Prince Skander Beg and was Albania's greatest hero. It is the same emblem worn by King Zog, and was a very common Albanian emblem. *U.S. National Archives.*

1944

By July, 1944 it was clear to the Germans that the Albanian collaborator forces and its civilian authorities were losing the guerrilla war. It was therefore decided in the end of August that the DGA office and its command were to be merged into the Higher-SS & Police Leader "Albania" under the command of *SS-Gruppenführer und Generalleutnant der Waffen-SS und der Polizei* Josef Fitzthum. *SS-Oberführer* Gstöttenbaur, of the German Consular Office in Tirana, would also be attached to the *HSS&PF* command.[649] Fitzthum's immediate problem was to organize (or rather, reorganize) the Albanian *Gendarmerie* and Army. In this he proved partly successful. By April, 1944 the total Albanian forces raised were two *"Jaeger"* (light infantry) regiments and four (4) militia battalions. The Albanian Order of Battle in this month looked as follows:

1. Albanian Jaeger Regiment 1
2. Albanian Jaeger Regiment 4

[649] NARS Microfilm T-501, Roll 258, Frame 000615.

3. Albanian Militia Battalion "Pec"
4. Albanian Militia Battalion "Pristina"
5. Albanian Militia Battalion "Prizren"

ABOVE: A Muslim farmer goes about his farming escorted by an Albanian Ushtar and two SS men of the SS "Skanderbeg" Division. *Bundesarchiv.*

Albanian Militia Battalion "Tetovo" This same German report stated that these formations were all fighting the guerrillas and under the control of the German Order Police.[650] The four militia battalions totalled around 2,000 men and were under the overall command of Hauptmann der Schutzpolizei Spruny. In addition to these forces, the Germans had been heavily recruiting Albanians (both by voluntary means and by forced conscription) for their planned Albanian-SS Mountain Division *"Skanderbeg."* They had been gathering recruits mainly from central and northern Albania and from the Kosovo region. The Balisti provided numerous recruits for this ill-fated formation.[651]

In fact, the first large-scale employment of the fledgling Albanian-SS division occurred between July 14th through the 30th 1944, when its 1st & 2nd Battalion/ 1st Regiment, and its 1st Battalion/ 2nd Regiment performed field maneuvers just south of Berane (Montenegro) and the northern Albanian border near Gusinje. During these maneuvers, the four entire Albanian militia battalions as well as the 14th SS Mountain Regiment of the *"Prinz Eugen"* Division also took part.[652]

---

650 NARS Microfilm T-175, Roll 174, Frame 2709461.

651 For a complete history of this ill-fated Albanian-SS division, please see "Forgotten Legions" by Antonio J. Munoz.

652 Munoz, op cit., page 233.

General Myrdatsch, the 70 year old Albanian officer who had served under the Italians was chosen to head the reorganized Albanian security police units, but he was almost immediately captured by Hoxha's Communists.[653] In his place, General Prenk Previsi was now selected.[654] Events in Albania took a turn for the worse for the Germans in late 1944. The Albanian SS *"Skanderbeg"* Division had proved too problematic, with hundreds of recruits deserting whenever they got the chance. Additionally, the *Gendarmerie* force and the militia battalions also suffered this problem which was in part due to the knowledge that the Allies were going to win the war. In Albania Enver Hoxha, the Communist leader, offerred no amnesty like Tito in Yugoslavia, but the writing was on the wall and those who could distance themselves from the Germans did so. When the Germans finally pulled out of Albania they took with them few Albanians. The Albanian collaborator simply disintergrated once the Germans left. They had proved a bit more useful in German than in Italian service, but this fact only gives credit to the superior military effecttiveness of the Germans.

LEFT: A closer look at the uniform of the Albanian Gendarmerie. This photo was taken during the Italian occupation. *U.S. National Archives.*

In the end, Albanian Axis collaborator forces proved to be poor quality troops, especially when not supported by strong Axis forces. This is not surprising, given that they were fighting alongside Axis partners who had no intentions of allowing real independence or choice to the Albanian people, so what were Albanians fighting for on the side of the Axis? The fight against the Communists had been a rallying cry for both the Italian & German occupation, and it must be said that it was a useful recruiting tool that the Axis forces used. However in the end, it proved inadequate and an insufficient reason for the majority of Albanians to fight for.

[653] NARS Microfilm T-501, Roll 258, Frame 000629.
[654] Ready, *Forgotten Axis*, op cit. Page 408.

ABOVE: General Myrdatsch, shown here flanked by Albanian Moslem officials in Tirana in 1941. An Albanian Fascist militiaman is seen behind the Albanian general. *U.S. National Archives.*
BELOW: An Albanian Fascist militiaman stands guard during a parade in Tirana, Albania during the Italian occupation. This picture was taken in 1940. Behind the Albanian Fascist militiaman is a member of the Albanian Gendarmerie. *U.S. National Archives.*

APPENDIX A

EASTERN LEGION BATTALIONS OPERATING IN THE CAUCASUS 1942-1943

BATTALION NO.:	COMMANDER(S):	STRENGTH:	HIGHER COMMAND:	AREA OF OPERATIONS:
450th Turkestani Infantry Battalion	Major Meyer-Mader; Major Bergen; Captain Kob	934 Turkestanis and 27 Germans	16th Motorized Division, 4th Panzer Army, Army Group B; Later: 3rd Panzer Corps, 1st Panzer Army, Army Group A	On Astrakhan direction (Kalmyk Steppe)
782nd Turkestani Infantry Battalion	1st Lieutenant (later Captain) Heise	900 Turkestani and 20 Germans	16th Motorized Division	On Astrakhan direction (Kalmyk Steppe)
811th Turkestani Infantry Battalion*	Major Kurth	820 Turkestani and 30 Germans	16th Motorized Division	On Astrakhan direction (Kalmyk Steppe)
452nd Turkestani Infantry Battalion	Captain Baumann	938 Turkestani and 12 Germans	97 Jäger Division, 44th Army Corps, 1st Panzer Army	Tuapse Region
781st Turkestani Infantry Battalion	Captain Niegsch	902 Turkestani and 28 Germans	101st Jäger Division, 44th Army Corps, 1st Panzer Army	Tuapse Region
I/370th Turkestani Infantry Battalion	1st Lieutenant Richter	928 Turkestani and 41 Germans	370th Infantry Division, 52nd Army Corps, 1st Panzer Army	Nal'chik and Mozdok Region
801st North-Caucasian Infantry Battalion	Captain Everling; then Captain Burkhardt	920 North-Caucasian and 27 Germans	370th Infantry Division, 52nd Army Corps, 1st Panzer Army	Nal'chik and Mozdok Region
802nd North-Caucasian Infantry Battalion	Captain Cap	900 North-Caucasian and 37 Germans	370th Infantry Division, then 3rd Panzer Division, 40 Panzer Corps, 1st Panzer Army	Nal'chik and Mozdok Region
800th North-Caucasian Infantry Battalion	1st Lieutenant Kurpanek	900 North-Caucasian and 40 Germans	125th Infantry Division, 5th Army Corps, 17th Army	Tuapse Region
804th Azerbaijani Infantry Battalion («Aslan»)**	Major Gloger	963 Azerbaijanis and 40 Germans	4th Mountain Division, 49th Mountain Corps, 1st Panzer Army	Direction on Suchumi
805th Azerbaijani Infantry Battalion	Captain Hoch	919 Azerbaijanis and 37 Germans	111th Infantry Division, 52nd Army Corps, 1st Panzer Army	Nal'chik and Mozdok Region
I/111th Azerbaijani Infantry Battalion («Dönmec»)	Captain Scharrenberg	929 Azerbaijanis and 33 Germans	111th Infantry Division, 52nd Army Corps, 1st Panzer Army	Nal'chik and Mozdok Region
806th Azerbaijani Infantry Battalion («Igit»)	Captain Ottendorf	911 Azerbaijanis and 44 Germans	50th Infantry Division, 52nd Army Corps, 1st Panzer Army	Nal'chik and Mozdok Region
I/73th Azerbaijani Infantry Battalion	Captain Franke	917 Azerbaijanis and 42 Germans	73rd Infantry Division, 5th Army Corps, 17th Army	Anapa and Novorossjsk Region
795th Georgian Infantry Battalion	1st Lieutenant Schirr	934 Georgians and 41 German	23rd Infantry Division, 3rd Panzer Corps, 1st Panzer Army	Nal'chik and Mozdok Region
796th Georgian Infantry Battalion	Captain Eismann	912 Georgians and 37 Germans	1st Mountain Division, 49th Mountain Corps, 1st Panzer Army	Tuapse Region
I/9th Georgian Infantry Battalion	1st Lieutenant Strack	927 Georgians and 38 Germans	9th Infantry Division, 5th Army Corps, 17th Army	Anapa and Novorossjsk Region
II/4th Georgian Infantry Battalion	Captain Bartscht	929 Georgians and Ossetians plus 36 Germans	4th Mountain Division, 49th Mountain Corps, 1st Panzer Army	Temrjuk and Anapa Region
808th Armenian Infantry Battalion	Major Kucera	916 Armenians and 41 Germans	1st Mountain Division, 49th Mountain Corps, 1st Panzer Army	Tuapse Region
809th Armenian Infantry Battalion	Captain Becker	913 Armenians and 45 Germans	13th Panzer Division, 3rd Panzer Corps, 1st Panzer Army	Nal'chik and Mozdok Region

* To October 1942 this battalion was re-named as the 444th Turkestani Infantry Battalion and became part of the 444th German Security Division.

** By the summer of 1943, this battalion became a part of the 314th Azerbaijani Infantry Regiment of the 162nd Turkoman Infantry Division.

Sources: *Bundesarchiv-Militararchiv (Freiburg); Oberkommando der 17. Armee; Oberkommando der 1. Panzerarmee.*

APPENDIX B

GENERAL STRENGTH TABLE OF THE FOREIGN VOLUNTEER FORMATIONS IN THE GERMAN ARMED FORCES 1939-1945

Respective Nationality of Volunteers	Numerical Strength
Volunteers from Western Europe	15,000
Volunteers from Citizens of the USSR	1,300,000-1,500,000
Muslim Volunteers within this figure:	
"HiWis"	200,000
Auxiliary police	40,000-45,000
Eastern Legions	150,000
Within this figure:	
Northern Caucasus	70,000-75,000
Volga Tartars	40,000
Turkestanis	180,000
Crimean Tartars	15,000-20,000
Volunteers from the Balkan States	270,000
Within this figure:	
Albanians	30,000
Bosnian Muslims	53,000-54,000
Kosovars	35,000-40,000
Volunteers from among the Arabs and inhabitants of North Africa	5,000
Volunteers from the peoples of India	3,000
Within this figure:	
Muslim-Indians	2,000
In all:	1,600,000-1,800,000
Muslim-volunteers within this figure:	510,000

Sources:

1. Drobyazko S.I. Vtoraya mirovaya voyna 1939-1945. Vostochnie legioni i kazach'i chasti v vermakhte.-M., 1999.
2. Strugar V. Yugoslaviya v ogne voyni. 1941-1945.-M., 1985.
3. Gunchak T. U mundirakh voroga // Biys'ko Ukraini.-1993.-No.6.-S. 6-156.
4. Caballero Jurado C., Lyles K. Foreign volunteers of the Wehrmacht. 1941-1945.-London, 1995.
5. Littlejohn D. Foreign Legions of the Third Reich (in four volumes).-San Jose, CA, 1979-1981.-Vol.3-4
6. Neulen H.W. An deutschen Seite. Internationale Freiwillige von Wehrmacht und Waffen-SS.-Muenchen, 1985.

APPENDIX C

COMPARATIVE TABLE OF MILITARY RANKS AMONG THE COMBATANTS

WEHRMACHT	WAFFEN-SS	EASTERN LEGIONS	RED ARMY
Schuetze (strelok)	SS Mann	Soldat	Ryadovoy
Oberschuetze (senior strelok)	SS-Oberschuetze	-	-
Efreytor	Stuermmann	Efreytor	Efreytor
-	Rottenfuehrer	Mladshiy unter-ofitser	-
-	Unterscharfuehrer	-	Mladshiy serzhant
Unter-feldwebel	Scharfuehrer	Unter-ofitser	Serzhant
Feldwebel	Oberscharfuehrer	-	Starshiy serzhant
Ober Feldwebel	Hauptscharfuehrer	Starshiy unter-ofitser	Starshina
Stabs-feldwebel	Stuermscharfuehrer	Feldwebel	-
Hauptfeldwebel	Stabsscharfuehrer	-	-
Fenrich	Standartenjunker	Kursant	-
Alt Fenrich	Standartenoberjunker	-	-
Leutenant	Untersturmfuehrer	Podporuchik	Ml. leytenant, Leytenant
Ober-leutenant	Obersturmfuehrer	Poruchik	St. Leytenant
Hauptmann	Hauptsturmfuehrer	Kapitan	Kapitan
Major	Sturmbanfuehrer	Mayor	Mayor
Oberst-leutenant	Obersturmbanfuehrer	Podpolkovnik	Podpolkovnik
Oberst	Standartenfuehrer	Polkovnik	Polkovnik
-	Oberfuehrer	-	-
General-Major	Brigadefuehrer	General-Mayor	General-Mayor
General-Leutenant	Gruppenfuehrer	General-Leytenant	General-Leytenant
General-roda voysk	Obergruppenfuehrer	General	General-Polkovnik
General-oberst	Oberstgruppenfuehrer	-	General Armii
General-Feldmarshall	Reichsfuehrer SS	-	Marshall Roda Voysk

Sources:

1. Zalesskiy K.A. Vozhdi I beonachal'niki tret'ego reikha. Biograficheskiy entsiklopedicheskiy slovar'.-M., 2000.-S. 494-499.
2. Caballero Jurado C., Lyles K. Foreign volunteers of the Wehrmacht. 1941-1945.-London, 1995.-P. 36.

APPENDIX D

MUSLIM VOLUNTEER FORMATIONS IN THE GERMAN ARMED FORCES, 1941-1945

1. Arabs and Muslim Indians

No.	Unit Designation	Years of Service	Contingent Nationalities	Fate
1.	Special Designation Unit 287 *(Sonderverband No. 287)*	1941-1942	Germans, Iraqis, Syrians, Palestinian Arabs, Arabs from North Africa	In 1942, reorganized as Special Designation Corps "F"
2.	Special Designation Corps "F" *(Sonderkorps "F")*	1942-1943	Germans and Arabs from Unit 287	In 1943 it was redesignated as 68th Army Corps (mot.)
3.	Legion of French Volunteers *(Legion Volontaire Francaise)*; it was the 638th Infantry Regiment of the 7th German Infantry Division.	1941-1944	Frenchmen living in France.	In 1944 was assigned to 33rd SS Division *"Charlemagne"*
4.	German-Arab Infantry Battalion No. 845 *(Deutsche-Arabische Bataillon No.845)* assigned to German 715th Infantry Division	1942-1943	Arabs living in France, plus other Middle East and North Africa Volunteers and Germans	In the Balkans, mainly Greece, then Yuigoslavia
4a	German-Arab Infantry Battalion No. 845 *(Deutsche-Arabische Bataillon No.845)* assigned to 41st Infantry Division in 1945	1944-45	Arabs living in France, plus other Middle East and North Africa Volunteers and Germans	Served in Yugoslavia from the fall of 1944 until spring 1945
5.	German-Arab Training Division *(Deutsche-Arabische Lehr Abteiling)* assigned to German 5th Panzer Army	1942-1943	Arabs living in France, and Germans	In 1943, capitulated in Tunisia
6.	"African Phalange" *("Phalange Africaine")*, from 1943, the Legion of French Volunteers in	1942-1943	French and Algerian Arabs	In 1943, capitulated in Tunisia.

	Tunisia *(Legion Volontaire Francaise en Tunisia)* assigned to German 334th Infantry Division.			
7.	"Legion of Free Indians" (Legion "Azad Hind"), from 1942 the 950th Indian Infantry Regiment *(Indisches Infanterie Regiment No. 950),* afterwards the 950th Indian Motorized Regiment *[Panzergrenadier Regiment 950 (indische)]*, from 1944 the Indian Volunteer Legion Waffen-SS *(Indische Freiwillige Legion der Waffen-SS)*	1941-1945	Indians (1/3 Hindus and Sikhs, 2/3 Muslims)	In 1945, capitulated in Southern Germany.

II. Balkan Muslims

1.	Kosovo Albanian Gendarmerie (HQ in Kosovska-Mitrovitse)	1941-1944	Albanians	In 1944, included in the 21st Division SS "Skanderbeg"
2.	"Balli Kombetar" organization battalions	1942-1945	Albanians	Destroyed by Partisan-Communists
3.	"Kosovo Regiment" *(Kosovksa-Mitrovitsa)*	1943-1944	Albanians	In 1944, included in the 21st Division SS "Skanderbeg"
4.	Pechskiy and Pristina Territorial Police Regiments	1944-1945	Albanians	Destroyed by Partisan-Communists
5.	Albanian Macedonian Militia	1943-1945	Albanians living in Macedonia	Destroyed by Partisan-Communists
6.	Croatian Legion (Hrvatska Legija): the 369th Croation Reinforced Infantry Regiment *(Verstärken Kroatischen Infan*terie Regiment No. 369), of the German 100th Jaeger Division	1941-1943	Croats, Muslims from Bosnia and Herzegovina	In 1943, destroyed at Stalingrad

7.	Khadzhieffendicha (Hadzifendic) Legion *(Hanziefendiceva Legija)*	1941-1943	Muslims from North-East Bosnia	In 1943, included in the 13th Division SS "Khandschar"
8.	Guski (Husko) Legion *(Huskina Legija)*	1943-1944	Muslims from Western Bosnia	In 1944, disbanded

9.	13th Mountain Infantry Division SS "Khandshar" *[Waffen-Gebirgsdivision der SS "Handschar" No.13 (kroatische No.1)]*	1943-1945	Croats and Muslims from Bosnia-Herzegovina	In 1945, capitulated in Austria
10.	23rd Mountain Infantry Division SS "Kama" *[Waffen-Gebirgs-Division der SS "Kama" No.23 (kroatische No.2)]*	1944	Croats and Muslims from Bosnia-Herzegovina	In 1944, disbanded
11.	21st Mountain Infantry Division SS "Skanderbeg" *[Waffen-Gebirgsdivision der SS "Scanderbeg" No.21 (albanische No.1)]*	1944-1945	Germans and Albanians	In 1945, disbanded

III. Muslim citizens of the USSR

1.	"Turkestan Regiment" *(Turkestaner Regiment);* also the 811th Infantry Battalion *(Infanterie Bataillon No.811)*	1941-1942	Germans and "Turkestanis"	In 1942 included in the Turkestan Legion
2.	Turkestan Legion *(Turkestanischen Legion)*	1941-1943	Uzbeks, Kazakhs, Kirgizians, Karakalpakians, Tadjiks	In 1943, disbanded
3.	Caucasus-Mohametan Legion *(Kaukasischer-Mohammedanischen Legion),* from 1942, Azerbadjianian Legion *(Azerbajdzanischen Legion)*	1941-1943	Azerbadjianians	In 1943, disbanded
4.	Georgian Legion *(Georgischen Legion)*	1941-1943	Georgians, Ossetians, Abkhazians	In 1943, disbanded

5.	Armenian Legion (Armenischen Legion)	1941-1943	Armenians	In 1943, disbanded
6.	Northern Caucasus Legion *(Nordkaukasische Legion)*	1942-1943	Adigeytsi, Cherkassians, Kabardinians, Balkarians, Karachaevans, Dagestanis, Ingushetians, Chechens	In 1943, disbanded
7.	Volga-Tartar Legion *(Wolgatatarische Legion)*	1942-1943	Volga Tartars, Bashkirians, Marians, Mordvians, Chuvashi, Udmurti	In 1943, disbanded
8.	Labor Unit *("Böhler Brigade")*	1943-1945	Germans and Turkestanis	In 1945, capitulated in Germany
9.	Volunteer Cadre Division *(Freiwilligen-Stamm-Division)*	1943-1944	Armenians, Azerbadjianis, Volga-Tartars, Cossacks, Ukrainians, Russians	In 1944, defeated on the Western Front
10.	12th (Caucasus) Tank-Destroyer Unit *(Panzerjaeger Waffenverband No. 12 – kaukasischer)*	1944-1945	Georgians, Armenians, Azeris, Kabardians, Balkarians	In 1945, destroyed in the Battle for Berlin
11.	162nd Turkish Infantry Division *(Turkomanische-Infanterie-Division No. 162)*	1943-1945	Germans, Turkestanis, Azerbadjianians	In 1945, capitulated in Austria
12.	Special Designation Unit "Gorets" *(Sonderverband "Bergmann")* from 1942 a regiment	1941-1944	Germans, Georgians, Armenians, Dagestanis, Azeris, Kabardinians, Balkarians	In 1944, disbanded
13.	Crimean-Tartar Self-Defense Companies *(Selbstschutz)* 1-14	1942	Crimean Tartars	In 1944, reformed into "Schuma" battalions

14.	Crimean-Tartar Auxiliary security police battalions *(Schutzmannschaft Bataillone-"Schuma")* No. 147-155; also the Crimean-Tartar Legion *(Krimtatarische Legion)*	1942-1944	Crimean Tartars, Germans	In 1944 a portion was disbanded, another portion defeated in the Crimea.
15.	1st Eastern-Muslim Regiment SS *(Ostmuselmanischen-SS-Regiment No.1)*	1944	Turkestanis, Azeris, Volga Tartars	In 1944 reformed as the Eastern Turkish Unit SS
16.	Tartar Mountain-Jaeger Regiment SS *(Tataren-Gebirgsjaeger-Regiment der SS)*	1944	Crimean Tartars, Germans	In 1944, reformed as the Eastern-Turkish Mountain-Jaeger Brigade SS No. 1
17.	Tartar Mountain-Jaeger Brigade der-SS No.1 *[Waffen-Gebirgsjaeger Brigade der SS (tatarische No.1)]*	1944	Crimean Tartars, Germans	In 1944, assigned to the Eastern-Turkish Unit SS
18.	Eastern-Turkish Unit SS *(Osttuerkischen-Waffenverband der SS)*	1944-1945	Volga Tartars, Turkestanis, Azeris, Crimean Tartars	In 1945, capitulated
19.	Caucasus Unit SS *(Kaukasischer-Waffenverband der SS);* also the Caucasus Cavalry Division	1944-1945	Georgians, Armenians, Azeris, North Caucasus tribes	Was not brought to full strength due to war's end.
20.	Sultan Kelech-Gireya Unit in Northern Italy	1945	North Caucasus tribes	In 1945 capitulated in Austria

Sources:

1. Bundesarchiv-Militaerarchiv (Freiburg):
2. Kommandeur der Osttruppen z. b. V. 710, RH 58/73, RHD 7/8a/2.
3. Kommando der 162. Infanteriedivision, RH 26-162/15.

APPENDIX E

TARTAR SELF-DEFENSE COMPANIES
(SPRING-AUTUMN 1942)

Company No.	Men	Platoon / Company	Location
1	100	-	Simferopol
2	137		Bijuk-Onlar
		1st platoon	Bijuk-Onlar
		2nd platoon	Bishak
		3d platoon	Terkundi
3	60	-	Beshuj
4	125	-	Baxan
5	150	-	Molbaj
6	175		Bij-Eli
		1st platoon	Bij-Eli
		2nd platoon	Koperlikoj
		3d platoon	Koktash
7	100		Alushta
		1st platoon	Korbek
		2nd platoon	Korbek
		3d platoon	Demergi
8	85	-	Bakhchisaraj
9	100	-	Koush
10	175	-	Yalta
11	175	-	Yalta, then Taraktash
12	100	-	Taraktash
13	100	-	Taraktash
14	50	-	Dgankoj

Source: Bundesarchiv-Militärarchiv (Freiburg), Oberkommando der 11. Armee, RH 19 VI/425

APPENDIX F

FOREIGN VOLUNTEER FORMATION STRENGTHS
IN THE GERMAN ARMED FORCES (1941 - 1945)

Nationality of the Volunteers	Numbers of Volunteers
Volunteers from Western Europe	15,000
Volunteers from Citizens of the USSR Muslims Volunteers From the USSR: In the *Hilfswilliger:* In the *Hilfsdienst & Ordnungsdienst* (police auxiliaries): In the *Ostlegionen* (Eastern Legions): North-Caucasians- Volga-Tartars- Turkestanis (inhabitants of Kazakhstan and Central Asia)- Crimean Tartars-	 1,300,000 – 1,500,000 200,000 Muslim *Hilfswilliger* 40-45,000 Muslims 150,000 Muslims (Divided as follows): 70-75,000 40,000 18,000 15-20,000
Volunteers from the Balkans Of that number: Albanians Bosnian Muslims "Kosovan" (inhabitants of Kosovo)	About 270,000 (including Croatians, Serbians, Slovenians, Macedonians, Albanians, Greeks). 30,000 53-54,000 35-40,000
Arab Volunteers from North Africa	About 5,000
Volunteers from Peoples of India:	About 3,000 (of which about 2,000 were Muslim)
Grand Total:	Around 1,600,000-1,800,000 (of which 510,000 were Muslims)

TABLE 1

Induction Process of Foreign Volunteers in the *Wehrmacht*

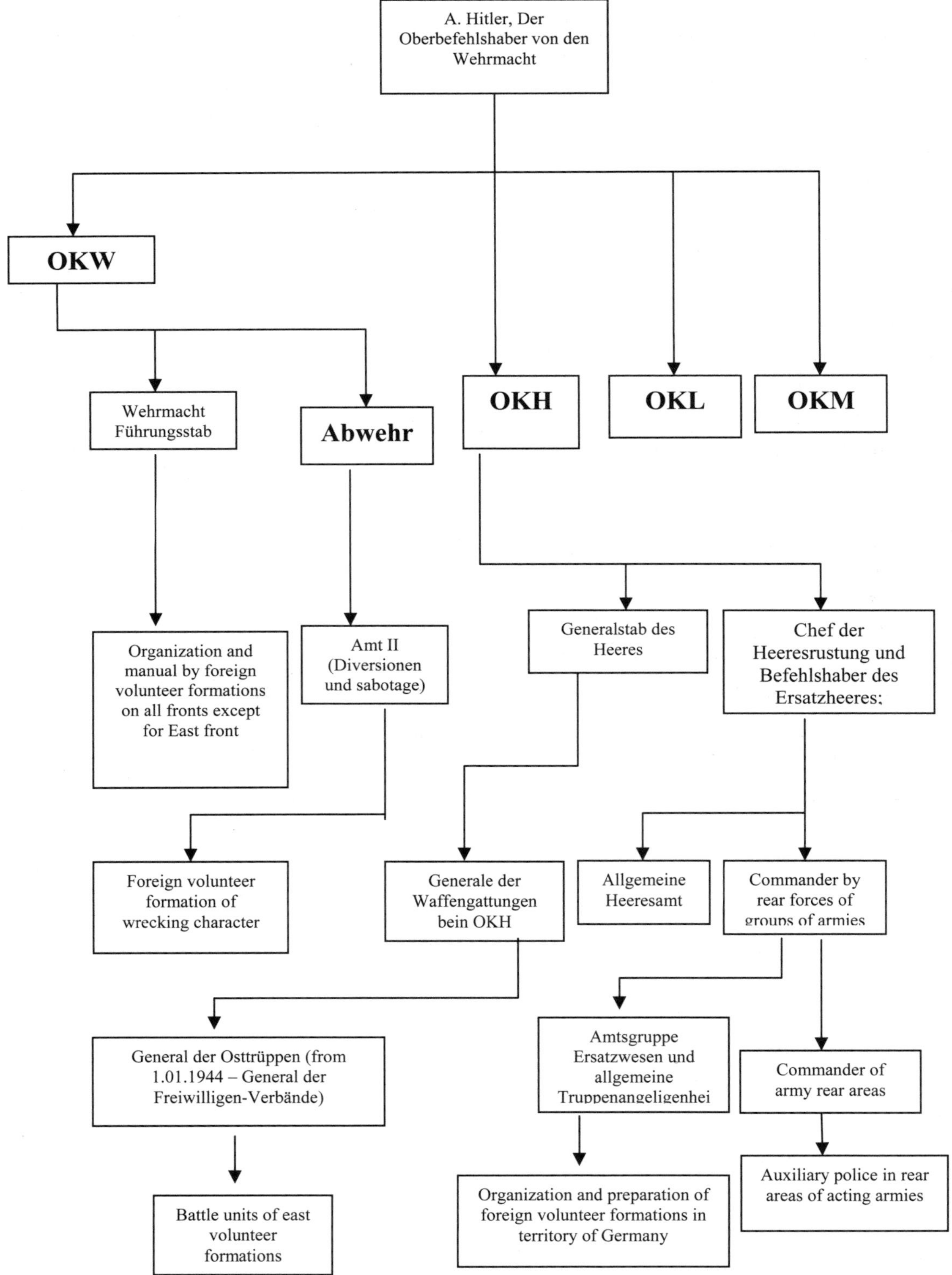

TABLE 2

Induction Process of Foreign Volunteers in the *Waffen-SS*

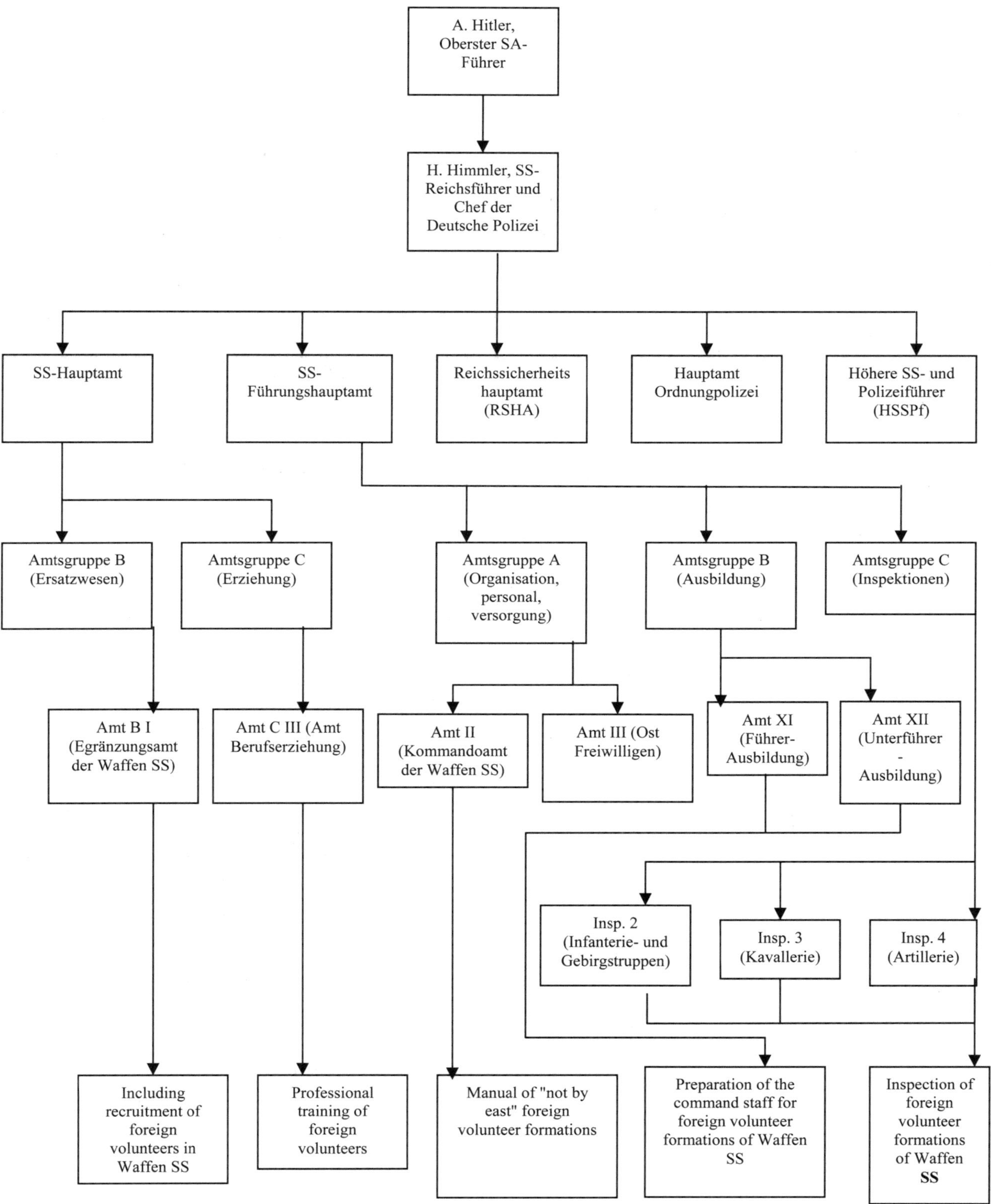

TABLE 3

Induction Process of Foreign Volunteers in the Ordnungspolizei

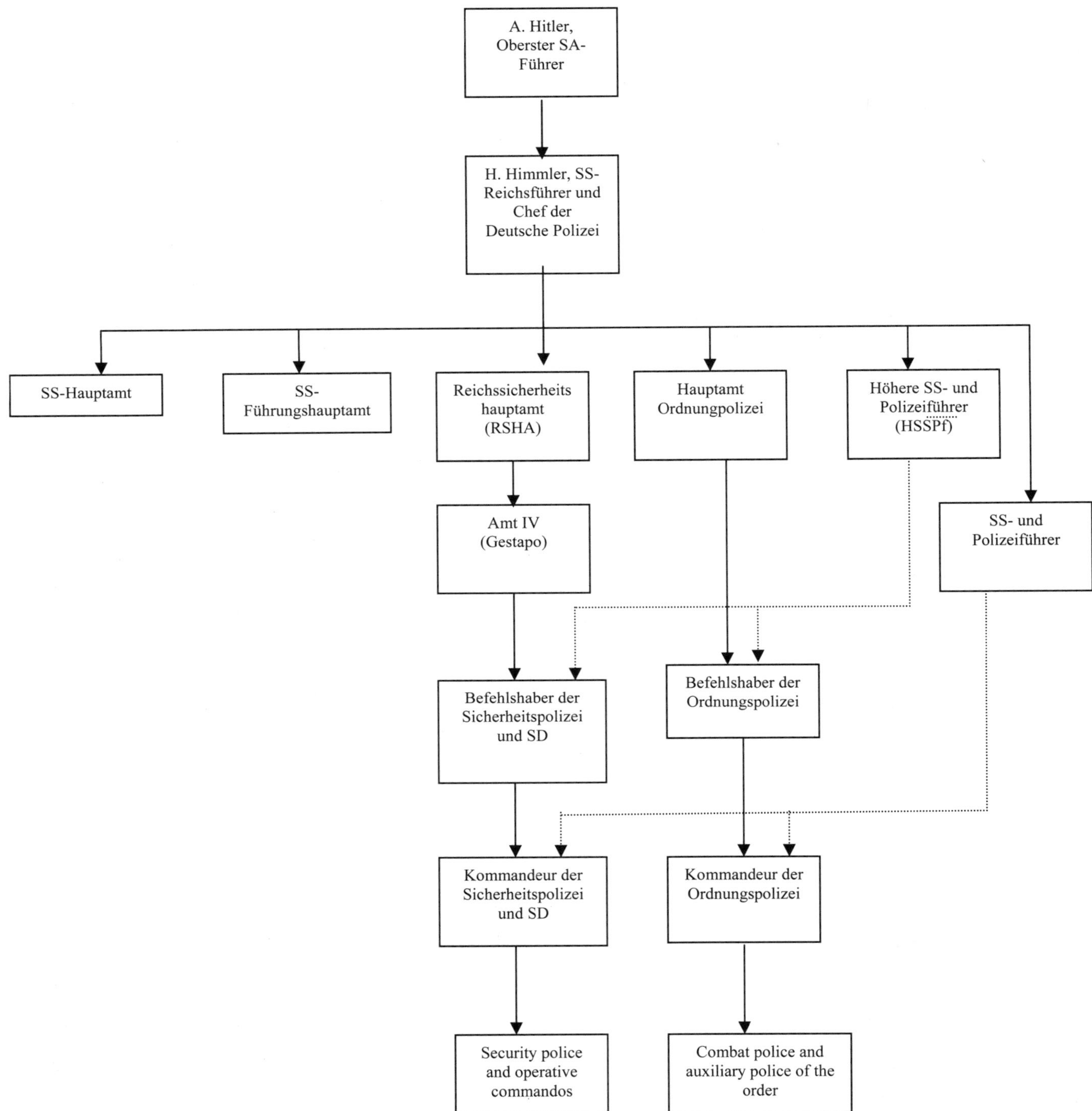

Selected Published References

Adair, Paul. *Hitler's Greatest Defeat. The Collapse of Army Group Center.* Sterling Publishing: New York, 1994.

Alexiev, Alex. *Soviet Nationalities in German Wartime Strategy, 1941-1945*. R-2772-NA. Rand Corporation: Santa Monica, 1982.

Anders, Wladyslaw. *Hitler's Defeat In Russia.* Henry Regnery Company: Chicago, 1953.

-----, Edited by A. Munoz. *Russian Volunteers in Hitler's Army, 1941-1945*. Axis Europa Books: Bayside, 1997.

Andreyev, Catherine. *Vlasov and The Russian Liberation Movement. Soviet Reality and Émigré Theories*. Cambridge University Press: Cambridge, 1987.

Armstrong, John A., editor. *Soviet Partisans in World War II.* University of Wisconsin Press: Madison, 1964.

Bethell, Nicholas. *The Last Secret. The Delivery to Stalin of Over Two Million Russians by Britain and the United States.* Basic Books Inc.: New York, 1974.

Birn, Ruth Bettina. *Die Höheren SS und Polizeifuehrer. Himmlers Vertreter im Reich und in den besetzten Gebieten*. Droste Verlag, 1986.

Browning, Christopher. *Ordinary Men: Reserve Police Battalion 101 and the Final Solution in Poland*. Harper Collins Publishers: New York, 1993.

Caballero-Jurado, Carlos. *La Espada del Islam: Voluntarios árabes en el Ejército alemán 1941-1945.* Garcia Hispan Editor: Alicante, 1990.

----------, *Commandos En El Caucaso: La Unidad Especial Bergmann; Volunterios Caucasianos en el Ejercito Aleman, 1941-1943.* Garcia Hispan Editor: Alicante, 1995.

----------, *Breaking the Chains: 14.Waffen-Grenadier-Division der SS and Other Ukrainian Volunteer Formations, Eastern Front, 1942-1945.* Shelf Books: Halifax, 1998.

Carnier, Pier Arrigo, *L'Armata Cosacca In Italia 1944-1945.* Mursia Editore: Milano, 1990.

Caroe, Olaf. *Soviet Empire. The Turks of Central Asia And Stalinism.* MacMillan & Co. Ltd.: New York, 1954.

Carell, Paul. *Hitler Moves East, 1941-1943.* Little, Brown, & Company: Boston, 1964.

-------, *Scorched Earth. The Russo-German War 1943-1944.* Little, Brown, & Company: Boston, 1970.

Cohen, Philip J. *Serbia's Secret War.* Texas A&M University Press: College Station, 1996.

Cooper, Matthew. *The Nazi War Against Soviet Partisans 1941-1944.* Stein And Day: New York, 1979.

Coudry, Georges. *Les Camps Sovietiques En France. Les Russes livres a Staline en 1945*. Albin Michel: Paris, 1997.

Dallin, Alexander. *German Rule In Russia 1941-1945. A Study of Occupation Policies*. MacMillan & Co. Ltd.: New York, 1957.

----. *Odessa, 1941-1944: A Case Study of Soviet Territory Under Foreign Rule.* RM-1875, ASTIA Document Number AD 123552 February 14, 1957. U.S. Air Force Project Rand. Rand Corporation: Santa Monica, 1957.

Dixon, C. Aubrey and Otto Heilbrunn. *Communist Guerrilla Warfare*. George Allen & Unwin Ltd.: London, 1954.

Dobrich, Momcilo. *Belgrade's Best: The Serbian Volunteer Corps 1941-1945.* Axis Europa Books: Bayside, 2000.

Drum, D. Karl, et al. *Airpower in Russian Partisan Warfare*. USAF Historical Study No.177. Arno Press: New York, 1968.

Erickson, John. *The Road to Berlin. Stalin's War With Germany.* Weidenfeld & Nicolson Ltd.: London, 1983.

Fischer, Bernd J. *Albania at War 1939-1945*. Perdue University Press: West Lafayette, 1999.

Fischer, George. *Soviet Opposition to Stalin. A Case Study in World War II.* Harvard University Press: Cambridge, 1952.

Franz, Hermann. *Gebirgsjäger der Polizei: Polizei-Gebirgsjäger-Regiment 18 und Polizei-Gebirgs-Artillerieabteilung 1942-1945*. Verlag Hans Henning: Bad Nauheim, 1963.

Gellermann, Guenther W. *Moskau ruft Heeresgruppe Mitte. Was nicht im Wehrmachtbericht stand: Die Einsaetze des geheimen Kampfgeschwaders 200 im Zweiten Weltkrieg*. Bernard & Graefe Verlag: Koblenz, 1988.

Gordon, Gary Howard. *Soviet Partisan Warfare, 1941-1944. The German Perspective*. University Microfilms: Ann Arbor, 1972.

Grenkevich, Leonid. *The Soviet Partisan Movement 1941-1944. A Critical Historiographical Analysis*. Frank Cass: Portland, 1999.

Goldhagen, Daniel Jonah. *Hitler's Willing Executioners. Ordinary Germans and the Holocaust*. Alfred A. Knopf: New York, 1996.

Hartog, Rudolf. *Im Zeichen Des Tigers: Die indische Legion auf deutscher Seite 1941-1945*. Busse Seewald Verlag: Herford, 1991.

Haupt, Werner. *Army Group North. The Wehrmacht In Russia 1941-1945*.Schiffer Publishers: Atglen, 1997.

------, *Die Schlachten Der Heeresgruppe Mitte 1941-1944*. Podzun Pallas Verlag: Friedberg, 1983.

-------, *Army Group Center, The Wehrmacht In Russia 1941-1945*. Schiffer Publishing Ltd.: Atglen, 1997.

-------, *Army Group South. The Wehrmacht In Russia 1941-1945*.Schiffer Publishers: Atglen, 1997.

-------, *Die 8. Panzer-Division im 2. Weltkrieg*. Podzun-Pallas Verlag: Friedberg, 1987.

Heer, Hannes and Klaus Naumann, eds. *Vernichtungskrieges Verbrechen der Wehrmacht, 1941-1944*. Hamburger Edition HIS Verlagsges: Hamburg, 1995.

Hehn, Paul N. *The German Struggle against Yugoslav Guerrillas in World War II. German Counter-Insurgency in Yugoslavia.* Columbia University Press – East European Quarterly: Boulder, 1973.

Hesse, Erich. *Der sowjetrussische Partisanenkrieg 1941 bis 1944*. Muesterschmidt Verlag: Gottingen, 1969.

Hilberg, Raul. *Perpetrators, Victims, Bystanders. The Jewish Catastrophe 1933-1945*. Harper Collins Publishers: New York, 1992.

Hilgruber, Andreas. *Die Räumung der Krim 1944*. Verlag E. S. Mittler & Sohn:Berlin, 1959.

Hinze, Rolf. *East Front Drama – 1944. The Withdrawal Battle of Army Group Center*. J. J. Fedorowicz Publishing: Winnipeg, 1996.

-------, *Rückzugskaempfe in Der Ukraine 1943/44.* Verlag Dr. Rolf Hinze: Neustadt, 1991.

Hnilicka, Karl. *Das Ende auf dem Balkan 1944/45*. Musterschmidt – Göttingen Verlag: Zürich, 1970.

Hoehne, Heinz. *The Order of the Death's Head. The Story of Hitler's SS*. Coward McCann, Inc.: New York, 1970.

Hoffmann, Joachim. *Kaukasien 1942/43. Das deutsche Heer und die Orientvolker der Sowjetunion*. Rombach Verlag: Friedberg, 1991.

------------, *Deutsche und Kalmyken 1942 bis 1945*. Rombach Verlag: Friedberg, 1986.

------------, *Die Ostlegionen 1941-1943*. Rombach Verlag: Friedberg, 1986.

------, *Die Geschichte der Wlassow-Armee*. Verlag Rombach: Friedberg, 1986.

Howell, Edgar M. *The Soviet Partisan Movement: 1941-1944*. Department of the Army: Washington, DC 1956.

Ignatov, P.K. *Partisans of the Kuban*. Hutchinson & Co.: New York, 1944.

International Military Tribunal. *Trial of the Major War Criminals*. IMT: Nuremberg, 1948. 24 volumes.

Jurado, Carlos Caballero. *Breaking the Chains. 14.Waffen-Grenadier- Division der-SS and Other Ukrainian Volunteer Formations, Eastern front, 1942-1945.* Shelf Books: London, 1998.

Jurs, August, editor. *Estonian Freedom Fighters In World War Two*. Voitleja Relief Foundation: Toronto, n.d.

Kamenetsky, Ihor. *Hitler's Occupation of Ukraine (1941-1944). A Study of Totalitarian Imperialism*. The Marquette University Press: Milwaukee, 1956.

Kannapin, Norbert & Georg Tessin. *Waffen-SS und Ordnungspolizei im Kriegseinsatz, 1939-1945.* Biblio Verlag: Osnabrueck, 2000.

Karashuk, A., editor. *Russkiya Osvobodetelnya Armia 1939-1945 (Russian Liberation Army, 1939-1945).* Act Publishers: Moscow, 1999. Vols. 1-3.

Klausch. Hans-Peter. *Antifaschisten in SS-Uniform*. Edition Temen: Bremen, 1993.

Kleitmann, Dr. K. G. *Die Waffen-SS – eine Dokumentation*. Verlag Der Freiwillige: Osnabrück, 1965.

Kumm, Otto. *Prinz Eugen: The History of the 7 SS Mountain Division "Prinz Eugen"*. J. J. Fedorowicz Publishing: Winnipeg, 1995.

---------,*"Vorwarts Prinz Eugen!" Geschichte der 7. SS-Freiwilligen-Gebrigs-Division 'Prinz Eugen'*. Munin Verlag: Osnabrück, 1978.

---------, 7. SS-Gebirgs-Division "Prinz Eugen" im Bild. Munin Verlag: Osnabrück, 1983.

Kurowski, Franz. *Deadlock Before Moscow. Army Group Center 1942-1943*. Schiffer Publishers: Atglen, 1992.

------------, *The Brandenburgers – Global Mission*. J. J. Fedorowicz Publishing: Winnipeg, 1997.

Krausnick, Helmut. *Hitlers Einsatzgruppen. Die Truppen des Weltanschauungskrieges 1938-1942*. Fischer Taschenbuch Verlag: Frankfurt am Main, 1985.

------------, editor. *Anatomy of the SS State*. Walker And Company: New York, 1965.

Kuehnrich, Heinrich. *Der Partisanenkrieg in Europa 1939-1945*. Dietz Verlag: Berlin, 1968.

Kurowski, Franz. *The Brandenburgers – Global Mission* -.J.J. Fedorowicz Publishing: Winnipeg, 1997.

Lepre, George. *Himmler's Bosnian Division. The Waffen-SS Handschar Division 1943-1945*. Schiffer Publishing: Atglen, 1997.

Littlejohn, David. *The Patriotic Traitors. The History of Collaboration in German-Occupied Europe, 1940-45*. Doubleday & Company: Garden City, 1972.

-----------, *Foreign Legions of the Third Reich, Volume III: Albania, Czechoslovakia, Greece, Hungary and Yugoslavia.* J. R. Bender Publishing: San Jose, 1985.

-----------, *Foreign Legions of the Third Reich, Volume IV: Poland, the Ukraine, Belorussia, Romania, Free India, Estonia, Latvia, Lithuania, Finland, and Russia.* J.R. Bender Publishing: San Jose, 1987.

Lucas, James. *War of the Eastern Front 1941-1945*. Janes Publishing Company: London, 1979.

MacLean, French L. *The Cruel Hunters. SS Sonderkommando Dirlewanger. Hitler's Most Notorious Anti-Partisan Unit*. Schiffer Publishers: Atglen, 1998.

-----------, *The Field Men. The SS Officers Who Led The Einsatzkommandos – the Nazi Mobile Killing Units.* Schiffer Publishers: Atglen, 1999.
Mehner, Kurt. *Die Waffen-SS und Polizei 1939-1945*. Militar-Verlag Klaus D. Patzwall: Norderstedt, 1995.

Manstein, Field Marshal Erich von. *Lost Victories*. Presidio Press: Novato, 1982.

Mellenthin, Major-General F. W. von. *Panzer Battles. A Study of the Employment of Armor in the Second World War.* University of Oklahoma Press: Norman, 1955.

Mehner, Kurt. *Die Waffen-SS und Polizei 1939-1945*. Verlag Klaus D. Platzwall: Norderstedt, 1995.

---------, *Die Geheimen Tagesbericht Der Deutschen Wehrmachtfuehrerung Im Zweiten Weltkrieg 1939-1945*. Biblio Verlag: Osnabrueck, twelve volumes. 1989-1994.

Mendelsohn, John, editor. *The Holocaust. Selected Documents in Eighteen Volumes. Volume 10 – The Einsatzgruppen.* Garland Publishing: New York, 1982.

Meyer, Brün. *Dienstalterliste der Waffen-SS - Stand vom 1. Juli 1944*. Biblio Verlag GmbH: Osnabrück, 1987.

Michaelis, Rolf. *Der Weg zur 36. Waffen-Grenadier-Division der SS*. Verlag fuer Militaerhistorische Zeitgeschichte: Rodgau, 1991.

-----------, *Die russische Volksbefreiungsarmee "RONA" 1941-1944. Russen im Kampf gegen Stalin.* Selbstpubliziert: Erlangen, 1992.

-----------, Ukrainer in Der Waffen-SS. Die 14.Waffen-Grenadier-Division der SS (Ukrainische Nr.1). Die Deutsche Bibliothek – CIP Einheitsaufnahme: Berlin, 2000.

Mollo, Andrew. *Uniforms of the SS. Volume 5 – Sicherheitsdienst Und Sicherheitspolizei 1931-1945.* Windrow & Greene: London, 1992.

Mulligan, Patrick Timothy. *The Politics of Illusion And Empire. German Occupation Policy in the Soviet Union, 1942-1943.* Praeger Publishers: New York, 1988.

Mueller, Rolf-Dieter & Gerd R. Ueberschaer. *Hitler's War In The East 1941-1945. A Critical Assessment*. Berghahn Books: Providence, 1997.

Munoz, Antonio J. *Hitler's Eastern Legions, Volume I – The Baltic Schutzmannschaft 1941-1945*. Axis Europa Books: Bayside, 1996.

---------, *Lions of the Desert: Arab Volunteers in the German Army 1941-1945.* Axis Europa Books: Bayside, 1997. 2nd Edition.

---------, *Hitler's Eastern Legions, Volume II – The Osttruppen.* Axis Europa Books: New York, 1997.

---------, *The Kaminski Brigade: A History, 1941-1945.* Axis Europa Books: Bayside, 1996.

---------, *For Czar and Country: A History of the Russian Guard Corps, 1941-1945*. Axis Europa Books: Bayside, 1999.

---------, *The Druzhina SS Brigade: A History, 1941-1943.* Axis Europa Books: Bayside, 2000.

---------, *Forgotten Legions Obscure Combat Formations of the Waffen-SS.* Paladin Press: Boulder, 1991.

---------, *Forgotten Legions Companion Booklet: Additional Data For The Classic Study*. Axis Europa Books: Bayside, 1999.

---------, *The Last Levy: Waffen-SS Officer Roster, March 1st 1945.* Axis Europa Books: Bayside, 2001.

---------, Editor. *The German Police*. Supreme Allied Headquarters, G-2 Section, prepared jointly with British MI-14(d). U.S. Army War Office: Washington, April 1945. Reprinted in revised and expanded format by Axis Europa Books: Bayside, 1997.

Nafziger, George. *The German Order of Battle: Waffen-SS and Other Units in World War II.* Combined Publishing: Pennsylvania, 2001.

----------, *Foreigners in Field Gray: The Russian, Croatian, and Italian Soldiers in the Wehrmacht.* Privately Published: Pisgah, 1995.

Neufeldt, Hans-Joachim, Jürgen Huck and Georg Tessin. *Zur Geschichte der Ordnungspolizei 1936-1945.* Schriften des Bundesarchiv: Boppard-am-Rhein, 1957.

Neulen, Hans Werner. *An deutscher Seite. Internationale Freiwilliger von Wehrmacht und Waffen-SS.* Universitas Verlag: Munich, 1985.

Newland, Samuel J. *Cossacks in the German Army 1941-1945.* Frank Cass: London, 1991.

Niepold, Gerd. *Battle For White Russia. The Destruction of Army Group Centre June 1944.* Brassey's Defense Publishers: New York, 1987.

Padfield, Peter. *Himmler.* Henry Holt & Company: New York, 1990.

Perro, Oskars. *Fortress Cholm.* Kurland Publishing: Toronto, 1981.

Piekalkiewicz, Janusz. *The Cavalry of World War II.* Stein & Day: New York, 1980.

Pohl, Otto J. *Ethnic Cleansing in the USSR, 1937-1949.* Greenwood Press: Westport, 1999.

Poirier, Robert G. and Albert Z. Conner. *The Red Army Order of Battle in the Great Patriotic War.* Presidio Press: Novato, 1985.

Prechtl, G. M. *Unsere Ehre Heisst Treue. Kriegstagebuch des Kommandostabes Reichsfuehrer-SS Taegtigkeitsberichte der 1. Und 2. SS Infanterie-Brigade, der 1. SS Kavallerie-Brigade und der Sonder- kommandos der SS.* Europaverlag: Vienna, 1965.

Preradovich, Nikolaus von. *Die Generale der Waffen-SS.* Kurt Vowinckel Verlag: Berg Am See, Austria. 1985.

Pronin, Alexander. *Guerrilla Warfare in the German Occupied Soviet Territories 1941-1945.* Georgetown University Graduate School: Georgetown, 1965.

Ramme, Alwin. *Der Sicherheitsdienst Der SS.* Deutscher Militaerverlag: Berlin, 1970.

Ready, J. Lee. *The Forgotten Axis. Germany's Partners and Foreign Volunteers in World War II.* MacFarland & Company, Inc.: Jefferson, 1987.

Reitlinger, Gerald. *The SS, Alibi of a Nation, 1922-1945.* William Heinemann Ltd.: London, 1956.

------------, *The House Built on Sand. The Conflicts of German Policy in Russia 1939-1945.* The Viking Press: New York, 1960.

-----------, *The Final Solution. The Attempt to Exterminate the Jews of Europe 1939-1945*. Thomas Yoseloff: South Brunswick, 1961.

Redelis, Valdis. *Partisanenkrieg*. Kurt Vowinckel Verlag: Heidelberg, 1958.

Schellenberg, Walter. *The Labyrinth. The Memoirs of Hitler's Secret Service Chief.* Harper & Brothers: New York, 1956.

Schramm, Percy E. *Kriegstagebuch Des Oberkommandos Der Wehrmacht 1940-1945*. Bernard & Graefe Verlag: Munich, 1982. 8 volumes.

Schuster, Peter & Harald Tiede. *Die Uniformen und Abzeichen der Kosaken in der Deutschen Wehrmacht.* Verlag Klaus D. Patzwall: Norderstedt, 1999.

Seewald, Dr. Heinrich. *Das toenende Erz. Deutsche Propaganda gegen die Rote Armee im Zweiten Weltkrieg*. Seewald Verlag: Stuttgart, 1978.

Seidler, Franz W. *Die Militärgerichtsbarfeit der Deutschen Wehrmacht 1939-1945*. Herbig Verlag: Munich, 1991.

--------, *Die Kollaboration, 1939-1945*. F. A. Herbig Verlag: München, 1995.

Senger und Etterlin. *Neither Fear Nor Hope*. Presidio Press: Novato, 1989.

Steenberg, Sven. *Vlasov*. Alfred A. Knopf: New York, 1970.

Strik-Strikfeldt, Wilfried. *Against Stalin & Hitler. Memoir of the Russian Liberation Movement 1941-1945.* The John Day Company: New York, 1973.

Shulman, Milton. *Defeat in the West*. E. P. Dutton: New York, 1948.

Smiley, David. *Albanian Assignment*. Chatto & Windus: London, 1984.

Tessin, Georg, et. al. *Zur Geschichte der Ordungspolizei, 1936-1945*. Bundesarchiv: Koblenz, 1956.

--------, *Verbaende und Truppen der Deutschen Wehrmacht und Waffen-SS, 1939-1945*. Biblio Verlag: Osnabrueck, 22 Volumes, 1979-1997.

Thomas, Nigel, et al. *Partisan Warfare 1941-45*. Reed International Books Ltd.: London, 1983.

Thorwald, Juergen. *The Illusion. Soviet Soldiers in Hitler's Armies*. Harcourt Brace Jovanovich: New York, 1975.

Thrams, Hermann. *Küstrin 1945. Tagebuch einer Festung*. Selbstpubliziert, 1992.

Tieke, Wilhelm. *The Caucasus and the Oil. The German-Soviet War in the Caucasus 1942/43*. J. J. Fedorowicz Publishing: Winnipeg, 1995.

Tolstoy, Nikolai. *The Secret Betrayal 1944-1947*. Charles Scribner's Sons: New York, 1977.

Tomasevich, Jozo. *The Chetniks: War and Revolution in Yugoslavia 1941-1945.* Stanford University Press: Stanford, 1975.

Tys-Krokhmaliuk, Yuriy. *UPA Warfare In The Ukraine. The Ukrainian Insurgent Army*. Vantage Press: New York, 1972.

United States Army. *Military Improvisations During the Russian Campaign*. Center of Military History: Washington, DC 1986.

Vakar, Nicholas P. *Belorussia. The Making of a Nation*. A Case Study. Harvard University Press: Cambridge, 1956.

Venohr, Wolfgang. *Aufstand der Slowaken. Der Freiheitskampf von 1944*. Verlag Ullstein: Frankfurt am Main, 1992.

Vukcevich, Bosko S. *Diverse Forces in Yugoslavia 1941-1945*. Authors Unlimited: Los Angeles. 1990.

Warlimont, Walter. *Inside Hitler's Headquarters 1939-1945*. Presidio Press: Novato, n.d.

Wicziok, Wilhelm. *Die Armee Der Gerichteten. Zur besonderen Verwendung – Bewaehrungsbataillon 500*. Heitz & Hoeffkes Verlag: Essen, 1992.

Yerger, Mark C. *Riding East. The SS Cavalry Brigade in Poland and Russia 1939-1942*. Schiffer Publishers: Atglen, 1996.

Ziemke, Earl F. and Magna E. Bauer. *Moscow to Stalingrad: Decision in the East*. Center of Military History, United States Army: Washington, DC, 1997.

---------, Stalingrad to Berlin. *The German Defeat in the East*. Center of Military History, United States Army: Washington, DC, 1968.

Selected Magazine & Newspaper Articles

Bernage, Georges. Musulmans D'urss. *39/45 Magazine:* Bayeux, No.80, 1993.

Daily Mail Newspaper. Front Page Article, *Death for Nazi Arab*. London - Saturday, April 1st 1944; No. 14.950.

Dallin, Alexander and Ralph S. Mavrogordato. Rodionov: A Case-Study In Wartime Redefection. *American Slavic and East European Review*, 18 (1959).

de Lannoy, Francois. De La Cagoule A La Brigade Nord-Africaine: L'Itineraire De Mohamed El Maadi, Alias "SS Mohamed". *39/45 Magazine:* Bayeux, No.80, 1993.

------------, Hitler et les Nationalismes Arabes. *39/45 Magazine:* Bayeux, No.80, 1993.

------------, L'Armée Vlassov. Les Soldats Russes De Hitler – Ukraine, Bielo-russie. *39/45 Magazine:* Bayeux, No.129, 1997.

Jurado, Carlos Caballero. Against Stalin & Stalinism: Count Grigori von Lamsdorff, 1936-1945. (part II). *Axis Europa:* Bayside, Issue 15 (Fall 1998).

Lamarque, Philippe. La Legion SS Turque. *39/45 Magazine:* Bayeux, No.80, 1993.

Masson, Philippe. Editor- Georges Lang. La Milice: La Collaboration en Uniforme. "La Phalange Africaine". Historia: Paris. Hors Serie No. 40, 1975.

Munoz, Antonio J. Nazi Racial & Recruitment Policies in the East. *Command*, Issue 35 (November 1995).

--------, German SS, Police, & Auxiliary Forces in Poland. Part V – 1944 and the Warsaw Uprising. Axis Europa Magazine, Issue 15 (Fall 1998).

--------, Twilight War: Northern Italy, 1945. *Command*, Issue 29 (July-August 1994).

--------, Occupying the Balkans. *Command*, Issue 38 (July 1996).

Westermann, Edward. Himmler's Uniformed Police on the Eastern Front: The Reich's Secret Soldiers, 1941-1942. *War In History*, Vol. 3, No. 3 (July 1996).

Military Studies

Bosse, Colonel Alexander von. *The Cossack Corps*. MS P-064 - Chief of Military History, US Army: Historical Division European Command, 1950.

Felmy, General Hellmuth and Walter Warlimont. *German Exploitation of Arab Nationalist Movements in World War II*. MS P-207 - Chief of Military History, US Army: Historical Division European Command, 1948.

Heygendorff, Generalleutnant Ralph von. *Commanding Foreign Peoples*. MS C-043 – Chief of Military History, US Army: Historical Division European Command, 1948.

Köstring, General Ernst. *Commentary on the Report of Dr. Seraphin Concerning Turkic Units*. MS C-043 – Chief of Military History, US Army: Historical Division European Command, 1948.

Seraphin, Major Dr. Hans G. *Caucasian and Turkic Volunteers in the German Army*. MS C-043 – Chief of Military History, US Army: Historical Division European Command, 1948.

Pamphlets

Odegard, Warren & Richard Deeter. *Foreign Volunteers of Hitler's Germany*. DO Enterprises: Los Angeles, 1968.

US Army. *Military Improvisations During the Russian Campaign*. Center of Military History, Washington, D.C., 1983. . DA Pamphlet 20-201, August 1951.

US Army. *Military Effects of Climate on Combat in European Russia*. Center of Military History, Washington, D.C., 1952. DA Pamphlet 20-291, February 1952.

SS Personnel Files, Interviews & Captured German Document Rolls

Zulukidse, Michael P.
Theurmann, Arved
Bey, Muhammed
Ulagaj, Kutschuk
Soobzokov, Cherim

NARS Microfilm T-78, Roll 410
NARS Microfilm T-78, Roll 645
NARS Microfilm T-501, Roll 256
NARS Microfilm T-175, Roll 140
NARS Microfilm T-175, Roll 168
NARS Microfilm T-175, Roll 174
NARS Microfilm T-175, Roll 191
NARS Microfilm T-311, Roll 286
NARS Microfilm T-313, Roll 194
NARS Microfilm T-314, Roll 661
NARS Microfilm T-501, Roll 249
NARS Microfilm T-501, Roll 256
NARS Microfilm T-501, Roll 258

Bundesarchiv-Militaerarchiv (Freiburg):
Kommandeur der Osttruppen z. b. V. 710, RH 58/73, RHD 7/8a/2.
Kommando der 162. Infanteriedivision, RH 26-162/15.
Bundesarchiv-Militärarchiv (Freiburg), Oberkommando der 11. Armee, RH 19 VI/425

1] FORGOTTEN LEGIONS: OBSCURE COMBAT FORMATIONS OF THE WAFFEN-SS, 1943-1945. by Antonio J. Munoz. 424 pages, hard cover, dust jacket, 104 photos, 64 maps. Details the many battle groups, divisions, & special units formed by the Waffen-SS. Many interesting first-person accounts, loaded with information on orders of battle, charts on manpower and casualties, foreign volunteers, etc. $50 ISBN- 0-87364-646-0

2] THE KAMINSKI BRIGADE: A HISTORY, 1941-1945. by Antonio J. Munoz. 64 pages, sc, color covers, 18 battle maps, 4 tables, and 31 extremely rare photos, 6 of which show the unit in Warsaw, Poland where it committed atrocities. Covers the complete & detailed history of the most effective & infamous collabora- tionist anti-partisan brigade formed by the Germans from Russian volunteers. Fully footnoted and documented! $20 *"This book deserves to be on the shelf of the serious student of WWII"*- Ray Tapio, CRITICAL HIT. ISBN- 1-891227-02-5

3] LIONS OF THE DESERT: ARAB VOLUNTEERS IN THE GERMAN ARMY, 1941-1945. by Antonio J. Munoz. 36 pages, sc color covers, numerous maps & drawings, plus 21 extremely rare photos of these Arab volunteers. The complete history of these units in Russia, the Balkans, North Africa, Italy, and even in front of Berlin as the Third Reich was collapsing! Includes 7 super rare photos of the elusive Arab 845th Battalion!!! ISBN- 1-891227-03-3 **NOW PUBLISHED IN EXPANDED FORMAT IN OUR NEWEST BOOK - *"THE EAST CAME WEST".***

4] SLOVENIAN AXIS FORCES IN WORLD WAR II, 1941-1945 by Antonio **J.** Munoz. 12 Color and b&w Plate illustrations by renowned military artist, Vincent Wai! Full color covers, perfect binding (flat spine), 84 pages plus covers, 165 extremely rare photos (100 never before published!), 35 tables, maps, line drawings, etc. Covers the complete history of all Slovenian collaborationist forces allied to the Italians and Germans during the war. Includes the "Blue Guard," "White Guard," with the Village Guard & Legion of Death, Slovene National Army, Slovene Home Guard, Upper Carnolia Defense Force, ethnic-German Defense Militia Regiment Lower Styria, etc.! An excellent reference source not only on the military history, but the organization, weapons, uniform, and insignia of the Slovene Axis forces! $22 ISBN- 1-891227-04-1

5] FOR CROATIA & CHRIST: THE CROATIAN ARMY IN WORLD WAR II, 1941-1945. by Antonio J. Munoz. 80 pages, case bound, color covers, numerous maps, tables, and photos. Complete history of the Croatian military, including the NDH, Ustashe, militia, Croat-German Legion divisions, Italian Legion, etc. Includes an excellent introduction by noted German military historian, Hans Werner Neulen. Most complete English language study on the subject! $35 ISBN- 1-891227-05-X

6] HERAKLES & THE SWASTIKA: GREEK VOLUNTEERS IN THE GERMAN ARMY, POLICE & SS, 1943- 1945. by Antonio J. Munoz 68 pages, Just reprinted! Case Bound color frontis-piece, 35 detailed maps, 36 very rare photos of these Greek collaborationist volunteers. Contains a wealth of data on Greek police, volunteer, and militia forces, troop locations, OB's, etc! A history which has never been detailed before, not even in the Greek language! $35.00 ISBN- 1-891227-06-8

7] FORGOTTEN LEGIONS BOOKLET by Antonio J. Munoz. This case bound, hard cover book contains additional data that only surfaced after the publication of book 1] FORGOTTEN LEGIONS. Has 55+ pages with complete, referenced listings, and additional photographs. $20.00 NOTE: not recommended unless you own "FORGOTTEN LEGIONS" (book 1 above). ISBN- 1-891227-07-6

8] THE HUNGARIAN ARMY & ITS MILITARY LEADERSHIP IN WWII by Andris Kursietis. Perfect bound, 88 pages, 60 photos, 11 maps, 7 Hungarian war posters (including recruiting posters for the 25th SS Hunyadi Division and even the Arrow Cross). Covers the complete history of the Hungarian officer corps and their impact on the army and its actions. Now in its 2nd, expanded and revised edition! $25 perfect bound or $35 hard cover. ISBN-1-891227-08-4 FEW COPIES LEFT! ORDER SOON.

9] HITLER'S EASTERN LEGIONS, Volume I - THE BALTIC SCHUTZ- MANNSCHAFT. by Antonio J. Munoz. 60 pages, sc, color covers, numerous detailed battle maps, 14 uniform plates by Sean Ryan. Covers the complete history of the Lithuanian, Latvian, and Estonian police, SS, Frontier Guard, *"Schuma"* & front battalions, regiments and army units which were raised by the Germans from 1941-1945. Much data on the anti-guerrilla war behind Army Group North. Also lists a complete, chronological listing of the history of these units. The 3-page index makes it easy to check all units. $21 perfect bound or $32 hard cover. ISBN- 1-891227-09-2

10] HITLER'S EASTERN LEGIONS, Volume II - THE OSTTRUPPEN by Antonio J. Munoz. Second volume in the series, this one on purely Russian and White Russian volunteer. 52 pages, sc color covers, 13 photos, full color shoulder board and collar insignia of these forces, 5 uniform plates by Sean Ryan, 4 maps, 3-page glossary. Includes a complete, chronological listing of each battalion and regiment. $21 perfect bound or $35 hard cover. ISBN- 1-891227-10-6

SPECIAL: Buy BOTH Hitler's Eastern Legions, Volumes I & II for ONLY $31 perfect bound or $48 hard cover.

11] THE GERMAN POLICE 442 pages, flat spine, sc color covers. Dozen's of rare maps, tables, photos, line drawings, etc.! Complete study on the history of the entire SS & Police system, including the military history of each battalion and regiment! *"Handsomely presented...must be consi- dered the Bible on the subject."*- Andris Kursietis, military historian. $42 perfect bound or $60 in a special 2 volume case bound edition. ISBN- 1-891227-11-4

12] EASTERN TROOPS IN ZEELAND, THE NETHERLANDS, 1943-1945 by Hans Houterman. 102 pages, flat spine, glossy color covers, sc, numerous maps, photos, tables, appendices. Covers the history of these Russian units in the Netherlands. The maps list the location of all eastern battalions in the West! $25 ISBN- 1-891227-00-9

13] RUSSIAN VOLUNTEERS IN HITLER'S ARMY, 1941-1945 by Wladyslaw Anders. 60 pages, sc color covers, flat spine, col ills of the emblems, Detailed ROA officer postings, numerous rare photos. Entire history of Vlasov & the ROA (Russian Army of Liberation).$13 perfect bound. ISBN- 1-891227-01-7

14] HRVATSKI ORLOVI: PARATROOPERS OF THE INDEPENDENT STATE OF CROATIA, 1942-45 by Josip Novak & David Spencer. 70 pages, hard cover book, color dust jacket, flat spine, 30 photos, maps, tables, appendices, color uniform plate, etc.! History of this formation in detail. $22 hard cover. ISBN- 1-891227-13-0

15] CHETNIK: The Story of the Royal Yugoslav Army of the Homeland, 1941-1945. by Momcilo Dobrich. Complete history of the Chetnik forces in WWII. Includes numerous detailed Orders of Battle for various years and dates, maps, photos, etc. The appendices include a complete history (detailed as well) of the Serbian State & Frontier Guard, as well as the Montenegro Volunteer Corps! $15.00 Saddle Stitched. Few Left! ISBN- 1-891227-20-3

16] THE ROYAL HUNGARIAN ARMY 1920-1945 Volume I Organization & History. by Dr. Leo W. G. Niehorster. Hard bound, with 100lb (heavy), glossy, full color dust jacket! This 317-page, oversized book (8 ½" by 11") contains the complete military history of the Hungarian Army from 1920-1945: a period which has been described as *the most* exciting, dramatic, and traumatic in the history of the Magyar military. This book is all encompassing and contains a wealth of data. Only $40. The book is already hailed as an instant classic and the definitive work on the Hungarian army in WWII! ISBN- 1-891227-19-X FEW COPIES LEFT!

17] MUSSOLINI'S AFRIKA KORPS: The Italian Army in North Africa, 1940-1943. by Rex Trye. 200 pages, hardcover, dozens of photos, line drawings, tables, orders of battle, uniform color plates, etc. The complete history of the Italian colony and the fight in North Africa from 1940-1943. This is the much awaited 2nd book by this authoritative author. PRICE: $36 hard cover. ISBN 1-891227-14-9

18] IRON FIST: A Combat History of the 17th SS Panzer Grenadier Division 'Gotz von Berlichingen', 1944-45" by Antonio Munoz. Perfect bound, color covers, dozens of tables, photos, illustration, line drawings, maps, orders of battle, etc. The history of this SS division. Eighty-two (82) pages, with several appendices (one on the 38th SS 'Nibelungen' Division!). Only $20.00 perfect bound. ISBN 1-891227-29-7

19] "GESTAPO VOLUNTEERS: The Oberkrainer Selbstschutz, 1943-1945" by Monika Kokalj Kocevar.
This is a perfect bound paperback book with an excellent text on the history of the German and collaborationist forces in northern Slovenia, which had been annexed by Germany. This story is not the one dealing with the Slovenian Domobran, but with the Gestapo/SD/Gendarmerie formations and their indegineous forces. Dozens of never before published photos. Noted WW2 military artist, Darko Pavlovic has done the color plates for the uniforms! Price: $10 perfect bound. ISBN- 1-891227-30-0

20] "For Czar & Country: A History of the Russian Guard Corps, 1941-1945" by Antonio J. Munoz. Saddle stitched, 54pp, 11 extremely rare illustrations, 17 maps, illustrations, tables and charts. The complete military history of a Czarist-era Russian volunteer force which aided the German occupation of Yugoslavia in World War II. One of the most esoteric and obscure units in the German army! Only $13 ISBN- 1-891227-23-8

21] THE DRUZHINA SS BRIGADE: A History, 1941-1943 by Antonio J. Munoz Hard Cover, 74 pages, oversized, five pages of color uniform plates. Complete history of the only German SD-sponsored Russian volunteer force. The rare photos and the detailed history has never before been published. Drawing on unpublished material and recently discovered pictures, Mr. Munoz has done justice to a little known part of the history of collaboration in Russia during World War II. Forward by author French L. MacLean. Only $15 perfect bound. ISBN: 1-891227-31-9

22] "DECIMA!: The Xth MAS & The Italian Social Republic, 1943-1945"
by A. Munoz & Prof. Marco Novarese. Case bound, hard cover book, 5 color battle maps, 10 photos, 4 full color uniform plates complete with orders of battle. 105 pp. Case Bound with full color dust jacket! Only $40! ISBN: 1-89227-32-7

24] "BELGRADE'S BEST: The Serbian Volunteer Corps, 1941-1945" by Momcilo Dobrich. 8 ½" by 11", 105 pp plus 105 photos in an additional 54 pages of photos! Numerous orders of battle, maps, tables, etc. The complete history of the most effective anti-partisan indigenous force in occupied Yugoslavia in World War II. Excellent study with a full color dust jacket Only $40.00 plus s&h. ISBN: 1-891227-38-6

25] THE LAST LEVY: Waffen-SS Officer Roster, March 1st 1945. 168 pages, case bound, color dust jacket. 8 ½" by 11" format. Waffen-SS Officer listing by unit, from *SS-Obersturmfuehrer* to *SS-Oberstgruppenfuehrer*. Each entry lists the officer's name, date of birth, date of promotion, and post within the unit. Over 100+ photos of SS commanders. Only $40.00 + s&h ISBN: 1-891227-36-X

26] THE EAST CAME WEST: Muslim, Hindu, and Buddist Volunteers in the German Armed Forces, 1941-1945. By Oleg V. Romanko, Antonio J. Munoz, and Dr. Martin J. Bamber. 332 pages, oversized, smythe sewn book, glossy color dust jacket, hundreds of color, b&w photos, diagrams, tables, charts, line drawings, etc. Complete history of these rare and esoteric Muslim, Hindu and Buddhist formations $50.00 + s&h ISBN: 1-891227-39-4

We accept ALL MAJOR CREDIT CARDS: VISA, MASTERCARD, DISCOVER, & AMERICAN EXPRESS.
Shipping and Handling charges apply. Please visit our web site at: http://www.axiseuropa.com
for a free catalog, or to order please write, fax, or call us at:
AXIS EUROPA BOOKS
53-20 207th Street, Bayside, New York 11364 USA
FAX: (718) 229-1352
PHONE: (718) 423-9893